By concentrating on five creative Christian thinkers of the second century (Justin, Athenagoras, Irenaeus, Clement of Alexandria and Tertullian), Eric Osborn shows how Christianity, using the Bible and philosophy, made monotheism axiomatic in its response to the hostile environment in which it developed. Christian theology argued for one God who was the rational 'clue to metaphysics, ethics and logic, and in so doing laid the foundations for the European intellectual tradition. This study casts new light on the lively beginning which brought Christianity and classical thought together.

THE EMERGENCE OF CHRISTIAN
THEOLOGY

THE EMERGENCE OF
CHRISTIAN THEOLOGY

ERIC OSBORN

Emeritus Professor, Queen's College,
University of Melbourne
Visiting Professor, La Trobe University, Melbourne

CAMBRIDGE
UNIVERSITY PRESS

Published by the Press Syndicate of the University of Cambridge
The Pitt Building, Trumpington Street, Cambridge CB2 1RP
40 West 20th Street, New York, NY 10011-4211, USA
10 Stamford Road, Oakleigh, Victoria 3166, Australia

First published 1993

Printed in Great Britain at the University Press, Cambridge

A catalogue record for this book is available from the British Library

Library of Congress cataloguing in publication data
Osborn, Eric Francis.
The emergence of Christian theology / Eric Osborn.
p.   cm.
Includes bibliographical references and index.
ISBN 0 521 43078 X
1. Fathers of the church. 2. Theology, Doctrinal – History – Early church,
ca. 30–600. 3. Bible – Philosophy – History. 4. Philosophical theology – History.
I. Title.
BR67.084   1993
230'.09'015 – dc20   92-11489   CIP

ISBN 0 521 43078 X hardback

To Genevieve

Contents

Preface

This is a study of the lively beginning which brought Christianity and classical thought together in Christian theology. The investigation began from the puzzle of how Christians could have believed in one God and worshipped Jesus as divine, only to find that this was not the chief threat to their monotheism. More importantly, the twofold division of God by Marcion denigrated the created world, while the Gnostic partition of God added a denial of free will and reason. Christian thinkers argued for one God, father and son, who was first-principle of physics, ethics and logic.

Of the three claims – that there is one God, that he is both father and son, that one God is first-principle of physics, logic and ethics – the third determines the structure of this book.

My gratitude is due to people in several places, from Queen's College, University of Melbourne, to Kingswood College, University of Western Australia, and now to La Trobe University, Melbourne. Beyond Australia, my debts for this book lie in Strasbourg, where I was guest professor in 1981–2, in Cambridge, where I spent study leave in 1985, and in Tübingen, where I enjoyed the generosity of the Alexander von Humboldt Stiftung in 1988. To colleagues and friends in these places I offer warm thanks. To C. Kingsley Barrett, Hans-Joachim Krämer and Malcolm Schofield, who have read appropriate parts of the penultimate manuscript, and to C. Behan McCullagh and John M. Rist, who read it all, I also offer my sincere thanks. I gratefully acknowledge the help of librarians in Tübingen and Melbourne: Frau I. Bethge, Miss Margot Hyslop and Dr Lawrence Macintosh, and the assistance of Miss Pamela Foulkes and Dr David Rankin who have checked references to Irenaeus and Tertullian.

Finally, my thanks go to Mr A. A. Wright of the Cambridge University Press, who, with intelligence and thoughtfulness, has piloted the manuscript to publication.

References

JUSTIN (Goodspeed's Edition)

1 apol. 14.1 refers to the *First Apology*, chapter 14, paragraph 1.
dial. 11.1 refers to the *Dialogue with Trypho*, chapter 11, paragraph 1.

ATHENAGORAS (Schoedel's Edition)

leg. 3 refers to *Legatio*, chapter 3
de res. 1 refers to *De resurrectione*, chapter 1.

IRENAEUS (Sources chrétiennes)

haer. 2.1.1 refers to *Against Heresies*, Book 2, chapter 1, paragraph 1.
dem. 14 refers to the *Epideixis*, or *Demonstration of the Apostolic Preaching*,
    paragraph 14 (J. Armitage Robinson's translation).

CLEMENT (Stählin's Edition)

prot. 4.63 refers to *Protrepticus*, chapter 4, paragraph 63.
paed. 1.3.24 refers to *Paedagogus*, Book 1, chapter 3, paragraph 24.
str. 7.1.2 refers to *Stromateis*, Book 7, chapter 1, paragraph 2.
ecl. 2 refers to *Prophetic Eclogues*, paragraph 2.
exc. Thdt. 2, refers to *Excerpta ex Theodoto*, paragraph 2.
*q.d.s.*4, refers to *Quis dives salvetur*, paragraph 4.

TERTULLIAN (Corpus Christianorum)

an. 27.1 refers to *De Anima*, chapter 27, paragraph 1.
The titles of Tertullian's works are abbreviated as follows:

an.   *De anima*
ap.   *Apologeticum*
bapt.   *De baptismo*

carn.	*De carne Christi*
cast.	*De exhortatione castitatis*
cor.	*De corona*
cult.	*De cultu feminarum libri II*
fug.	*De fuga in persecutione*
Herm.	*Aduersus Hermogenem*
idol.	*De idololatria*
iei.	*De ieiunio*
Jud.	*Aduersus Judaeos*
Marc.	*Aduersus Marcionem libri V*
mart.	*Ad martyras*
mon.	*De monogamia*
nat.	*Ad nationes libri II*
orat.	*De oratione*
paen.	*De paenitentia*
pall.	*De pallio*
pat.	*De patientia*
praescr.	*De praescriptione*
Prax.	*Aduersus Praxean*
pud.	*De pudicitia*
res.	*De resurrectione mortuorum*
Scap.	*Ad Scapulam*
scorp.	*Scorpiace*
spect.	*De spectaculis*
test.	*De testimonio animae*
val.	*Aduersus Valentinianos*
virg.	*De uirginibus uelandis*
ux.	*Ad uxorem libri II*

Abbreviations

ABR	*Australian Biblical Review*
ACW	*Ancient Christian Writers*
ANRW	*Aufstieg und Niedergang der römischen Welt*
Apoll.	*Apollinaris.* Civitas Vaticana
AThR	*Anglican Theological Review*
Aug.	*Augustinianum*
BSGW	*Berichte der sächsichen Gesellschaft der Wissen-schaften* Leipzig
BJRL	*Bulletin of the John Rylands Library*
BKV	*Bibliothek der Kirchenväter*
CCh	*Corpus Christianorum*
ChH	*Church History*
CQ	*Classical Quarterly*
EL	*Ephemerides Liturgicae*
EThL	*Ephemerides Theologicae Lovanienses*
FZPhTh.	*Freiburger Zeitschrift für Philosophie und Theologie*
Greg.	*Gregorianum*
HTh.	*History and Theory*
HThR	*Harvard Theological Review*
HThS	*History and Theory, Supplement*
HUCA	*Hebrew Union College Annual*
JAC	*Jahrbuch für Antike und Christentum*
JHS	*Journal of Hellenic Studies*
JRS	*Journal of Roman Studies*
JSJ	*Journal of the Study of Judaism in the Persian, Hellenistic and Roman period*
JThS	*Journal of Theological Studies*
Lat	*Lateranum*

Laur.	*Laurentianum*
LCC	*Library of Christian Classics*
LCL	*Loeb Classical Library*
MThZ	*Münchener theologische Zeitschrift*
NAWG	*Nachrichten der Akademie der Wissenschaften in Göttingen*
NRTh.	*Nouvelle revue théologique*
OrChrP	*Orientalia Christiana Periodica*
Orph.	*Orpheus*
PhAnt.	*Philosophia Antiqua*
PhP	*Philosophia Patrum*
REG	*Revue des études grecques*
RevSR	*Revue des sciences religieuses*
RFIC	*Rivista di filologia e d'istruzione classica*
RFNS	*Rivista di filosofia neo-scolastica*
RGG	*Religion in Geschichte und Gegenwart*
RHPhR	*Revue de histoire et de philosophie religieuse*
RMet.	*Review of Metaphysics*
RMP	*Rheinisches Museum für Philologie*
RQ	*Römische Quartalschrift für christliche Altertumskunde*
RSLR	*Rivista di storia e letteratura religiosa*
RSR	*Recherches de science religieuse*
RThAM	*Recherches de théologie ancienne et médiévale*
RThPh.	*Revue de théologie et de philosophie*
Sal.	*Salesianum*
Schol.	*Scholastik*
ScrTh.	*Scripta Theologica*
SE	*Sacris Erudiri*
SR	*Studies in Religion*
StPatr.	*Studia Patristica*
StTh.	*Studia Theologica*
SVF	*Stoicorum Veterum Fragmenta*
ThPh.	*Theologie und Philosophie*
ThRv	*Theologische Revue*
ThR	*Theologische Rundschau*
ThZ	*Theologische Zeitschrift*
TRE	*Theologische Realenzyklopädie*

TS	*Theological Studies*
TU	*Texte und Untersuchungen*
TyV	*Teología y vida*
VC	*Vigiliae Christianae*
VetChr.	*Vetera Christianorum*
WUNT	*Wissenschaftliche Untersuchungen zum neuen Testament*
ZKG	*Zeitschrift für Kirchengeschichte*
ZNW	*Zeitschrift für die neutestamentliche Wissenschaft*
ZThK	*Zeitschrift für Theologie und Kirche*

CHAPTER I

One God: questions and opposition

The emergence of Christian theology and the beginning of
European culture are closely entwined. Remove Christian ideas
from Europe, and its philosophy, art, literature and music
cannot be understood. Yet the emergence of Christian thought
was precarious, 'the nearest run thing you ever saw in your
life',[1] and its survival has been through challenge and dispute.

Such challenge brings special times of movement in the
history of ideas. Christian thought displayed fresh vigour in the
second half of the second century. In contrast to the Apostolic
Fathers, who were largely concerned with domestic affairs,
Christian argument developed rapidly in the highly original
writings of Justin, Athenagoras, Irenaeus, Clement of Alexandria and Tertullian. We witness an intellectual acceleration
when, for the first time, there was a Christian Bible to expound
and when New Testament ideas took off with such speed that
the opposition became increasingly irrelevant. This is one of
those brief periods of human invention when earlier concepts
become museum pieces. Any such expansion requires at least
four things: some thinkers to think, new resources to use,
questions to answer, and an opposition to challenge.

The theologians who followed on from the writings which we
call the New Testament were several and their contributions
were of unequal worth. Of those who made the great leap
forward in the second half of the second century, we shall
consider five. Justin came from Nablous in Palestine but lived,

---

[1] A. Wellesley, concerning the battle of Waterloo. He added, 'I don't think it would
have done if I had not been there.' *The Creevey papers: a selection from the correspondence
and diaries of the late Thomas Creevey,* ed. Sir Herbert Maxwell (London, 1905), 236.

I

taught and died a martyr in Rome. He saw Socrates as the embodiment of his own love for truth and as a Christian before Christ. Athenagoras was described as a Christian philosopher from Athens and wrote good Greek in his defence of Christians and their doctrine of resurrection. Irenaeus went from Asia Minor to be bishop of Lyons and to write the major criticism of heretics in the cause of Christian unity and peace. He saw the full sweep of human history under the guiding hand of God. Clement came to Alexandria at the end of his quest for knowledge and found there a Christian teacher who distilled the highest truth from scripture. He placed equal stress on the value of logic and of imagination. Tertullian, turbulent in temper and style, an orator with a passion for argument, had an incisive mind which often descended to personal abuse. His savage humour and vigorous style set him aside from others.

The place where these writers faced their problems was the meeting of two great cultures – Israel and Greece, the Bible and philosophy. This is where they were and the unchosen source of weapons for their attackers and for their defence. It was a turning-point of *Geistesgeschichte* and the beginning of European culture.

The new resources included, after Justin, a Christian Bible which set scriptures of the new covenant alongside those of the old. The story of salvation, from creation to apocalypse, found its centre in Jesus Christ. This story could be compatible with elements of both Judaism and Hellenism, for the Septuagint and Philo had mingled both[2] and Numenius defined Plato as 'Moses speaking Attic dialect'.[3] Here, in passing, is a useful clue to transition: the distinction between translation and philosophy. It was easy to translate biblical or pagan traditions into philosophical concepts, without doing any philosophy.[4] Many

---

[2] See *Le monde grec ancien et la Bible*, ed. C. Mondésert, *Bible de tous les temps*. 1 (Paris, 1984), 19–54.   [3] *str.* 1.22.150.

[4] This was not enough for Christian apologists because of the strength and plurality of their problems. It was however the method followed in the twentieth century by P. van Buren who, in his book, *The secular meaning of the gospel* (London, 1963), accepted the definitions of logical analysis and translated Christian doctrine into empirical forms of Christian practice. The project was of uncertain value because it avoided the argument which analysis required.

had found Greek philosophical ideas in the Pentateuch, when it was allegorically interpreted, without committing themselves to the peril of dialectic. This was insufficient since, for philosophers, especially Plato, the path to the end was as important as the end. Fortunately for posterity, Christian apologists had to argue for their lives.

Three questions stood out. First, was there one God who was both the father of Jesus Christ and the creator of this world of evil and chaos? Second, was Christian faith monotheist? Christians claimed that Jesus was God, yet insisted that there was only one God. There was no difficulty with an incarnate saviour, who was greater than men; there had been several of those. But according to John, the son was divine, one with the father. Third, what followed from such affirmations? Christians claimed that this belief had coherent consequences for true being, right living and sound thinking. The incarnation was not just a pretty story. If one accepted this divine identity, then, like Plato's first-principle, it made sense of things divine and human, of right and wrong, of true and false. It gave a better account of physics, ethics and logic than other starting-points. The three claims – one God, one God as father and son, one God as first-principle – provide the structure of this book and of the earliest Christian theology. The problem to which they pointed was the problem of one God. It was not the only problem which had to be faced; but it was the distinctively theological one.[5]

For Aristotle, a first-principle is a 'first point from which a thing either is or comes to be or is known' (*Metaph.* 1013a). After describing the son as a cosmic unity in which all things meet, Clement claims that God, as being, is first-principle of physics (theology, metaphysics), as good, first-principle of ethics, and as mind, the first-principle of logic (*str.* 4.25.162). This threefold division is found first in Xenocrates (frag. 1),[6] later in Alcinous (*Did.* 3) and elsewhere; but it is implicit in the *Republic*, where Plato 'treats as inseparable three notions which may well seem to us to be entirely unconnected. The Good, for

---

[5] The importance of this problem has been recognised in the works of R. M. Grant and M. Simonetti (see Appendix 1).

[6] *Xenocrates*, ed. R. Heinze (Leipzig, 1892).

Plato, is first and most obviously the end or aim of life, the
supreme object of all desire and aspiration. Second, and more
surprisingly, it is the condition of knowledge, that which makes
the world intelligible and the mind intelligent. And third and
last and most important, it is the creative and sustaining cause
of the whole world and all its contents, that which gives to
everything else its very existence.'[7]

An extended treatment of the earliest Christian philosophy
showed that, with all its Platonism and Stoicism, it ended on the
claim that Jesus was God.[8] The accounts of God, the world,
humanity and history pointed to this conclusion; but how could
one God be two? Who could accept faith in two or three divine
beings as the way to a monotheism which rejected faith in more
than one God? Christians could see the difficulties in their
monotheistic faith. The word was with God and the word was
God. There were quick ways out of the problem: Modalists
insisted on the unity without a clear distinction between father
and son; Adoptionists affirmed that distinction without adequate respect for the unity. Each ignored part of the problem.

Origen states the problem most clearly in his *Dialogue with
Heraclides*, where he speaks of 'two Gods'. The expression is new
for Christians, although Justin and others had used the phrase
'let us make' (Gen. 1:26) to prove plurality within the godhead.

ORIGEN: While being distinct from the father is the son himself also
   God?
HERACLIDES: He himself is also God.
ORIGEN: And do two Gods become a unity?
HERACLIDES: Yes.
ORIGEN: Do we confess two Gods?
HERACLIDES: Yes. The power is one.[9]

Origen proceeds to show 'in what sense they are two and in
what sense the two are one God'. Adam and Eve became one
flesh and he who is joined to the Lord is one Spirit (1 Cor.
6:17).[10] When the scriptures speak about the one and only

[7] J. E. Raven, *Plato's thought in the making* (Cambridge, 1965), 130.
[8] E. Osborn, *The beginning of Christian philosophy* (Cambridge, 1981).
[9] *dial. Her.* 124; H. Chadwick translation, *Alexandrian Christianity* (London, 1954).
[10] Cf. *Cels.* 2.9; 6.47.

God (Isa. 43:10; Deut. 32:39), they do not mean the father without the son. 'In these utterances we are not to think that the unity applies to the God of the universe... in separation from Christ, and certainly not Christ in separation from God. Let us rather say that the sense is the same as that of Jesus' saying, "I and my father are one".'[11] Elsewhere, Origen replies to Celsus that there is no difficulty in the father and the son being one God, since unity of mind is possible between many minds and, indeed, the first Christians were of one heart and mind.[12]

However christology was neither the whole nor the origin of the problem. We may consider the three questions as three aspects of one central problem. The first asks whether there is one God, first cause and creator. The second asks how faith in one God depends on faith in two, father and son, or even three, father, son and spirit. The third asks why there is one God and offers him as first-principle of physics, ethics and logic. In time, the second question would seem most difficult. For the second century, the first question, whether there is one God, was a greater threat; but all three were parts of the one problem. The Christian response was that it was easier to believe in one God who was saviour as well as creator, who was end as well as beginning, and that the word made flesh in Jesus Christ was a more useful first-principle of physics, ethics and logic than any God-shaped blank.

Such claims make the emergence of Christian theology from these questions one of the most enticing puzzles in the history of thought. Its logical interest is well matched by its historical consequences, because from the threefold structure of Christian theology came the philosophy and culture of Europe. For this is the system which Nietzsche saw as 'the longest lie', the belief that there is something beyond our random efforts which, as God, Science or Truth, will save us if we do and say the proper things.[13] Secularised by the Enlightenment, denounced by Nietzsche, it is still the pain of Derrida who is dedicated to the 'systematic crossing out of the ἀρχή' and the critical rejection of

---

[11] *dial. Her.* 128.　　　　　　[12] *Cels.* 8.12.
[13] R. Rorty, *Consequences of pragmatism* (Minneapolis, 1982), 208.

all 'that retains any metaphysical presuppositions incompatible with the theme of différance'.[14]

The opposition was at least fourfold. It came from pagans, Gnostics, philosophers and Jews. Gnostics and Marcion were persistently dualist; the God of creation could not be the supreme God. Pagans regarded the abolition of the lesser gods as a disaster and a transcendent God without minor gods as a nonentity. Philosophers, like Celsus, cleverly noted that Christians talked more about Jesus than about God and rejected this practice as inconsistent with one first cause. Jews regarded the deification of a crucified man as blasphemous and absurd.

The importance of monotheism for Christianity has, of course, been challenged. The cry of 'one God' characterised all monotheistic missionary preaching.[15] However, according to one rapid verdict, there was too much tension in Christian monotheism which then produced christology and trinitarianism and left the conflict between one God and many gods behind.[16] Others have claimed that with the trinity, not to mention the angels, Justin and Athenagoras were unacknowledged polytheists.[17] Such claims are wrong, unsubtle, but usefully provocative.

Christians had to answer the charge of atheism and they responded by showing the richness of their account of God. Athenagoras describes the son who creates as 'the word of the father in form and energising power' and the spirit as the ἀπόρροια of God who creates the word in the beginning of his ways and works (*leg.* 10.4 including Prov. 8:22). The trinity has power in unity and the angels are placed by God to look after all things in heaven and earth (*leg.* 10.5). Some of the angels fell and became pagan deities; but there are plenty of good angels left to keep the divine providence going (*leg.* 24.3). They do this as God's ministers, not as supernumerary gods.

Because the persons of the trinity are divided by rank some

---

[14] J. Derrida, *Speech and phenomenon, and other essays in Husserl's theory of signs*, trans. D. B. Allison (Evanston, 1972), I, 46. Quoted Rorty, *Pragmatism*, 98.

[15] P. W. van der Horst, *The sentences of Pseudo-Phocylides* (Leiden, 1978), 151. See also R. Kerst, 1 Kor. 8.6. – ein vorpaulinisches Taufbekenntnis, *ZNW*, 66 (1975), 130–9.

[16] So claims W. Schmauch, Monotheismus und Polytheismus, *RGG*, 3 Aufl., 4, 1116.

[17] F. Loofs, *Leitfaden zum Studium der Dogmengeschichte*, 7th edn (Tübingen, 1968), 95.

interpreters have suggested a political model; but this falls far short of proof. Certainly Maximus of Tyre gives a useful account of 'one God, king of all and father, and many gods, sons of God, fellow-rulers with God',[18] which would, however, have made nonsense of the Christian rejection of polytheism. An earlier clue is found in Justin's answer to the charge of atheism. He denies the charge, except with reference to the wicked demons or pagan gods, and declares belief in the most true God who is father of all righteousness. This God, with son, spirit and angels, is honoured in reason and in truth (1 *apol*. 6).

This does not mean that Christians were half-way between the monotheism of the Jews and the polytheism of pagans.[19] They declared one transcendent God who precluded all compromise. He was so transcendent as to seem useless and irrelevant to the universe. Belief in such a God could be regarded as a form of atheism; so it was essential for Christians to show that their God was an energising power in son and spirit, the source of all righteousness and the highest truth.

All this was evangelical. Faith in God, father and son, had coherent consequences for true being, right living and sound thinking. If one accepted this divine identity, then, like Plato's first-principle, it made sense of things divine and human, of right and wrong, of true and false. It gave a better account of metaphysics (or physics), ethics and logic than any other starting-point. God as ἀρχή provided both cause and structure.

What appeared at first to be a weakness therefore became a major strength. A transcendent God, without a son who saved the world, quickly became a nonentity. A son of God, who was Alpha and Omega, provided a saving monotheism and good news of God. The detail of this claim became accessible through the formidable opposition of the pagan state, Gnostics, some philosophers and Judaism. The rational exuberance of Justin, Athenagoras, Irenaeus, Clement and Tertullian drew stimulus from opposition. Whether this was why Christianity spread so

---

[18] *Or*. 11.5, cited W. R. Schoedel, A neglected motive for second-century trinitarianism, *JThS*, 31 (1980), 362.

[19] As was later claimed by Gregory of Nazianzus (*Or*. 38.8) and Gregory of Nyssa (*Or. cat.* 3).

effectively is not our concern. In the search for a comfortable theory a recent writer claims, 'But that Christianity came to maturity in the Greek world and represents the blend of hellenistic Judaism, hellenized Christianity, and Greek ideas and Greek religion and Greek spirit, gives the answer for me as to how Christianity came to rise to the ascendancy it achieved'.[20] Our first concern is with development of ideas, not with prizes, and the ideas are more complex than this account allows. Of the four centres of opposition, Judaism is the most complex.

ROME AND HER GODS

Christians found different things in the world around them. For Clement, paganism was the sordid scene of many gods and unspeakable mysteries, with some residual gleams of light from the universal Logos. For Justin and Tertullian, it was the world of good order and a promise of justice, compromised by the power of demons. The pagan gods were deceitful demons, hostile to Christians, who knew the truth about them. For Irenaeus, paganism hardly mattered; there were too many troubles at home and too much to defend and to declare. He thanked Rome for peace and safe travel (*haer.* 4.30.3).

The pagan world was marked by exuberant variety, the 'shapeless profusion of polytheism',[21] where all were tolerated and reverence for the past ensured that none was lost. Tolerance was balanced by hostility to atheists or monotheists. Christians were worse than Jews because they had left the faith of their fathers. Besides the masses of evidence for pagan religion in temples and inscriptions, there is detailed information in poets and philosophers. Dancers and actors drew crowds to theatres for religious spectacles. Processions of different kinds dominated the annual cycle of events and travel was governed by religious shrines. The gods were honoured by eating, drinking and energetic orgies.

[20] S. Sandmel, Palestinian and Hellenistic Judaism and Christianity: the question of the comfortable theory, *HUCA*, 50 (1979), 148. Apart from the illogicality of the claim that x represents the blend of a, px, b, c, d, (one cannot define x in terms of x), the key terms here are far too general.

[21] R. McMullen, *Paganism in the Roman Empire* (New Haven and London, 1981), 5.

Criticism of the gods in Xenophanes, Heraclitus and Plato, was balanced by Plutarch and others who extolled their goodness. Christian apologists drew on the sceptical literature and shared the same presuppositions as pagan critics.[22] Such denigration of the gods was far less effective than moderns might expect. 'But who cared? The inappropriateness of common forms of worship, seen through the eyes of Seneca or Porphyry, appears not to have deterred a single soul from the inheritance of his tribe.'[23] Inertia could be aided by not taking any accounts of the gods literally and revelling in their enigmas, or by transferring cruder elements to demonic intermediaries. Order emerged with the dominance of sun-worship to which other cults were subordinated, until Constantine, a 'convert to the Sun himself, changed faith a second time and so became a Christian'.[24] For a long time polytheism persisted in an hierarchical pyramid. 'Christ and Yahweh were drawn into polytheism on the latter's terms, simply as new members in an old assembly.' To the more traditional system must be added the dynamic new cults, like Mithraism, which spread vigorously in the second century.

By the end of the second century, Christianity was on the way to dominance in the Roman empire. At the end of the first century it did not count, yet at the end of the fourth century it reigned supreme and other religions did not count. 'Among all leisurely developments, *de longue durée*, this one of the period AD 100–400 might fairly be given pride of place in the whole of Western history.'[25] Christianity began in the Roman world as a religion whose founder and followers worked miracles.[26] By the end of the second century, Celsus could claim that Christians had gone underground (*Cels.* 8.69), for few were being martyred (*Cels.* 3.8). While Origen insisted that Christians were dedicated to the universal diffusion of the gospel, Celsus had claimed that Christians, like Gnostics, did not want a lot of converts (*Cels.* 3.9), that they approached only the intellectually feeble,

[22] *Ibid.*, 75 and 176; Eusebius, *Praep. ev.* 4.2 and 3, 5.22; Lactantius, *Div. Inst.* 2.17.
[23] McMullen, *Paganism*, 77.   [24] *Ibid.*, 85.
[25] R. McMullen, *Christianizing the Roman Empire* (New Haven and London, 1984), viii.
[26] *Ibid.*, 22. Eusebius, *h.e.* 3.24.3.

slaves, women and children, and that they ran away when someone intelligent appeared.[27]

It is odd that Christians should seem both widespread and isolated, tolerated and persecuted. '*As Christians*, declaring themselves in that role to the public, preaching, holding meetings, or the like, they were very little in evidence... But simply as neighbors, they were naturally everywhere.'[28] Conversion may have been public but the long period of growth which belonged to every Christian received little notice. Under Constantine there was a sudden change and the number jumped rapidly (perhaps, from five million to thirty million) within a hundred years, with the intellectuals bringing up the rear.[29] The motives leading to conversion to Christianity included a desire for blessings, a fear of pain and a belief in miracles.

The state made life difficult, if not impossible, for Christians. It might have found justification in the alleged extravagance of Christian orgies.[30] Justin was concerned that these should not be taken as typically Christian (1 *apol.* 26.7). Clement of Alexandria attacked the promiscuity of Carpocratians (*str.* 3.2.10). The Christian name was associated with some questionable if not criminal activities. Pliny, Tacitus and Suetonius reveal various negative opinions which Christians had to dispel.[31] Lucian's Peregrinus showed the affinity between Christian and Cynic. The charges of sexual libertinism and cannibalism were Fronto's chief objections. The holy kiss was another ground for criticism. Even Clement compared it with a serpent's sting. Christian exorcism, which Justin boasted was more effective than other forms of exorcism, gave pagans good reason for linking Christians with magic, and the veneration of relics confirmed this charge.

Pliny had been satisfied that Christians were guilty only of a form of worship which venerated Christ as a god (*Epp.* 10.96).[32]

---

[27] *Ibid.*, 37. *Cels.* 3.44, 53 and 55.   [28] *Ibid.*, 40.
[29] *Ibid.*, 68. Jerome, *In Jovin.*, 3.6.   [30] Minucius Felix, *Octavius* 9.5f.
[31] S. E. Benko, *Pagan Rome and the early Christians* (Bloomington, 1986), 4–24. See also S. E. Benko, Pagan criticism of Christianity during the first two centuries AD, *ANRW* 23/2 (1980), 1055–118.
[32] For an introduction to Pliny's account of the Christians, see R. L. Wilken, *The Christians as the Romans saw them* (Yale, New Haven and London, 1984), 1–30.

Elsewhere, confession of the name of Christian could be enough to justify execution. Some were required to sacrifice to the statues of the emperor and gods and to curse the name of Christ. Those who denied the accusation and passed the test were free (*Epp.* 10.44). The Christians were seen as a club (ἑταιρία or *collegium*) which might have a professional, burial or religious significance. Their creed was a *superstitio* which denied the current religion of Roman life. After Trajan's rescript to Pliny there is no change in the legal position of Christians until Decius. Christians were a special kind of criminal, to be punished not for what they had done in the past, but for what they were in the present.[33]

However the legal grounds for the persecution of Christians are far from clear. There are three main views:[34] (i) that there was an imperial and general edict against the practice of the Christian religion, (ii) that Roman governors punished Christians in the interests of public order, at their own discretion,[35] or (iii) that Christians were prosecuted for specific criminal offences such as illegal assembly or treason. Sporadic and limited persecutions show that there was no general law against Christians; they were not important enough. All attempts to vindicate this theory have failed. Proponents of the *coercitio* theory have had difficulty in finding a reason why governors would want to coerce Christians. The most useful version of the specific charge theory allows for variety. 'As fast as one *crimen* proved baseless, another took its place, better substantiated, as the *cohaerens scelus*.'[36] Stubbornness seems the most common charge, but this could not be the primary accusation; contempt of court is not possible until one has been taken to court on other grounds. Incendiarism, illegal assembly and disregard for the gods are all frequently found. Lucian identifies the fault as atheism.[37] 'No doubt the official policy was far from clear to the persecuted who, accused technically of the Name, did not perceive the underlying cause, and it did not suit the Apologists

---

[33] T. D. Barnes, Legislation against Christians, *JRS* 58, 9 (1968), 48.
[34] A. N. Sherwin-White, *The letters of Pliny: a historical and social commentary* (Oxford, 1966), Appendix 5, 772–87.   [35] Mommsen's theory of *coercitio*.
[36] Sherwin White, *The letters of Pliny*, 783.   [37] *de morte Peregrini* 11–14.

to be fair to the imperial policy on this point.'[38] In the confusion, it is hard to see how fairness would bring clarity.

The second half of the second century was, for Christians, a time when precarious existence alternated with intervals of quiet expansion. Darker days were to come with Maximin and Decius. A useful plan speaks of the false dawn (135–65), the years of crisis (165–80), the turn of the tide (180–235).[39] During the false dawn, Christians accepted the continued existence of the Roman state, since the law which threatened Christians was used leniently. Antoninus Pius sought to protect them from the violence of mobs; but individual Christians still died a martyr's death. Aristides pointed to Christians as the world's chief hope and the writer to Diognetus called them the soul of the world. Justin claimed Christ as the culmination of philosophy as well as of prophecy, and died as a martyr rather than sacrifice to the gods. Outside Rome, Christians attracted much less attention. Yet opposition to atheists, who were suspected of magic, darkened the dawn of tolerance.

In the years of crisis (165–80) which followed, procedures were modified so that action against Christians could be more effectively carried out. Martyrdom became more frequent. Lucian and Celsus pointed to Christian weaknesses, which included a lack of patriotism and loyalty to the nation's gods. Tatian's violence was matched by the plea of Athenagoras for a fair deal. Montanism offered a protest of prophecy against accommodation with the world. The martyrs of Scilli responded with African rigour and volunteer martyrs were sent away unpunished by the proconsul of Asia in 185.

By 180, the achievement of the church had reached a high point and the tide began to turn against the growing movement. Mithraism, syncretism and local cults flourished; but splendid temples united the empire whose citizens were required to honour the protecting gods. In 212, 'The *constitutio Antoniana* made general persecution possible', because all could now be required to offer sacrifice to the gods and pray for the well-being

[38] Sherwin-White, *The letters of Pliny*, 785.
[39] W. H. C. Frend, *Martyrdom and persecution in the early church* (Oxford, 1965).

of an emperor whose *genius* Christians believed to be a demon.[40] Swearing by the *genius* of the emperor was the accepted response to the accusation of *laesae Romanae religionis* and *titulum laesae augustioris maiestatis*. Commodus was persuaded to treat Christians kindly by his mistress Marcia who viewed them with favour. Under Severus monotheistic disloyalty to imperial cult brought sporadic persecution, which in Alexandria was harsh in face of triumphant Christian response. Assimilation with the world had not dampened the zeal of the martyr. That was to happen, according to Cyprian, in the years which preceded the violence of Maximin and Decius.

With this attempt to trace a pattern in the relation of Christians to their rulers, the difficulty of generalisation becomes apparent. The shock of particular personal loss and the recurring possibility of persecution moulded the minds of the growing Christian community. One turning-point might be selected. In the New Testament, the state is something indifferent, appointed by God, whose judgement it will face at the coming Eschaton. However, about the middle of the second century, the conviction emerges that God has postponed his judgement of the world for the sake of its conversion. God wills that men might be saved and, to give time for this, he provides that the world continue to exist (Justin, 1 *apol.* 45; *dial.* 39.2). The state ceases to be neutral; its rejection of the Christian offer becomes as significant as the Christian refusal to comply with the requirements of the state. Only under Constantine, when state and church accept one another, is the conflict resolved.[41]

Was Christianity a political religion?[42] Did the fact of persecution, like the crucifixion of Jesus, prove that the Christian message was a political threat? Christians insisted that it did not. They kept the laws, they looked to a kingdom beyond the present age, and they prayed to their God for their rulers. Unfortunately that was not what their rulers wanted.

---

[40] *Ibid.*, 312.

[41] K. Aland, Das Verhältnis von Kirche u.Staat in der Frühzeit, *ANRW* 23, 1 (1979), 246.

[42] Did it have consequences for the secular state? Jürgen Moltmann has argued in several places that Christianity was and is inevitably political. This paragraph owes much to lively discussion with him on this point.

Few have felt kindly towards those who have prayed for their conversion. Christians would not worship the emperor and would not honour the gods who had made Rome great. Their situation varied from time to time and the attitudes of Christian writers were diverse. Irenaeus and Clement seem to have no problem with the performance of political duties. Justin is critical of the state and its injustice towards Christians: killing Christians is irrational, unjust, demonic, and disastrous, because persecutors face divine judgement and condemnation to eternal punishment. Tertullian relishes, in prospect, the conflagration of Christian persecutors. At the same time he applauds and congratulates potential martyrs. They will do well from their martyrdom and so will the church.

Christians did not produce a political theology, but their existence contradicted the Roman political ideology. Their God was not an alternative, but a different kind of ruler. Monotheism required no positive political action; but its God was universally supreme, for every soul was naturally Christian. It did not draw inspiration from earthly kingship. Its royal language came from ancient Israel and the psalms which Christians used in prayer and praise.

In moral matters there could be open conflict. Justin (*2 apol.* 1f.) tells of a case where Roman law was put on the wrong side of justice.[43] On the other hand, much that the Stoics had praised could be found in Christian practice.

GNOSTICS AND MARCION

Gnosticism began from a vision of the universe, in response to the great questions of human origin and destiny. There was some thought behind the myths or pictures; but vulgarisation and proliferation stifled the processes of reason. This was not accidental. No one has given an explanation why the capacity for reflective thought is so unevenly distributed within the human race. Gnosticism overcame this inequality by a redistribution of talent on its own terms. Those who accepted its

---

[43] See R. M. Grant, A woman of Rome, *ChH*, 54 (1985), 461–72, for an interesting piece of nescience fiction. Also see below, chapter 7, note 67.

doctrines were thereby proved superior. Its communities were syncretistic and continued to produce new groups,[44] governed by a conviction that the first-principle of all things was a strange God who had no relation to this world and its creator.[45] While at some points it drew on Hellenism for its material,[46] its small quota of argument is not impressive and it eventually fell victim to logic for which it had no answer. Basilides argued (*str.* 4.12.82) that martyrs died because of their desire to sin, even if they had done nothing wrong. This may well be the most foolish and insensitive argument in the history of the human race, which would have long since perished, if every desire to sin brought violent death.

The logical inadequacy was evident if not decisive. Gnostics committed the fallacy of infinite regress, forever adding more aeons. They were pioneers in the bureaucratic fallacy which claims that multiplication of intermediaries makes it easier to move from particulars to first-principle and from first-principle to particulars.[47] But no logical objection could be final against Gnosis which was a higher way than argument. Therefore the criticism of Gnostic systems required an approach which went beyond logic to what was fitting or aesthetically appropriate. This was found in the humour of Irenaeus, which showed that Gnostic myths were inappropriate and genuinely funny.[48]

Because of its general lack of argument, Gnosticism is properly seen as theosophy. Just as the weaker student will remember the allegories of the Sun, Cave and Divided Line in the *Republic*, when the structure of Plato's argument is beyond him, so Gnosticism was able to help those simpler folk who thought in pictures and found argument about theology difficult and irreverent. They were offered a picture-book Platonism. Gnosticism provided philosophy without argument, which is like

---

[44] A. Böhlig, *Zum Hellenismus in den Schriften von Nag Hammadi* (Wiesbaden, 1975), 10.

[45] *Ibid.*, 40. 'Die ἀρχή des Alls bildet bei den Gnostikern der fremde Gott.'

[46] *Ibid.*, 53.

[47] One might add the 'space travel fallacy' that divine transcendence could remotely cause the world when it emanated enough platforms to fill the infinite gap. On the bureaucratic fallacy see E. Osborn, Clément, Plotin et l'Un, in ΑΛΕΞΑΝΔΡΙΝΑ, *FS Claude Mondésert* (Paris, 1986), 188.

[48] E. Osborn, Irenaeus and the beginning of Christian humour: The idea of salvation, Supplement to *Prudentia* (1989), 64–76.

opera without music, ballet without movement, or Shakespeare without words. Its influence on Christianity has been seen more favourably within the recent flight from authority which has favoured losers against winners.[49] However, the variety of Christian belief in the second century, as shown by Bauer and confirmed by le Boulluec,[50] proves not merely that heresy was common, but that authority was not powerful. Sympathy for the underdog is misplaced. The Gnostics did not lose because they were suppressed by dominant authority; they lost because they would not think.

A case for similarity of method between Clement and the Gnostics has been based on their common use of allegorical method and Clement's readiness to use Gnostic material.[51] A generous but implausible case for Gnostic influence on second-century fathers deserves attention.[52] Irenaeus, we are told, develops the central objection that there is only one God who made the world and all mankind. It is 'perhaps not an exaggeration' to say that Irenaeus developed all his theology from this thesis, and 'it could be' that it was only in opposition to Gnosticism that he was able to develop his own systematic theology.[53] Yet Irenaeus insists that Gnostics were entirely irrational (*irrationabiliter, inflati, haer.* 2.28.6; *irrationabiles igitur omni modo, haer.* 4.38.4). Irenaeus is seen as a defender of the traditional confession of one God (*haer.* 4.33.cf.4.6.1) so that his logical objections to Gnostic arguments may be ignored.[54] This is seriously wrong because Irenaeus' concern for argument springs from his belief in one God who is the first-principle of truth and logic; his demand for reason was part of his demand for God. Irenaeus is concerned, as are the Gnostics, with likeness to God, but rightly argues that by ignoring the difference

[49] See Jeffrey Stout, *The flight from authority* (Notre Dame, 1981), 2f.
[50] W. Bauer, *Orthodoxy and heresy in earliest Christianity* (Philadelphia, 1971), eds. R. A. Kraft and G. Krodel, translated from the second German edition, ed. G. Strecker (Tübingen, 1964). A. le Boulluec, *La notion d'hérésie dans la littérature grecque IIe–IIIe siècles*, 2 vols. (Paris, 1985).
[51] M. Mees, Rechtgläubigkeit und Häresie nach Klemens von Alexandrien, *Aug.*, 25 (1985), 722–34.
[52] Barbara Aland, Gnosis and Kirchenväter, Ihre Auseinandersetzung um die Interpretation des Evangeliums, in *Gnosis, FS Hans Jonas*, ed. B. Aland (Göttingen, 1978), 158–215.   [53] *Ibid.*, 165f.   [54] *Ibid.*, 167.

between man and God and the need for human obedience, the Gnostic cannot become God's *perfectum opus* (*haer.* 4.39.2).

Immortality comes from submission to God (*haer.* 4.38.3). From this, we are told, it is clear that Irenaeus understood Gnosticism and attacked it where it threatened the theology of the church.[55] His defence of the incarnation is based on the distinctness of the creature which was to be saved (*haer.* 3.18.1). Yet it is claimed that, 'while Irenaeus lived entirely from the tradition of the church, the great Gnostic opponent deepened and unified his thought'. The opposite is true. Simple loyalty to a tradition was on the Gnostic side and the thinking was all with Irenaeus. Claims for the greatness of the Gnostic achievement[56] have nowhere been substantiated. They employ the simple but serious fallacy that the stimulus to a major intellectual work must be commensurate to the response it evoked. In many cases, the trivial and foolish have exasperated better minds into singular achievement.[57]

Tertullian's claim that Gnostics are only interested in their own salvation is confirmed by the Gospel of Truth.[58] Also he saw clearly that the crucial issue between Gnostics and others lay in the disputed difference between Christ and Christians. Yet it is claimed that, as a defence mechanism, he deliberately misunderstood Gnostics. This was not the case; indeed Tertullian was kind to Gnostics, crediting them with intellectual concerns and denigrating Athens against Jerusalem because of their poor performance.

Clement's approach, the argument continues, is different because he deals with particular issues and argues the inadequacy of the Gnostic account. The Gnostic myth, which was their rule, is ignored by him. On four particular issues, Gnostic argument is found to be deficient. The desire to make Clement a naïve defender of the church's faith leads to the claim that the

---

[55] *Ibid.*, 172–6.
[56] 'a breathtaking world of fantastic symbols, beautifully intricate myths, weird heavenly denizens and extraordinary poetry.' B. Layton, *The Gnostic scriptures* (London, 1987), xviii.
[57] The Fallacy of the Hopeless Historian sees every movement of thought as an equal and opposite reaction to what has preceded it. The fallacy has no proper place in the history of ideas.   [58] Aland, *Gnosis*, 179.

λογικὴ συγκατάθεσις of faith is a simple acceptance of God's offer of salvation, without reference to reason;[59] on the contrary, the point of Clement's argument is that such logical assent is grounded on reason.

The position of Clement, in contrast to Irenaeus and Tertullian, is that he considers the peripheral arguments of Basilides to deserve refutation. Irenaeus and Tertullian concentrated on the Gnostic myth, where difference of genre made argued refutation a limited form of attack. The second century is seen to centre on the anthropological consequences of the gospel and the new creation. We are told that, without the Gnostic contribution it cannot be understood, and without the Gnostic provocation, it could not have happened.[60]

Now it is true that Justin, Irenaeus and Tertullian would not have written works against Gnostics if there had been no Gnostics, nor would they have tried so hard to get things right if others had not got them wrong. Whether credit should go to the Third Reich for the United Nations Organisation or whether credit should go to Gnostics for the emergence of Christian theology is doubtful. Certainly the Gnostics were not the mothers of Christian theology nor the first Christian theologians. Perhaps the Gnostic was not always a fool about everything, for that would be a remarkable achievement. He claimed that ordinary Christians were inadequate rather than wrong; it was a mistake to take the norm of Christian behaviour as the limit of Christian achievement.[61] The demiurge, who foolishly claimed to be unique and exclusive was the type of the common Christian. Origen and Clement were similarly embarrassed by the *simpliciores*. Mediocrity and complacency were not consistent with the gospel; there were higher planes to be sought.[62]

A total assessment of Gnosticism will always be elusive

---

[59] *Ibid.*, 214.
[60] Aland, Gnosis und Kirchenväter. See Fallacy of Hopeless Historian, above, note 57.
[61] K. Koschorke, *Die Polemik der Gnostiker gegen das kirchliche Christentum* (Leiden, 1978), 232.
[62] Marcionites and Manichees were in a different league, as indicated by Koschorke, *ibid.*, 238–41. Advocates of perfection may present a sorry picture of personal achievement.

because of its concern for secrecy and originality. It was the claim of each sect that it possessed a new and higher grasp of truth. Whatever was derivative tended to be suppressed. Any comprehensive theory must be vulnerable.[63] Even Harnack did not hold to his definition of Gnosticism as 'acute hellenisation'.[64] Norden's account of an oriental beginning is implausible; he denied that 'knowledge' of God could be a purely Hellenistic idea since neither ἄγνωστος nor γνῶσις is ever linked with θεός in the Platonic lexicon![65] (It was odd not to see the logic of negative theology in *Republic* 508e–509b or *Parmenides* 134bc.)

One interpretation starts from Platonism as theology, and knowledge as the quest of the classical world.[66] It then claims that Gnosticism is simply an interpretation of Pauline theology, since this is where the key words, γνῶσις, πίστις, σοφία are found, one generation earlier.[67] The striking characteristic of Christianity was its newness and it was this that Gnosticism sought to exploit. Paul's concern for wisdom, knowledge and righteousness was central to his thought;[68] the knowledge of the spiritual man is now imperfect and there is no rejection of the knowledge which was there before Christ came.[69] For Plato as for Paul, God, not man, was the measure of all things, and for Isaiah as for Paul, all wisdom without God was folly.[70] The veil of mystery must be lifted so that the truth may be seen; in Christian Platonism as in Paul, Christ takes the veil away.[71]

Claims for Gnostic originality on any logical point have yet to be substantiated. Perhaps Basilides saw the reason behind *creatio ex nihilo*;[72] but Hermas had already made it fundamental to Christian belief. Theophilus also insisted that all things came from God alone (*Autol.* 2.4), so that it would be odd to attribute the origin of the idea to Basilides, who used the formula without abandoning the dualism against which it was directed.

---

[63] See the critique of H. Jonas, in H. Langerbeck, *Aufsätze zur Gnosis* (Göttingen, 1967), 21–8.   [64] *Ibid.*, 29.
[65] *Ibid.*, 33. This is a splendid example of philological stamp-collecting, which ignores the central principle that different words can mean the same thing and that the same words can mean different things.   [66] *Ibid.*, 37. This was Jaeger's view.
[67] *Ibid.*, 81.   [68] *Ibid.*, 93–9.   [69] *Ibid.*, 107.   [70] *Ibid.*, 117 and 121.
[71] *Ibid.*, 137.   [72] G. May, *Schöpfung aus dem Nichts* (Berlin, 1978), 63–85.

Three grounds for the rejection of Gnosticism by other Christians are commonly selected: non-conformist ethical behaviour, denigration of the creator God and docetic christology.[73] There was a more fundamental ground: the method by which these and other opinions were reached. Gnostics avoided the processes of reason and claimed a higher way. Ordinary Christians looked for faith, reason and knowledge. Gnostics wanted to solve the problem of God with a story. That had been done before, in the beginning of the gospel; but the problem had changed into a logical or a philosophical one. What was needed was not more stories but philosophical thought. This was, from the evidence we have, beyond the scope of Gnostics and so they faded into relative oblivion until hungry publishers recently discovered them. The simplicity of the difference has been missed because nothing was monolithic. Theologians used symbol and enigma as well as argument; but theosophy had little argument and its God was not the ἀρχὴ τοῦ λογικοῦ τόπου.

Marcion was a dualist, but not a Gnostic. His main work was called *Antitheses* and that of his follower Apelles *Syllogisms*. Because he employed argument, he was at once a more serious and a more useful threat. He saw the newness of the gospel, and the wonder of the love revealed in Christ. Such love was plainly incompatible with the biblical creator of this world, because of the imperfections of the world and the barbarities of the Jewish God. Therefore there were two Gods: the strange god who was father of Jesus and the demiurge whose poor record was due to his limited knowledge and power. Paul, he claimed, had seen the contrast. No one has ever been able to avoid it. Marcion did not expound a special knowledge, but took his stand on faith, the Gospel and Epistles which he edited into a canon, and on argument. Yet he attacked the central claim that God was one. Tertullian put the argument against him: it was all a matter of number and God was not God if he was not one.

[73] G. W. MacRae, in *Jewish and Christian self-definition*, ed. E. P. Sanders, 1 (London, 1980), 128–33.

PHILOSOPHERS: WHAT HAS ATHENS TO DO WITH JERUSALEM?

Widely different answers were given to this question. Eusebius[74] tells of a group of Christians who applied logic to scripture under the guidance of Theodotus, a cobbler. They finished up without scripture and with Euclid, Aristotle, Theophrastus and Galen. However Galen[75] saw logical argument for the few and parable or miracle for the many; while fideist Christians belong to the second group, he said, they act like philosophers in their moral restraint and their contempt for death. Justin found Christianity to be the only sure and useful philosophy (*dial.* 8); but Galen found the arbitrary actions of the creator of Genesis plainly inferior to the rational design of Plato's demiurge.[76] Creation out of nothing was not acceptable to classical thinkers.[77]

Celsus complains concerning Christian fideism (*Cels.* 1.9; 3.55); he charges Christ with miracles through magic (*Cels.* 1.6), and his followers with magical incantations (*Cels.* 1.68). Although Celsus insists that he had encountered no Christian intellectuals, it has been claimed that he wrote in response to Justin.[78] The evidence for this hypothesis is limited,[79] and some of it has been shown to point the other way. For example, the lists of deified men (*Cels.* 3.22 and 1 *apol.* 21) suggest that Celsus did not know Justin.[80] However we shall see that the total argument supports the hypothesis.[81] Celsus objects to the incarnation as indicating mutability and limitation in God (*Cels.* 4.2 and 14), to resurrection as a sign of irrationality in God who is sovereign pure reason (*Cels.* 5.14), and finally to the worship of Jesus (*Cels.* 8.14) as inconsistent with monotheism.

---

[74] *h.e.* 5.28.13–25, 'Little Labyrinth'.

[75] R. Walzer, *Galen on Jews and Christians* (Oxford, 1949), 15.

[76] *De usu partium*, 11.14.

[77] Aristotle, *Physics* 187a, 33f., Lucretius *de rerum natura* 1.160, Plutarch, *de anim. procr. in Tim.*, *Moralia* 1014b, Celsus, *Cels.* 5.14.

[78] See C. Andresen, *Logos und Nomos, Die Polemik des Kelsos wider das Christentum* (Berlin, 1955), 308–72.

[79] See E. F. Osborn, *Justin Martyr* (Tübingen, 1973), 168–70.

[80] G. T. Burke, Celsus and Justin: Carl Andresen revisited, *ZNW*, 76 (1985), 114.

[81] See below, pp. 197–9.

The story of Jesus is unreliable and improbable (*Cels.* 1.41 and 2.55) and the abandonment of the Jewish Law removes the one ancient security which Christians might have used (*Cels.* 2.4 and 10).

Celsus made the perceptive comment that Christians were more concerned with Jesus than with God (*Cels.* 8.12, 14, 15). This criticism confirms a central problem of this book: why must God be one and more than one? Morally, Christians faced the future like worms, who hoped to be lifted out of the ground (*Cels.* 5.14). Atheists, they could not be trusted by honest god-fearing Romans.

Lucian regarded Christians as naïve and credulous, ready prey for any trickster. Jesus was nothing but a charlatan, but so were most other religious figures of Lucian's day.[82] Lucian would not have called Christianity a 'detestable superstition', as Tacitus did, but saw it as yet another of the new cults which proved the credulity of mankind. Peregrinus (alias Proteus) discovered that Christians reverenced the crucified bringer of a new mystery, despised death because they hoped for immortality, renounced the gods of Greece, held their goods in common and were wonderfully gullible. Nevertheless, a reading of Lucian convinced one classicist that Christianity faced no serious challenge. 'Christianity had no rival in its power to quicken the spiritual life of men, to satisfy their higher aspiration, to give life a zest which would have been incomprehensible to the Epicurean, to inspire a fortitude in the presence of suffering and death which transcended the teaching of the Porch, to concentrate unselfish energies on noble aims, and to sustain them by an ideal loftier than any which had been presented to the ancient world by religion, by patriotism, or by speculative thought.'[83]

Sophists were attacked by Clement, because they replaced philosophy with rhetoric and used words to make falsehoods appear true (*str.* 1.8.39). If rhetoric and disputation are not joined to philosophy, they can do nothing but harm. Plato called sophistry an 'evil art' and Aristotle declared it to be

---

[82] Cf. H. D. Betz, *Lukian von Samosata und das Neue Testament* (Berlin, 1961), 11f.
[83] R. Jebb, *Essays and Addresses* (Cambridge, 1907), 192.

dishonest and specious.[84] Euripides laments the power of skilful speech to destroy truth.[85] Plato, ruled by a love for truth, said, as if inspired by God, that he would obey only the reason which seemed to him best (*Crito* 46b). Those who are ruled by pleasure or fear are easily seduced by falsehood (*Rep.* 413).

To the Sophists, Clement gives the credit for the disordered structure of his *Stromateis* which demand thoughtful analysis from their readers. This is enough to keep the Sophists away from the secret of the true philosophy, for they will neither dig deep for what is hidden nor hunt after an elusive quarry (*str.* 1.2.21). They are marked by indefatigable mouths and a lust for trivia. They chatter like turtle-doves, they scratch and tickle the ears of those who like their sort of thing. As in old shoes, only their tongue is intact (*str.* 1.3.22). Greeks, like Democritus and Solon, have always warned against them (*str.* 1.3.22f.). Clement's great concern for logic springs from opposition to those who misuse it, as well as to those who think they are above it.

In Justin's *Dialogue*, Trypho voices the simpler Jewish objections which run back to the opponents of Paul. How could those who venerated a man, be judged true worshippers of God? What is the use of keeping half the Law? What moral or metaphysical insight could flow from a criminal on a cross? What sense could be made of human history after Abraham and Moses if the Law were not supreme? Judaism's diversity in faith and practice leaves us with a very complicated picture.

Near but still so far

In recent investigation the gap between first-century Jewish and Christian theology has narrowed. There was a second divine being in Jewish thought and this 'incipient binitarianism' could provide ground for *rapprochement*.

---

[84] Neither statement is a citation from Plato or Aristotle but each reflects a tradition linked with one of them. Cf. Sextus Empiricus Adv. Math. 2.12 and Aristotle *Top.* 126a.   [85] *Antiope*, frag. 206.

Paul's faith in one God and one Lord (1 Cor. 8:6) suggests a twofold structure which is close to much of Judaism. The break must occur when the worship given to Jesus goes beyond that normally given to divine agents in Judaism.[86] There is ample evidence that, 'within the first two decades of Christianity, Jewish Christians gathered in Jesus' name for worship, prayed to him and sang hymns to him, regarded him as exalted to a position of heavenly rule above all angelic orders, appropriated to him titles and Old Testament passages originally referring to God, sought to bring fellow Jews as well as Gentiles to embrace him as the divinely appointed redeemer, and in general redefined their devotion to the God of their fathers so as to include the veneration of Jesus'.[87]

Judaism had recognised three kinds of divine agents who shared in God's rule. There were personified divine attributes such as Wisdom or Logos,[88] exalted patriarchs like Adam, Seth, Enoch, Abraham, Jacob and Moses,[89] and chief angels like Michael and Yahoel.[90] There were permutations and combinations between these categories. The Gnostic demiurge, it has been claimed, might have been anticipated by the creative work of the divine Name and of the Angel of the Lord, who possessed the Tetragrammaton.[91] Clement of Alexandria, quoting the Preaching of Peter, accuses Jews of worshipping angels (*str.* 6.5.39–41). Their worship of angels and archangels, of months and of the moon, discredits their claim to exclusive knowledge of one God. Origen defends the Jew against the accusation of angel worship which was, he maintained, incompatible with their beliefs (*Cels.* 5.6). Philo refers to Moses as divine in the limited sense that the wise man is a god to a foolish man (*det.* 161). Perhaps Philo is inconsistent on this point and he does indeed deify Moses,[92] for example, in the prayer to

---

[86] L. Hurtado, *One God, one lord: early Christian devotion and ancient Jewish monotheism* (Philadelphia, 1988), 8.   [87] *Ibid.*, 11.   [88] *Ibid.*, chapter 2.

[89] *Ibid.*, chapter 3.   [90] *Ibid.*, chapter 4.

[91] See J. E. Fossum, *The name of God and the angel of the lord* (Tübingen, 1985). See also A. F. Segal, *Two powers in heaven: early rabbinic reports about Christianity and Gnosticism* (Leiden, 1977), 244–59.

[92] See E. R. Goodenough, *By light, light: the mystic gospel of hellenistic Judaism* (New Haven, 1935), 223–34.

Moses as hierophant (*somn.* 1.164f.).[93] In the second century, Jews had no problem with a chief angel; the question for the Rabbis was whether, in some cases, such a belief compromised monotheism.[94] Generally, Jewish chief angels were not sufficiently important and independent to fall under the censure which 'two powers' drew from the Rabbis.[95]

In contrast, Christians and Gnostics were regarded as heretical dualists by the Rabbis. Gradually, Christians and Jews came to see that Christianity stood for something different and 'that earliest Christian devotion constituted a significant mutation or innovation in Jewish monotheistic tradition.'[96] This devotion is found in hymns and prayers to Jesus, the confession of faith in him, the use of his name, the Lord's Supper and prophetic oracles attributed to the risen Christ. Yet such worship was not far from the veneration offered to angels in Jewish mysticism.

Apocalyptic, mysticism and riders 'in the chariot'

How much information concerning Judaism can be drawn from apocalyptic and mysticism? Recent enthusiasm insists that 'the language of the apocalypses is not descriptive, referential, newspaper [!] language, but the *expressive* language of poetry, which uses symbols and imagery to articulate a sense of feeling about the world'.[97] Yet here we find a Judaism which is not far from Christian faith. Merkabah mysticism, concerned with chariot visions, is a still more profitable area with its figure of the Metatron who shares the throne of God but remains subject to him. He is 'the most powerful figure... a minor god, but at the

[93] Hurtado, *One God*, 67, regards this as a rhetorical flourish.
[94] Segal, *Two Powers*, 187. Hurtado, *One God*, 91.
[95] Segal, *Two Powers*, 200f., goes on to hedge his claim by acknowledging the limits of our knowledge of first-century Judaism and allowing the possibility that the opposite of his conclusion might be true.
[96] Hurtado, *One God*, 99.
[97] 'Their abiding value does not lie in the pseudo-information they provide about cosmology or future history, but in their affirmation of a transcendent world.' J. J. Collins, *The apocalyptic imagination* (New York, 1984), 214. Such language is commissive and more congenial to the dynamics of political power. *Ibid.*, 215.

same time he is a servant, a slave of his master'.[98] Here also the positive affirmation of this world precludes both an apocalyptic vision of imminent destruction and Gnostic pessimism. If the mystic does not return from his journey above but dies in his journey, this is sufficient proof that he did not 'deserve to see the king in his beauty'.[99] Because both mysticism and Gnosticism are careless of logical consistency, there was mutual borrowing between the two; 'people were attracted by complex pictures even when these pictures were composed of the most heterogeneous elements'.[100] Christian Gnosticism came on the scene after Jewish traditions had absorbed Gnostic elements, and took over the mixture.

For example, parts of Clement's *Excerpta ex Theodoto* (37–9) clearly derive from Merkabah mysticism. In *Excerpta* 38 and 62 it is evident that 'the place' and 'the creator' are identical and this depends on Jewish sources where a parallel usage is widespread.[101] Further there are clear links between the Book of Elkasai, (commonly regarded as a Jewish-Christian work) and Merkabah mysticism.[102] Since Gnostic influence denigrated the creator, the Rabbis of the second century censured that part of the Haggadah on Gen. 1:26 which, by assigning the creation of the human body to the angels, thereby opened the way to dualism.[103]

Even Palestinian Judaism was affected by the environment of Gnosticism and mystery cult. Israel, as the vineyard of the Holy One, became a mystical body, inaccessible to outsiders, and the term μυστήριον was applied to the divine name, to circumcision, to the paschal sacrifice and especially to the Mishnah.[104]

Not all was mysticism and apocalypse. Some movement from Jerusalem to Athens is observable in Aristobulus. In the second

[98] I. Gruenwald, *Apocalyptic and Merkavah mysticism* (Leiden, 1980), 238.
[99] *Ibid.*, 111.   [100] *Ibid.*, 118.
[101] G. G. Scholem, *Jewish Gnosticism, Merkabah mysticism and Talmudic tradition* (New York, 1960), 34f.
[102] J. M. Baumgarten, The Book of Elkasai and Merkabah mysticism, *JSJ*, 17 (1986), 223.
[103] Jarl Fossum, Judaism, Samaritanism and Gnosticism, *JSJ*, 16 (1985), 238.
[104] J. J. Petuchowski, Judaism as 'Mystery' – the Hidden Agenda?, *HUCA*, 52 (1981), 152.

century BC, Pseudo-Aristeas has Moses as a philosopher whose starting point is one God whose power is evident in all creation.[105] The Wisdom of Solomon (13:1-9) perceives the creator in the beauty of his works, while 4 Maccabees indicates a knowledge of philosophy.[106]

Yabneh and one God

Yabneh, by fixing a canon, made a statement of belief, just as the Christian canon of scripture declared a rule of faith. Its militant monotheism is indicated by the Jewish wars and Jewish treatment of Christians. Sects persisted and there were plenty of visions and secrets; but, for Justin's Trypho, the sects were already outside Judaism. This can mean either that the reforms of Yabneh were speedily effective or that Justin was concerned with Jews who were hostile and that hostility came from the stricter monotheists.

Yabneh had become a centre for Jewish learning after the destruction of Jerusalem, and in the years 70–80, conservative tendencies were active to preserve Judaism. Christianity was now emerging as a distinctive group. The so-called Synod of Yabneh has been credited with two things: the introduction of liturgical cursing into the synagogue service and the fixing of the canon of Jewish scripture. The cursing was directed against Rome and against various groups of heretics.[107] Jewish Christians were not the sole target, but were included and thereby discouraged from attending services.[108] The canon of scripture came slowly from synagogue usage. The separation of Jews and Christians was not a direct result of either the cursing or the canon; both sides moved apart over a period of time.[109]

[105] J. J. Collins, *Between Athens and Jerusalem: Jewish identity in the Hellenistic diaspora* (New York, 1983), 179. See below, chapter 4, conclusion.
[106] R. Renehan, The Greek philosophic background of Fourth Maccabees, *RMP*, 115 (1972), 223–38.
[107] P. Schäfer, Die sogenannte Synode von Jabne, in *Studien zur Geschichte und Theologie des rabbinischen Judentums* (Leiden, 1978), 62.   [108] *Ibid.*, 52.
[109] *Ibid.*, 62. Schäfer (p. 1) begins from a discussion of the difficulties attached to the study of rabbinic or talmudic literature, because it is *Traditionsliteratur*, formed over a very long time and not the work of identifiable authors at identifiable times.

Another view maintains that Yabneh was concerned to tolerate, not to expel.[110] For the first time, Jews 'agreed to disagree',[111] so that the Mishnah emerged as a work with many conflicting opinions. Justin (*dial.* 80), we have seen, refers to Jewish sects which are not tolerated.[112] This indicates a more complex state of affairs than 'a grand coalition', where 'Perhaps some sects, aside from Samaritans and Christianizing Jews, lingered on for a while.'[113] It seems that Yabneh made a desert and called it peace. All who refused to join the coalition and insisted on sectarian definition were branded *minim* and cursed. 'Those Rabbis who could not learn the rules of pluralism and mutual tolerance were banned'; so that we are left with a society which was based on the doctrine that while some 'conflicting disputants may each be advancing the words of the living God', other disputants certainly were not.[114]

Within Judaism, heresy is serious because of birth dogma. Anyone who is born into an authoritarian religious community becomes automatically a member 'so that without his confessing to its dogmas, they are nevertheless obligatory upon him, and he is deemed a heretic should he ever reject them'.[115] Heresy should carry a death penalty.[116] 'Yahweh would never consent to forgive him... every curse recorded in this book would settle on him; Yahweh would blot out his very name from under the heavens, and Yahweh would single him out from all the tribes of Israel for doom, by all the curses recorded in this book of the law' (Deut. 29:19f.). This raises serious problems for philosophic religious faith which has to be 'free and justified assent to the truth of an intelligible proposition'.[117] It makes the whole issue of Jewish heresy more formidable and worthy of sympathetic consideration when 'cannons of controversy' are fired

---

[110] S. J. D. Cohen, The significance of Yavneh: Pharisees, Rabbis and the end of Jewish sectarianism, *HUCA*, 55 (1984), 27–53.   [111] *Ibid.*, 29.

[112] Cohen overstates the view which he wishes to disprove: Jewish sectarianism was 'not *flourishing*' despite Justin's evidence, because Justin, he discovers, was not a sociologist. Jewish society was 'not *torn*' by sectarian divisions. (My emphasis.) 'This conclusion cannot be upset by a lone baraita and by an elusive passage of Justin.' p. 36.   [113] *Ibid.*, 42 and 35f.   [114] *Ibid.*, 50f.

[115] A. J. Reines, Birth dogma and philosophic religious faith, *HUCA*, 46 (1975), 298.

[116] *Sanhedrin* 10:1; cf. Gen. 17:1–3 and 7–14, Deut. 29:8–14 and 17:20.

[117] *Ibid.*, 309.

in anger.[118] Christianity could not creep unnoticed into the world.

Rabbis used the criterion of 'two ultimate powers' to define heresy.[119] How it may be related to accounts of a 'second god' is not clear, since Philo, Numenius and Origen all meant something different by that term. Nor can dualism be explained in terms of social opposition. 'No doubt, some social and political forces were being expressed in the religious controversies'[120] is a safe platitude which does not explain the puzzle of dualism or the diversity within Judaism.

The tradition of two ultimate powers begins from biblical theophanies, where God is seen as a man or angel.[121] Paul uses 'two powers' polemic against Jews and, in the Fourth Gospel, Jews charge Christians with the same error. The issue is central to the division of Jew and Christian. In radical Gnosticism the second power was seen as hostile rather than complementary, and therefore Jewish criticism became stronger. Christians were classed with other 'apocalyptic or mystical groups who posited a primary angelic helper for God'.[122] The Rabbis claimed that all these groups had abandoned the monotheism of Deut. 32, Isa. 44:7 and Exod. 20. Dualism was sometimes based on strained exegesis of God's justice and mercy or of his *shekhina*. The accounts of Logos and Christ, which are given by Justin and Theophilus, use scripture in a way which the Rabbis condemn.

The limitations of rabbinic argument may be seen from one example: because God said publicly 'I am the Lord thy God' and no one protested, therefore there was no one else.[123] (Gnostics claimed that the members of the pleroma laughed at his ignorance.) In order to survive amidst growing confusion, the Rabbis adopted stricter standards,[124] which Christians and

[118] S. M. Passamaneck, Cannons of controversy, *HUCA*, 18 (1977), 265–99.
[119] A. F. Segal, *Two powers*.
[120] *Ibid.*, 267. The writer's difficulty is illuminated by an earlier comment, p. 14, 'Obviously all the scholars who have written on the problem of the "two powers" have seen Gnosticism, Judaism and Christianity as related phenomena, but I have not discussed that aspect of their thought yet because no two scholars agreed completely on the causal nexus between them.'   [121] *Ibid.*, 261.
[122] *Ibid.*, 262.   [123] Rabbi Nathan, *Mekhilta Bahodesh*, 5; cited Segal *ibid.*, 57.
[124] Segal, *Two powers*, 264.

'other' sectarians did not meet. Against Jewish adherence to formulae, the Gnostic movement flourished by equally arbitrary counter-assertion.

Synagogue cursing

Jewish hostility to Christians is recorded by Paul, first as persecutor and second as persecuted. For John, the expulsion of Christians from synagogues (John 9:22; 12:42; 16:1f.) is also clear. In rabbinic texts, Christians are included under the general terms of apostates, *minim*, Roman collaborators.[125] Justin (1 *apol.* 31.6) tells how Christians were persecuted under Bar Cochba and compelled to curse Christ; he frequently refers to the cursing and abuse of Christ and Christians by Jews (*dial.* 16.4; 47.4; 93.4; 95; 96; 108.3; 117; 123; 133.6; 137). This included but was not confined to a liturgical practice (*dial.* 47.4): the twelfth 'benediction' of the prayer of eighteen petitions. Here again the *minim* and the *Nazoreans* are cryptic terms which were taken to include Christians, although what the speaker meant was known only to him.[126] It was common to designate heretics or apostates in veiled speech: Matthew speaks of 'swine' and Paul speaks of 'dogs'.[127]

The formal cursing of Christians was taken up within the prayer and there was also subsequent abuse of Christ. Justin speaks of insults to the king of Israel, 'in accordance with the teaching of the heads of the synagogue, after the prayer' (*dial.* 137.1). Abuse of Jesus would be more distressing, as Justin says, than abuse of Christians. 'Do not, my brothers, say any evil against the crucified one and do not mock at his stripes, by which all may be healed as we have been healed.' ἐπισκώπτω and λοιδορέω are nasty words (*paed.* 1.7.66 and 74). Jews also cursed Christ to escape Roman persecution; but Justin speaks of a persistent practice, directed towards Christian expulsion rather than Roman appeasement. Justin knows that Jews regard at least five Christian claims as blasphemous and this

---

[125] J. Maier, *Jüdische Auseinandersetzung mit dem Christentum in der Antike* (Darmstadt, 1982), 131.   [126] *Ibid.*, 141.
[127] Ambiguity was to play an important role under the Christian empire. See T. C. G. Thornton, Christian understanding of the BIRKATH HA-MINIM in the Eastern Roman Empire, *JThS* 38, 2 (1987), 419–31.

would make cursing more probable. Christians were commonly regarded as Jewish apostates because they used Jewish scriptures, and the later case of Chrysostom is not 'abundant evidence that Christians were welcome in the synagogue'.[128] Evidence for the persecution of Christians by Jews and by Romans at the instigation of Jews, is strong.[129] It was a major stimulus to Justin in his apologetic writing.

The evidence of Justin is supported on many sides. The diversity of Jewish attack on Christianity confirms the accuracy of his account of ritual cursing.[130] The cursing of heretics, approved at Yabneh, found in different verbal forms, was a bond of Jewish unity and expressed liturgically the separation effected in the second half of the first century.[131] Conflicting evidence on the exclusion of Christians from synagogues may be explained by the different stages of separation between Jew and Christian. At first Christians were punished within the community; when this proved ineffective, exclusion followed. Gentile visitors to synagogues were welcomed in hope of their conversion; but Christians were cursed because they had rejected the claims of Judaism. This could also discourage them from taking cover, under Judaism, from the persecution of Rome.

The Jews, for Justin, were a hostile group, who ill-treated the Christian minority and needed to be conciliated by extended apologetic. They had their variety and divisions;[132] but there was a moral majority with strong ideas on monotheism and apostasy, and these were the object of Justin's respectful scriptural debate and plea for brotherhood. Justin's restrained manner and respect for his Jewish colleagues provide strong arguments for his reliability. So we may accept also the accuracy of Justin's account (1 *apol.* 31.6) of the persecution of Christians

[128] R. Kimelman, Birkhat ha minim and the lack of evidence for an anti-Christian Jewish prayer in late antiquity in *Jewish and Christian self-definition*, ed. E. P. Sanders, II (London, 1981), 244.   [129] Maier, *Jüdische Auseinandersetzung*, 133–5.
[130] 'The curse, one of a number of measures against emergent Christianity, was a form of the benediction of the *minim*'. W. Horbury, The benediction of the *minim* and early Jewish Christian controversy, *JThS* 33, 1 (1982), 59.   [131] *Ibid.*, 61.
[132] There was great variety within Judaism in the second century, as in the Middle Ages and indeed today. Justin cannot speak to all Jews but he clearly represents a Judaism which he knows.

by Bar Cochba,[133] who was ruthless against any who would not
follow him. His revolt was patently messianic in its inspiration
and Christians could hardly follow another Messiah.[134] The
accuracy of Justin is further confirmed by Tertullian's use of
similar material in his *Adversus Judaeos*. For Tertullian began
from the prolonged chaos of an actual dispute between a
Christian and a Jewish proselyte. The disputants were aided by
supporters who barracked, shouted and prevented elucidation
point by point. Therefore Tertullian was determined to set
down, in his most irenic writing, the details of relevant
argument. Much of the material is also found in Justin, who had
similarly complained of noise in debate and found it necessary
to return to the same theme more than once.

Christianity and Judaism were divided in common possession
of the same scriptures. Justin talks of the validity and limits of
the Law, Jesus as Messiah and the church as the true Israel.[135]
Before the Jewish war Christians were punished in the synagogues, during the war they were persecuted as traitors, and
after the war they were expelled from the community of
Israel.[136]

The story is complex. Christian awareness of discontinuity
with Judaism began early. Christian preaching of the cross,
resurrection and return of Jesus as Messiah, ensured alienation
from Judaism. Yet strong links with temple and synagogue
persisted (Acts 2:46; 3:11; 5:12; Matt. 17:24-7; 5:23f.;
10:17; 24:20; Mark 2:20). Peter and James were responsible
for a new legal direction in Jerusalem.[137] With James, a rational,
nomistic form of the gospel emerges, which reaches a climax in
the Jewish Christianity of the Clementines and rejects Paul in

---

[133] P. Schäfer, *Der Bar-Kochba-Aufstand* (Tübingen, 1981), 60. I am also indebted to
Professor Schäfer for discussion on the previous question concerning the variety of
Judaism.

[134] Messias gegen Messias, N. N. Glatzer, *Geschichte der talmudischen Zeit* (Berlin, 1937),
40. See also E. Schürer, G. Vermes, F. Millar, *The history of the Jewish people in the age
of Jesus Christ (175 BC–AD 135)*, (Edinburgh, 1973), I 545, cited Schäfer, *Bar-Kokhba*,
60.

[135] L. Goppelt, *Christentum und Judentum im ersten und zweiten Jahrhundert* (Gütersloh,
1954), 288–301.   [136] *Ibid.*, 312.

[137] G. Strecker, Christentum und Judentum in den ersten beiden Jahrhunderten, in
Eschaton und Historie (Göttingen, 1969), 295.

favour of Peter and James.[138] Yet conflict between Judaism and Christianity is intensified. In Pauline and other gentile churches, the influence of Jewish teaching is evident in church order and ethics. Justin and Irenaeus distinguish the natural law from the ephemeral parts of Mosaic Law. The love command fulfils the law of nature (*haer.* 4.12.1f.) and the gospel is the law of freedom and life (*haer.* 4.34.3f.). Yet it is important to see that the rejection of Marcion is more important than a *rapprochement* with Judaism. An insistence on rationality and free choice was characteristic of the later period and it was directed against blind obedience to the Mosaic Law.

Ignatius directs his hostility against Christians who want to improve their Christianity with Jewish supplements.[139] Saving history shows that Jewish doctrines are old and useless fables (*Magn.* 8.1) and to accept them would be to deny the grace received from Christ. The authoritative Christian documents are not the Jewish scriptures but the cross, resurrection and faith (*Magn.* 8.2). For Christianity did not 'believe on' Judaism but Judaism 'believed on' Christianity. Its scriptures pointed unambiguously to Christ (*Magn.* 10.3). Any interpreter of Judaism who does not speak of Christ, belongs to a past which is irrevocably dead (*Phil.* 6:1). With Theophilus the position changes in Israel's favour against Marcion. The Law is divine, Moses is God's servant and our prophet, and wonderful David is our ancestor (*Autol.* 3.9, 18, 25). The excellence of the Law is guaranteed by the separation of the ten κεφάλαια (*ibid.* 3.9) from the ritual law which is secondary.[140] Yet the scriptures belong to the Christians rather than to the Jews and there is little evidence of social relations between Jew and Christian.

To sum up, Judaism was, by its mysticism, closer to Christianity than is commonly recognised; but there was still a gulf fixed by the claims made for the crucified man, Jesus. Judaism was, by conviction, aggressive towards heretics, especially after Yabneh. Christians did not like being cursed, and they wanted to live at peace with most men.

[138] *Ibid.*, 302.
[139] W. A. Meeks and R. L. Wilken, *Jews and Christians in Antioch* (Missoula, 1978), 20.
[140] M. Simon, *Verus Israel* (Paris, 1964), 114–17; Meeks and Wilken, *Antioch*, 46.

GENEROUS ENEMIES

The pagan state, Gnostics, Marcionites, philosophers and Jews, all made life difficult for Christian believers. Yet at the same time, they contributed to the progress of the faith. Paganism embodied a rich heritage of classical culture without which theologians could not have written as they did. The state provided the stability of public order for which Christians prayed and the totalitarian structure which could later be used by a Christian emperor. The Roman achievement in distant places still bewilders the traveller to Africa, northern Europe and the East. Gnostics and Marcion were, from the volume of literature which they provoked, the greatest threat. Yet they reminded Christians of the newness of the gospel and showed that theosophical maunderings were not enough. Knowledge was always something more than one had, and without vision, people perish. Philosophy, chiefly Platonism, had no friendship for ignoble fideists; but the One, which was Nous and beyond Nous, provided a monism which was readily consistent with God and his only-begotten. Judaism, in Philo and elsewhere, by a simple translation of concepts, assimilated the Bible to Greek metaphysics. In apocalyptic mysticism, it produced close companions for God, so that monotheistic pluralism was no strange thing.

Clement's respectful and frequent use of Philo can lead his interpreters to overstate Philo's influence.[141] To select two examples, Philo is cited in Clement's account of God and of the good as assimilation to God. Nevertheless Paul and Plato (or other philosophers) are explicitly the sources of Clement's account of these topics, and Paul, as a renegade Jew, would have been lynched if he had fallen into Philo's hands. Paul is cited four times as often as Philo and Plato twice as often as Philo. Many of Clement's citations of Philo are inexact and unacknowledged. There is no problem here. Oral citation could be the explanation since the *Stromateis* come from the words of

---

[141] For a valuable recent discussion, see A. van den Hoek, *Clement of Alexandria and his use of Philo in the Stromateis* (Leiden, 1988).

Clement's teachers. More probably, inexact citation could point to written sources as is evident in the *Deipnosophistai* of Athenaeus where details of authorship are omitted and the substance of a citation is reproduced in a way appropriate to its new context: 'this may be in a straightforward way, a speaker simply using a quotation as his own words or incorporating it into them, or there may be interruption by the "narrative" such as it is. In general, there may be disruption of the original order of words... transference into *oratio obliqua* and in extreme cases paraphrase or adaptation to the context of the dialogue, even by facile substitution of words.'[142] The *Deipnosophistai* of Athenaeus[143] are filled with hundreds of citations concerning the place of food, cooking and wine in the Alexandrian good life of Clement's day. They show why it was necessary for Clement to write his *Paidagogos*, and why he uses so many citations from other authors. 'Ancient authors often cited each other inaccurately through misunderstanding or carelessness.'[144]

In spite of the mass of Philonic material, Clement's and Philo's interests were very different.[145] It has been said, of the exegetical borrowings from Philo, that for Clement 'encore ne sont-elles pas les plus intéressantes ni pour lui, ni pour nous.'[146] It has been pointed out that Clement's 'main problems (notably faith and logic, free will and determinism, and the correct evaluation of the natural order) are different from Philo's and are approached from quite another angle'.[147] Again there is no problem. However bulky the material which is lifted into a new context, it will take on a new meaning, which may or may not be consistent with its origin. Clement used Philo as a statement of the barbarian philosophy, and hoped that Jews would turn

---

[142] C. Collard, Athenaeus, the Epitome, Eustathius and quotations from tragedy, *RFIC* (1969), 157.

[143] Athenaeus, *The Deipnosophists*, with an English translation by C. B. Gulick (7 vols.), Loeb Classical Library (London, Cambridge, Mass., 1927–41).

[144] R. W. Sharples and D. W. Minter, Theophrastus on fungi: inaccurate citations, *JHS*, 103 (1983), 154.

[145] The question is discussed at greater length in my article, Philo and Clement: citation and influence, to appear in *FS for H.-J. Vogt*, edited by N. El-Khoury.

[146] C. Mondésert, *Clément d'Alexandrie, introduction à l'étude de sa pensée religieuse à partir de l'écriture* (Paris, 1944), 183.

[147] H. Chadwick, *Early Christian thought and the classical tradition* (Oxford, 1966), 142.

from what they had believed to the Christ on whom they had not believed (*str.* 2.1.2).

Rarely was the line of battle firmly drawn. Jews were indeed hostile to Christians, yet Justin allows that a Christian may keep the Mosaic Law provided that he does not make others do so. Jewish Christians could display various permutations. Imperial authority was recognised by Paul (Rom. 13:1–7) and Jesus (Mark 12:17). The Augustan empire and the Christian church had risen together and their mutual dependence was evident to Melito of Sardis (Eusebius, *h.e.* 4.26.7f.) and many other Christians. The Roman destruction of the Jewish temple validated the claims of the new Israel, and the Christian hope of Roman conversion postponed the end of the world which promised to be an unforgettable experience (*ap.* 32; *res.* 24). On the other side, Roman governors found it difficult to explain why Christians should be persecuted. 'It was easy to apply tests of loyalty... But men like Pliny were clearly embarrassed to have to do that.'[148]

Gnosticism was even harder to identify and isolate in the second century than it is today. The non-literal exegesis of scripture was widely practised. Those who took logic seriously, still had time for symbols and allegory. Clement was happy to borrow isolated points of enigmatic exegesis which he thought were right. Marcion's rejection of the Old Testament scriptures grew from a deep awareness of the newness of the gospel, an awareness which all Christians shared. Philosophers and Christians were selective in their praise and blame of one another. Justin and Clement gave to philosophy a subordinate but significant place. Tertullian rejected the pseudo-dialectical mythology which he found in heretical thought, but was able to own Seneca as *saepe noster* and to demand that secular culture be used for the furtherance of the gospel.[149] *Gaude pallium et exsulta!* (*pal.* 6.2).

Yet the opposition remained formidable. Jews denied that

---

[148] A. Momigliano, Some preliminary remarks on 'religious opposition' to the Roman empire, in *Opposition et résistances à l'empire d'Auguste à Trajan*, Fondation Hardt, Entretiens, XXXIII (1986), 123.

[149] J. C. Fredouille, *Tertullien, et la conversion de la culture antique* (Paris, 1972), 357. Osborn, *Christian philosophy*, 105–7.

Jesus could be God since God was one. The state religion claimed that Christians were atheists and immoral; they had no ethics. Philosophers said they were believers, not thinkers; they had no logic. Heretics, like Marcion and the Gnostics, declared that God could have no contact with the world; there could be no physics. All this opposition could not be ignored. Jews denied Christians the right to Old Testament scripture, which was the first source of their apologetic. The state denied their right to exist and offered martyrdom from time to time. Some Christians welcomed the criticism of the philosophers, since the cross was folly to the Greeks. Fideism remained an option and another evasion lay in Gnostic élitism; some Christians have always been happy to excel their fellow believers and the heresies were powerfully divisive.

The Christian answer to the question of one God in physics, ethics and logic began from two different concepts. God was one because of his sole rule (*monarchia*) and because of his recapitulation (*anakephalaiosis*), one as A and one as Ω: there had to be one beginning and one end, and God had to be both. The second-century account of one God spoke of the unbegun beginning and the summing up of all things. On the first account, the son had to seem subordinate to the father; on the second account the father was eclipsed by the son. Neither of these alone would do; both were needed. The two concepts were presented together and the intricacy of their relations produced complexity; but it did justice to the biblical account.

The emergence of Christian theology is our concern, the examination of its context and meaning. We have begun with the historical reconstruction of intellectual, social and political forces to which Christians were subjected. We turn next to the other element in their context: the ideas available in philosophy and the Bible. Then the question of meaning will lead to logical reconstruction of the thought of our five writers and their response to the problems of one God. God is the one first cause and *consummator*. He is son in father and father in son. He is first-principle of physics, ethics and logic.[150]

---

[150] The christological claim is only remarkable in conjunction with the primary claim that God is first cause.

The Old Testament had spoken of one God whose sole rule was declared in the Shema, in the conflict of Elijah and Elisha with the prophets of Baal, and in the reformation of Josiah. It spoke also of a new beginning and an end which would vindicate this God in the restoration of all things. The apocalyptic hope looked to the day when the lion would eat straw, when the wilderness would blossom as a rose, when sorrow and sighing would flee away.

Greek philosophy had shown a parallel concern for unity in complexity. The first-principle of all things was a recurring quest and the metaphysic of mind showed how all things became one. The puzzle of the concept of unity had long provoked discussion, so that contemporary philosophy, especially that which owed allegiance to Plato, was rich in intellectual resources for Christian use. In the next two chapters we shall examine the contributions of philosophy and the Bible to the Christian problems.

CHAPTER 2

The One and the Mind

Since, among philosophers, the one first-principle was not commonly called 'God', our three questions require translation into: Is there one first-principle of all things? Is there plurality within the first-principle? Is there one first-principle of physics, ethics and logic? Adequately to cover all these questions would take twenty books, not twenty pages. In Plato and his successors we shall find answers to all these questions. After Xenocrates we further note, in answer to the second question, the way in which mind becomes first-principle, in what has been called the metaphysic of mind or *Geistmetaphysik*.

The claim that there was one first-principle of all things, runs back to the beginning of Greek thought. Yet the diversity of Greek thinkers shows that the meaning of this claim was always changing. Monists argued with pluralists, but never in the same way, for the problems did not stay the same. Aristotle divided the early philosophers into those who derived all things from one first-principle and those who did not (*Ph.* 184b); but this was a particular use of ἀρχή and not even Plato used it in this way. According to Simplicius (*Ph.* 24.13), Anaximander was the first to use the word. Aristotle sets out six meanings of ἀρχή and concludes, 'It is common, then, to all first-principles to be *the first point from which a thing either is or comes to be and is known* ... Hence the nature of a thing is a first-principle, and so are the elements of a thing, and thought and will, and essence, and the final cause – for the good and beautiful are the first-principle

both of the knowledge and of the movement of many things'
(*Metaph.* 1013a).[1]

Plato answers our first and third questions, by arguing for one
first-principle of all things, and the same first-principle of
physics, ethics and logic. We find all this in the *Symposium* and
Republic. The *Symposium* shows in a lucid manner: first, the
movement from physical to spiritual beauty–goodness and from
many examples to the one lasting substance, secondly, the
negative element in this process which is constantly rejecting
something and moving on to something else, and finally, the
end, where perfect beauty–goodness is seen and contemplated.

Man seeks eternal glory either through his children or, better,
through the spiritual offspring which will live after him. The
poetry of Homer or Hesiod and the laws of Solon show that men
can produce things which are lovelier, wider in influence and
more permanent than human progeny. We are able to move
from the beauty of many bodies to an awareness of lovely form,
because the beauty of each body is the same form. Moving from
many to one, from the particular to the universal, we are saved
from a servile and illiberal devotion to the individual loveliness
of a single man or an institution. By saying 'no' to bodies and all
particular instances, we come in the end to knowledge of 'an
everlasting loveliness that neither comes nor goes, that neither
flowers nor fades; for such beauty is the same on every hand, the
same then as now, here as there, this way to that way, the same
to every worshipper as to any other. Nor will his vision of the
beautiful take the form of a face or of hands or anything that is
of the flesh; it will be neither words nor knowledge...but

---

[1] My emphasis. Earlier he claims a common nature for 'cause' and 'first-principle'
(1003b). Ambiguities of cause and first-principle are parallel, 'for all causes are first-
principles' (1013a). Nous or intuitive reason grasps first-principles (*EN*1141); but
there is no consistency in his terminology on this point. See W. K. C. Guthrie, *A
history of Greek philosophy*, VI, *Aristotle, an encounter* (Cambridge, 1981), 178–86, for
comment on some of the problems.

subsisting of itself and by itself in an eternal oneness while every lovely thing partakes of it in such a way that however much the parts wax or wane it will be neither more nor less, but still the same, inviolable whole.' Movement to the one beauty involves rejection of physical objects and their plurality. Yet while the many are not to be confused with the one, every lovely thing partakes of the one ultimate beauty. This beauty is apprehended directly when we 'gaze on beauty's very self, unsullied, unalloyed, free from the mortal taint that haunts the frailer loveliness of flesh and blood'.[2]

Plato's most extended account of the first-principle of being is found in the *Republic*, where his dialectic is supported by the three allegories of Sun, Divided Line and Cave.[3] Plato has made the distinction (505) between appearance and reality, between many and one. Some may prefer appearance to reality, but no one is satisfied with appearances when he comes to the question of the good. It is then objected (506) that Socrates has said what the good is not (such as knowledge and pleasure), but he has not said what the good is. To this Socrates replies, 'Then do you want a poor, blind, halting display from me when you can get such splendid accounts from other people?' He is pressed to give an account of the offspring of the good and moves into the allegory of the Sun. He distinguishes many particular things that are good from the single form of goodness (507b). The form of the good gives truth to the objects of knowledge and the power of knowing to the mind; it is the cause of knowledge and truth but is other and still fairer than they (508e). It is beyond all that man can think just as the sun is beyond the light and the sight which it causes. Both sun and good transcend the things which they cause. The form of the good is 'beyond the reality of the forms and superior to it in dignity and power'. In the Divided Line, the sight moves from images to objects in the visible sphere and the mind moves from geometrical objects to forms in the intelligible sphere (511). Finally in the Cave, the reflections and shadows have to be rejected in favour of the light

---

[2] For the Symposium I have followed, with modifications, the translation of Michael Joyce, in *Five dialogues of Plato*, Everyman edition (London, 1942).

[3] See translation of H. D. P. Lee, Penguin Books (Harmondsworth, 1980).

and the sun, and for the prisoner who ascends, 'the process
would be a painful one, to which he would much object, and
when he emerged into the light his eyes would be so dazzled by
the glare of it that he wouldn't be able to see a single one of the
things he was now told were real... Later on he would come to
the conclusion that it is the sun that produces the changing
seasons and years and controls everything in the visible world,
and is in a sense responsible for everything that he and his fellow
prisoners used to see' (516). Similarly in the intelligible realm,
the last thing to be perceived is the form of the good which
causes whatever is right and good in anything, and all truth and
intelligence (517). The conversion which leads to this vision
turns the mind away from the world of change until it can
endure to look straight at being and at the brightest being of all,
which is the good (518). Those who have seen the good should
return to the cave and rule those who are below. Once they are
accustomed to the dark then they will see a thousand times
better than others, will distinguish the different shadows and
know the forms behind them, because they have seen the truth
of what is just and good (520). In the *Phaedrus* Plato speaks of the
ascent of the soul to the place of true being, accessible not to the
senses, but to reason alone, and the source of all true knowledge
(247ce).

Plato moves towards an answer to our second question, 'Is
there plurality in the first-principle?' in his enigmatic *Parmenides*. Today many readers take this dialogue as a purely logical
exercise; in the second century, some readers took it as a
metaphysical statement. It is worth while to look at it more
closely. In the *Parmenides* Plato indicates four sets of contradictions or antinomies, which follow from the proposition, if
unity is (i.e. if there is a one), and its negation. The argument
may be set out in four hypotheses:[4]

1 if unity is, what follows for unity;
2 if unity is, what follows for other things;
3 if unity is not, what follows for unity;
4 if unity is not, what follows for the others.

[4] R. E. Allen, *Plato's Parmenides*, tr. and analysis (Oxford, 1983), 185.

The first movement of the first hypothesis argues that if there is a one, the One will not be many, cannot have any parts or be a whole. It has no beginning, middle, limits or shape; it is not anywhere, being neither in itself nor another, neither at rest nor at motion; it cannot be either the same as itself nor another, cannot be like or unlike either another or itself. It cannot be either equal to or not equal to itself or another; it has nothing to do with time and does not occupy any stretch of time. Finally, the One in no sense is, is not named or spoken of, is not an object of opinion or of knowledge, nor is perceived by any creature (137c–142a).

The second movement of the first hypothesis speaks of a complex unity. If a one is, it is one entity, a whole of parts, indefinitely numerous and also limited, with extension and shape, both in itself and in another, having motion and being at rest. The One is the same as, and different from, both itself and others. It is like and unlike itself and others, with which it both has and does not have contact, is both equal and unequal in magnitude and in number. The One exists in time, both is and is not, becomes and does not become, is older and younger than itself and others. It can be known and named and discussed (142b–155e).[5]

Each of the other three hypotheses is argued out in a similar manner with equally paradoxical results. The argument may be seen as an exercise in dialectic which draws contradictory consequences from the proposition 'if unity is' or 'if there is a one'. It is an answer to Zeno's answer to the pluralists' answer to Parmenides. Zeno showed that the pluralists could not avoid contradictions. Plato, in turn, showed the weaknesses of Zeno's monist position by indicating the contradictions which follow from each of four hypotheses. The end of the exercise is ἀπορία. A useful analysis of the dialogue shows that the puzzle in each of the antinomies is a worthwhile problem and not just a verbal

---

[5] F. M. Cornford, *Plato and Parmenides* (London, 1939), 102–245, divides each antinomy into two, separating the One and the One-many, so that the two movements in each refer to different things, namely, if unity is when unity is a one, and if unity is when unity is a one-many. He finishes up with nine hypotheses, calling the third movement within the first antimony 'Hypothesis 2a'.

quibble.[6] In this piece of serious reasoning it is clear that certain common assumptions will inevitably end in contradictions.

The first set of assumptions is that the One cannot be many, that the One possesses the attributes of being, and that the possession of more than one attribute pluralises the subject. The first antinomy claims that if the One exists it is already more than one, because it has both unity and being. This became an important principle and the basis of much negative theology. For if anyone says that the One has being, he should proceed to say all sorts of other things; therefore it would seem necessary to place the One beyond being and to deny its existence.

In the *Parmenides*, we are close to an answer to our second question: is there plurality in the One? Plato is able to talk about a one and a one-many which are the same thing, yet are contradictory and necessary. A drastic modern explanation might be found in Wittgenstein, who suggests that the difference between a simple and a complex entity is in the mind of the beholder, which sees One now *as* simple and now *as* complex.[7] This would not have satisfied Plato, but it is useful in the later Middle Platonic and Neoplatonic development.

It should be noted that Plato did not abandon the forms or the form of the good after he wrote the *Parmenides*.[8] The *Sophist* and the *Timaeus* still maintain, in different ways, the importance of the forms. The form of the good plays a part in the argument of the *Philebus*, as a conjunction of beauty, proportion and truth (65a). What is measured or appropriate stands above all other goods (66a), and by it, the priority of reason over pleasure is decided (66e). Plato's famous lecture on the good belongs to the later period of his life. Therefore, the *Parmenides* did not dislodge either the forms or the form of the good from their place in Plato's thought. He had shown the necessity of plurality within one first-principle; but he continued to affirm the unity of the

[6] M. Schofield, The antinomies of Plato's Parmenides, *CQ*, 27, 1 (1977), 139–58.
[7] L. Wittgenstein, *Philosophical investigations* trans. G. E. M. Anscombe (Oxford, 1963), 46f. Wittgenstein cites Plato's *Theaetetus*.
[8] D. Ross, *Plato's theory of ideas* (Oxford, 1963), 87. On the ideas, 'Plato nowhere answers Parmenides' argument; but he continued to hold the theory of Ideas, and therefore plainly thought the argument not fatal to the theory'.

first-principle. At some stage he identified the good and the One.[9]

Also important for our discussion is the argument for a first mover in Book 10 of the *Laws*, where it is proposed that false belief about the gods be considered a crime against the state and suppressed by magistrates. There are three heresies which are pernicious; atheism (that there are no gods at all), indifferentism (that the gods are indifferent to human behaviour), and opportunism (that divine judgement can be evaded by gifts and offerings). Plato further undertakes to prove that all bodily movements must be dependent for their cause on movements of the soul which alone generates its own movement. The world is the work of a soul or souls, these souls are good and have as their head a supremely good soul ἀρίστη ψυχή. The enemy is atheism which combines the materialism of the Ionians with the moral relativism of the Sophists. To prove that bodily movement is always caused by movement of the soul, which is prior to body, Plato analyses ten kinds of movement and shows that whatever possesses spontaneous or self-generated movement is called ἔμψυχον. ψυχή is what we call self-initiated movement, 'the same reality which has the name "soul" in the vocabulary of us all has self-movement as its definition' (Laws 896a) and it must be the cause of all movement in the cosmos. The soul may function with or without a body and the supremely good soul, which rules the heavens, is divine. 'This soul, whether we take it to bring light to the world by driving the sun as its chariot, or from outside, or in whatever way, each of us should esteem a god' (*Laws* 899a). Yet the question whether there was one god or many was not regarded by Plato as an important question,[10] and θεός did not carry the same connotation for him as 'god' does for us.

A similar argument leads to *one* first mover in Aristotle, who concludes 'Since motion must always exist and must not cease, there must necessarily be something eternal, either one thing or many, that first initiates motion and this first mover must be

---

[9] J. M. Rist, *The mind of Aristotle: a study in philosophical growth* (Toronto, 1989), 199.
[10] A. E. Taylor, *Plato, the man and his work* (London, 1949), 492.

unmoved' (*Ph.* 258b). Since all movement requires a mover, the only way to avoid infinite regress is to posit an unmoved mover.

The prime mover must be pure actuality and in no way potential, for 'if there is something that is capable of causing movement or acting on things, but is not actually doing so, there will be no movement; for that which has a potentiality need not exercise it '(*Metaph.* 1071b). The unmoved mover is the final cause of all things and produces motion by being loved, whereas other things produce motion by being moved themselves. Its actuality means that it 'exists of necessity; and in so far as it exists by necessity, its mode of being is good, and it is in this sense a first-principle' (*Metaph.* 1072b). As the best, it is pure thought and the object of thought. 'If the God is always in that good state in which we sometimes are, this compels our wonder... And life also belongs to God; for the actuality of thought is life, and God is that actuality; and God's self-dependent actuality is life most good and eternal. We say therefore that God is a living being eternal, most good, so that life and duration continuous and eternal belong to God; for this is God' (*ibid*). This eternal, immovable substance, without magnitude, indivisible, impassive and unalterable 'thinks itself, seeing it is the best thing, and its thinking is a thinking of thinking' (*Metaph.* 1074b).

The 'unwritten doctrines' of Plato establish the One and the indefinite dyad as first-principles (Arist. *Metaph.* 987 ab). Plato differed from the Pythagoreans because he accepted the Heraclitean flux, and Socrates' unchangeable essences, which he called 'forms', and made them the causes and the elements of things. From the great and small and the One come the forms as numbers. Plato's dyad consists of great and small. The One imposes limit on the formless dyad which is both indefinitely great and indefinitely small.[11]

On the basis of the dialogues, a modern writer proposes

---

[11] On this topic, see K. Gaiser, *Platons ungeschriebene Lehre* (2nd edn., Stuttgart, 1968); H.-J. Krämer, *Arete bei Platon und Aristoteles. Zum Wesen und zur Geschichte der platonischen Ontologie* (Heidelberg, 1959), 380–486, and W. K. C. Guthrie, *A history of Greek philosophy*, V, *The later Plato and the Academy* (Cambridge, 1978), 426–42.

Plato's 'unwritten *dialectic*', which concerns the relation of the One and the Two. In the *Phaedo*, Plato discusses the puzzle of how the number two is reached (96e–97b). According to the unwritten dialectic, everything comes from the One *and* from the Two. The monad and dyad are equally fundamental, because 'Someone understands what cognition, knowing, insight, is, only when he also understands how it can be that one and one are two and how "the two" is one'.[12] Further, for Plato, number needs both unity and plurality. 'The number consists of units each of which by itself is one and nevertheless the number itself, according to the number of units it includes, is not many but a definite "so-many", the unity of a multiplicity bound together: ἀμφότερα δύο ἑκάτερον δὲ ἕν [both two, but each one] (*Theaetetus* 185ab). Every logos has this formal structure.'[13] Knowing that Socrates walks means for Plato that he knows who Socrates is and what walking is and that the noun and the verb can be woven together. The example in the *Sophist* 263a 'Theaetetus flies' contains two ideas which cannot be woven together. Logos, insight, knowledge, always depends on joining *a* with *b* and seeing them as one.

Speusippus regarded the One as the seed or potency of all else. The seed does not possess the attributes of the plant which grows from it. The One causes goodness and being but cannot be good or be (frag. 34, Lang). Therefore it cannot be the first-principle of things, but needs plurality in order to produce things. From the viewpoint of later Platonism, 'And so, considering that if they took the One in itself, thought of as separate and alone, adding no other element to it, nothing else at all would come into being, they introduced the Indefinite dyad as the first-principle of beings.'[14] Iamblichus tells how Speusippus saw the progression from the One of different, successive first-principles: 'The elements from which numbers

---

[12] H.-G. Gadamer, *Dialogue and dialectic: eight hermeneutical studies on Plato* (New Haven and London, 1980), 135. Some philosophers see more Gadamer than Plato in this account.   [13] *Ibid.*, 147.

[14] *Procli commentarius in Parmenidem*, eds. Klibansky, Labowsky, Anscombe (London, 1953), 38, 31–41, 10. This account cannot stand unchallenged. See L. Tarán, *Speusippus of Athens* (Leiden, 1981).

derive are themselves not yet either beautiful or good; but out of the union of the One and the Cause of Multiplicity, Matter, there arises Number, and it is in this realm that there first appears Being and Beauty; and next in order there has arisen out of the elements of lines the geometrical realm, in which likewise there is Being and Beauty.'[15] The One is prior to mind.

METAPHYSIC OF MIND AND MIDDLE PLATONISM

Xenocrates gives a clear answer to our second question (Is there plurality in the one first-principle?), by affirming plurality in the first-principle which is both one and mind. He has been named as the founder of the *Geistmetaphysik* or metaphysic of mind which dominates later ancient philosophy. He presents the original sketch of the *Geistmetaphysik*.[16] He is also the first to distinguish explicitly between the three parts of philosophy which concern us, physics, ethics and logic (frag. 1),[17] although Aristotle may sometimes make the same distinction (*Top.* 105b). The monad is mind (frag. 16) which contemplates the ideas. Here again, we find the beginning of a central theme of later Platonism, that the ideas exist in the divine mind. Equally important is his concern for triadic distinctions. Ἐπιστήμη, αἴσθησις, δόξα, are the criteria of three forms of being: intelligible, sensible and mixed.[18]

While others may provide the beginning of Middle Platonism, it is to Alexandrian thinkers that we turn for fresh development. Here, for Eudorus, the One is the ground of all being and above attributes of any kind.[19] Then follow monad and dyad, as opposites, the former being good, limit and form, the latter being bad, limitless and formless matter. There is a tendency to greater unity. 'The postulation of a supreme, utterly tran-

---

[15] Iamblichus, *Comm. Math.* p. 16 (Festa), cited J. Dillon, *The Middle Platonists* (London, 1977), 16.
[16] H. J. Krämer, *Der Ursprung der Geistmetaphysik. Untersuchungen zur Geschichte des Platonismus zwischen Platon und Plotin* (Amsterdam, 1964), 126.
[17] Heinze, *Xenocrates*.
[18] Sextus Empiricus, *Adv. Math.* VII 147–9, cited Dillon, *Middle Platonists*, 30.
[19] Simplicius, *In Phys.*, 181, 10f., cited Dillon, *ibid.*, 126f.

scendent First Principle, which is also termed God, is a most fruitful development for later Platonism... The One is the ground of all existence; it is also the causal principle of Matter. This doctrine of Eudorus', which contradicts... strict Platonism, leads to a monism more extreme than that favoured by later Middle Platonism.'[20] Its appeal for later Christian tradition is clear; God would not be God if he were not the source of all being and the cause of matter if matter existed.

Following Jewish tradition, Philo of Alexandria[21] identifies the One with the God of the Old Testament, variously described as τὸ ὄν and ὁ ὤν. The monad is the incorporeal image of God, who is above all.[22] His transcendence requires a statement of negative theology, where God is ἀκατονόμαστος, ἄρρητος, κατὰ πάσας ἰδέας ἀκατάληπτος.[23] The stars are not gods, there is only one God and Lord of all; on him alone depends the preservation of all things.[24] Because he is one and indivisible, God is incomprehensible. The intellectual world can be grasped clearly, but God cannot. 'Moses desired insatiably to see God and to be seen by him, so he asked him that he should show clearly his reality which was difficult to comprehend. He wished to exchange his uncertainty for a firm faith... He penetrated into the darkness where God is, that is, in the hidden ideas of formlessness of being. For indeed, the cause is neither in darkness nor in space but transcends time and space;... so that the soul, which is friendly to God, when it seeks true being, discovers what is invisible and without form. From here it comes to the greatest good of all, to grasp that the being of God is beyond the grasp of every creature and to see that he is invisible.'[25] The flight to transcendence has no limit, and goes beyond the good, the One and the monad.[26]

Philo remains one of the riddles of intellectual history. His enthusiasm for his Jewish heritage inspires both a verbosity which can estrange serious readers, and a zeal which requires

---

[20] Dillon, *ibid.*, 127f.
[21] 'un élément étranger irreductible à la tradition platonicienne...la transcendance absolue du Dieu biblique'. J. Daniélou, Bulletin d'histoire des origines chrétiennes, *RSR*, 54 (1966), 300.   [22] *Spec. Leg.* 2,176.   [23] *Somn.* 1.67.
[24] *Spec. Leg.* 1.13 and 20.   [25] *Post.* 13–15.   [26] *Vita contemp.* 2.

the lynching of any apostate.[27] Yet he is an important figure and
a careful examination of his account of creation reveals a
knowledge of Plato and a subtlety of expression which will
reward his patient reader.[28]

Plutarch speaks of God as the good (*de def. or.* 423d) and One
(*de E.* 393bc). While there are dualistic tendencies, the One
remains supreme and controls the disorder of the dyad; 'but the
nature of the One limits and contains what is void and irrational
and indefinite in ἀπειρία, gives it shape, and renders it in some
way tolerant and receptive of definition' (*de def. or.* 428f). There
are four first-principles of all things: life, motion, generation,
decay and the first two are joined together by the monad (*de
facie* 591b).

Moderatus of Gades derives his scheme from the first
hypothesis of Plato's *Parmenides*, each of its movements corre-
sponding to an hypostasis.[29] He believed that Pythagoras had
said everything needful and that Plato, Aristotle, Speusippus,
Aristoxenus and Xenocrates took what they wanted from
Pythagoras, made it their own and then described as Pythagorean all the trivia they had not stolen.[30] This is, indeed, how a
Pythagorean might see the matter. The unity of mind, the
second One which truly is and is thought, mediates between the
transcendent first One and the realm of soul, which participates
in the two higher hypostases. The realm of sense and matter
does not share in being, but merely reflects as a shadow that
which is above it.[31] The dialectic of monad and dyad begins the
exposition of the decad. 'Thus the principle of Unity and
Sameness and Equality, and the cause of the σύμπνοια and
συμπάθεια of the Universe and of the preservation of that which
is always one and the same they call One, while the principle of
Otherness and Inequality and of everything that is divisible and
in the process of change and different at different times, they
termed the dual principle of dyad; for such is indeed the nature

[27] *Spec. leg.* 1.54f.
[28] See D. T. Runia, *Philo of Alexandria and the Timaeus of Plato*, 2 vols. (Leiden, 1986).
[29] See E. R. Dodds, The Parmenides of Plato and the origin of the Neoplatonic 'One',
     CQ, 22 (1928), 129–42.   [30] Porphyry, *Vita Pyth.* 53.
[31] Simplicius, attributed to Moderatus rather than to Porphyry, Dillon, *Middle
     Platonists*, 347.

of two in the realm of particulars.'[32] The subtlety of the account is notable. The second One generates beings by withdrawing its ἑνιαῖος λόγος, to make room for quantity without form, quantity as privation, dispersion and severance. What follows is the realm of matter, of the indefinite dyad, of particulars. The second One is not an opposition of monad and dyad, but a dialectic which is both single and twofold.

For Alcinous, the ideas are thoughts in the divine mind, and indicate plurality within the One. 'Whether God is mind, or a being with mind, in either case he must have thoughts and these must be eternal and unchanging; if this is so the ideas exist' (*Did.* 163). The descriptions and attributes of God are not ways of defining him but ways of giving him a name. Three ways of speaking of God are by negation, as in the first hypothesis of the *Parmenides*, by analogy, as in the allegory of the Sun in *Republic* 6, and by transcendence or ἀναγωγή, as in the speech of Diotima in the *Symposium*. God is without parts, unchanging and incorporeal (*Did.* 165). Philosophy is concerned with physics, ethics and logic.

The first God of Numenius is simple and indivisible, separate from the demiurge and from the created world (frag. 11). These constitute three gods, the first 'father', the second 'creator' and the third 'creation' (frag. 21). The first God is outside action, entirely given to contemplation, while the second God is double, both goodness and being, creating both his own form and the cosmos which is the third God. The triadic structure is as imprecise as it is in the *Second 'Platonic' Epistle* (312e), 'All things are related to the king of all, and they are for his sake, who is the cause of all things fair. The second things are related to the second, and the third things are related to the third.' While the first God is at rest and concerned with the intelligible realm, the second is in motion and concerned with the intelligible and sensible (frag. 15). Here we find a divergence from the *Geistmetaphysik* of Xenocrates: while the first god is pure unity, the second god is twofold (frag. 25).[33] In Xenocrates, the first god was both nous and monad.

---

[32] Porphyry, *Vita Pyth.*, 48.   [33] Krämer, *Geistmetaphysik*, 126.

Middle Platonism, which contains the background for the present study, provides its own response to several important puzzles.[34] The chief problem is the relation between simple and complex unity, between the simplicity and negativity of the first God and his designation as the mind which contains the world of ideas. 'The origin is on the one side the absolute simplicity which withdraws from any closer definition and can only be understood adequately in terms of the perfect abstraction of the *via negativa* (ἄφελε πάντα), but at the same time seems to be positively defined as νοῦς and moreover dismantled into the explicit plurality of the pyramid of ideas.'[35] Whereas Xenocrates solved the contradiction between simplicity and plurality by the analogy of the thinker and his many thoughts, in Numenius and others there is a substitution of a hierarchy for the unity found in those who followed the *Geistmetaphysik*.

CLEMENT OF ALEXANDRIA

Clement's account of the One is both a response to the challenges which confronted the Christian doctrine of God and an original contribution to the *Geistmetaphysik* of Middle Platonism. How far he was dependent on unknown sources we cannot be sure. He did not depend on Alcinous for his account of the One. Perhaps both used a lost commentary on the *Parmenides* or perhaps they made their own commentary within a common tradition.

For Clement, God is both mind and beyond mind, one and powerful. His account of the One still provides difficulties for interpreters and must therefore be considered in detail. For the common-places of negative theology change their meaning in different contexts; there are many varieties of silence about the same God. All the subtleties of the *Geistmetaphysik* are found in

---

[34] Which are not accessible to *Quellenforschung* because of its purely verbal character. However the parallels listed in Stählin's footnotes and set out in S. R. C. Lilla, *Clement of Alexandria: a study of Christian Platonism and Gnosticism* (Oxford, 1971), 119–226, are useful when they serve rather than replace the text.

[35] Krämer, *Geistmetaphysik*, 119.

his theology, especially the insistence that God is both nous and beyond nous, simple and complex unity, devoid of attributes yet infinitely powerful, one and yet beyond the monad. He is the ground of being and of goodness, for the end of faith is to become μοναδικός and the end of virtue is assimilation to him in undivided freedom from passion. God is the first-principle, mind, good, measure and number of all things (*prot.* 6.69.2 *et passim*). God is the One (*str.* 5.12.81 *et passim*) and beyond the One and monad (*paed.* 1.8.71), beyond the world of ideas (*str.* 5.6.38). The Logos is also one, a complex unity into which the believer is united (*str.* 4.25.156f.). The father is simple, one thing as one, and the son is complex, one thing as all things. Yet the son is in the father and the father is in the son, just as for the *Geistmetaphysik* the One is both simple and complex, as for Plotinus the three hypostases, according to some interpreters, retain some kind of unity or 'telescope' into one another, and as for Wittgenstein the same unity may be simple and complex depending on the way in which it is viewed.[36] Any unity may be 'seen as' both simple and complex.

According to Clement, the way to the knowledge of God is, as Plato has said, the way of symbol and of costly sacrifice (*pseud. Ep.* 2 and *Rep.* 2). Such a sacrifice has been made for us in Christ our passover (*str.* 5.10.66), and requires from us the sacrifice of all physical distraction and passion. This is why philosophy was for Socrates the practice of death, the concentration on purely mental objects, and why, says Clement, Pythagoras required five years silence from his pupils. All these ideas came from Moses (*str.* 5.11.67) who required that the holocaust be skinned. The soul which wishes to know must be free from matter, passions, lusts or else it will project all these things on God. Just as snails and hedgehogs roll themselves into a ball in which they can see only themselves, so men turn in on themselves and can see only a God who has all their material lusts. The Greeks longed in vain for the higher knowledge and mysteries. That

---

[36] For Plotinus the soul is simple (*Enn.* 1.1.2), mind is simple (*Enn.* 5.3.11 and 5.3.13) and not the simplest (*Enn.* 5.3.13). For Wittgenstein, see *Philosophical investigations*, tr. Anscombe, 21–4, 193–212.

way is now open in Christ, and is described in detail beginning from the elements of mathematics.

1 All physical properties must be abstracted: first depth, then width and length.
2 From the remaining point, position must be removed, to leave simple unity.
3 From this unity we throw ourselves into the μέγεθος τοῦ χριστοῦ and then, by holiness, advance into the ἀχανές, so that we come to a νόησις of the παντοκράτωρ, knowing not what he is but what he is not *(str.* 5.11.71).

Continuing with Clement, knowledge of God, as Moses and Solomon declared, can only come from God. The gift of knowledge comes from the son who is the tree of life and knowledge, bearing blossom by his knowledge in the garden of the earth. To the mysteries of the third day, which Abraham saw from afar (Gen. 23:3f.), the mind gains access through the teacher who rose on the third day. 'God's country is hard to reach; Plato called it the land of ideas, having learnt from Moses that it was the place of all things universally' *(str.* 5.11.73). Paul's vision face to face will come, said Plato, only when, from within the world of things that are, the mind, by itself, moves to the God who transcends them *(Rep.* 7.532; *str.* 5.11.74). Moses built only one temple to God, because there was only one world and only one God. (Basilides knows that there is one world but not that there is one God.) Moses, Isaiah, Euripides, Plato, Paul, Zeno and Zephaniah all said that earthly temples were inappropriate to the highest God.

To know this inaccessible God, Moses had to enter thick darkness and Paul had to ascend to the third heaven. Plato thought that there was only one heaven; but Clement of Rome and Paul saw infinity in the judgements and ways of God. The mysteries of the kingdom of heaven, hidden in three measures of meal, point to the threefold soul which is drawn by the power of the word into unity. ἕλκει καὶ τὸ πᾶν αὐτοῦ σύστημα εἰς ἑνότητα συνάγει *(str.* 5.12.80). Solon, says Clement, spoke of God's infinity[37] and Empedocles insisted that God, though inaccessible

---

[37] Diels, frag. 16. Clement, not Solon, transfers the reference to God.

to the senses, could be grasped with the mind. John tells of the only begotten God, who is in the bosom of the father, and who declares the God whom no one has seen. The invisible and ineffable has also been called Depth, by some people (Valentinians), because it contains and embraces all things, being inaccessible and without limit (ἀνέφικτόν τε καὶ ἀπέραντον) (*str.* 5.12.81). Then comes Clement's most pungent paragraph.

1 As ultimate first-principle, God is the most difficult principle to express in words.
2 None of the categories can apply to him.
3 He cannot be described as the 'whole' because he is father of all things and beyond magnitude.
4 Nor can any parts be predicated of him, the indivisible One.
5 His indivisibility makes him infinite, not in the ordinary sense that one cannot give a complete account of him, but,
6 in the sense that he cannot be broken up into logical parts, has no limit, and is therefore without form and name.[38]
7 The names we give him are props to our minds but do not express him.
8 The names indicate his almighty power and are not his predicates in any way.
9 He cannot be demonstrated because there is no more ultimate principle from which he may be inferred.
10 So God is known by his grace and the word which comes from him. This is what Paul told the worshippers of the Unknown God.

Three problems have arisen in recent interpretation, each concerning the indivisible One and each capable of easy solution.

---

[38] O. Stählin (Klemens von Alexandrien, *BKV*, 2, 19 (München, 1937), 4, 189) supports the interpretation which I have taken here:' nicht in dem Sinn, dass man es nicht erschöpfend behandeln kann '. The temptation is strong to take the antithesis ἀδιεξίτητον–ἀδιάστατον as 'infinitely extended–unextended' but this does not fit with Clement's account of the one as beyond categories and already devoid of properties other than oneness.

(i) It has been argued that, in Clement, the One is infinitely small, the smallest possible entity. Plutarch and Anaxagoras are quoted in support of this view.[39] However illuminating the claim, it cannot be true. The One is part of a *Geistmetaphysik*. Physical numbers have long been left behind. Clement's way to the One (*str.* 5.11.71) is reached by abstraction which takes away all dimensions and position. The many names of the nameless God indicate his almighty power. As Plotinus later argued, the One is not like other elements, the smallest of all, but the greatest, great in limitless power. 'It is not without parts in the way the smallest particle has no parts. For it is the greatest of all things, not in size, but in power... The infinite, indeed, must be understood, not within the categories of unlimited magnitude or number, but in terms of unbounded power (*Enn.* 6.9.6).

(ii) Infinity can be reached by pushing logical limits so far apart that a complete account cannot be given. The indivisibility of the One produces a different kind of infinity for in the One the logical limits are brought together so that they coincide and disappear.[40] On a spatial analogy, infinity can be achieved by pushing two points further and further apart, or by bringing them closer and closer together, until they coalesce. The infinite smallness which has been rejected above (i) provides an analogy of what is logically without limits. This gives it an infinity, which is here explained by Clement and which has been generally ignored.

(iii) While God is One and beyond the monad, this is not the only infinity which he possesses. As father of all he is beyond magnitude and dimensions. (As Depth, according to the Valentinians, he embraces all things and is inaccessible and infinite (*str.* 5.12.81).) Clement of Rome speaks of a limitless ocean and Paul speaks of the depth of the riches of the wisdom and knowledge of God.[41] Beyond all dimensions, and by way of the μέγεθος τοῦ χριστοῦ we reach God in the void (*str.* 5.11.71).

---

[39] John Whittaker, Philological comments on the Neoplatonic notion of infinity, in *Studies in Platonism and patristic thought* (London, 1984), 156.

[40] See Aristotle, *Ph.* 218a and *Metaph.* 1002b, for temporal and spatial analogy.

[41] 1*Ep. Cor.* 20.8; Rom. 11.33, cited *str.* 5.12.80.

It cannot therefore be claimed that God is infinite only in his indivisibility.[42] He is infinite as τῶν ὅλων πατήρ. The question is susceptible of extended analysis. Clement's position approaches that of Plotinus for whom the One is infinite in itself as it is infinite in power. For Plotinus, 'the One is infinite, the others finite, the One is creator, the others creatures, the One is entirely itself, entirely infinite, the others are both finite and infinite... the One has no otherness, the others are other than the One'.[43]

How then, says Clement, is the unknown God to be known (*str.* 4.25.156)? He is known, according to Plato, as mind by those who live as gods among men. The Eleatic stranger (*Sophist* 216ab), a dialectician, is such a stranger because he lives among the eternal ideas. What Plato attributed to the Coryphaeus in the *Theaetetus* (173c) is now found in perfect contemplation, in the life Christ gives in the midst of death. The life-giving power of one spirit can be known in the son.

1 The indemonstrable God is known in the son who is wisdom, knowledge and truth.
2 In him the powers of the spirit come together so that he is ὡς πάντα ἕν (*str.* 4.25.156).
3 As Alpha and Omega he joins the end to the beginning.
4 Faith in him means that the believer becomes one as he is drawn together in an indissoluble unity (*str.* 4.25.157).
5 The transformed life is described in heavenly dimensions.
6 God is the unbegun first-principle and the highest mystery. As being, he is the first-principle of physics, as good he is the first-principle of ethics and as mind he is the first-principle of logic.

Here the concepts of the all-powerful One, who is both mind and beyond mind, which are so important for Middle Platonism, and Paul's concept of the powers of the spirit, are evident.

---

[42] As was argued by E. Mühlenberg, *Die Unendlichkeit Gottes bei Gregor von Nyssa* (Göttingen, 1966), 75f., but denied by Whittaker, Philological comments, 168.

[43] J. M. Rist, *Plotinus, the road to reality* (Cambridge, 1967), 37. See also p. 25, 'Within recent years there has been a long and learned discussion on the infinity of the Plotinian One and from it we can learn much. The chief participants are now in basic agreement that the One is infinite in itself as well as infinite in power.'

'All the powers of the spirit, becoming together one thing, converge in the same point, the son; he cannot be described by listing each concept of his powers. For the son is not simply one thing as one, nor many things as parts, but one thing as all things. All things come from him. For he is the circle of all the powers rolled into one and united.'[44]

The power is universal, belongs to the father and especially provides the knowledge which gives life. Christ is the power of God, active everywhere and always (*str.* 6.6.47). The son is the power of the father, governing all things to the last detail (*str.* 7.2.9), working all things with untiring and invincible power according to the father's will (*str.* 7.2.5), as the undivided universal watchful power of God (*str.* 3.10.69). All things are filled by our teacher's holy powers of creation, salvation, providence, prophecy and teaching (*prot.* 11.112).

The powers belong to the father, whose word is his wisdom, goodness and almighty power. The divine word remains unknown to those who do not confess him (*str.* 5.1.6). The son is God's will, symphony and harmony, word of God, arm of the lord, power of the universe and the will of the father (*prot.* 12.120). God's power leads men to his knowledge. It spreads through the universe to declare the light inaccessible (*str.* 6.3.32). His providence works on us so that we must confess the only God (*prot.* 10.103). The true gnostic knows the son of God through the power of the father (*str.* 6.15.132).

In what other ways has Clement elucidated the problems of Middle Platonism and the *Geistmetaphysik* which confronted him?

(i) Clement stays with the unity of the monad and dyad as found in Xenocrates. Father and son draw the world together. The distinction between the father and the son is matched by an emphasis on their unity. The son is God in God (*exc. Thdt.* 8) and almighty God (*paed.* 3.7.39). His unity and being are the unity and being of the father (*paed.* 2.8.75; *prot.* 10). Both father and son are the ἄναρχος ἀρχή of all things (*str.* 4.25.162; 7.1.2). Reciprocity is a constant theme: 'O the great God! O the

---

[44] *str.* 4.25.156f. Cf. Plotinus, *Enn.* 5.1.7.

perfect child! Son in father and father in son!' (*paed.* 1.5.24) and 'God in the form of man undefiled; servant of his father's will, the logos who is God, who is in the father, who is at the right hand of the father and with the form of God is God' (*paed.* 1.2.4). Against any form of dualism, Clement insists that God cannot hate creation because it was made by his word or by himself and 'both are one, that is God' (*paed.* 1.8.62).

(ii) Clement retains the dialectic between the One and the two, through the notion of power. The word became flesh that he might be seen (*str.* 5.3.16). The mysteries of divine love, the bosom of the father have been declared by the only God. 'God himself is love and for love became visible to us' (*q.d.s.* 37). The universal activity of God is not restricted to creating and sustaining the universe. A divine dialectic is needed for God to be one and universal. The salvation of men is the work of the son to whom all men belong. 'How could he be saviour and lord if he were not the saviour and lord of all?' (*str.* 7.2.7). The divine saving power works like a magnet, through many rings of steel which represent the saving circles of different parts of salvation history. The law was given to the Hebrews and philosophy to the Greeks. 'Everything, then, which did not in any way obstruct man's free power of choice, he made conducive to virtue and showed it to be so. So that in some way or other, even to those who see only dimly, the true, only one almighty good God, might be manifest from eternity to eternity saving by the son and in no way whatever the cause of wickedness' (*str.* 7.2.12). Divine unity is not merely an external power, for the Logos enters the soul of the true Christian. 'In this soul, through obedience to the commandments, the ruler of all things mortal and immortal is consecrated and set apart. He is the king and author of good things. He is truly law, ordinance and eternal logos and he is individually to each and in common to all, one saviour. This is in truth the μονογενής, the stamp of the majesty of the king of all and the almighty father, who impresses on the perfect Christian the seal of perfect contemplation in accordance with his own image. So there is now a third divine image, which is made as like the second cause as possible and made like that life which is life indeed, the life through which we live the true life' (*str.* 7.3.16). The divine dialectic is complete. God has become man that man might become God. The unity of the many with the one is achieved by two moves, by a universal cause and dialectic of God becoming man, not by a hierarchy or causal chain. Some hierarchies persist in pockets; but they are logically subordinate to universal cause and dialectic. Clement's rejection of hierarchy is a deliberate choice on theological and logical grounds. Gnostic heretics chose the way of hierarchy and competed in their picture-book Platonism. Valentinus had thirty aeons, while Basilides had three hundred and sixty five. Clement's energetic insistence on God's unity and universality and his account of dialectic were aimed against three forms of divine pluralism: traditional polytheism, Gnostic multiplicity and Marcion's dualism.

THE ONE AS POWER, BEYOND THOUGHT AND BEING

Here we return to our first question: how can the One be first-principle and cause of all things? The One,[45] said Speusippus, was the seed of all else and in Plotinus the One is the source, root and seed from which the end unfolds (*Enn.* 4.8.6: ἐξιλιττέσθαι οἷον σπέρματος ἔκ τινος ἀμεροῦς ἀρχῆς εἰς τέλος cf. *Enn.* 6.9.9). These metaphors point to the One as power. (*Enn.* 5.3.15; 5.4.2; 3.8.9f.). To this set of images may be added the mathematical symbol of the circle whose radii meet in the One. The centre is that from which the circle unfolds (*Enn.* 6.9.8). As what is simple is the ἀρχή of what is not simple, so the One is ἀρχή of existing things, not as a genus, but as the number one is the element from which all numbers come (*Enn.* 6.2.10). As the point is common to all lines and the one is common to all numbers, so the first can turn into the last and the simple into the compound (*Enn.* 6.2.11).

The One is the first-principle and element of the intelligible numbers and consequently of all that is, including arithmetical numbers (*Enn.* 5.5.4).[46] The simplicity of the One is the

---

[45] This section is indebted to Krämer, *Geistmetaphysik*, 338–69.
[46] Krämer, *ibid.*, 343.

condition of its being first-principle and excludes all synthesis (*Enn.* 5.5.13). The One therefore is everywhere and nowhere for to possess anything more than its simplicity would deprive it of ultimacy. Addition causes diminution and defect (*Enn.* 3.9.4– 9). Yet at this very point, Plotinus insists that the One is the first-principle, source and power of all things.

Plotinus' account is corroborated from early Neopythagorean number theory where the One as δύναμις is seed, source and root. 'The monad is first-principle of all things... and from it come all things while it comes from nothing, indivisible and potentially all things.'[47] In the first half of the second century, Nicomachus, in his *introductio mathematica* uses the potential–actual relation to describe the relation of the monad to the series of numbers.[48] Later the same logic and metaphor are found in Iamblichus. More interesting is the Gnostic use of these ideas in a mythological form, replacing the mathematical argument with a story; the indivisible small point will become great. All these ideas, which derive from the early Academy, are widespread in Middle Platonism. Plotinus states them with greater clarity. Aristotle twice[49] indicates that Speusippus, like the Pythagoreans, bases his negative account of the One on its function as seed and potentiality. 'In that Speusippus', writes Krämer, 'excludes ὄν, οὐσία, ἀγαθόν, καλόν, νοῦς and θεός from the first-principle and thereby – at least in the case of ἀγαθόν – goes well beyond all Academics, he constitutes in fact with all its consequences, the pure first-principle free from all additives, or more precisely the στοιχεῖον idea of the Academic metaphysic.'[50]

But within the Academy the problem emerged: Was the One, like the Pythagorean mathematical στοιχεῖον, just the smallest finite particle, or was it the greatest and infinite? Plotinus distinguishes the One from the arithmetical monad (*Enn.* 6.9.6). As first-principle, it is the greatest, not like the other elements, the smallest. It is the greatest in its 'infinite power'. The fixed intensive infinity is the reason why it can be called elsewhere

---

[47] Theon of Smyrna, *Expositio* (Teubner, Leipzig, 1878), 99f., cited Krämer, *ibid.*, 346.
[48] e.g. 2.16.8 and 2.8.1.   [49] *Metaph.* 1072b 30ff. and 1092a 11ff.
[50] Krämer, *Geistmetaphysik*, 353.

'formless' and 'measureless'.[51] All of which is reminiscent of Plato's account of the good as prior to being which it excels in age and power, and of Clement's account of the infinite One.

Plotinus' rejection of Aristotle's divine mind leaves him terms like κατανόησις (*Enn.* 5.4.2.17) and ὑπερνόησις (*Enn.* 6.8.16) and a state of awareness which is transparent to itself. The One is the maker or creator, but does not use pre-existent matter, being concerned with existence not with the imposition of order.[52] Plotinus did not strip the One of teleological relevance; he wished simply to underline the mystery of ultimate causation. 'The role of the One is both to support existence rather than no existence, and to organize and (indirectly) arrange the rational movements of what exists.'[53] There is activity from the One and of the One (*Enn.* 5.4.2.27). Instead of mind, the One is seen as will, not merely cognitive but productive.[54] This points to the important sense in which a first-principle is sole cause and not dependent on forms or matter to produce the universe. 'Creativity, will, power, non-contingent cause and supporter of existence, first cause irreducible to conceptual analysis: it is a much more full-blooded concept of a first cause than Aristotle had proposed.' However these very attributes make the One closer to us and more like us, which is what it cannot afford to be.[55]

Plotinus does not depend on Middle Platonism so much as clarify the problems with which it was concerned. Plato in *Parmenides* and *Republic* 509 spoke of a transcendent first-principle which was beyond the being of the forms. Speusippus also placed the One beyond mind and God.[56] Xenocrates, however, gave transcendence to the Nous-monad as first God, One, king and element. The theology of Nous combined transcendence with immanence and provided the basis of most metaphysics of late antiquity. In Plotinus, the transcendence of

---

[51] *Ibid.*, 362.'d.h.als Unendliches im Intensiven, und kann darum zugleich in noch höherem Grade Einheit sein als die mathematische Monade.'

[52] J. M. Rist, The One of Plotinus, *RMet.*, 27,1 (1973), 83. 'It separates Plotinus from the metaphysics of Plato and Aristotle, for whereas these "classical" thinkers are concerned with a metaphysic of order, of the imposition of pattern or form on the indeterminate or chaotic, Plotinus' arguments are concerned with existence.'

[53] *Ibid.*, 84f.   [54] *Ibid.*, 68 *et passim*.   [55] *Ibid.*, 86f.   [56] frag. 38, Lang.

the One went beyond mind; but the three hypostases exhibited unity and might be merged together. The One is ὑπερνόησις or νόησις which does not think but is the cause of thinking in another.[57]

THE UNITY OF HYPOSTASES

Middle Platonism is inconclusive because it turns its first-principles into hypostases and arranges them in a religious hierarchy. Two options were open if not always clear for later Platonism. Plotinus avoided hierarchy by merging the hypostases, soul into intelligence and intelligence into One, and by a dialectic which held together the monad and the dyad. Iamblichus chose the way of hierarchy and multiplied triads without regard for logic. His imparticibles were based on the fallacy of the 'Third Man', a fallacy which Plato had clearly exposed in his *Parmenides*.[58] Proclus developed the same error in his many triads. All of which, it has been claimed, made the highest principle more transcendent and more accessible.[59] Nothing is stranger than this 'bureaucratic fallacy'. If one doubles the steps in a causal sequence, one doubles the number of relations which must be proved. Yet this was the way Platonism chose when it abandoned the insight of the *Geist-metaphysik* and the dialectic of monad and dyad. Gnostic theosophy had anticipated the hierarchy of later Platonists.

Since Plotinus builds on earlier Platonism to produce a scheme of thought which avoids later pitfalls, we shall briefly examine his position to decide whether there is plurality within the One. He links his metaphysic with Plato's *Parmenides*: a one which is nothing but one and is beyond language, a one which is all things and to which no limit may be fixed and a one which is also many. These three concepts point to the hypostases of the One, Nous, and Soul.

The problems of the ultimate One and the way to it are elucidated in extended discourse. How can the One produce

---

[57] *Enn.* 6.8.16 and 6.9.6. Despite the subtlety of Plotinus' account of the One, it has been argued (Krämer, *Geistmetaphysik*, 401) that most of this can be found elsewhere in the Pythagorean monad which is ἀρχή, στοιχεῖον, δύναμις.   [58] 131e–132b.

[59] A. C. Lloyd, The later Neoplatonists, in *The Cambridge history of later Greek and early medieval philosophy*, ed., A. H. Armstrong (Cambridge, 1967), 282.

what it does not contain? How can the One be described
positively? It has no common term with anything beyond itself
(*Enn.* 5.5.13). It can have no limiting condition (*Enn.* 5.5.6 and
6.8.11). This means that it cannot be part of a hierarchy or a
series. Yet the One must produce plurality because plurality is
inferior to it (*Enn.* 5.3.15). The One is all things in a transcendent mode and analogies can therefore be drawn. The One
is 'all things and none of them' (*Enn.* 5.2.1 and 6.7.32). It is the
power of all things (*Enn.* 3.8.10 and 5.1.7 and 5.3.15).

There is ample evidence that Plotinus merges his three
hypostases together. For example, we learn (*Enn.* 5.1.6) that
the One is immobile and can neither have assented nor decreed
nor stirred in any way towards the existence of a secondary
entity. A few lines later we are told that the soul is an utterance
and act of Nous 'as Nous is an utterance and act of the One'. In
the same section we are told that the offspring is always lesser
than that which begets it, but that, when the begetter is the
highest good, the offspring is separated only by being distinct.
While we are told (*Enn.* 5.1.5–7), that the One is simple, we
learn (*Enn.* 5.1.7) that Nous is part of the contents of the first,
although Nous is undivided and without parts. We are told
(*Enn.* 5.1.6) that the One has 'unfailing self-intention', while
Aristotle is criticised (*Enn.* 5.1.9) for allowing the One to have
the power of thought, because if any being has the power of
thought it cannot have primacy over other beings. After citing
Plato's *Parmenides* concerning pure unity, a one-many and a
third which is one and also many (*Enn.* 5.1.8), Plotinus tells of
the obligation to ask whether the principles in Aristotle's Nous
are one *or* many (*Enn.* 5.1.9). Finally (*Enn.* 5.5.9), God is an
instantaneous presence everywhere and while nothing is contained and nothing left empty, everything is fully held by God.
This has to be reconciled with the claim (*Enn.* 5.5.4) that there
is a simplicity in the One which rejects all participation and also
(*Enn.* 5.5.6) that absolute simplicity must be maintained.

The account of Nous gives similar evidence of the merging of
hypostases. Plotinus, like the Middle Platonists, distinguishes
between discursive thought which he places within the Soul and
intuitive thought which he places within the Nous. Discursive

thought moves from premiss to conclusion or from one object to another, while intuitive thought sees all things at once and is a special prerogative of Nous which shares the simultaneity which is the One (*Enn.* 1.8.2). While Soul moves (*Enn.* 5.1.4) and divides the life of Nous, Nous itself is a unity which embraces all. Soul cannot achieve unity but Nous possesses unity of subject and object (*Enn.* 3.8.8 and 5.3.2). Soul deals with images and words (*Enn.* 4.3.30) while Nous deals with forms. These may be distinguished but never separated (*Enn.* 5.9.6 and 3.9.2). Nous is alive and contains individuals, intelligences and forms within its unity. Plotinus identifies Nous with the perfect living creature of Plato's *Timaeus* 30c (*Enn.* 5.9.9; 6.2.21; 6.6.7; 6.7.8). The forms are themselves living and conscious intelligences (*Enn.* 5.1.4; 5.9.8; 6.7.9). The intelligible world is brimming over with its own vitality (*Enn.* 5.3.12). Although subject and object are not separate in the Nous, the contents of vision are still plural and therefore Nous may be separate from the One (*Enn.* 5.3.13). The One may have a self-apprehension, an awakening or a superior kind of thought (*Enn.* 6.7.38); but it remains prior to the emergence of subject and object (*Enn.* 6.7.37; 6.9.6). For Plotinus, both Nous and the One can be the occasion of a mystical experience (*Enn.* 5.8.10; 6.7.15). There is a way to the One through the Nous (*Enn.* 6.9.3) and the highest level of Nous is united to the One (*Enn.* 6.7.35).

The Soul and Nous are easily joined since every soul contains the intelligible world. Spiritual entities are not cut off from one another. Just as the highest level of Soul remains in union with Nous so the highest level of Nous remains in contact with the One (*Enn.* 6.7.35).

For Plotinus the union of the individual soul with the One is its final goal. By turning from the world of sense, man comes to know himself and the One which is his source (*Enn.* 6.9.7). This is, in Plotinus' final exhortation, the flight of the alone to the alone through the stripping away of all things, that is, removing the multiplicity which is foreign to the One (*Enn.* 6.9.11). The soul moves through Nous and beyond the forms. The division of subject and object is removed and the soul reaches that high level of Nous which is not distinguishable from the One. Here the soul waits calmly until the One appears (*Enn.* 5.5.7 and 6.7.34 and 6.7.36). Contact with the One is made through the centre of an individual soul (*Enn.* 2.2.2 and 5.1.11). The One is the centre of man's innermost self and to this source man is joined from within. This experience goes beyond knowing, because knowing involves plurality (*Enn.* 6.9.3f.). Although it is a union of the alone with the alone, it is also a joining in a chorus at the end of the soul's journey (*Enn.* 6.9). Whether the joining of Nous to One and Soul to Nous and One is best described as 'telescoping'[60] or not, it is clear that they cannot be separated.

CONCLUSION

Plato provided immediate answers to the first and third questions (Is there one first-principle? Is there one first-principle of physics, ethics and logic?). The second question (Is there plurality in the One?) is raised in the *Parmenides* and becomes explicit in the *Geistmetaphysik* of Xenocrates. Clement is able to answer all three questions with remarkable clarity.

The value of Plotinus for the present study is that he continued the discussion which engaged his predecessors and which was important for Christian thought.[61] Plotinus answered the first and second questions with the concepts of power and simplicity. The One must be power to be first-principle and to bring all else into being. On the question of plurality within the One, Plotinus had his ambiguities and there is disagreement concerning his merging of the hypostases. One of his interesting attempts to cope with plurality in the One was to make simplicity and plurality a matter of degrees. Simplicity was a quality of each hypostasis. Soul is simple in substance (*Enn.* 1.1.2), Mind is simple but not entirely simple (*Enn.* 5.5.11 and 5.3.13) and not the simplest (*Enn.* 5.3.13).

The subsequent history of later Platonism illuminates the question of one first-principle and gives some occasion for

---

[60] I have spoken of 'merging' rather than 'telescoping' because the second word has been used in different senses.

[61] These problems indicate the only sense in which we may speak of a Christian Platonism. H. Dörrie, Was ist spätantiker Platonismus?, *ThR*, 36, 4 (1971), 285–302.

lament. Iamblichus objected to the merging of hypostases and introduced an explicit causal chain in his account of the imparticibles (ἀμέθεκτα). The triad of unparticipated, participated and participating, dominated his view of reality. The basic theorem of Proclus' *Elements of Theology* is also concerned with this distinction (*Elements* 24). It was the canonisation of the logical error indicated by Plato in the 'Third Man' Argument (*Parmenides* 131e–132b). Plotinus' account of emanation provided some basis for this move (*Enn.* 5.2.2), but not for the excesses which followed. We have noted the false claim that the introduction of more rungs in the causal ladder would make the summit more transcendent and more accessible.[62] The same move can be justified either as a separation or as a joining of first-principle or form and particular.[63] The move of Iamblichus has been properly designated as the bureaucratic fallacy.[64] Not all hierarchies commit this fallacy[65] in which the successive members are related causally or by participation. By good thinking and some good luck, most Christians, in their monotheist concern, were spared from it.

For a later Christian writer was able to answer the question concerning the plurality of the One and to state clearly[66], that father and son are one, neither as two parts of one whole nor as two names for one being. Father is father and son is son. Μία δὲ ἡ φύσις. For that which is begotten is like the one who begets so that the son is not a different God. The son and father are the same τῇ ἰδιότητι καὶ οἰκειότητι τῆς φύσεως, καὶ τῇ ταυτότητι τῆς μιᾶς θεότητος. Just as the brightness of the sun is not a second entity, nor another light, nor a participator in light, ἀλλ ὅλον ἴδιον αὐτοῦ γέννημα.

To this Platonic story a sturdy Stoic footnote must be added. The other great philosophy of the first Christian centuries was Stoicism. The most thorough treatment of its influence finds in Clement the end of the Stoic epoch and the beginning of the

---

[62] Lloyd, The later Neoplatonists, 282.
[63] See R. Williams, *Arius, heresy and tradition* (London, 1987), 194, for creative division. This is the centrifugal rather than the centripetal mode of the bureaucratic fallacy.
[64] Osborn, Clément, Plotin et l'Un, 188.
[65] Cf. 'Hierarchies are and must be independent of reality', L. Wittgenstein, *Tractatus logico-philosophicus* (London, 1974), 113.   [66] Athanasius, *Contra Arianos* 3.4.

Platonic dominance.[67] However, we shall see much Stoicism in Tertullian. Initially unattractive to Christians because of its immanent God, some have found evidence for a transcendent God in its teaching.[68] Tertullian follows Stoicism with his double claim that the idea of God may be proved from creation (*Marc.* 5.16), and is also natural and spontaneous.[69] 'What is God', says Seneca, 'but universal reason' (*Quaest. nat.* 1, *praef.* 13). Many Stoic arguments are to be found in the fathers.[70] The δύναμις λογική of Justin (*dial.* 61.1) and the son who is a derivation and part of the father (*Prax.* 9), indicate a Stoic contribution to trinitarian thought. But it is the cosmic presence of the word which provides the clearest affinity with Stoicism.[71] Since early Christian theology fits more readily into the development of Middle Platonism, Stoic affinities will be dealt with in their appropriate places.[72]

---

[67] M. Spanneut, *Le stoïcisme des pères de l'église* (Paris, 1957).   [68] *Ibid.*, 271.
[69] *Ibid.*, 276–88.   [70] *Ibid.*, 294.   [71] *Ibid.*, 324–45.
[72] Finally we must note the anti-philosophical lobby in early Christian thought. Tertullian and Hippolytus claimed that philosophy and heresy went together. Tertullian, we shall consider later. I have discussed Hippolytus in chapter 4 of the forthcoming work: A. di Berardino and B. Studer (eds.), *Storia del metodo teologico I, Età patristica* (Edizioni Piemme).

CHAPTER 3

The Bible as the material of theology

How important was the Christian Bible, which came into existence at this time, for the problem of the divine unity? If philosophy provided the method, it was the Bible, including the very new testament, which provided the material for an argued account of one God. This is not surprising since the origin of Christian scriptures is tied closely to the problems and challenges with which we began. 'It rests on a broad foundation, a rich experience, which allows it to grasp the One in the Many and again and again to bring it out forcefully and afresh.'[1] Clement quotes the Old Testament 3,200 times and the New Testament 5,000 times. We cannot, in one chapter, present all that the New Testament says about God, goodness and truth; but we are obliged, at least, to show that these subjects are as widely present in the New Testament as the first theologians took them to be, and that they are dominated by the 'feeling for the essential and unitary: the one God, the one Christ and the one salvation which God has given'.[2]

How did the second-century writers use the Bible[3]? There were at least two methods of handling scripture. The first was through symbol or allegory and was directed chiefly to the Old Testament. This is not a method which can be exactly tested,

---

[1] H. von Campenhausen, *The formation of the Christian Bible* (London, 1972), 207.

[2] *Ibid.*, 206.

[3] The material which scripture provides concerning one God, could be handled in several ways. One might begin with explicit references to one God: the unique divine goodness of Mark 10:18 and Matt 19:17, the universalism of Rom. 3:30, the rejection of idols in 1 Cor. 8:4, the divine family of John 17 and the trinitarian formulae; an alternative method would be to examine the titles given to Christ. Neither of these would show the wider presence of the theme of one God.

because symbols grow differently in different hands. For this reason, it was found less helpful against Gnostic fantasy. The second method was to handle the text in a logical way, to treat it as any other writing might be treated and to set out its teaching. This method enables us to satisfy ourselves that there was no gap between the claims of the New Testament and the claims of the earliest Christian theology.

When Irenaeus and Tertullian use New Testament scriptures, they take them as contemporary documents and simply work through them. They set down what the text has to say on the relevant issue. If we are to see the influence of the New Testament on their thought, we must take those books which are commonly used, and ask what the text has to say about the one God, who is known to those who believe that Jesus is God, about the world, human life and human thought. Were being, goodness and truth relevant questions or did the first theologians impose them on the documents of piety? Is the unity of God a common theme? Is it related to the other two questions (ethics and logic)? For it would appear that there is much said about God as being, but less about ethics and almost nothing about logic. We shall look at Matthew, Paul and John. Matthew tells of one son of God who fulfils and will fulfil. Paul tells of one Christ who reconciles and brings all together. John declares the one word, the fullness of God, the one son who reveals the unknown father. In my concentration on text, I shall make minimal reference to the vast secondary literature.

In this way I shall follow a method used by our five writers, a method which came from philosophy. Clement named dialectic as the essential tool for interpretation of scripture (*str.* 1.28). The chief cause of error was failure to distinguish between universal and particular and the chief aim was to find the ἀκολουθία or logical sequence. For Justin and Irenaeus, the argument of scripture must be understood. Gnostics neglect the canon and order of truth. They multiply names without any rational control (*haer.* 1.11.4). They jumble the order of the Johannine prologue to produce a strange concoction, just as others jumble genuine lines of Homer to produce a story Homer never told (*haer.* 1.9.4),[4] Tertullian makes the same objection and comparison (*praescr.* 39).

All this clarifies a distinction and a decision of method. In the history of ideas, we combine, but do not confuse, historical reconstruction with rational reconstruction.[5] Historical reconstruction understands a writer in terms of his environment; rational reconstruction understands him in terms of his own language and ideas. For second-century writers, the historical environment of scripture was commonly irrelevant. There can be only four Gospels because there are four life-giving winds and because the four evangelists were sent by the same spirit to preach and to write (*haer.* 3.11.8). This means that only rational or logical reconstruction of scripture was appropriate and that such exegesis will differ from modern accounts. This is evident in their long passages of exposition, where they are concerned to connect logically whatever is relevant to their account of God.[6]

So another principle emerges: in order to apply historical reconstruction to our five writers, to understand how they approached scripture, we must apply only rational reconstruction to scripture. This might seem a truncated form of exegesis; but anything else would be anachronistic. Authorship and origin are important for the identification of a work and its validity as prophetic or apostolic. In the task of interpretation they have nothing more to offer for the early Christian writers. A similar non-historical approach may be found today among some literary critics, for whom the text is all that matters and

---

[4] A similar concoction came from the speaking statue of Alexandria. See G. Kaibel, *Epigrammata* (Berlin, 1878), 1009. J. Daniélou (*Message évangélique et culture hellénistique* (Tournai, 1961), 82–4) considers Irenaeus' cento to be a composition of Valentinus. An opposing view is presented by R. L. Wilken (The Homeric cento in Irenaeus' 'Against Heresies', 1.9.4, *VC*, 21 (1967), 25–33).

[5] See R. Rorty, The historiography of philosophy: four genres in *Philosophy in history*, eds. R. Rorty, J. B. Schneewind and Quentin Skinner (Cambridge, 1984), 49.

[6] Interpreters of Origen have noted a similar thing. 'Origen plods through the Bible, deaf to its music, like a scientist trying to distil chemical formulae from Shakespeare.' R. P. C. Hanson, Review of H. Crouzel, Origène, *ZKG*, 92/2 (1986), 279. Cf. M. Harl, *Origène et la fonction révélatrice du verbe incarné* (Paris, 1958), 363. Clement's *Hypotyposeis* provide an exception to this rule; but they are still not within the framework of historical exegesis.

has within it an 'unexamined and a priori principle of internal coherence'.[7]

Yet the plain text is not entirely plain. Justin regards scripture as 'the mind and will of God' (*dial.* 68). The prophets saw and declared the truth, as they were filled with the holy spirit (*dial.* 7). Philosophers and poets obtain their seeds of truth from the prophets (1 *apol.* 44). Even Plato learned from 'our teachers', the prophets (1 *apol.* 59). Scripture as a complex world of divine truth takes the place of the Platonic forms.

For Clement, spirit is the strength of word as blood is of flesh (*paed.* 2.2.19). The rational gates of the word are opened by the key of faith (*prot.* 1.10). The prophetic and teaching spirit works through the mind (*str.* 1.9.45). The truth of scripture comes from the divine word, because Plato insisted that truth could only be learnt from God or from the offspring of God (*str.* 6.15.123).

Mind is the place of the ideas and God is mind. 'All the powers of the spirit become collectively one thing and come together in the same point which is the son' (*str.* 4.25.156). In this account of the word[8] the manifold powers of the spirit come together in the son, as in Justin they are said to rest on him (*dial.* 87). The intimate relation of prophetic scripture, spirit and word, gives to scripture a divinity. This carries over to the writings of the New Testament as Clement calls them (*str.* 5.13.85). Justin finds inner fire and true philosophy in love for the words of the prophets and the friends of Christ. 'For they have a dread power (δέος) in themselves and are sufficient to shame those who turn away from the right path and to bring sweet rest (ἀνάπαυσις) to those who practise them' (*dial.* 8).

BACKGROUND OF THE NEW TESTAMENT

Any examination of the New Testament requires some account of the Old Testament. The questions of God, goodness and truth were already old when Jesus came, and Justin confines his citations almost entirely to the Jewish scriptures. The Old

---

[7] E. Said, Roads taken and not taken in contemporary criticism, Contemporary Literature, 17 (1976), 367; cited R. Rorty, Idealism and textualism, in *Pragmatism*, 151.   [8] See above, pp. 57f.

Testament is about one God who is above all time, measure, likeness and limits, who cannot be touched or seen, yet is ever present and inescapable.[9]

The God-who-is is the source of all creation. From his being and power comes the creation and on his saving care that creation depends. His uniqueness is shown in creation (Deut. 4:32f.) and requires total obedience (Deut. 4:37–40), which the long record of apostasy (Judg. 2:11–19; 3:7–11; 10:6–16) denies. God's autonomy is evident in his prophets, who do not talk about God but receive his word. In Second Isaiah we find, at last, an extended statement concerning the only God (45:14–25); but the concern with one God is evident from the patriarchs onwards.[10]

What is said about goodness? Ethical demands of this God are clear in his calling and his command to love. Deuteronomic and Deuteronomistic writers point to the ethical demands of the unique God who has delivered Israel. He requires total love from heart and soul (Deut. 6:5). He loved and chose the fathers and their children (Deut. 4:37), so they must love the only God in earth and heaven and keep his laws.

What is said about truth? Wisdom followed from the keeping of the same laws, and all will recognise 'the wise and understanding people' (Deut. 4:6). The fear of the lord is the beginning of wisdom to which an entire literary genre is devoted. There is one source of wisdom: the one God who alone is truly wise and whose wisdom in the beginning established the earth (Prov. 3:19 and 8:22–31). Wisdom is not a matter of logic and science. It dominates metaphysics and ethics in later Judaism and forms a link with Hellenistic thought. It becomes the supreme ethical value and a divine entity beside God; it was

---

[9] It reaches its high point in the monotheism of Second Isaiah after a long and confused journey. The official monotheism of one God and his law, found in priests and prophets is in conflict with popular syncretism. Those who kept the first commandment were a minority, but they pointed to the distinctive centre of the religion of Israel

[10] Even with Canaanite compromise, God could be considered one, with many names; but there was confusion for all between the one God and the many gods of Canaan. The Deuteronomic reformation led through monolatry ultimately to monotheism, to a belief in one God who creates all things.

to provide Paul with a concept to explain the place of Jesus in the universe.

In Prov. 8:1–31, wisdom is a divine figure, the source of strong and sound judgement, the first of all creatures and the link between God and man.[11] In Sirach 24, there is a more colourful description of a divine being who proceeds from the mouth of the most high God and covers the earth as a cloud. Moving through the universe, she finds rest and inheritance in Israel, whence she sends out her eternal light.[12]

Wisdom (Wisd. 8:1) reaches from end to end of things, bringing order to all. God gives knowledge of the making of the world and of the ordering of its seasons, and of the beginning, ending and midst of the times (Wisd. 7:18). Wisdom is universal. 'For she is the breath of the power of God and a pure influence flowing from the glory of the Almighty... the brightness of the everlasting light, the unspotted mirror of the power of God, and the image of his goodness: and being but one, she can do all things, and remaining in herself, she makes all things new, and in all ages entering into holy souls, she makes them friends of God and prophets' (Wisd. 7:22–7).[13]

At the same time prophecy and apocalyptic do not die out. Justin, who is our first source for the use of scripture, sees all fulfilled in Christ. His Dialogue is dominated by the recapitulation of all things and the fulfilment of all prophetic hopes.[14] The use of Old Testament writings in all early Christian writings will be governed by the notion of fulfilment. This developed into the concepts of reconciliation and consummation. The mystery of the gospel is that in the οἰκονομία of the fullness of the times the universe has been summed up in Christ.

---

[11] In Egypt, Judaism made contact with the cult of Isis as creator and sustainer of the universe as well as the teacher of ethical principles.

[12] Hellenistic philosophy joined Stoic immanent and universal reason to the Platonic forms. Aristobulus joins this idea to wisdom (Eusebius, *Praep. ev.*, 13. 12f.) quoting Orpheus and Aratus concerning the all-pervading power of God. Clement claims that the Stoics learned of their immanent God through the biblical account of wisdom (*str.* 5.14.89).

[13] Later Stoicism developed such a close relation between God and the soul that it was possible to join its immanent God to the Old Testament spirit of God. See also Baruch 3 and 4.

[14] See P. Prigent, *Justin et l'ancien testament* (Paris, 1964), 319–36.

The movement from fulfilment of scripture is made easy by a
high doctrine of biblical inspiration. For Justin, we have seen,
scripture is the mind and will of God, taking the place of
Platonic forms as the reason of things. The joining and dividing
of the Platonic dialectic is the way to the form of the good, the
mind of God, the fullness and recapitulation of all things. Justin
began from the summing up of all things in Christ, just as a
Platonist would take the good as the key to coherence. It was
long thought that Justin's proofs against Trypho were based on
testimonia – loose lists of messianic prophecies. This is not the
case.[15] Behind the Dialogue stands Justin's lost work against
heresies which centres on the recapitulation of all things in
Christ. This same work is a source for Irenaeus and for
Tertullian. From here we grasp the theme of the first Christian
theologians. Just as all prophecies came together in Christ, so
the divine purpose and plan was complete in him. We turn now
to those parts of the New Testament, which were most
frequently used by our five writers: Matthew, Paul and John.

Anyone who is unable to look for the principle of coherence in
the biblical material which follows, will miss the point of the
exercise. As Justin insisted, there is no profit in repeating texts
unless one grasps the argument behind them (*dial.* 92).

MATTHEW

Continuity with Old Testament concepts is most evident in
Matthew where the same source of being, goodness and truth is
found in God. This emerges as an affirmation of life, goodness
and wisdom and a negation of death, sin and falsehood.
Matthew maintains:

1 There is one God whose kingdom has come near in Jesus
   Christ.
2 There is one Jesus Christ who fulfils the work of salvation.
3 There is one law, one way of righteousness, which is
   corrected and fulfilled in Jesus Christ.
4 There is one mystery and one wisdom, made known in Jesus
   Christ.

[15] *Ibid.*

One God the father

God's kingdom at hand

The Baptist preaches that the kingdom is at hand (Matt. 3:2) as
he prepares the way for the lord (Matt. 3:3). The preaching of
Jesus declares the kingdom of heaven (Matt. 4:17). Jesus
preaches the good news of the kingdom (Matt. 4:23) which is
confirmed by his casting out demons (Matt. 12:26). Parables
tell what the kingdom is like (Matt. 13:24–47). The king sends
his servants into the streets to invite whoever is there. All is done
by his sovereign command (Matt. 22:10).

The commandments of the lord God

The first commandment is total love of the one God
(Matt. 22:37). One God requires unqualified obedience.[16] Jesus
resists temptation by declaring the commandments of God: not
by bread alone, but by the word of God comes life (Matt. 4:4).
You shall not tempt the lord (Matt. 4:7); you shall worship and
serve him only (Matt. 4:10).

The father in heaven

The good works of the disciples are seen that the father might be
glorified. The perfection of the father is his universal goodness to
all (Matt. 5:45). The nearness of the father rewards secret
prayer (Matt. 6:4 and 6). He is owned as father by those who
pray for the coming of his kingdom (Matt. 6:9), he knows and
cares for the needs of his children (Matt. 6:26 and 32), and he
gives good gifts to those who ask him (Matt. 7:11).

Father and son

The kingdom comes when the son casts out demons
(Matt. 12:26). He is the Christ, the son of the living God
(Matt. 16.16), transfigured before his disciples and confessed by
the father as beloved son (Matt. 17:5). The unity of father and

---

[16] This is also part of ethics. See below, pp. 79f.

son is declared, 'Father, if it be possible, let this cup pass, nevertheless not what I will but what you will' (Matt. 26:39). Jesus is asked whether he is the Christ, the son of God (Matt. 26:63), and is taunted because he said he was son of God. He trusted in God, let God deliver him (Matt. 27:43). The cry of dereliction, 'My God, my God, why have you forsaken me' (Matt. 27:46), is balanced by the centurion's confession, 'Truly, this was a son of God' (Matt. 27:54).

One son of God, lord of history and final judge

Universal saviour
He is called Jesus because he will save (Matt. 1:21), he cures all sickness (Matt. 4:23), and drives out unclean spirits (Matt. 8:16). At sea, he saves those who are about to perish (Matt. 8:26). The sick touch him in order to be healed (Matt. 9:21). His universal healing power (Matt. 9:35, 10:1 and 12:15f.) fulfils the prophecy of Isaiah 42:1–4 (Matt. 12:17). As saviour he goes to his death (Matt. 26:66) and is mocked because he cannot save himself (Matt. 27:42).

Fulfilment and correction
Jesus comes to fulfil, not to destroy (Matt. 5:17 *et passim*). The antitheses of the Sermon on the Mount underline the totality and contradiction of this fulfilment: 'You have heard ... but I say to you ...' (Matt. 5:22, 28, 32, 34, 39). Jesus' authority is universal and his fulfilment corrects what has gone before.

He comes to call sinners (Matt. 9:13) and to end fasting (Matt. 9:15). New wine will not fit in old skins (Matt. 9:16f.). The sign he gives is the sign of Jonah with a difference (Matt. 12:39) and he is greater than Solomon (Matt. 12:42).

King, lord, son of man
The star leads to the king (Matt. 2:2). John points to one who is mightier than he (Matt. 3:11), and whose baptism is with spirit and fire (Matt. 3:17). He teaches with authority (Matt. 7:28f.), is recognised as son of God by terrified demons

(Matt. 8:29), forgives sins (Matt. 9:6) and defeats demons (Matt. 9:34). The son of man will come before the disciples have passed through all the cities of Israel (Matt. 10:23). He is the coming one (Matt. 11:3). As son of man and κύριος he is lord of the sabbath (Matt. 12:8) and declares that it is lawful to do good on the sabbath.

History is in his hand. Tares and wheat grow together until harvest (Matt. 13:30). The sower is the son of man (Matt. 13:37) and the reapers are his angels. He shares his cup with his disciples (Matt. 20:22), and gives his life as a ransom for many (Matt. 20:28). Hailed as lord and son of David by those who seek his mercy (Matt. 20:31) and who shout, 'Hosanna!' (Matt. 21:9), his authority is beyond question (Matt. 21:24) and he becomes the head of the corner (Matt. 21:42). He is the lord who sits on the lord's right hand (Matt. 22:43f.) in a recognition of plurality in God. At the end of history the son of man will separate the nations into sheep and goats (Matt. 25:31f.) and as king he will call the righteous into his kingdom (Matt. 25:40). He establishes a covenant in his blood (Matt. 26:28), foretells his coming in glory (Matt. 26:29), wears a crown of thorns (Matt. 27:29), is hailed as king of the Jews (Matt. 27:30) and, possessed of all authority, sends disciples to all the nations (Matt. 28:18–20).

The good is one

The good is one, God (Matt. 19:17).

The way of righteousness

The theme of Matthew – Jesus comes 'to fulfil all righteousness' (Matt. 3:15) – is declared at the baptism of Jesus. John the Baptist came 'in the way of righteousness' (Matt. 21:32). This righteousness is declared in the Sermon on the Mount, especially in the beatitudes which promise that they who hunger and thirst after righteousness will be filled (Matt. 5:3–12). Righteousness is a matter of doing good works and avoiding evil. He who does and teaches the commandments will be called

great in the kingdom of heaven (Matt. 5:19), and his righteousness must exceed that of scribes and pharisees (Matt. 5.20).
Swearing is not permitted because it is against God
(Matt. 5:34). The narrow gate must be entered (Matt. 7:13).
For not every one, who says 'Lord! Lord!', will enter the
kingdom, but only he who does the will of the father
(Matt. 7:21). Many will come in the last day to claim the lord
as their own, but, because of their actions, they will be dismissed
with the words, 'I never knew you' (Matt. 7:22f.). Hearing and
doing must be kept together. He who does, builds on the rock
and he who does not, builds on the sand. Each will stand or fall
by this test (Matt. 7:24–7). The good tree is known by its fruits
(Matt. 12:33f.) and the good man produces good from the
treasure within him (Matt. 12:35). Every idle word will be
judged (Matt. 12:36f.).

At the last judgement, the son of man declares the universal
law of doing good. Those who have fed the hungry, clothed the
naked, visited the sick and the prisoners, will inherit the
kingdom prepared for them from the foundation of the world.
Whatever they have done to the least of his brothers, they have
done to him who is king and judge of all (Matt. 25:34f.).

Obedience to the commandments
Jesus has set the pattern of obedience and triumphs in
temptation by observing a specific commandment (Matt. 4:4–
10). Speech is no substitute for obedience. The hypocrites
already have their reward (Matt. 6:5) and the heathen think
that they will be heard for speaking a lot (Matt. 6:7). Obedience
to one master prevents anxiety. No one can serve two masters
(Matt. 6:24f). To those who seek first the kingdom, all other
things will be added (Matt. 6:33). The hypocrite must recognise his own disobedience and remove the beam from his eye
(Matt. 7:5); but to him who asks, it will be given. He that seeks
will find, and to him that knocks, it will be opened (Matt. 7:8).
The son of man will give to each, according to what each has
done (Matt. 16:27).

The way of obedience allows no compromise. If hand and
foot offend, they must be cut off (Matt. 18:8). Some will be

eunuchs for the kingdom of heaven. The rich young ruler has kept all the commandments (Matt. 19:20) and will find perfection in selling all his goods and following (Matt. 19:21), for the good is one. Two great commandments require total allegiance (Matt. 22:37–9). He who endures to the end will be saved (Matt. 24:13). Vigilance is required of all who watch, for they do not know the day or hour of coming judgement (Matt. 25:13).

Sovereignty of love

Righteousness finds perfection in the love of enemies by the children of the father, who exhibits unqualified love (Matt. 5:44–7). Love requires that others be forgiven and only thus may the forgiveness of God be received (Matt. 6:12). Singleness of eye brings light (Matt. 6:22) for one master only may be loved. A second 'master' will be hated (Matt. 6:24).

The disciple follows

The call 'Follow me' (Matt. 4:19), is met by a total response (Matt. 4:22). The hesitant disciple is rebuked by the son of man who has nowhere to lay his head (Matt. 8:20) and the dead must be left to bury their dead (Matt. 8:22). The place of the call does not matter. Matthew leaves all to follow (Matt. 9:9).

The twelve are chosen and sent out as sheep among wolves (Matt. 10:16); but they should not worry, when they are brought to trial, since the holy spirit will speak through them (Matt. 10:19). He who endures will be saved (Matt. 10:22) and it is enough for the disciple to be as his master (Matt. 10:25). There is no place for fear (Matt. 10:26) nor for rival affections, since he who loves father or mother more is not worthy of his lord (Matt. 10:37). He who finds his soul will lose it; but he who loses will find (Matt. 10:39).

The cost of discipleship includes loss of family, as for Jesus his disciples become his mother and his brothers (Matt. 12:49). The kingdom is the pearl of great price for which a disciple gives all that he has (Matt. 13:45f.). The demands of the law go beyond the human stomach for a man is defiled by what comes out of him, not by what goes in (Matt. 15:11). The way of the cross is solitary (Matt. 16:24); it drinks the cup of Jesus (Matt. 20:22) and takes the place of the servant (Matt. 20:26). The rich cannot enter the kingdom of heaven (Matt. 19:24). The fragility of the disciple is seen in Peter who swears his loyalty and then denies three times (Matt. 26:33f. and 26.75), as well as in Judas who kisses and betrays his master (Matt. 26.49). Yet the way of righteousness is the way of obedience to all commands and of discipleship which spreads among all nations to the end of time (Matt. 28:18–20).

Faith and mystery

The power of faith
Faith, which moves mountains (Matt. 17:20 and 21:21), has more to do with power than with knowledge. The centurion's faith is greater than the faith of Israel (Matt. 8:10) and as he believes so he receives (Matt. 8:13). In the storm the disciples are rebuked for their little faith (Matt. 8:26). The sick are healed (Matt. 9:22) and the blind see (Matt. 9.29), according to their faith. There can be no miracles in Nazareth because there is no faith (Matt. 13:58) and fear is rebuked (Matt. 14:27) among those of little faith (Matt. 14:32).

The mystery of the kingdom
The truth has been hidden from the wise but revealed to babes, (Matt. 11:25) for no one knows the son but the father, and no one knows the father but the son and those to whom the son reveals (Matt. 11:27). The weary are called to rest and to bear the easy yoke. The mystery of the kingdom is declared in parables and those who see, do not see and understand (Matt. 13:13). This fulfils Isaiah's prophecy of blindness (Matt. 13:14f.). Yet Jesus makes clear the parable of the sower (Matt. 13:18) and of the tares (Matt. 13:36). At the conclusion of the discourse, his hearers have understood (Matt. 13:52), like the scribe of the kingdom who produces new things and old (Matt. 13:52). The teaching of Jesus, the son of the carpenter, brings astonishment (Matt. 13:55); disciples are slow to understand (Matt. 16:9) and truth is known only through the father

who reveals (Matt. 16:17). Many are called but few are chosen
(Matt. 22:14) and none but the father knows the day or hour of
the coming of the son of man.

Those who do not know, make the word of God futile through
their tradition (Matt. 16:6). They honour God with their lips
only, and teach the commandments of men. Those who
understand are disciples who recognise the truth of Jesus
(Matt. 22:16), their one teacher (Matt. 23:10) and who are
sent to make disciples of every nation in the name of their lord
(Matt. 28:18f.).

In Matthew, the sole rule of one God the father is declared in
his kingdom, his commandments and his heavenly perfection.
The coming of his kingdom, the fulfilment of his commands and
the last judgement of the world are the work of the son. From his
saving actions came both ethics and knowledge. In Matthew,
the dialectics of beginning and end, of God's sole rule and
summing up, provide the basis for participation in being
goodness and truth.

PAUL

A logical or rational reconstruction of Pauline argument may be
set out under four headings of Pauline theology: one sovereign
good God, one world for one Christ, one way of faith and life,
one truth of one gospel. Ephesians is a postscript which simplifies
and develops Paul's thought to include the key concept of
recapitulation. Unity means universality.

Power of righteousness

There is one sovereign good God who is creator of all that exists.
His unity and goodness are seen in his sovereign grace and the
power of his righteousness.

The living and the true
The hope of the letters to the Thessalonians turns on the one
God who rules all things and on his elect (1 Thess. 1:4), who
have left the worship of idols and serve the living and true God
(1 Thess. 1:9). Paul turns for confirmation to this God (1

Thess. 2:10). As the one father of all, God directs the ways of his people (1 Thess. 3:11), whose one concern is to please him (1 Thess. 4:1).

Sovereign lord

For the Galatians, Paul begins from the sole authority of God who raises the dead (Gal. 1:1) and is praised to all eternity (Gal. 1:5). He has no favourites, but is the sovereign God of all (Gal. 2:6). Before him, none may stand justified through works and obedience to law (Gal. 2:16), and to believe in him is to be crucified with Christ (Gal. 2:20f.). We deal directly with this God alone, for when there is one God, there is no need for a mediator and God is one (Gal. 3:20).[17] It is not what men know about God that matters, but what God knows about them (Gal. 4:9).

Strength of the weak

One God is the source of peace (1 Cor. 1:3). His autonomy chooses the weak and brings confusion to the strong (1 Cor. 1:20). No flesh may be proud in his presence (1 Cor. 1:29). Believers have received their righteousness, wisdom, holiness and redemption from him alone (1 Cor. 1:30). None should boast except in the lord (1 Cor. 1:31). The cross is based solely on God's power (1 Cor. 2:1–5). The kingdom of God is not man's proud talk but the power of God (1 Cor. 4:20). Idolatry, which worships anything other than God, is the archetypal sin. An idol is nothing because there is only one God (1 Cor. 8:4). For others there are many gods, but for believers there is one God the father, the source and goal of all things, as there is one

---

[17] 'Unlike the law, the promise is absolute and unconditional. It depends on the sole decree of God. There are not two contracting parties. There is nothing of the nature of a *stipulation*. The giver is everything, the recipient nothing. Thus the primary sense of "one" here is numerical.' J. B. Lightfoot, *Saint Paul's Epistle to the Galatians*, 7th edn (London, 1881), 147. Lightfoot considers this affirmation of the oneness of God to be 'quite unconnected with the fundamental statement of the Mosaic law, "The Lord thy God is one God," though resembling it in form'. He comments also (p. 146) that 'The number of interpretations of this passage is said to mount up to 250 or 300'.

lord Jesus Christ who brings all into being (1 Cor. 8:6). Jesus is not described as God; but his lordship here means that he stands in close relation to God, and his messiahship is affirmed by the title of Christ.[18] God is unique, the beginning and end of all things.[19]

All spiritual gifts are traced to one God who gives in different ways (1 Cor. 12:6), but works in all. Christian worship should so turn to him as to evoke the cry, 'Truly God is among you' (1 Cor. 14:25). Peace, not disorder, comes from this God (1 Cor. 14:33).

Paul denies his own resources and depends on the God who raises the dead (2 Cor. 1:9), has fulfilled all the promises of the old covenant (2 Cor. 1:20), and, as creator, brings light out of darkness (2 Cor. 4:6). The strength of the sovereign God is perfected in weakness and his grace is always sufficient (2 Cor. 12:9).

Righteousness of God

Paul's apostleship points to one God, who calls and separates, and whose gospel saves all (Rom. 1:16f.). One God will justify Jew and gentile (Rom. 3:30). Divine unity means universality: God cannot be the exclusive possession of Jews.[20] The one God must be creator and saviour of all. *Sola gratia* can only be based on *solus deus*, on the omnipotence and freedom of God as creator and judge. 'As merely the God of the Jews, he would cease to be the only God. The full force of this revolutionary statement is seldom perceived.'[21]

---

[18] Paul neither denies nor affirms the existence of other spiritual beings, but recognises for the Christian only one God who is the source of life and redemption, because of what he has done in history through his son. He is our creator and our destiny, and Christ is his agent in creation. C. K. Barrett, *The first epistle to the Corinthians* (London, 1968), 192f.

[19] E. B. Allo, *Saint Paul, Première épître aux Corinthiens*, 2nd edn (Paris, 1956), I, 201. 'A l'affirmation de l'unité de Dieu, Paul ajoute celles que Dieu, le Père, est l'unique premier principe et l'unique fin dernière, et que Jésus-Christ, l'unique Seigneur, a été médiateur dans la création du monde comme il l'est pour le salut des hommes... C'est la première fois dans le Nouveau Testament qu'une part est assignée au Christ dans l'œuvre de la création.'

[20] C. K. Barrett, *A commentary on the epistle to the Romans* (London, 1957), 83f.

[21] E. Käsemann, *Commentary on Romans* (Grand Rapids, 1980), 104.

Paul returns to boast in the one God who has poured out his love by his spirit (Rom. 5:5). God commends this love through the death of Christ (Rom. 5:8) and his act for sinners gives them confidence to boast in him (Rom. 5:11). Life in the spirit derives from the God who sent his son (Rom. 8:3) and who now gives life to mortals (Rom. 8:11). The one God works all things for good (Rom. 8:28). Through foreknowledge, election, adoption, calling, justification and glorification (Rom. 8:29f.), all is governed by the question, 'If God be for us, who can be against us?' (Rom. 8:31). Nothing can separate from his love, so when Paul speaks of God's concern for Israel, he bases his argument on one God who rules over all and who is blessed to all ages (Rom. 9:5). This universal mercy is the ground (Rom. 12:1) for the new life in Christ (Rom. 12:2). The problem of obedience to rulers is solved by dependence of all on God. The ruler is a servant of God, for good or evil, according to the conduct of the citizen. All stand under the one God (Rom. 13:4).

God alone

For the Philippians Paul begins with a prayer to God who began and will finish the good work among them (Phil. 1:3–6). To live is Christ and to die is gain (Phil. 1:21). All comes from God who works in his people to will and do his pleasure (Phil. 2:13). Worship in spirit rejects confidence in flesh (Phil. 3:3), and seeks only knowledge of Christ (Phil. 3:8). From this God come joy and peace beyond understanding (Phil. 4:4–7).

Lord in heaven

To the Colossians, Paul, an apostle by the will of God, sends grace and peace from God the father (Col. 1:1f.). He reminds slaves and masters that they have a just lord in heaven whose impartiality they should reflect (Col. 3:22–4:1).

One God, above, through and in all

In Ephesians, Paul's theme of unity is developed and extended. From a doxology for God's grace to all men in all ages (Eph. 1:3–9) the writer goes on to speak of the work of Christ in bringing all things together (Eph. 1:10). When he speaks again of the body of Christ, he begins from the one God and father of all who is above, through and in all (Eph. 4:6).

To sum up, the one God is unconditioned by anything human. The living and true sovereign God is the strength of the weak. In the power of righteousness, he alone is justifier, all-sufficient to his children on earth as in heaven. He is one God above, through and in all.

One world and one Christ

Apart from the work of Christ, the world lacks coherence and unity. Out of confusion, the one Christ who is restorer of all things, will bring this world in subjection to his father. Then, God will be all in all. This unity depends on the work of Christ, which is done through his body, the church, as his members, by his spirit, work his will in the world. All things are reconciled to the one God.

Waiting with the word

Paul reminds Thessalonians of the effect of the gospel (1 Thess. 1:5), and the ever-spreading word (1 Thess. 1:8). They wait for the son of God, their deliverer (1 Thess. 1:10) and the word is active among them (1 Thess. 2:13–16. All points to the return of the lord, with voice of archangel and trumpet of God, to raise the dead, so that the saints may be forever with the lord (1 Thess. 4:13–18).

Word and history

For the Galatians, the saving history, where the law prepares for Christ (Gal. 3:24), contains different dispensations within the unity of God's saving work. Hagar and Sarah point to enduring conflict between flesh and spirit (Gal. 4:29). In Romans, the unity of history is again clear. God's wrath and mercy are displayed, and Israel and others are judged by the only God (Rom. 10:1f.). God places all in the same category of disobedience, so that he might show mercy on all (Rom. 11:32). 'For from him, and through him and to him are all things. To whom be glory for ever, Amen' (Rom. 11:36).

Body of Christ

The unity of Christ requires that Corinthian schisms should cease (1 Cor. 1:10–13). His ministers should display the unity of his power. Paul planted, Apollos watered and God made the church grow. The church is God's building and he will destroy those who destroy his temple (1 Cor. 3:4–17). Those who receive all by grace, belong to Christ as he belongs to God (1 Cor. 3:21–3), and although present objects of derision (1 Cor. 4:9), they will judge men and angels (1 Cor. 6:3).

The world is transformed by the working of Christ's body within it (1 Cor. 12). There is one God, whose power stretches through the many gifts of his spirit.

Victory in Christ

Christ will bring all things under his sway, and will hand to the father the kingdom (1 Cor. 15:23–8). Death shall be destroyed and God will be all in all. The last Adam is a life-giving spirit who will transform those who die in him; in this way, the spirit, who is the power which raised Christ from the dead, will bring the corruptible to incorruption and the mortal to immortality. This victory begins now, and our work is not in vain (1 Cor. 15:57f.).

Dialectic and reconciliation

Affliction is overcome by the comfort of God, despair points to divine power, and death finds hope. All of which leads to thanksgiving for triumph in Christ; to some, Christians are a sign of death, and to others, a sign of life (2 Cor. 2:14–16). The life of the spirit brings a new covenant of spirit instead of letter (2 Cor. 3:6). Such treasure in earthern vessels points to the dialectical existence of Christians, who carry about the dying of Jesus so that his life might also be plain (2 Cor. 4:7–10). Outwardly they may fade away, but inwardly they are renewed each day (2 Cor. 4:14–16). Reconciliation is a negation of negation. One died for all so that they should live for him (2 Cor. 5:15). All things come from God who has reconciled us to himself through Christ and has given us the ministry of reconciliation (2 Cor. 5:17–21). The signs of an apostle reveal the same dialectic of weakness and the power of God (2 Cor. 13:4).

Reconciliation in process

Confidence in God springs from reconciliation and atonement (Rom. 5:11). As in Adam's one disobedience many died, so in Christ the grace of God has overflowed from one to many (Rom. 5:15) and now the kingdom of death is challenged by the kingdom of grace, through Christ the lord (Rom. 5:21).

The process, by which the one Christ brings one world to God, is still subject to frustration (Rom. 8:18). Yet sufferings point to the glory to be revealed in the sons of God. Within the world, there are already those who have the spirit and who wait for liberation. They are saved by hope and wait in patience (Rom. 8:25).

Yet their waiting is not inactive for the word must be preached, and the feet of those who bring good news are beautiful upon the mountains (Rom. 10:14f.). While the good news is received with blindness and deafness (Rom. 11:7), the new life of Christ is lived out. By the grace which God gives to all members of the body, through their obedience and their different gifts, the saving work of Christ goes on (Rom. 12:4f.).

Glory and light

The 'Great Christology' (Col. 1:15–23) declares the divine status of Christ. He is the origin of all things and the goal to which they move. The perfect likeness of God, supreme over creation, he holds all together. All things cohere in him, who is head of the church and the first-principle of the new creation, indwelt by the divine fullness and reconciling all things in cosmic peace by his cross.[22] Reconciliation of all things is a consequence of the divine fullness in Christ.[23] Christ will dwell in all who believe (Col. 1:27f.). His fullness is life out of death and forgiveness for sinners (Col. 2:13). When he appears, his own people will share his glory (Col. 3:4). In the new humanity there is no Greek, Jew, circumcision, uncircumcision, barbarian, Scythian, slave, or free, for Christ is all in all (Col. 3:11).

Recapitulation of all things

Ephesians develops, after Paul, the unity of reconciliation. The calling of the Christian is part of a divine plan which ends in the summing-up of all things in Christ (Eph. 1:10). He who was raised by God, now has all things beneath his feet, and is head to his church (Eph. 1:22). Those who were dead in sins have been raised to life and seated in the heavens (Eph. 2:5). Christ, as peace, has broken down the dividing wall and made one new humanity, reconciling Jew and Gentile in his body on the cross (Eph. 2:14–16). This is the dispensation of God's grace (Eph. 3:2) which ends in the fullness of God (Eph. 3:19) who is able to do more than men can ask or think, by his power at work in them (Eph. 3:20). By truth in love they grow up into him (Eph. 4:15), and put on the new humanity which is created in righteousness, holiness and truth, by God (Eph. 4:24).

One Christ brings unity to a divided creation. Those who wait for his final victory become part of the process of reconciliation through his body in the world. At every point the nature and purpose of his work springs from his unity with the father for whom he reconciles all things.

One way of faith and life

In response to the sovereign grace of God, all who have sinned are justified by faith. From beginning to end this is the work of God. The alternative is the way of the flesh, of autonomy against God, boasting which denies creaturehood and leads to

---

[22] C. F. D. Moule, *The epistles of Paul the apostle to the Colossians and to Philemon* (Cambridge, 1957), 58–74.
[23] E. Schweizer, *Der Brief an die Kolosser* (Zürich, Einsiedeln, Köln, 1976), 67.

death. Life follows the second Adam in obedience, instead of the first Adam in sin. Under the cross, creaturehood is restored and faith knows only Christ and him crucified. In metaphysics, the unity of God means that there is one world united by one Christ. In ethics, there is one way which derives from the love shown in the cross of Christ by the only God. The whole of life is to be lived to God's glory.

Coram deo

Paul thanks God for the constancy of hope fixed on one lord and one God (1 Thess. 1:2f.). All that matters is to live in the presence of God (1 Thess. 2:5), serving God and his gospel alone (1 Thess. 2:8). God requires purity of life, love and concern in the way of holiness (1 Thess. 4:3). For the sin which wrongs man also wrongs the God who has given his holy spirit to men (1 Thess. 4.8); he will bring them to perfect holiness so that they may be free from sin when their lord returns (1 Thess. 5:23f.).

Spirit not flesh

The slave of Christ has one loyalty and does not try to please men (Gal. 1:10). Crucified with Christ, he now lives by the faith of Christ (Gal. 2:19–21). Reversion to the law denies God's order; for how can one begin with spirit and end up with flesh (Gal. 3:2)? All that matters is faith which works by love (Gal. 5:6). This means freedom (Gal. 5:13), for the whole law has been summed up in love to neighbour (Gal. 5:14). The fruit of the spirit must be seen in love, joy, peace, long-suffering, kindness, faith, meekness and self-control (Gal. 5:22). Those who belong to Christ have crucified the flesh and its lust so that they may live and walk by the spirit (Gal. 5:24–6).

Charisma and God's will

Apostleship depends on the will of God who has made his apostles an object of shame in the world (1 Cor. 4:9). The human body, a temple of the holy spirit, bought with a price, is to be used to the glory of God (1 Cor. 6:20). Each has his own charisma which God has given (1 Cor. 7:7). The rights and freedom of an apostle express what he knows of Christ (1 Cor. 9:1–18). The single allegiance remains. No one may share both the table of the lord and the table of demons (1 Cor. 10:21). All must be done to the glory of God (1 Cor. 10:31). Even the argument that women's heads should be covered is derived by way of Gen. 1:27 and 2:22f. from the one God: the man is the head of the woman, Christ is the head of the man and God is the head of Christ (1 Cor. 11:3). Yet, since all things are of God, man and wife, in common dependence on one source, live in mutuality rather than hierarchy (1 Cor. 11:11f.). The supreme and necessary gift is love (1 Cor. 13) which endures forever (1 Cor. 13:12f.). The grace of God changed Paul from a persecutor to a preacher (1 Cor. 15:10f.). As a child of light, the believer lives in response to the creative power of God (2 Cor. 4:6). There can be no place for idols in one who is a temple of the living God (2 Cor. 6:16). All Paul's future is in God's hand and, on his next Corinthian visit, God might well bring him low (2 Cor. 12:21); this also would have its place in the one plan.

Law and judgement

The sin of mankind is a rejection of the one way which God has given, and a preference for the many paths of wickedness (Rom. 1:18f.). God gives men over to themselves and the result is a spectacular plurality of vice (Rom. 1:28–32). God judges the wicked and gives glory, honour and peace to those who do good (Rom. 2:10). The true Jew is inwardly obedient not outwardly busy in the service of God. He follows the one way of the spirit as against the ever-multiplying way of the letter (Rom. 2:28f.). Since all have sinned, the one way of grace is offered to all (Rom. 3:23f.). God's unity implies his universality (Rom. 3:30). This is the only way in which the Law has a future (Rom. 3:31).

New humanity

Baptism brings new life (Rom. 6:4), which is lived to God alone
(Rom. 6:13). Those who were slaves to sin are now slaves to
righteousness. Human existence is determined by the lord who
is served. The lordship of sin and death is past, and the lordship
of Christ leads on to life eternal (Rom. 6:18–23). Yet sin remains
and the struggle finds victory only through God (Rom. 7:24f.).
Life in the spirit alone fulfils the law (Rom. 8:1f.). Spirit
supersedes flesh (Rom. 8:12) and confirms that believers are
God's sons (Rom. 8:16).

While Israel failed to reach the law of righteousness
(Rom. 9:31), the new life in Christ is daily sacrifice which fulfils
God's perfect will (Rom. 12:2). In the variety of charismata the
one way is followed and the one spirit is active. Grace is given in
different ways within the body where all are members of one
another (Rom. 12:5f.).

Summing up the law

The unity of Christ's way is the love of neighbour, which sums
up the law. (Rom. 13:8–10). In life and death, we belong to the
lord (Rom. 14:8f.). Faith governs every act, even the choice
between eating or abstaining; whatever is not of faith is sin
(Rom. 14:23).

The single goal

For the Philippians, the one rule is to walk worthily of the
gospel, firm in one spirit, striving with one soul. Suffering for
Christ is a gift and an athletic contest (Phil. 1:27–30), which
concentrates on one thing (Phil. 3:13). The believer forgets the
past and reaches out for the prize. Nothing should be a cause for
care as the peace of God watches over those who are in Christ
(Phil. 4:6f.).

Risen with Christ

Those who follow the Christ who has reconciled all things, must
walk worthily and please him in all things (Col. 1:9f.).
Wholeness and perfection mark the risen life in Christ and
destroy the greed which is idolatry (Col. 3:1–5). There can be

no compromise with the old way. The elect must show that they
are holy and beloved (Col. 3:12f.). This will be evident from
their compassion, kindness, humility, meekness and forbear-
ance. Forgiving all wrongs, they will be ruled by love, the bond
of perfection (Col. 3:14f.). Watchfulness brings perseverance in
prayer and thankfulness to God (Col. 4:2).

Perfection in love
The growth to perfection (Eph. 4:1–16) is a growth into the
unity of faith and knowledge, because there is a new humanity
created by God in righteousness, holiness and truth (Eph. 4:24).
It begins by putting away falsehood and living the truth
(Eph. 4:25). Kindness follows and reflects the forgiveness
received from Christ (Eph. 4:32). The believer moves from
darkness to light, with all goodness, righteousness and truth
(Eph. 5:8f.).

The unity of the moral life derives from its being lived in the
presence of God, where unity of spirit is set in contrast to the
plurality of flesh and its demands. God's will works through the
one charisma given to each believer. One God gives law and
that gospel which alone saves all. The new humanity is delivered
from the struggle against the many powers of sin by its one lord.
The law is summed up in a single command and Paul strains
towards a single goal. Those who are risen with Christ grow to
perfection in unity of faith and knowledge of one God. At every
point the good life is united by the work of one God.

One wisdom of God

There is only one gospel. The wisdom of the world and the
sophistry of Greeks have no place. The whole of truth derives
from the spirit which is active against the letter.

Paul's antithesis, of spirit which gives life and letter which
kills, is found in three short accounts: Rom. 2:27–9, Rom. 7:6,
2 Cor. 3:6. An analysis of these passages elucidates the key
idea.[24] Letter means the Law of Moses in its written form, seen

[24] The following account is indebted to E. Käsemann, *Perspectives on Paul* (London,
1971), 138–66.

by the Jew as the source of his unique salvation and as identical
with holy scripture. The scripture has been known as 'sacred
letters' and Paul is probably the first to refer to it by the singular
'letter'. Jewish tradition has misunderstood the intention of the
divine will. The Law confirms this misunderstanding by its
demands for works, perverting the relationship between God
and the pious Jew, and bringing sin and death. Letter can only
mean slavery. Freedom comes from the spirit, which means
participation in the event of Jesus Christ and starts from the
revelation of God as one who creates out of nothing and raises
the dead. By contrast the letter kills because it ties man to his
own strength and piety, taking him away from the sovereign
grace by which alone he can live. The spirit gives life because it
is the power which reveals the presence of the risen lord. The
Old Testament may be read through a veil and misunderstood
as a demand for works. On the other hand, when the veil is
taken away by Christ, the message of justification may be seen.

There can be only one gospel because there is only one Christ
and one God, from whom comes the only knowledge and
revelation.

The power of the gospel

The gospel proves the power of God (1 Thess. 1:5); and tells
the truth about God in every place (1 Thess. 1:8). With God as
witness, Paul gave himself solely to the preaching of the gospel
(1 Thess. 2:1–6), the true word of God which is effective in
those who believe (1 Thess. 2:13).

No other gospel

The entire theme of the letter to the Galatians is the one gospel;
there is no other (Gal. 1:6). This has several consequences.
Anyone who comes with another gospel, is under a curse
(Gal. 1:9). Truth is not a matter of opinion. Separated from
before birth, called by divine grace, Paul went off into Arabia
before he consulted other apostles (Gal. 1:15–17). The law as
tutor had prepared God's people for faith in Christ (Gal. 3:24).

However allegiance cannot be divided between the tutor and the truth; those who circumcise will lose the benefits of the gospel (Gal. 5:2).

Knowledge and wisdom

Paul prays that the Philippians might excel in knowledge, perception and judgement (Phil. 1:9f.). Knowledge of Christ in resurrection and suffering is the highest excellence (Phil. 3:10). God's unique wisdom is the word of the cross (1 Cor. 1:18), wiser than human wisdom (1 Cor. 1:24f.), perfect, divine and mysterious, hidden to the princes of this world who ignorantly crucified the king of glory (1 Cor. 2:7f.). Eye has not seen, nor ear heard, what God has prepared for those who love him. Christians already have the mind of Christ (1 Cor. 2:16). Knowledge goes back to the first act of creation when God commanded light out of darkness; this same God has enlightened the hearts of believers with the knowledge of his glory (2 Cor. 4:6).

Truth and reason

Universal guilt is a sin against truth (Rom. 1:18), as it rejects what God has made clear through his creation. Although men professed to be wise, they became fools when they exchanged the glory of God for images of men and animals. Their mindless hearts had been darkened (Rom. 1:21) so that they changed the truth of God for a lie (Rom. 1:25). The same God spoke in creation, law, prophets and gospel. He is worshipped with reason by those whose minds have been renewed (Rom. 12:2).

Mystery and wisdom

To the Colossians, Paul proclaims the mystery of the indwelling Christ who points the way to perfection (Col. 1:28). In contrast to this teaching philosophy is deceitful (Col. 2:8). False teaching demands ascetic practice and is a shadowy nothing beside the reality of Christ (Col. 2:16f.); freed by Christ from the elements of this world, believers should not be influenced from such a source (Col. 2:20). Raised with Christ, they should seek things above, where Christ is at the right hand of God (Col. 3:1). When his word lives in them in its fullness, then all wisdom is theirs and their life and worship are governed by one devotion and one power.

Unity of faith and knowledge

In Ephesians the opening prayer, for wisdom and revelation in the knowledge of God, is to be fulfilled, as hearts are opened to the hope of God's calling. His plan and purpose are a mystery (Eph. 1:17–23), a secret which has remained with God until now: that gentiles should share in the promise of Christ through the gospel (Eph. 3:6). The one body, built on one faith in one God grows by holding to the truth in love (Eph. 4:5 and 15). The goal is a maturity which is free from deceit and possesses a unity of faith and knowledge.

The gospel is one because its power springs from one God, who gave the law to prepare for it within his one dispensation. His unique wisdom, found in the cross, annihilates the wisdom of the world and shines creatively by the light of Christ's knowledge. Sin against God's truth is the root of human folly; from irrational worship of idols, the believer turns in rational worship to the God who renews the mind. The true mystery of Christ comes from God alone. So in knowledge as elsewhere, one God is the source. His unity defines the sovereignty and uniqueness of his truth.

Paul was concerned with theology, ethics and logic, and with one God as being, goodness and truth. Two comments are appropriate: first, God must repeat himself in a new creation through Christ, in order to overcome death, evil and error. The god who commanded the light to shine out of darkness, shines again in the face of Christ to give knowledge. Secondly, Paul develops a Christian use of argument, which is accelerated in the second-century writers who are our chief concern. 'Judaism might care little for logical conclusions, and Paul might be equally willing to ignore them. But he was the Apostle of the Gentiles: and the Greek world demanded a consistent scheme of thought; and if Paul was pressed to provide one, he could only do so by assigning to Jesus a position in the order of reality which could scarcely be made acceptable to the unitarian monotheism of Judaism.'[25]

FOURTH GOSPEL

Here the unity of God is affirmed in a striking way, from a beginning where the word is God and is with God, to a climax in the prayer for the unity of believers in the God who is one.

1 There is one God the father, from whom all things come and to whom all is referred.
2 There is one word, who is the fullness of God and who reveals the father.
3 There is one way of life and love, to be followed in Christ.
4 There is one word of God, who brings light and truth.

One God, the father

Invisible and anonymous
The light shines in darkness and there are negative moments in the apprehension of God. For no one has ever seen him; the μονογενὴς θεός has declared him. The positive claim 'God is spirit' (John 4:24) has a negative context: the time is coming when neither in Samaria nor in Jerusalem will he be worshipped. God as spirit is known by his voice but 'You have not heard his voice, nor have you seen his face and you do not have his word abiding in you' (John 5:37). Anonymity is stressed by the frequent title 'He who sent me' and 'I am'. Yet he so loved the world as to send his son (John 3:16) and he is constantly active in creation (John 5:17). His mystery and anonymity indicate his transcendent sovereignty.

The contrast between God and the world is contrast between one and many, light and darkness, spirit and flesh. Everyone needs to be born again, to be born of the spirit (John 3:8). We have nothing except what has been given from heaven (John 3:27). He who comes from above, is over all things

[25] W. L. Knox, *St Paul and the church of the gentiles* (Cambridge, 1939), 110.

(John 3:31). The time has now come, when God must be worshipped in his own way (John 4:23), in spirit and in truth (John 4:24).

Son in father

Yet it is easy to speak of one God in the Fourth Gospel because the father is inseparable from the son whom he sends. The perpetual activity of the father is the continuation of his creative strength (John 5:17) and the son merely follows what the father does (John 5:19). The father has given to the son the work of judgement (John 5:22), so the son is honoured as the father (John 5:23), who provides evidence for his authority (John 5:37). The son is the heavenly bread whom the father gives (John 6:32f.). In controversy Jesus points to the father who sent him and who is the source of his teaching and glory (John 7:17f.). Jesus does nothing from himself, but speaks according to the instruction of the father (John 8:28). He does not glorify himself; but the father glorifies him (John 8:54). He was before Abraham (John 8:58). When Jesus raises the dead (as only God can do), he prays 'Father, I thank you that you heard me', so that others should learn of his unity with the father (John 11:41f.). As the cross draws near, a voice from heaven confirms the glory of the father's name (John 12:28). To the fearful disciples, Jesus tells of many rooms in the fathers's house, where Jesus will prepare a place (John 14:1).

Reciprocity

The father is in the son as the son is in the father. Jesus speaks no words from himself and the father who is in him works as well as speaking words (John 14:10). The reciprocity of father and son is total. Knowing Jesus is knowing the father (John 14:7) and seeing Jesus is seeing the father (John 14:9). 'The reason why it is Jesus and not another who is the way to the Father is because it is only Jesus of whom it can be said that the Father is in him and he is in the Father (John 10:38; 14:10f.). Never is that kind of reciprocity in the Gospel extended to anyone else. Only Jesus stands in perfect solidarity with the Father'.[26] The

[26] M. L. Appold, *The oneness motif in the fourth gospel* (Tübingen, 1976), 18.

sending motif mixes reciprocity with subordination. Son points
to the father, and father points to son. No one lives and learns
from the father without coming to Jesus. Jesus' witness is true
because the works are done in the father's name (John 10:25).
Some subordination remains, for the works which the father has
given him, bear witness that the father has sent him (John 5:36).
Glorification of father and son is also reciprocal, however odd
and singular this may be (John 13:31f.).[27] Reciprocity in
mutual knowledge, glory, love, witness and work, points to the
unique oneness of father and son.

This means that those who hate Jesus, hate his father
(John 15:23). Jesus possesses all that the father possesses, and is
God from God (John 16:15). Prayer offered to the father in his
name will be answered with affirmation (John 16:23). The
divine glory which was shared before the beginning of the world
is to be revealed on the cross (John 17:5). The final confession
of faith in Jesus is 'My lord and my God' (John 20:28).

One word

Divine word
Everything depends on the word who was God and with God in
the beginning (John 1:1). He became flesh with glory full of
grace and truth (John 1:14), to declare the God whom no one
can see (John 1:18). As lamb of God he takes away the sin of the
world (John 1:29, 36), and he calls disciples who follow
(John 1:37, 46, 47) and confess him (John 1:49).

Signs of glory
Signs show his glory (John 2:11). He can remake the temple in
three days (John 2:19) and knows what goes on in human
hearts (John 2:25). He brings new birth and will be lifted up
like the serpent in the wilderness so that believers may find life
eternal (John 3:14, 15). Although he was sent not to judge but
to save the world (John 3:17), yet he does judge. The Baptist,
who goes before him is different (John 3:28) for the distinction
between heaven and earth is the distinction between God and

---

[27] *Ibid.*, 31. 'Jesus comes and he goes; he is sent and he returns; but his glory, though
extending into different spheres, remains the same.'

man (John 3:31). From his fullness flows life eternal, which he
alone can give (John 4:14). He is indeed Messiah (John 4:29)
and his time is close at hand (John 4:34). His word brings life to
a dying son (John 4:49, 53) and raises a paralytic (John 5:8).
Foretold by Moses (John 5:46), he is recognised as the prophet
who should come into the world (John 6:14). Yet, time and
again, the words 'I am' show that he is more than Messiah and
prophet. Only as God, can he give the unending life, which
comes from God alone (John 6:26f.). Those who come to him
will know neither hunger nor thirst (John 6:35). He has come
down from heaven to do the father's will and to own those
whom the father has given to him (John 6:37–40). His words
are spirit and life (John 6:63) and apart from him, there is
nowhere to go (John 6:68f.).

Dialectic and darkness
As surely as some believe, so others hate. The world hates him
because he condemns evil works (John 7:7). He brings division
as men decide for or against him (John 7:12). Yet his works
bring belief, for what more could Christ do than what has been
done in him (John 7:31)? From him will come the gift of the
spirit and life eternal (John 7:38f.). Since he is the light of the
world, those who follow him will not walk in darkness
(John 8:12). So long as he is in the world he remains the light
of the world (John 9.5). He continues his work of creation,
placing mud on blind eyes so that they are perfected and healed
(John 9:15). In all this he is entirely dependent on God from
whom his power comes (John 9:33).

   As good shepherd, he gives his life for the sheep (John 10:11),
has power to lay down his life and to take it up, as his father
commands (John 10:17). Predictably, he is condemned as a
blasphemer because he makes himself God (John 10:33), so he
points to the work of the father which he is doing (John 10:37).
Through his deeds the glory of God, father and son, is fulfilled
(John 11:4). As resurrection and life, he gives life to all who
believe (John 11:25). Yet his anointing points to his death and
he must go away (John 12:7f.). At the hour of his glory, like a
seed he must be buried in the ground, that life might come. Yet

after his humiliation he will be exalted and will draw all men to himself (John 12:23–32).

Finishing the work

He approaches the end with knowledge of his father's will (John 13:1) and with authority over all that he does (John 13:3). Yet distress comes because of the failure of one of his disciples (John 13:21). As way, truth and life, he is one with the father; he is in the father and the father is in him. His father speaks and works through him (John 14:10). He is the source of life, the true vine, cultivated by the father (John 15:1). He loves his disciples as his father has loved him and he invites them to remain in that same love (John 15:9). Those who are joined to him will share his love and share also the persecution of the world (John 15:20). In the hour of his arrest and trial he rules as lord. He goes to meet his accusers with the words 'I am' (John 18:5). He declares that all his speech and action have been public and not secret (John 18:20). His kingdom is not of this world, but he is a king (John 18:36) and by his crown of thorns he is recognised, 'Behold the man' (John 19:5). Offered as a king to the Jews he is rejected (John 19:14f.), yet he completes the work of his father and rises from the grave. The words of peace and victory are spoken to the frightened disciples (John 20:19) and he is acclaimed as lord and God (John 20:28).

Recapitulation

The idea of recapitulation which is expounded by Irenaeus,[28] includes concepts which are found in the Fourth Gospel. The summing up of all things or their fullness in Christ is a matter of history, metaphysics and redemption: it tells how the long exposition of man was concluded in Christ, it moves from the partial to the whole, and it tells of *Christus Victor* and the liberation which he brings. Secondly, recapitulation implies totality, correction and perfection: all things must be summed up, what is wrong must be corrected, and the final unity must be the last and perfect word.

---

[28] See below, pp. 147–71. Pauline ideas are also very important.

All these concepts may be found in the Johannine Prologue, and it has been argued on independent grounds that re-capitulation is the central idea of this thematic statement.[29]

The first verse establishes the framework: in the beginning was the word. History begins with creation (v. 3) and moves through the witness of John, to the coming of the word into his own territory (v. 11) and the faith of those who believe in his name (v. 12). The climax is the joining of λόγος and σάρξ and the glory which is made manifest. Since word is the beginning of creation while flesh or man is the end so the joining of end to beginning brings the fullness of grace and truth. John gives testimony to the upward movement whereby the word, who comes after, takes precedence because of his priority in time (v. 15). Grace upon grace points beyond Moses to the coming story of God.

Metaphysics or ontology begins with the word who was God and was near to God. He was the source of all that is (v. 3), the life and light given to men (v. 4) and the light which shone in darkness (v. 5). A metaphysical distinction is made by the claim that he was the *true* light (v. 9). By him believers are changed into children of God (v. 12) so that their being comes not from man, but from God himself (v. 13). The ontological climax is the joining of word with the flesh he had once made, in the fullness of grace and truth. The pre-existent word becomes incarnate yet remains identical with the father as μονογενής.

The redemption wrought by *Christus Victor* requires a dualism in which the word overthrows his adversaries. He is the light of men (v. 4), a light which shines in darkness, is not overcome, but gives light to all (v. 9). Yet the world which he made did not know him (v. 10) and his own people did not receive him (v. 11). The rejection is cancelled by the gift of authority to become sons of God (v. 12). The word transforms flesh to a thing of glory and grace surmounts the limits of the law.

Other concepts are also necessary for recapitulation. *Totality* and universality in time and space belong to him who was in the beginning and who made all things. His offer of salvation

---

[29] G. Siegwalt, Introduction à une théologie chrétienne de la récapitulation, *RThPh.*, 113 (1981), 259–78.

overcomes rejection through the universal gift to all who believe (v. 7); all who receive him obtain the power to become sons of God (v. 12).

The concept of *correction* is linked with the three negatives in the prologue. His own did not receive him, but those who did receive him became children of God (v. 11). These were born not of flesh and blood but of God (v. 12). Man has never seen God; but the μονογενής has told his story. His rejection is corrected by the sonship of those who believe, human flesh is corrected by new birth from God, and human ignorance is corrected by the revelation of the son. The Law of Moses is corrected by the grace and truth of Jesus Christ.

Finally *perfection* is plain in the fullness of the son whose incarnation is revealed in glory (v. 14). It is not remote and inaccessible, for from this fullness all who believe have received grace upon grace (v. 16). The inferiority of the Law of Moses is surpassed by the true grace or the gift of truth which comes through Jesus Christ.

All these concepts, plainly present in the prologue, are woven together in many ways.[30] Irenaeus produced and elaborated the term 'recapitulation' as a summary of this logic. Gnostics used Johannine language as a source of symbols uncontrolled by logic.[31]

Subordination of son to father remains, for the fullness of the son is linked to the transcendence of the father by the dependence of the son. Jesus is dependent on the father for power, knowledge, mission, instructions, message, life, destiny, authority, love, glory, disciples' testimony, gift of spirit, all other gifts, guidance, union and communion.[32] This dependence is

---

[30] Historical parallels cannot help much with the idea of recapitulation, since πλήρωμα and its related ideas may be found in Jewish, Gnostic and Jewish–Gnostic writings. None of the Gnostic or Jewish–Gnostic writings can be dated prior to John, and therefore we may speak of pre-Gnosis if we wish to define Gnosticism as a second-century phenomenon. It should be remembered that in holding to this definition, we are not disputing facts or concepts but the appropriateness of a name. The Jewish–Gnostic writing most relevant is the 'Three Steles of Seth'. Most important is the fact that verbal parallels are of secondary significance when terminology is vague and ambiguous. Only the use of a word within a coherent context can determine its meaning.   [31] Irenaeus, *haer.* 1.8.5.

[32] J. E. Davey, *The Jesus of St John* (London, 1958), 77f., cited by C. K. Barrett, *Essays on John* (London, 1982), 22f.

declared by his obedience and sonship. With remarkable subtlety, the titles which are linked with his 'I am' also indicate dependence, obviously in the case of way, door and vine, and indirectly in the case of light, life and truth.

The difficulty of presenting separate accounts of father and son points to the success of the Johannine account of one God. The monarchy of the father, who sends the son, seems to imply subordination; but the total subordination of the son points to his identity with the father and the unity of subordination brings divine fullness. He who accepts the cup which the father has given, is able to cry 'It is finished'. We are left with 'that twofold presentation of Jesus that is characteristic of John, who asserts both the equality of Jesus with the Father as God (1:10; 10:30; 20:28), and his subordination (14:28)'.[33] Equality without subordination would produce two gods.

In John christology and theology cannot be separated. This emerges in what has been called 'prosopographical' (person-related)[34] exegesis of the discourses concerning the spirit in chapters 14–16. The term was coined to explain the argument used by Justin and Philo to prove plurality within the Godhead. When God said, 'Let us make...', there had to be more than one person in the subject of the sentence. Similarly in John the use of the same predicates with different subjects and the use of the same subjects with different predicates can only be justified by the concept of three persons and one God. That this is stated obliquely adds to the mystery and force of the claim.

One way

Obedience

Only in Jesus can obedience, love and life be found. The law came through Moses, but grace and truth come through Jesus, who is the fullness from whom comes grace upon grace. The disciples are invited to come, see and be with Jesus (John 1:39,

---

[33] C. K. Barrett, *The Gospel according to John*, 2nd edn (London, 1978), 71.

[34] See C. Andresen, Zur Entstehung und Geschichte des trinitarischen Personbegriffes, *ZNW*, 52 (1961), 1–39. The use of the term 'prosopographical' by Andresen and other theologians is not identical with its use by ancient historians. See also R. Cantalamessa, *La cristologia di Tertulliano* (Freiburg, 1961), 156, and the discussion below, chapter 6.

46). They go with Jesus to Cana and Capernaum (John 2:1, 12). The coming of Jesus divides his disciples from those who reject him. He comes as light and judgement into the world. Evil-doers hate light, but those who do the truth come to it. By their choice all are judged (John 3:19–21). Faith is the only way, and work is to believe on him, whom the father has sent (John 6:29). God draws, teaches and will raise up those who come. They hear and learn from the father (John 6:44f.). As they remain in the word, they truly become disciples, knowing the truth which sets them free (John 8:31f.). The shepherd is both door and keeper of his flock (John 10:9); his own know him and he knows them (John 10:14). In the hour of crisis they are children of light (John 12:35f.).

Unity in love
They follow the example of their lord who washes his disciples' feet (John 13:14) and receive his new commandment that they should love one another as he has loved them. This love will be the mark of their discipleship (John 13:34f.). As his love rules their lives so he becomes the way as well as truth and life (John 14:6). Love is the way of obedience to his commands. Those who love him keep his words; in turn they are loved by the father who sent him (John 14:15, 21, 23).

United to him as a branch to a vine, they remain in him apart from whom they can do nothing (John 15:4), keeping his commandments and loving one another (John 15:9, 11, 12). Joy marks this love; but the world will hate them, as it has hated him (John 15:18f.). Soon they will not see him; then they will see him again and their sorrow will turn to joy. In that day all will be fulfilled (John 16:16, 24). God will keep them in the world, because they are his and because the world is hostile to them, as they keep the word of the father (John 17:14, 26).

One truth and light

Light in darkness

The true light brings light to every man (John 1:9). Grace and truth came through him (John 1.17), who is recognised by Nicodemus as a teacher from God (John 3:2). His truth is testimony, which points to the truth of God (John 3:33). The truth concerning Jesus is declared outside the limits of faith, by Caiaphas, who foretells that one man must die to gather into one the scattered children of God (John 11:50-2). Yet the disciples do not understand the entry into Jerusalem until afterwards (John 12:16). The ignorance of others has been foretold by the prophet. Their blindness comes because they love the glory of men rather than the glory of God (John 12:38-43). Yet the word that he speaks will judge them at the last day (John 12:48).

Knowing the truth

He knows the truth about all whom he meets, and astounds both the woman of Samaria, and the Samaritans, who hear for themselves and believe (John 4:39, 42). His enemies judge according to appearance instead of judging justly, and are met by sustained argument (John 7:24). Jesus proclaims in the temple that they do not know the God of truth who sent him (John 7:28). The time for learning the truth is short and, when he has gone, it will be too late (John 7:34, 36). He brings confusion to those who cannot decide whether he is prophet, Messiah or someone else (John 7:40-3). Yet it is plain that he speaks in a way that no man has spoken before (John 7:46). His testimony and judgement are true because he knows where he comes from and where he goes (John 8:14, 16). As his disciples remain in his word, truth will set them free (John 8:31f.). Believing is more than merely observing his presence and his words, for only faith can remove the blindness of sin (John 9:37, 39). Unbelievers reject the works of Jesus and do not belong to his flock (John 10:26). Yet many do believe (John 10:42), drawn by his works to faith (John 11:15). Faith confesses that Jesus is son of God (John 11:27).

Truth and discipleship

To the disciples he is truth and life and way (John 14:6). When truth is revealed by the spirit, they will know that Jesus is in the father and that they are in him (John 14:20). The spirit will lead into all truth (John 16:13), and make all things clear. Parables will give away to open speech (John 16:25). Although their faith is still weak (John 16:31f.), Jesus prays that they might receive the knowledge of God and his son, which is life eternal (John 17:3). His holiness brings them to holiness and truth (John 17:19) and the world will believe (John 17:21). The world has not known God, but Jesus and his disciples have known and will pass on their knowledge (John 17:26). In the hour of judgement Jesus points to the testimony of truth and leaves Pilate with the question 'What is truth?' (John 18:37). The purpose of John's written Gospel is that men might believe that Jesus is the son of God and by this faith find life in his name (John 20:31).

CONCLUSION

In each of the three writers, God is lord of life, goodness and truth. As being, he creates, gives life and raises the dead. As good, he requires and gives righteousness. As truth, he reveals his mystery and gives the light of knowledge to those who are in darkness. There are differences between the three accounts of being, goodness and truth; but the questions are asked and answers are given.

Secondly, there is persistent duality in the one God. Matthew's approach is linear and historical: there is one son of God who fulfils and will fulfil. Paul is concerned with universal salvation: the one Christ reconciles and restores, bringing all things together. For John, the mystery of this salvation is revealed by the word who is the fullness of the God, the one son who reveals the father. The saving efficacy of Christ confirms the reality of one God, for God must not only create but resurrect, not only give law but justify, not only reveal but enlighten.

Thirdly, the theme of the gospel in each case is one of completion and finality. The saviour fulfils the law and the promises; he remains with his disciples to the end of the age. In him all the promises of God are realised, 'Yea' and 'Amen'; in the fullness of the times he recapitulates all things. The word becomes flesh, full of grace and truth, to give his fullness, grace upon grace. He works to finish what the father has given him to do and his last utterance is: 'It is finished'.

This theme emerges in ever stronger terms. Christ sums up all things in heaven and earth (Eph. 1:10). The father has made him ruler of all things and head of the church, as he fills all in all. Fulfilment, taken as a power, brings in Christ a finality which has a future, a perfection which overflows into the emptiness beyond it. These are the ideas which, with Platonic elaboration, will guide the development of Christian thought.

Fourthly, while the one God determines the account of truth, wisdom and knowledge, these questions are not worked out and commonly appreciated, as are those concerning being and goodness. There appears to be plenty of material for physics and ethics in New Testament writings, but less for logic, which is largely concerned with the interpretation of Jewish scriptures. As apostle to the gentiles, Paul sees a wider need for argument and John begins 'In the beginning was the λόγος'; but it is this area of Christian thought which will prove vulnerable to heresy and in need of development by apologists.

CHAPTER 4

One God as cause and father

With the resources of the Bible and philosophy, how do the first theologians respond to the fourfold challenge of state, heretics, philosophers and Jews? They reject the many, fallible gods of the state, and the separation of old and new testaments by Jews and heretics; they claim the transcendence of the philosophers' first cause and the truth of divine creation. God is one, father, cause, creator, spirit, lord of history and entirely good. They begin from the unity of God. We have already considered part of Clement's response in an earlier chapter.

MYSTERY AND THE MONAD

God is one, says Clement, and beyond the monad (*paed.* 1.8.71). He is outside language and cannot be described in writing. The use of riddles is recommended so that anything written about God will do less harm should it fall into the wrong hands. Indeed, it is better not to write, but to learn (*str.* 5.10.65). God is beyond the reach of logic or the practice of speech; yet the riddles, which express him, act as a safeguard and deepen his mystery.

Mystery

Plato and other Greeks believed that truth was linked with mystery.[1] The philosopher followed the path of the initiate (*Phdr.* 249a–250c). Diotima spoke of the highest mysteries (*Symp.* 210a–212c). Persian and Jewish thought produced a

[1] A. Böhlig, *Mysterion und Wahrheit* (Leiden, 1968), 15.

religious ethos which readily joined the Platonic quest for higher knowledge. For Paul, the mystery of God is the heart of scripture and the wonder of salvation. Paul (1 Cor. 4:1) writes as a steward of mysteries, and imparts the secret and hidden wisdom of God. Clement joined Paul's mystery with Plato's account of philosophy as the true mystery (*Phd.* 8od), which was central to Philo's allegorically interpreted Torah.[2] Hellenistic Judaism had turned to higher revelation in hymn, drama, narrative and apocalypse.[3]

God's mystery is ever-present, for a Christian, says Justin, begins from baptism which declares the God whose name cannot be uttered (1 *apol.* 61). The mystery of the cross, found in the blessing of Joseph, endures in its strength (*dial.* 91). Egyptians used symbolism to describe God who, in many forms, sees and hears all things (*str.* 5.7.42). Christian mystery is unique and open to all. Christians worship differently, not like Jews or Greeks, but with a new and third kind of worship (*str.* 6.5.41). They are not an exclusive sect, for their secret is open. Christian workmen find the God who, according to Plato, is difficult to discover and impossible to declare (*ap.* 46); but this claim of Plato (*Ti.* 28c) calls for silence and negation (2 *apol.* 10).

Negative theology

God is the only unbegotten, uncaused being, and whatever is unbegotten is identical with all else that is unbegotten (*dial.* 5). His negative attributes (uncreated, eternal, invisible, impassible, incomprehensible, without limits) are part of his definition (*leg.* 10). From the concept of unity, the *via negativa* takes away physical dimensions and then position to finish in the magnitude of Christ (*str.* 5.11.71). For Clement, any first-principle is hard to describe. God, the indivisible one, is the ultimate first-principle and hardest of all (*str.* 5.12.81f.). This unique God is also called the first-begotten by whom all things were made (*str.* 6.7.58).

---

[2] See Goodenough, *By light, light.*
[3] Collins, *Between Athens and Jerusalem*, 195–236.

There are practical as well as logical difficulties in talking of God. We cannot properly name God because the giver of a name must be older than the receiver, and there is no one older than God; the names which we give to God are ways of addressing him, and derive from his good deeds and functions (*2 apol.* 6). It is foolish to accuse Christians of being atheists because they do not worship the gods of a particular city, since everyone is an atheist when he moves to a new city where different gods are worshipped (*leg.* 14). One could say that God is mind or light, but this does not mean that he is like a human mind, nor like the light which our eyes behold (*haer.* 2.13.4). He may be seen as a circle which contains all things, or a square which contains many smaller squares; but this is a difficult way of talking (*haer.* 2.13.6). Free from passion, he controls human desires (*str.* 4.25.157).

Men are like snails or hedgehogs who curl up in themselves and think of God in terms of their own nature (*str.* 5.11.68). He does not live in a house; both Paul and Zeno saw the inappropriateness of temples made by hands. Zeno insisted that temples should not be built, or if built, should not be regarded as holy (*str.* 5.11.76). Human confusion about gods was widely discussed: Ethiopians, said Xenophanes, had black gods, and Thracians had red gods. Everyone makes gods like themselves (*str.* 7.4.22); but God is like a universal consciousness without eyes and ears, aware of all that happens (*str.* 7.7.37). Philosophers differ on whether God is inside or outside the world – the Stoics put him outside the world, while the Platonists put him, like a pilot, within the ship of the world (*ap.* 47).

Negative theology, which declared what God was not, had been well established by the second Christian century.[4] Jewish polemic against idolatry had developed in Philo, and become more mystical in the Hellenistic Gnosis which derived from Palestinian apocalyptic. In Middle Platonism, the first-principle was unspeakable and invisible. Gnosticism appeared to be more negative: God was absolutely unknown even to the heavenly powers (*haer.* 1.23.2). With a multiplication of nega-

[4] Daniélou, *Message*, 297–316.

tive attributes, Gnostics could insist that they alone had knowledge of the unknowable. On the other hand, Alcinous and Maximus of Tyre specified three ways of knowing the unknown: abstraction, analogy and eminence, while Celsus spoke of synthesis, analysis and analogy. Clement established the term ἄγνωστος in the theology of the church; by grace and the word, we know the unknown (*str.* 5.12.82), who knows us. Clement moves by systematic abstraction to the magnitude of Christ, the abyss, and to the knowledge of the Almighty. He begins from the hidden God of the Bible, follows apocalyptic traditions and underlines the distinctive Christian revelation of the son.[5] The more transcendent God became, the greater was the need for a word who could declare him.

Simplicity and ἀπάθεια

The simplicity of God, for Clement as for Philo, follows from his unity.[6] As unmixed simplicity, God evades all categories except that of the pure unity which he himself exhibits.[7] The contemplation of this divine unity brings purity and simplicity to the soul.[8] For Irenaeus, divine simplicity means that God is entirely like himself and equal (*haer.* 2.13.3). Man, who is flesh and soul, also possesses spirit which is uncompounded and simple (*haer.* 5.7.1).

The New Testament links simplicity and giving. As God does not grudge his gifts so the believer gives and gives again. The apostles taught in this way (*haer.* 3.14.2). God gives in the simplicity of his goodness (*haer.* 4.38.4).

God's freedom from passion made it difficult to relate him to his world.[9] Yet, said Tertullian, while God's anger is not like that of man, it has the movement of feeling and sensation (*Marc.* 2.16). Clement talked much of divine passionlessness (*str.* 2.16.72; 2.18.81; 4.23.151), which was compatible with

[5] See above, chapter 2, pp. 52–60.   [6] *Immut.* 82, *fuga.* 164, *Abr.* 122, *heres* 183.
[7] *Leg. all.* 2.3. See W. Pannenberg, Die Aufnahme des philosophischen Gottesbegriffes als dogmatisches Problem der frühchristlichen Theologie, *ZKG* 70 (1959), 9–11, 33–6, and Daniélou, *Message*, 355f.
[8] *migr.* 153. On this question see J. Amstutz, Ἁπλότης (Bonn, 1968).
[9] See M. Pohlenz, *Vom Zorne Gottes* (Göttingen, 1909).

infinite love. How a changeless God may be involved in history is a persistent problem in Christian thought.[10] It is not merely a philosophical issue, for divine identity and faithfulness are central to human trust in God. Platonism was able to reinforce the claim for an immutable, autonomous, omnipresent and good God.[11]

Jewish division

In Judaism the names and attributes of the nameless God provided pragmatic and less consistent approaches. The divine name must not be pronounced (Lev. 24:15f.) and Philo, Josephus and Aquila agree with the LXX on this point. However the Mishnah gives an official list of many divine names in the Bible. These include: father of mercy, father in heaven, father of the world, lord, mighty.[12] The attributes of God are omnipresence, omniscience, omnipotence, eternity, truth, justice, goodness, purity and holiness.[13] The anthropomorphic tendencies of Jewish scriptures caused a tension between those who chose literal meaning and those who required allegory. Different degrees of literalism were proposed. The God who walks in the garden and rests on the sabbath, is, according to a first-century source, a God who has figure, limbs and enormous physical proportions. Psalm 104 says that God literally wrapped himself in a garment of light.[14] God is a student of the law, weeps and needs a house.[15] The division between literalists and allegorists is confused, because some Rabbis, who are steeped in Greek philosophy and culture, are opposed to allegory and welcome anthropomorphism, while others, who have no philos-

---

[10] 'Gott ist unendlich vollkommen und zugleich unendlich einfach, er ist absolut notwendig und absolut frei, er ist welttranszendent und weltimmanent, er vergilt gemäss seiner Gerechtigkeit und verzicht zufolge seiner Barmherzigkeit. Desgleichen verbindet er Statik mit Dynamik; er ist immerdar unveränderlich und zugleich ewige und höchste Aktivität.' H. Pfeil, Die Frage nach der Veränderlichkeit und Geschichtlichkeit Gottes, MThZ 31 (1980), 22.

[11] Provided its later accounts of the procession of hypostases and the generation of the world were set aside. See J. de Blic, Platonisme et christianisme dans la conception augustinienne de Dieu créateur, *RSR*, 30 (1940), 188–90.

[12] A. Marmorstein, *The old rabbinic doctrine of God* (New York, 1968), 56f.

[13] *Ibid.*, 148–217.

[14] A. Marmorstein, *Essays in anthropomorphism* (New York, 1968), 51.

[15] *Ibid.*, 65–79.

ophy, favour allegory. Philosophical Jews are aware of the dangers of allegory and its tendency to Gnosticism.[16] Both literalists and allegorists found supporters, and a legend claimed that, at the climax of conflict between the schools of Shammai and Hillel, a heavenly voice declared that both proclaimed the words of the living God.[17]

Unity and enclosure

Athenagoras sets out a logical basis (λογισμός) for belief in the unity of God.[18] In a way similar to Alcinous, he argues (*leg.* 8) that to be a god means to be ἐξ ἀρχῆς and ἀγένητος. To establish the uniqueness of God, he considers where one could put a plurality of gods. They cannot be in the same place, for ἀγενήτοι do not come from a common pattern and must be unlike one another. Could many gods be parts of a larger unity? Alcinous denies this possibility, because a God with parts could not be ἀρχικός, since a part is prior to its whole (*Did.* 10.8). Athenagoras argues also that the ἀγένητος is indivisible and cannot have parts. Finally, other gods could exist, neither in this world for God made it and controls it, nor in another world, for God has filled all things. Another god could have neither place nor function. Therefore God is one. εἷς οὗτος ἐξ ἀρχῆς καὶ μόνος ὁ ποιητὴς τοῦ κόσμου θεός.[19]

The discussion of place requires a God who encloses all things and is not enclosed.[20] The idea of enclosing has its beginnings in Presocratic philosophy and in Aristotle's *Physics* (3.4–8). In Philo, if God be the encloser, he must be immaterial, not in a place, unknowable in his essence and creator of all things.[21] Philo argues similarly for an enclosing God who fills and pervades all.[22] Hermas begins his *Mandates* (1.1) with the claim that God encloses all things and alone is uncontained. Irenaeus

[16] *Ibid.*, 155. [17] *Ibid.*, 157.

[18] A. J. Malherbe, Athenagoras on the location of God, *ThZ*, 26 (1970), 47–52.

[19] Athenagoras draws on Middle Platonic discussions of God and space. Cf. Alcinous, *Did.* 10; Plutarch, *De comm.not.* 30, 1073f.

[20] W. R. Schoedel, Enclosing, not Enclosed: the early Christian doctrine of God, in *Early Christian literature and the classical intellectual tradition, FS R. M. Grant*, eds. W. R. Schoedel and R. L. Wilken (Paris, 1979), 75–86. [21] *Migr. Abr.* 183.

[22] *Conf. Ling.* 136, *Leg. All.* 1.18.

(*haer.* 2.1.2) criticises the Gnostic account of fullness. If there were more than one fullness (pleroma) or God, then there would be no fullness. If something exists outside the fullness, then it either encloses or is enclosed by it. If it is separate, then there exists a third thing which separates it from the first fullness and this leads to infinite regress (*haer.* 2.1.3). Irenaeus leads up to the all-seeing, all-thinking, all-hearing One of Xenophanes. Plurality must be rejected.[23]

Stoic theology

Negative theology, of Platonic origin, has been given great importance because its formulae are so easily identified.[24] The more positive theology of Stoicism was also influential in the religious syncretism of the second century.[25] The world was studied, not for itself, but as a way to the transcendent being who would bring salvation through vision, action and knowledge. In contrast to Gnosticism which separated nature and grace, immanent soul and transcendent spirit, world and God, reason and knowledge, Stoicism joined λόγος with νόμος and gave ethics priority over logic and physics.

The Stoic account of God balanced positive and negative theology. God was ζῷον ἀθάνατον λογικὸν τέλειον ἢ νοερὸν ἐν εὐδαιμονίᾳ, κακοῦ παντὸς ἀνεπίδεικτον, προνοητικὸν κόσμου τε καὶ τῶν ἐν κόσμῳ (*SVF* 2,1021). Stoics were philosophers of the divine existence, of a God who was immanent and yet whose transcendence was maintained by a negative tradition. Following this balanced tradition, Athenagoras speaks of God known by νοῦς and λόγος (*leg.* 4, 10, 23), and Tertullian combines the invisible and visible, the incomprehensible and what is declared by grace, the unthinkable and that which is thought (*ap.* 17). Irenaeus tells of his God who is invisible and

---

[23] 'For if there were two or more he would no longer be mightiest and best of all'. Xenophanes, 3, 977a, 24.

[24] A useful collection of doxographical parallels is found in John Whittaker, ΑΡΡΗΤΟΣ ΚΑΙ ΑΚΑΤΟΝΟΜΑΣΤΟΣ, in *Platonismus und Christentum, FS H. Dörrie*, eds. H.-D. Blume and F. Mann (Münster, 1983), 303–6.

[25] See Spanneut, *Le stoïcisme des pères de l'église*, 77; Christian writers were influenced by Stoic ideas indirectly rather than by direct allegiance.

ineffable for all his creatures but not unknown (*haer.* 4.20). For Clement, Athenagoras and Irenaeus, as for Stoics, God is known through the harmony and providence of the world, common notions and anticipations (προλήψεις), through his works and through testimony to him.[26]

FATHER, CAUSE, CREATOR

God and the world

The negative account of God has answered the objections of philosophers and attacked the prevailing polytheism. It preserved the simplicity and integrity of one God. Indeed, the heart of the Christian message lay in the novelty and unity of the Christian God who was proclaimed.[27] However, can this one God create and care for the world? Does he not by his transcendent perfection, leave behind a blank which can only be filled by a lesser creator god?

Here lay the more pressing challenge to the divine unity. Marcion declared a strange god of the gospel whose goodness was incompatible with the evil of this world, which he placed under a creator who could be identified with the just God of Moses and the prophets. Against Marcion, God was defended as the morally good father and creator and as the logically necessary first cause. He is the lord God of Sinai, sovereign spirit, the ruler of history, who holds in his hands the beginning, middle and end of the times. If he were not all these things, he would be less than he is; perfect goodness must overflow in beneficence.

There is one father from the beginning and we should not look for another (*haer.* 5.16.1). There is one God who, as Paul said, is above, through and in all (*haer.* 5.18.2) and this one God who was in the beginning will at the end be present as the same God and father. While God is above all change and corruption (1 *apol.* 20), Marcion is wrong to say that there can be a God

---

[26] Spanneut, *ibid.*, 270–88. See below, pp. 262–8, for fuller account of the various forms of the knowledge of God.

[27] Cf. E. Peterson, ΕΙΣ ΘΕΟΣ (Göttingen, 1926) 213ff.

who is greater than the first cause and maker of the universe (1 *apol.* 26). Justin never calls Christ 'son of God' without specifying God as the 'father of the universe' (1 *apol.* 67). God is unchanging and, at the same time, universal in his action (*dial.* 3). He who made heaven and earth, is the only God, only lord, only creator and only father. So Marcion is wrong when he talks about a second god and Gnostics are wrong with their divine pleroma, which is separate from the creator God (*haer.* 2.1).

Christians know that their account of God is different. While Stoics say that God will be broken up into pieces when the world is made again, and the Sibyl thinks that everything will disintegrate, Christians insist that the first cause, God, is above the things which he made (1 *apol.* 20 and *dial.* 5). Justin was disappointed in the philosophers from whom he sought to learn about God. Some had little interest in the subject and some claimed that God cared for the world, but not for men (*dial.* 1). Nearly everyone confesses one God and it is therefore foolish to restrict the Christian proclamation (*leg.* 7). The only God, the only lord, the only creator, the only father (*haer.* 2.1.1), is the one maker of all things (*haer.* 2.9.1). The hidden causes of things, unknown to us, are known to God. They may be left to him and to his word who sits at his right hand. We do not sit on the throne of God, and our knowledge is so partial, that we must leave difficult questions in the keeping of a supreme and gracious God (*haer.* 2.26).

Gnostics wrongly declare that the prophets spoke by inspiration of other gods. All the prophets proclaimed one God, the maker of heaven and earth, and they all announced the coming of his son; similarly, the apostles declared one God, maker of all things (*haer.* 2.35.4). The simple elements of the gospel are that there is one God who made the universe, who was announced by the prophets, declared in the law, and revealed in Christ. There is no other God beside him (*haer.* 3.11.7). As absolute truth, Jesus would not have acknowledged an imperfect being as God, nor do his disciples mention any other, but the one true God and lord of all (*haer.* 3.5.1). The church takes up the confession (Acts 4) that the lord God made heaven and earth and sea (*haer.* 3.12.5). He, who was uncreated and without beginning or end, made all things (*haer.* 3.8.3). The one creator determines the whole economy of salvation – its beginning, middle and end (*haer.* 3.24.1). In this the maker, who is always the same, differs from that which is made, for that which is made has a beginning, a middle and can be increased (*haer.* 4.11.2).

Creator and cause

The good creator is remembered each Sunday. Christians gather for worship on the day when God changed darkness and matter to make the world (1 *apol.* 67). As Isaiah (42:8) says, God made the heavens, fixed the earth, called men to righteousness and gave them strength. As the lord God, he will not give his glory to another (*dial.* 65). Since Christians believe in a universal creator God and his word, they cannot be called atheists (*leg.* 30). Sunday means both creation and resurrection, for the God who formed things, says Athenagoras, will be able to form them again at the resurrection. He is able to raise from the dead what he first created (*de res.* 2). Paul had linked creation with resurrection in the great antitheses of Romans 4: justification of the ungodly (4:5), resurrection of the dead (4:17), creation out of nothing (4:17). God's justice raises, unharmed, those natures which need resurrection (*de res.* 10). Only the creator, in his power and wisdom, can raise to life what has been dissolved (*de res.* 11).

Between creation and resurrection, the same God works continuously for man's salvation. In patience and long-suffering, the one God made all things, spoke to different prophets, gave different covenants, until his word became flesh and suffered. The different dispensations moved Paul to speak of God's wisdom, knowledge and unsearchable judgements (*haer.* 1.10.3), for the one God is creator, father, founder, maker, just and good. He shaped man, planted paradise, made the world, sent the flood and saved Noah. The God of Abraham, Isaac and Jacob, the God of prophets and law, was revealed by Christ and declared by the apostles. The eternal son reveals the father to angels and to all whom he wills (*haer.* 2.30.9).

God's unchanging transcendence is balanced by his universal and saving goodness. As he is the one creator so he is always revealed by his creation (*haer.* 2.9.1), and governs the whole dispensation from beginning to end (*haer.* 3.25.1). God is cause, is ultimate and yet immediate and universal. His solitary perfection and creative goodness always interact. The creator is perfect while the creature is imperfect; for the creature never excels the creator (*haer.* 4.38.1). There cannot be another God beyond the creator; indeed, Marcion's God would not be good but negligent, because he is not effective within creation and certainly does not raise the dead (*haer.* 5.4.1).

Creation, said Plato (*Laws* 715), is under the control of the ancient word, who acts rightly and moves from beginning to end of all things to produce justice (*haer.* 3.25.5; *str.* 2.22.132). One God rolls up the heavens like a book and renews the face of the earth. He made temporal things for man so that man might grow to immortality. He bestows present grace so that, in future ages, the fullness of his goodness may be known (*haer.* 4.5.1).

Plato can help, as we search, beyond his works, for God himself, because Plato saw the distinction between the works of God and their inaccessible Maker (*prot.* 6.68). Indeed there is a universal human awareness that God is one, indestructible, unbegotten, and that somewhere above, he has an existence which is true and eternal. This God is king of all and the measure and balance of all (*prot.* 6.69). The Sibyl speaks of one God who sends winds, rain and earthquakes and who truly exists (*prot.* 8.77). Contrary to Marcion, Clement claims that God is good and does good. His justice and goodness are one (*paed.* 1.8.62–74) and testimony to this one God is true martyrdom (*str.* 4.4.17). Sophocles spoke of the one creator (*str.* 5.14.113). God is not made but makes; works of art cannot be sacred or divine because they are made by man. God is not fixed in any one place, but may be found whenever his people meet (*str.* 7.5.28f.).

Pagan gods could only exist if there were a higher god who made them, and this is absurd, for no high god would do such a thing (*ap.* 11.4). There is one God who made the cosmos (*ap.* 17) and philosophers should pay more attention to the creator and not be so obsessed with natural things; like Thales, they fall into a well while gazing up at the stars (*nat.* 2.4.18). Paul believed in the creator and did not introduce a new God (*Marc.* 1.21.1). The question of God to Adam 'Where art thou?' did not imply that God was ignorant – heaven is his throne and earth is his footstool (*Marc.* 2.25.1).

Clement tackles the crucial concept of cause, setting out different kinds of causes (*str.* 8.9) and indicating the causal content in the concepts of creator, maker and father (*str.* 8.9.29). Justin argues very simply that there must be one unbegotten first cause. If there were two, we should have to look for the cause of the difference between them. Infinite regress engenders frustration. Sooner or later, the exhausted mind stops on one thing, the unbegotten cause of all (*dial.* 5). While Justin and Irenaeus use similar arguments to prove the oneness of the first cause and necessary being, Clement has a special interest in the cause of ultimate truth and goodness. Understanding the first cause brings knowledge of good and evil (*str.* 7.3.17), and from such knowledge comes true humanity which is immune to opinion and hardship (*str.* 7.3.18). Man is always morally inferior to the first cause (*str.* 6.14.114), whence he receives a knowledge of truth from truth itself (*str.* 6.9.78f.).

God, says Irenaeus, would not be God if there were anything beyond him. One of many gods would lack what the other gods possessed. When heretics, in their desire to surpass others, suppose another pleroma beyond the first, they start an infinite regress. There is either one God or there is no God (*haer.* 2.1.1f.). For Tertullian, the principle of Christian truth is 'God is not, if he be not one' (*Marc.* 1.3.1). God is the great most-high (*summum magnum*),[28] eternal, unbegotten, unmade, without beginning or end. He must be unique. Two gods are even less credible than many. Marcion starts with two gods and finishes with nine (*Marc.* 1.15). Valentinus starts with two, but like the sow of Aeneas (*Aeneid* 8.43), finishes with a brood of thirty aeons

---

[28] This term is not found elsewhere; it has some affinity with a Neopythagorean abstraction. See A. Bill, *Zur Erklärung und Textkritik des 1. Buches Tertullians 'Adversus Marcionem'* (Leipzig, 1911), 20. Bill's work provides an extended discussion of the argument and reveals subtleties.

(*Marc.* 1.5.1). Marcion's strange God is still more incredible because he has caused no world which might prove his existence. He has not even produced the tiniest vegetable (*Marc.* 1.11.5). He either would not or could not create; neither hypothesis is appropriate to God.

Furthermore, the universal efficacy of God as cause is shown in the variety of his work; the many parts of the human frame point to his intricate wisdom (*haer.* 5.3.2). In the creator we find the love which points to him as father, the power which shows him as lord, and the wisdom by which he is both maker and restorer (*haer.* 5.17.1). From the beginning, rational creatures have existed in the eye or word of God, and even the grasshoppers sang to the all-wise God (*prot.* 1.2). Not only Plato, but others spoke of the only true God; he is, as the Pythagoreans say, one God, not outside the universe but within it (*prot.* 6.72). This immanence, according to Clement, is a form of providence planted in the world (*str.* 4.12.88), and Christians are joined together in the one economy of divine work. All things are full of Zeus, said Aratus, the poet who was quoted by Paul at Athens (*str.* 5.14.101). The immanent God of the Stoics, says Clement, (*str.* 5.14.101) echoes the truth of the Christian God, who is everywhere and who is perceived by the soul directly (*str.* 6.3.33f.). The finger of God is simply his creative power (*str.* 6.16.133). He is Alpha and Omega which means that he first made all things and that he does not cease to do good (*str.* 6.16.141). All that is, is willed by God (*str.* 7.12.69). From nature we may learn that God is the maker, that the universe is good and that all things are his free gift to us (*spect.* 2.4). We do not begin from the unknown but from the known within nature, that is, from the God who is known universally through his creation (*Marc.* 1.10.4). This world is worthy of God (*Marc.* 1.13.2) and all creation, especially the smaller animals, show his greatness (*Marc.* 1.14.1). The one God, who made man and all things, is capable of more than Marcion's god (*Marc.* 1.16.1), and all his goodness is evident (*Marc.* 2.4.6).

So the balance continues, between the unknown God or ultimate cause, and the richness of his creation. There could not be another God or father beyond the good creator, who alone can raise the dead (*haer.* 5.4.1). God is a great king, alone, unique and yet the world is held together by a cosmic sympathy which depends upon him (*str.* 5.14.133).

The universal activity of God is seen in his word, the one only-begotten whom the Gnostics do not accept. They divide Jesus from the only-begotten (*haer.* 1.9), but the church universal believes in one God and one incarnate Jesus and one holy spirit (*haer.* 1.10.1). This one universal word of God means that whatever has been rightly said belongs to Christians, and Christians worship him next to God (2 *apol.* 13).

Ex nihilo

In early Christian thought the idea of creation is enriched in several ways which remove the anonymity of the first cause. Is there a consistent account?

Creation *ex nihilo* is a consequence of monotheism. This is clearest in Hermas' account of 'one God who founded and created all things, and brought all things into being out of what is not, and who contains all things while he alone is not contained (*Mand.* 1), and also in Theophilus for whom there is nothing coeval with God (*Autol.* 2.8).

In Justin matter is ordered to produce existing things (1 *apol.* 10 and 59); it is clear that matter is not a second principle alongside God, for there can be only one unbegotten (*dial.* 5). In Clement there are several expressions which could be taken to refer to relative non-being as the object of creative power; but there is no clear account of this non-being and Clement is unambiguous that all creation owes its being to God (*prot.* 4.63; *paed.* 1.6.26). Tertullian, against Hermogenes and all dualism, explains why creation from nothing is the only reasonable monotheist option. Hermogenes' error lay not in his claim that matter was the stuff of creation, but in his claim that it was a second principle beside the creator (*Herm.* 4).

Irenaeus gives more detail on the manner and consequence of man's creation. All is the work of God with his two hands, the son and the spirit. No angels are needed. The father wills, decides, commands and makes the substance of created things.

The son executes, forms, shapes and models, while the spirit
finishes, arranges and adorns, nourishes and gives growth.[29]
Creation is the more significant because it begins the process
which leads to man's glory. Here commences the economy of
divine grace which includes many dispensations and which
culminates in the recapitulation of all things. Man is seen in the
light of creation where his lord shaped and prepared man to be
with him and share his glory.[30] Adam is the κεφάλαιον, to which
man is restored in Christ, who joins the end to the beginning
(*haer.* 3.22.3). Flesh comes from creation and will receive
ἀφθαρσία from God. For this world and man's flesh are not
temporary episodes; but flesh is related constantly to the spirit,
first in Christ, then in the sacraments and finally in the glory of
the resurrection.[31] The same defence of the flesh becomes
passionate in Tertullian, when he tells of all that the flesh can do
for God (*res.* 8). Further, the flesh of Christ is essential to the
necessary dishonour of Tertullian's God.

The doctrine of creation offers examples of the way in which
problems change, the need for awareness of logical structure
and the chameleon qualities of words. Justin says that God
created the world out of formless matter and that Plato found
this idea in Moses. Matter is in no way a second power beside
God. (This is the truth, he says, and Plato's adoption of the idea
does not make it truer or less true.) God did not need a pattern
of forms or a second God to bridge the gap between him and
matter; some Platonists thought that he did and Justin's account
of Plato might be questioned. Forms were part of the Platonic
ladder which Justin threw away when he read the prophets and
the friends of Christ who had direct encounter with God. Forms
are for Clement, as for most Middle Platonists, thoughts within
the divine mind.[32]

With Tertullian, matter is rejected. He is convinced, as much
as Justin, that there is only one unbegotten being. The rival
power, proposed by Hermogenes, is now matter. Matter is

[29] *haer.* 2.30.9; 3.24.2; 4.20.1; 4.20.6; 4.38.3; *dem.* 5; see Y. de Andia, *Homo vivens, incorruptibilité et divinisation selon Irénée de Lyon* (Paris, 1986), 67.
[30] Andia, *Homo vivens*, 344.   [31] *Ibid.*, 337.
[32] See Clement, *str.* 4.25.155; note the later problem of the hypostatisation of the divine ideas, G. C. Stead, *Divine substance* (Oxford, 1977), 278.

rejected, because God is one and omnipotent. Tertullian makes the same move as Justin, though with different pieces. Clement brings out the same issue by talking of the will of God as sufficient cause of creation from 'the things which are not'.[33] From 4 Maccabees to Paul and Hermas, the account of creation *ex nihilo* is concerned to declare one all-sufficient God. For Paul, God creates out of nothing, just as he raises the dead (Rom. 4:17) and justifies the ungodly (Rom. 4:5).

Now, all of this becomes clear when we take the context of each statement seriously. Two difficulties emerge. Writers commonly have several axes to grind. Tertullian will not allow the dualism of Marcion, nor that of Hermogenes, nor that of the docetist denigration of flesh. Justin simply wants to discredit Marcion as often as he can, since nothing is worse than a second God, and it would be easier to talk to Jews if Marcion were not so critical of their God. Marcion was so impressed by the wonder of the gospel, that he could not understand how this world could have come from the same God.

The second difficulty is evident in the assumption by some critics that Justin must have been dualist because he spoke about formless matter as the stuff of creation. Ambiguities are ignored by the fallacy of the humourless historian, (much humour depends on changes of meaning in words), who finds parallel phrases and is unaware of those changes in meaning which are the basis of thought and humour. On this topic, we are told, Justin 'understands things less as a disciple of Jesus and the prophets than as a disciple of Plato and of Greece'.[34] Yet Justin's several references make it clear that the world owes both its being and its order entirely to God, by whom all things were ordered and brought into being (1 *apol.* 20). Matter is not a second power beside God.

---

[33] *str.* 5.4.89 and 92. See discussion, Osborn, *Christian philosophy*, 280f.
[34] E. de Faye, *De l'influence du Timée de Platon sur la théologie de Justin Martyr* (Paris, 1896), 183.

ONE LORD

Bible

The God of the Christians is the God of the Christian Bible. The lord God is one lord to be loved with heart and soul and might. His biblical name points to his activity throughout the story of salvation. For all time and eternity, says Justin, there is but one God, who led the Hebrews out of Egypt and in this one God the Christians trust (*dial.* 11). He is great and mighty, terrible lord of lords and no respecter of persons (*dial.* 16). Where he is described as God of gods and lord of lords, scripture does not acknowledge other gods, but refers to those who are falsely reputed gods (*dial.* 55). Because the lord is not like earthly rulers, he does not need the world as a place to live in. He is all things to himself (*leg.* 16). Apostles, prophets and Christ did not acknowledge another lord besides him (*haer.* 3.9.1). He is the one God of Moses ('I am that I am'), and the God of Abraham, Isaac and Jacob. The first, second and fifth commandment, all point to the one God beyond whom there is no other (*str.* 6.16.133f.). The Greeks have indeed some knowledge; but they need the law and the prophets to teach them that there is only one God. An idol is nothing, because nothing can resemble God (*str.* 6.17.151; *str.* 6.18.163). From the beginning, the lord has forbidden the worship of any other gods.

Philosophers

The lordship of God, testified in scripture, receives support from logic and philosophers. God is not, if he be not one (*Marc.* 1.3). There is no sound argument which can point to another god beyond the lord. Since the so-called gods were once human, who had the authority to turn them into gods (*nat.* 2.13.1–4)? Marcion with his two gods is shown to be in double trouble: the strange god cannot be proved, the inferior creator cannot be denied.

Plato tells of a great ruler in the sky, the maker of the universe, who orders all things and is followed by a host of gods (*leg.* 23). The same philosopher speaks of a lord who is god of gods, the father and king of all (*str.* 5.14.102f.). The poets criticise the many gods for their weakness and frailties (*prot.* 7.75). Indeed Socrates subverted the worship of the gods and would not swear by them (*ap.* 14.7); for these reasons he was put to death (*nat.* 1.10.42).[35] The intelligent activity of the one God in his works points to divine providence (*str.* 5.1.6). Because there is one lord of all men, one God who is good and just, it follows that just men do not differ from one another as they reflect his goodness and justice (*str.* 6.6.47). Nothing can stand against him who is lord almighty (*str.* 1.17.85); he has absolute sovereignty (*str.* 6.17.151), his knowledge is universal (*str.* 6.17.156), and he needs nothing (*str.* 7.3.15). Since God is everywhere, a true Christian speaks the truth in every place (*str.* 7.8.51).

The sovereignty of God, declared in the Old Testament, confirmed by logic and philosophy, emerges with greater clarity in the New Testament. There could not be another god, according to the declaration of Christ (*haer.* 4.27.4). One lord dispenses the treasures of his goodness, and teaches by one instructor, the word (*paed.* 3.12.87). All the apostles speak of one creator God, announced by law and prophets, and one Christ (*haer.* 3.1.2). All who preach truth have declared one true God, one father and one word (*haer.* 3.15).

Contrast

While the God of the Christians is wrongly depicted as a crucified ass, he is rightly indicated by the cross, which is to be respected in many forms throughout the world (*ap.* 16.8). Christians worship the one God (*ap.* 23.11), who is lord of the emperor for whom the Christians pray (*ap.* 30.1). Idolatry is forbidden so Christians do not frequent idolatrous theatres and games (*spect.* 13.3). Their one master is God (*Scap.* 5.4), whom they declare although it gives offence (*test.* 2.1). While the one lord has, for the present, given earthly power to Rome, only the

---

[35] Yet Socrates was not consistent because, while he denied the gods, he ordered a sacrifice to be made (*an.* 1.6).

Christians know what he intends for the future (*nat.* 2.17f.). Tertullian indignantly attacks the pagan gods: why should Christians be persecuted for not worshipping what they regard as vile? As a convert, he sees a great gulf between the Christian God and the many members of the Pantheon. The vehemence of his attack declares his sole concern for the Christian God.[36]

Monotheism alone

The persistent monotheism of the second-century apologists had its dangers. For the sake of debate, they frequently presented a caricature of paganism and reduced Christianity to unqualified monotheism.[37] Aristides simply denies accusations of atheism and expounds Christian monotheism. Theophilus discusses divine unity (*Autol.* 2.1–33), Tatian contrasts one lord with many demons, the writer to Diognetus describes the Christian God as one alone and Justin argues against both pagan and Jew that Christians are true monotheists. It might appear that in their concern for monotheism, Theophilus, Tatian and Athenagoras find no place for the historical Jesus.

Similarly, Tertullian takes seventeen chapters of his Apology to discredit polytheism. Christianity simply *is* monotheism: 'quod colimus, deus unus est' (*ap.* 17.1). To one God, the soul gives testimony (*ap.* 17.5). The ban on idolatry is 'lex nostra... propria Christianorum, per quam ab ethnicis agnoscimur' (*idol.* 24.3). When Tertullian does talk about Jesus he simply hammers the paradox of Jesus and one God.[38] When he passes to 'pauca de Christo ut deo' (*ap.* 21.3), he speaks of the divinity of Christ as known through the moral change in believers (*ap.* 21), of the power of Christ's name over demons, of his works

---

[36] J. M. Vermander, La polémique de Tertullien contre les dieux du paganisme, *RevSR*, 53 (1979), 122f.

[37] Because 'ein Gegner eben besiegt werden muss' Christianity is seen 'in einer stark vereinfachten Form', 'einfach als Monotheismus', J. Lortz, Das Christentum als Monotheismus in den Apologeten des zweiten Jahrhunderts, in *Beiträge zur Geschichte des christlichen Altertums und der Byzantinischen Literatur*, FS A. Ehrhard, ed., A. M. Koeniger (Bonn, 1922), 302.

[38] *Ibid.*, 309. 'wie Tertullian das erreicht, durch enge Verbindung des monotheistischen und christologischen Vorstellungkreises, durch Behandlung der Christologie als Funktion des Monotheismus, gehört zum Wundervollsten, was dieser eminent Taktiker im Apologeticum (Kap. 17–21) vollbracht hat.'

which bring faith in God and of his judgement at the last day
(*ap.* 23). This is not enough, it has seemed to some, to place the
mystery of Christ in the centre of faith.[39] Christology, they
claim, is also neglected in Tertullian's other apologetic writings
(*nat.* 1, 2, *test.*, *Scap.*) and in other apologists, with the exception
of Justin, who proves that Christ is God (1 *apol.* 30–53).[40]

On the contrary, all we have is practical apologetic. The
apologists saw the opposition between monotheism and polytheism as the best place to fight their battle. They took
monotheism from Judaism, enlightened it with philosophy and
removed its legal restrictions. This monotheistic concentration
may explain their measure of success,[41] for a debater works by
leaving some things out and making the same point in many
ways. Their claim was based on reason and used a long tradition
of arguments against polytheism. Nor was there religious
impoverishment for, as in the Areopagus speech (Acts 17), there
was a strong sense of the nearness of God.[42] Indeed, for
Tertullian, it was through the paradox of Jesus and one God,
that the divine unity could be grasped. God was one in a new
way, through the son and spirit.

Divine unity is the persistent theme of Tertullian's polemic
against four opponents: the polytheism of pagan religion, the
materialist dualism of Hermogenes, the biblical dualism of
Marcion and the Gnosticism of Valentinus.[43] Against polytheism he attacks philosophers, poets and people (*nat.* 2), while
against Hermogenes and Marcion the problem of evil is his chief
concern. Athenagoras balances unity with trinity. He argues
that it is absurd to charge Christians with atheism when they
have a 'plural conception of deity'.[44] After the father and the
son and holy spirit, there is a host of angels and ministers whom
God has appointed by his word.[45] John 1:3 and 10:38 provide

[39] As was maintained by J. Heinze, Tertullians Apologeticum, *BSGW*, 62, 10 (Leipzig,
1911), 489.
[40] Justin's concern is the eternal Logos rather than the historical Jesus.
[41] J. Lortz, Monotheismus, 315 and elsewhere.
[42] Lortz (Monotheismus, 322) finds only one place (*cor.* 15), where there is a 'gewisses
intensives Christospathos'.
[43] A. D'Alès, *La théologie de Tertullien* (Paris, 1905), 41.
[44] W. R. Schoedel, *Athenagoras, Legatio and De Resurrectione* (Oxford, 1972), xviii.
[45] W. R. Schoedel, Neglected motive, 356–67.

a christology, but there is only an oblique reference to the incarnation (*leg.* 21).[46] Exclusive worship of one God is contrasted with idolatry, where the offensive element is identified as service to something lower than the only God.[47] The notion of *idolum* also conveyed the concepts of falsehood, image and shadow.[48] At the general level, every honour taken from God is a victory for the devil, and every sin becomes a form of idolatry.[49]

Polytheism's last plea

Finally, it should be noted that, then as now, all may not be won over to monotheism. In spite of logic, some have wistful longings for divinities in the natural world where Greek poets once blended divine plurality with divine unity.[50] The monism of Plotinus can be made compatible with many gods[51] and later Neoplatonists derived many henads from one henad. 'These last Hellenes wanted to find the divine presences that they and their ancestors and all mankind had known and loved in their cities and villages, their trees and springs and rivers and mountains, all together yet still distinct with the One, to meet the Unknowable in the likeness of many familiar friends.'[52] The claim, we are told, for divine action in history and incarnation places limits on God and makes humans too important. At the end, this case for polytheism is reduced to an emotive plea.[53]

---

[46] There can be no doubt of the importance of Athenagoras' contribution to the theology of the trinity. See L. W. Barnard, *Athenagoras* (Paris, 1972), 182. 'The Holy Spirit is the "effulgence" or "outflow" from God resembling the sun's rays. Within the inner life of the Godhead there exists between the persons unity (ἑνότης, ἕνωσις), fellowship (κοινωνία) and diversity (διαίρεσις). These later became technical terms in Trinitarian theology and in Athenagoras they appear for the first time applied to the Father, Son and Holy Spirit.'

[47] J. C. M. van Winden, Idolum and Idololatria in Tertullian, *VC* 36 (1982), 108–14.

[48] *cor.* 7.8. 'Si enim mendacium divinitatis diabolus operatur.'   [49] *praescr.* 40.

[50] A need for fairies at the bottom of the garden has been maintained by A. H. Armstrong. Some advantages of Polytheism, *Dionysius*, 5 (1981), 181–8.

[51] *Ibid.* 185f. Oddly the attack on the Gnostics (*Enn.* 2.9) is seen as an attack on exclusive monotheism.   [52] *Ibid.*, 187.

[53] 'We may perhaps be being called, more urgently than ever before to a very difficult sort of humility, which, if we ever attained to a decent measure of it, might establish our unique spiritual greatness among the beings we know by our very capacity of denial of that greatness... This is difficult to do properly. It is easier to proclaim that we are nothings before God or miserable sinners before God, often in a way which enhances our own importance, than to accept quietly that in the divine sight we may

SPIRIT

Positive meaning

The concept of spirit, again, like unity and lordship, has both positive and negative content, pointing to what God is and what he is not. On the positive side, it means that God has moral qualities and is above material needs (1 *apol.* 10). According to Plato, he is seen by the mind, or seen by the soul, if the soul has affinity with him (*dial.* 4). The Stoics speak of God as an all-pervading spirit who is eternal, and is distinct from all temporal, physical shapes (*leg.* 22). The gods who are spirits have no passions (*leg.* 21) and the heart of man can enter into eternal communion with God (*leg.* 31). God is all mind and comprehends (*haer.* 2.28.4f.). He is a pure and holy essence in contrast to the gods of the heathen (*prot.* 4.50). The soul, which is by nature Christian, testifies to the one creator God (*ap.* 17). Plato, however, is wrong in making the soul entirely equal to God (*an.* 24). Finally, God's spiritual goodness must be rational and not the irrational goodness of Marcion's most high God (*Marc.* 1.23).

Negative meaning

The negative aspects of spirit are clear. Faith in God means, for the Christian, the ability to distinguish God from the work of human hands; matter is one thing and God is another. The Athenian, who used a statue to boil his turnips, was a real atheist who did not believe in any god at all (*leg.* 4). Christians can see the difference between matter and God, between worship of idols and prayer to an unseen God, between his creatures and the uncreated God, between what is not and what is, between what the senses perceive and what the mind grasps (*leg.* 15). Christians have abandoned false material gods for the unbegotten and impassible God (1 *apol.* 25). Philosophers are better than idolaters, but still do not grasp the first cause of things. They venerate elements instead of stones or ibises.

be insignificant somethings in a very small corner of space and time.'. *Ibid.*, 188. Aggressive humility is a highly competitive virtue.

Christians acknowledge the one first cause, the spirit of God, who is neither a physical object nor a philosophical element (*prot.* 5.66). Because idols are false no free man should be compelled to sacrifice to them (*ap.* 28); indeed the worship of idols is the chief human crime – a form of self-slaughter, falsehood and fraud against God (*idol.* 1).

Powers of the spirit

The concept of spirit introduces a complex, all-embracing view of the divine unity. For Justin the word does it all, as the spirit speaks through the prophets and is consummated in Christ. All the powers of the spirit, elsewhere divided among many, rest on him (*dial.* 87f.). In Clement, word and spirit make God known, comprise reality and work salvation. Word is universal, accessible to faith and knowledge. Spirit is active to join intelligence with holiness. All the powers of the spirit come together in the son or word (*str.* 4.25.156).[54]

While Clement uses the trinitarian formula, his chief concern is with the activity of the spirit as present in Jesus, in the world and in men. The dynamic spirit overshadows its *persona*, as word and spirit act together universally. The spirit is life and Christ gives the spirit. Yet spirit is a personal reality, a subject, who is seen as the divine nature of the son, the force communicated by the father to Jesus. It is the means by which man receives the power of God to become spiritual.[55]

Athenagoras speaks of the holy spirit as an emanation (ἀπόρροια) of God (*leg.* 10.3).[56] The work of the spirit in creation is the same as that of the Platonic world–soul.[57] So spirit and word unite, with word being responsible for creation and spirit for sustaining and governing the world.[58] Tertullian plays on the ambiguity of body (*corpus*). Spirit is body but

---

[54] E. F. Osborn, Word, spirit and Geistmetaphysik: the concept of spirit, Supplement to *Prudentia* (1985), 65–8.

[55] L. F. Ladaria, *El espiritu in Clemente Alejandrino* (Madrid, 1980), 264–70.

[56] Quoting Prov. 8.22, with support from Wisd. 7:25.

[57] Cf. Plutarch, *Isis and Osiris*, 49, 371b.

[58] A. J. Malherbe, The Holy Spirit in Athenagoras, *JThS*, NS 20, 2 (1969), 538–42, concludes that Middle Platonism is the chief influence.

spiritual body differs from natural body. Spirit is body of a distinctive kind, yet because God is spirit, he must be body.[59] God is reason, rational (*Marc.* 1.23) and eternal voῦς (*leg.* 10). Reason is the constant mark of the divine being (*Prax.* 5; *Marc.* 1.24); all the arguments from a Stoic theology of divine reason are scattered through early Christian writings.[60]

HISTORY AND THE ECONOMY OF SALVATION

The patient God

The God of history is patient and long-suffering, as he showed himself with Jonah (*haer.* 3.20.1). His long-suffering can be reflected in that of those who worship him, just as a doctor is proved by those whom he has cured (*haer.* 3.20.2). God is never violent or unjust (*haer.* 5.1.1) and shows mercy in his age-long dealings with man (*prot.* 1.8). His eternal goodness and justice (*paed.* 1.8.71) are shown in the order and arrangement of things (*str.* 1.29, 182) and in his perpetual patience (*pat.* 15.1).

God's work in history shows that he acts differently at different times (*Marc.* 4.1) or in different dispensations (*haer.* 4.20.11). Yet Christ came for all ages of man, not just for one. There is one God who judges all (*haer.* 4.40.2). He is the God of two testaments (*haer.* 4.32.2 and 4.34). The one God is seen clearly in the Old Testament (*haer.* 4.7), and remains sole author and end of both covenants (*haer.* 4.9.3); therefore we do not differ from the Jews in our account of God (*ap.* 21).

God and change

Is a God of history a God of change? Tertullian insists that God can change[61] and questions the unchanging goodness of Marcion's strange God (*Marc.* 1.22f.). For God's goodness must be eternal, rational and perfect and the goodness of Marcion's

---

[59] Spanneut, *Le stoïcisme*, 288–90.

[60] *Ibid.*, 293f. See also J. Stier, *Die Gottes- und Logoslehre Tertullians* (Göttingen, 1899). 56–8.

[61] J. M. Hallman, The mutability of God: Tertullian to Lactantius, *TS*, 42 (1981), 373–93.

God is none of these. A good God must be angry and punish evil-doers; so , after man's fall, God became a severe and cruel judge (*Marc.* 2.11). In response to sin, God's perfect goodness became justice (*res.* 14). In different situations, God acts differently, becoming angry to the proud, merciful to the sinner, patient with the stubborn, all in his own distinctive way (*Marc.* 2.16.7). Tertullian is not able to maintain this view consistently; he shows the strength of Marcion's objection when he makes God the father invisible, inaccessible, placid like the God of the philosophers, and gives the son those qualities which Marcion regards as unworthy of God (*Marc.* 2.27.6). Yet against Praxeas, Tertullian maintains the divine immutability of the word, whose incarnation is simply the putting on of flesh (*Prax.* 27.6f.).

God in history

How is the knowledge of God in history related to the inner testimony of the soul? Tertullian saw a possible tension between the inward and outward pursuit of divine knowledge. The soul returned into itself to find the knowledge of God; but this knowledge was expressed in the rule of faith and the divine economy, in God's relation to the cosmos and history.[62]

History becomes important for all who see Christ as its culmination. After Christ, says Clement, philosophy is no longer relevant (*prot.* 11.112); it made a fuss of many things, but now one teacher teaches everything. For Tertullian, Christ, who is the Alpha and Omega, is the sum of truth, both old and new.[63] His view of history helps him to understand philosophy and faith, 'But our lord Jesus Christ declares himself to be truth, not custom; just as he was always Christ and before all things, so he is truth eternal and ancient' (*virg.* 1.1f.).

Enthusiasm for history opposes the Gnostic denial of divine activity outside the pleroma. There were two Gnostic worlds

---

[62] A. Meis Wörmer, 'Pero es el gran mérito de este pensador primitivo el que, pese a sus arriesgados avances *ad intra*, nunca pierda de vista la proyección de este misterio *ad extra*.' El problema de Dios en Tertulliano, *TyV*, 21 (1980), 286.

[63] 'Die in der Fülle der Zeit erschienene veritas ist auch die ewige veritas'. M. B. von Stritzky, Aspekte geschichtlichen Denkens bei Tertullian, in *Platonismus und Christentum*, ed. Blume and Mann, 266.

and the higher world, not the human world, was the one that counted. Irenaeus argued for one world and one God; any world beyond God would make him incomplete (*haer.* 2.8.3 and 2.4.3).[64] Salvation history overcomes the contradictions between this world and its God, and the difference between the two testaments: the world is not yet complete but its fulfilment has been declared. The Valentinian learns by detaching his spiritual seed from history; Irenaeus learns within the world where man grows from law to freedom, for God is found within the plan of history and to flee from history is to flee from God.[65] This is apparent in the entirely historical content of the *Demonstration*. God is proved by the many instances of prophecy and fulfilment.

One God and the economy

The unity of God is essential to the existence of οἰκονομία. Son and father are lord because he who is born of God is God. There is one God, son and father, who is known through 'the economy of our redemption' (*dem.* 47). It has been argued that this economy is a function of the Godhead not of the history of salvation;[66] but an 'economic trinity' cannot exist without an economy of salvation, and the latter is the concern of Irenaeus.[67] Within the total economy there were various economies which were harmonious within the whole; but there was one and the same God, from the beginning to the end, helping the human race.

---

[64] 'Any attempt, like the gnostics', to sever a perfect and complete world outside and beyond history from this world which derives from it...involves imperfection and defect within the Pleroma itself' (*haer.* 2.4.2f.). R. A. Markus, Pleroma and fulfilment, The significance of history in St Irenaeus' opposition to Gnosticism, *VC*, 8 (1954), 212.

[65] Irenaeus 'substitutes for the gnostic redemption-physics a Christian redemption-history. The gnostics had seen their salvation as *by* nature *from* history: Irenaeus sees salvation as *by* history, *in* nature. '*Ibid.*, 219.

[66] M. Widmann, Der Begriff οἰκονομία, im Werk des Irenäus und seine Vorgeschichte (Dissertation, Tübingen, 1956), 78f.

[67] *Ibid.*, 80. 'Was für ihn nämlich alle Geschichte, von der Schöpfung bis zum Ende, zusammenhält und eint, das eben ist der Plan Gottes mit der Menschheit, der jede Phase der Geschichte umfasst und durchwaltet.'

The word οἰκονομία was adapted by Paul who saw the extended responsibility of stewards of the mysteries of God (1 Cor. 4:1), in their faithfulness to the vast economy of salvation.[68] In the Deutero-Pauline literature it covered the breadth of the divine purpose, realised in Christ, to restore the universe (Eph. 1:10). Ignatius wrote of the same theme (*Eph.* 6:1; 18:2; 20:1), while Justin used the word to speak of the incarnation (*dial.* 45.4; 67.5; 87.5; 103.3; 120.1), of the cross (*dial.* 30.3 and 31.1) and of the divine plan in general (*dial.* 107.3, 134.2 and 141.4). Tatian extended the term to refer to the internal disposition of the trinity (*orat.* 5.1). Hippolytus and Tertullian both used the term in this way to combat the Monarchian heresy. By the end of the third century the reference to the trinity was abandoned and the word became the common designation for the incarnation and its consequences.[69]

Irenaeus uses the term one hundred and twenty times, of which thirty three refer to the Gnostic ordering of the pleroma, especially in the formation of the saviour. In his own account, it covers the several dispensations of the one God (*haer.* 4.33.7) or the mystery of the cross which repeats and unites (*haer.* 5.17.4). The difference between Irenaus' historical use of the term and the Gnostic use ('la plus nébuleuse théosophie') is clear.[70] In Gnosticism, the concept of οἰκονομία may refer to the rule of the demiurge, to this world in distinction from others (cf. *haer.* 1.7.4) and is linked with fate; but it may simply refer to any order (*haer.* 1.16.2; 1.14.9). In Valentinian and Basilidean Gnosis it may refer to the descent of the redeemer into the lower world (*haer.* 1.24.1; 1.14.6).[71] The Stoic use of the term merits more attention.[72] Chrysippus speaks of ἡ τῶν ὅλων οἰκονομία which governs all by immanent reason and fate.[73] This is taken up by Irenaeus when he speaks of the *verbum dei gubernans et disponens omnia* (*haer.* 5.18.3).

The word, neutral enough in its usual meaning (plan of

[68] A. D'Alès, Le mot οἰκονομία dans la langue théologique de S. Irénée, *REG*, 32 (1919), 1–9. [69] *Ibid.*, 9. [70] *Ibid.*, 8.
[71] Widmann, Diss., 114–23; the evidence does not suggest significant use.
[72] *Ibid.*, 123–33. [73] H. von Arnim, *SVF*, 2, 937.

management), is used, in Christian writing, chiefly to describe the total plan of salvation. Not all world history is part of the economy, but all the economy *is* part of world history. This is supported in Irenaeus by Stoic natural theology for which the cosmos is permeated and ruled by the one God. Once again Stoicism, not Platonism, provides the philosophical structure.[74]

The apparent disunity of *Against heresies* has been attributed to multiple sources which provide a barrier to any exposition of its ideas.[75] For example, it is argued that what is said about image and likeness in one place cannot be explained by what is said elsewhere.[76] However, these are fluid terms about which few, if any, are consistent. Unity is found at a deeper level in Irenaeus.[77] The latter part of Book Three speaks of an economy of salvation which springs from the one creator God, is directed to the salvation of man in his physical creaturehood, works through the whole biblical history from beginning, to middle, to end and is entirely fulfilled in the incarnation of God's only son.[78]

The oneness of God provides the integrating theme of *haer.* 4. Recent study has shown that older hypotheses of multiple sources cannot be applied to this book. There is a formal unity to the book, based on the words of the lord.[79] The coherence of the argument is even more striking. Book 3 proves that there is one God who creates, and one incarnate word. Book 5 deals with eschatology, with further reference to one God. Book 4 joins the two by an account of saving history, in which the unity of the dispensations points to the unity of God.[80] The different themes of human evolution (from Adam-child) and human

---

[74] Diverse elements like the Adam–Christ dialectic and the long-term education of man's free will are joined within this scheme. M. Widmann, Der Begriff οἰκονομία im Werk des Irenäus und seine Vorgeschichte (Dissertation, Tübingen, 1956), 172f.

[75] F. Loofs, Theophilus von Antiochien Adversus Marcionem, und die anderen theologischen Quellen bei Irenaeus, *TU* 46, 2 (Leipzig, 1930).

[76] H. Koch, *ThStKr.* (1925), 187, cited, Widmann, Der Begriff οἰκονομία, 3. See also D. P. Minns, The will of the father and the obedience of the son in the writings of Justin Martyr and Irenaeus, (Dissertation, Oxford, 1984), 174–242.

[77] P. Bacq, De l'ancienne à la nouvelle alliance selon S. Irénée (Paris, 1978) established beyond question the unity of *haer.* Book 4, despite widespread earlier acceptance of its disunity.   [78] Widmann, Diss., 31f.

[79] Bacq, De l'ancienne à la nouvelle alliance 282–90.   [80] *Ibid.*, 290.

catastrophe (from Adam-sinner) are shown to be two aspects of the same mystery of salvation.[81] Irenaeus works always with logical rigour and fidelity to scripture. Within the one economy or universal history of salvation, there are many divine interventions or economies which find their unity in the same God and father (*haer.* 4.28.2). While salvation is given once for all in the recapitulation of Christ, it extends to every stage of human growth.[82]

GOODNESS

The one God is uniquely and actively good.[83] Justin speaks much of the goodness and justice of God, who made the world. As good and unbegotten, his goodness is ultimate (1 *apol.* 14f.). Yet divine goodness calls man to follow, to imitate God in self-control, righteousness, love and all that is fitting before him (1 *apol.* 10). Every form of evil is excluded from the father of righteousness and other virtues (1 *apol.* 6).[84]

The goodness of God is, for second-century writers, the theme of their opposition to Marcion, who separated a good God from a just creator. Clement argues at length against those who consider that the just is not good (*paed.* 1.8.62f.), to prove that goodness and justice mutually entail one another. God's chief concern is the work of salvation and, as the only saviour, his goodness is unique (*str.* 5.10.63; *str.* 7.7.41; *prot.* 11.116).

In the debate against Marcion, the words of Jesus, 'There is none good but God' had to be linked with the creator. Justin expands the verse: 'None is good but God alone, *who made all things*' (1 *apol.* 16.7).[85] The great commandment is to love and serve the lord God 'who made you' (1 *apol.* 16.7). Clement uses the verse twelve times to declare that the one God is good and the good God is one (*paed.* 1.8.71 and 1.8.74). Unique goodness

---

[81] *Ibid.*, 294.　　　　　　[82] *Ibid.*, 383.

[83] E. Osborn, ' Origen and justification: the good is one, there is none good but God (Matt. 19:17 *et par.*)', *ABR* 24 (1976), 18–29.

[84] As von Engelhardt points out, Justin does not refer to the ἀγάπη of God. See M. von Engelhardt, *Das Christentum Justins des Märtyrers, Eine Untersuchung über die Anfänge der katholischen Glaubenslehre* (Erlangen, 1878).

[85] My emphasis. Similarly at *dial.* 101.2 there is both a supplement καὶ γὰρ ἐπὶ γῆς τὸ αὐτὸ ἔπραξε and further modification.

belongs to the one saviour (*str.* 5.10.63). Ignorance of God brings death; to know the only father is to share in his eternal life and power, for he alone is good and saviour (*str.* 7.7.41).[86]

Natural precepts, common to Christians and Jews, depend upon assent to God, and upon following his word in a total love of the one God (*haer.* 4.13.4). The goodness of God cares for all who are estranged from him (*str.* 2.16.73). Piety points to the first cause, father and maker, whose image is to be seen in human goodness (*str.* 2.18.78). In his own being, God shows that goodness, justice and forgiveness cannot be separated (*str.* 2.15.66). All natural righteousness points to the one God who is good and just (*str.* 5.14.141). Some things come directly from him, and some things do not (*str.* 7.7.39). Because God's judgement is irrevocable, it must be complete (*an.* 33). God is without sin, and Christ is without sin because he is God. Only man can sin (*an.* 41).

A weak God, like the god of Marcion, would be a danger to religion and morality (*Marc.* 1.27). God's entire goodness, foreknowledge and power are plainly proved, says Tertullian (*Marc.* 2.5). From the beginning, his severity has been directed against man's sin, and his goodness and justice have been joined in his perfection (*Marc.* 2.11). If God did not threaten, his goodness would be ineffective (*Marc.* 2.13). On all occasions God confronts us, whether to punish or to do good (*Marc.* 2.14). His goodness is natural and always has purpose (*Marc.* 2.16); he first chose and then rejected Saul with perfect consistency (*Marc.* 2.23). Paul speaks of the depth of the riches and wisdom of God because law and gospel are bound together in one God (*Marc.* 5.14).

[86] Origen uses the verse against Celsus to deny that the world is full of gods (*Cels.* 5.11f.), and against Gnostic dualists to affirm that God is the source of all being, creator of the world, yet other in substance from all that he has made (comm. in John 2:13; 6:39; 13:25). He turns the text against Marcion to claim that the father sent the son ὄντα πρὸς ἑτέρους καὶ εἰκόνα 'τῆς ἀγαθότητος' τοῦ θεοῦ (comm. in Matt. 15:10). Again Origen argues (*princ.* 2.5) for the goodness of justice, citing Paul, 'The law then is good and the commandment holy and just and good' (Rom. 7:12). The Marcionites had claimed that Matt. 19:10 refers to the father of Christ who is not the creator; but in the Psalms, God is described as 'good' and in John 17:25, Jesus addresses his father as 'just'. Origen's thought is dominated by the twin themes of divine unity and goodness. See Osborn, *Origen and justification*, 23.

From negative beginnings, the apologetic account of God moves forward to great strength, for monotheism expects a lot from its one God. At first he seems a paradox – transcendent monad and omnipotent creator. Yet the polarisation has point. In order to create and govern, God must be other than his creature. So he is utterly transcendent, cause and creator, lord of patriarchs and prophets, sovereign spirit, perfect goodness and ruler of history. But why does he have to do anything? The answer lies in his perfect goodness which must be active. 'It is not that God, in virtue of his essential goodness, remains blessed and immortal, "neither troubled nor causing trouble"; but because he does good in his own unique way, and, being and becoming *true God and good father* in his own unceasing doing of good, he remains changeless in the identity of his goodness. *For what is the use of good which is not active and never does good?*' (*str.* 6.12.104. My emphasis.).

CONCLUSION

The similarities between Christian and Jewish accounts of God have led to rash generalisations, like the claim that Christians simply took over the Jewish version, which was a naïve blend of devotion and philosophical jargon,[87] and had no desire to go further.[88] Yet Justin, the earliest of the writers we have considered, moved well beyond this position. God is the father of righteousness and all virtues (1 *apol.* 6), father and maker of all (1 *apol.* 8).[89] His activity in history leads up to the coming of Christ.

It has been argued that Justin was not able to unify the philosophical and the biblical accounts of God.[90] A fierce debate on this point, one hundred years ago, took formulae at their face value and did not allow for the polysemous flexibility

---

[87] Goodenough, *The Theology of Justin Martyr* (Jena, 1923), 123. Greek Judaism 'philosophised about an Absolute but prayed to God the Father. Ordinary Greek Jews would only have understood the Jewish God of Abraham, while they would have used the philosophical phrases with the indiscrimination of unintelligence.'

[88] *Ibid.*, 124.

[89] Justin inverts the titles given by Plato to the maker and father of all (*Ti.* 28c).

[90] G. T. Purves, *The testimony of Justin Martyr to early Christianity* (London, 1888), 145.

of words about God. Few realised how philosophical terminology was already endowed with religious overtones by non-
Christian writers such as Maximus of Tyre.[91]

Indeed, the most important move lay in the strength with
which the unification of the philosophical and biblical accounts
of God was carried out. Today, for many, the contrast remains
striking. A contemporary apologist sees faith in the biblical God
as a distinct step after belief in the God of the philosophers. 'The
conflict between the "God of the philosophers" and "the God
of Abraham, Isaac and Jacob" – as Pascal formulated it against
Descartes and others – has remained open up to now. Can it
really be settled at all?'[92]

In the second century, the biblical account of God had long
been considered as the barbarian philosophy. Greek witnesses
had presented the Jews as philosophers because of their more
philosophical account of God.[93] Hecateus of Abdera, as early as
the fourth century BC, described the Jewish state in terms
reminiscent of Plato's Republic[94] and Theophrastus, Aristotle's
pupil, writes of the Jews as philosophers.[95] Megasthenes finds
philosophers outside Greece, first in the Brahmans of India and
then in the Jews (*str.* 1.15.72). Josephus quotes Clearchus,
another pupil of Aristotle, in similar terms.[96] The link lay in the
Greek belief in one God, who was called by many names.
'There exists one God and spirit and fate and Zeus, who is also
named with many other names.'[97] The Letter of Aristeas
presents Judaism as a universal, monotheist philosophy and
Aristobulus supports the same idea.

Against this background, Justin and Clement made the new
move which was crucial for Christian thought. Support may be
found, plainly in Athenagoras, and in Irenaeus, who argued
about the Bible. Even Tertullian, who denounced philosophy,

[91] *Ibid.*, 147. This point is made by Purves in his brief discussion of the disputants:
   Weizsäcker, Von Engelhardt, Stählin and Hilgenfeld.
[92] H. Küng, *Does God exist?* (London, 1980), 613.
[93] M. Hengel, *Judaism and Hellenism* (London, 1974), 1, 255. This paragraph depends on
   Hengel's useful work.
[94] F. Jakoby, *Fragmente der griechischen Historiker*, 262, frag. 6.
[95] *Ibid.*, 737, frag. 6.   [96] *contra Ap.* 1.176–82.
[97] *SVF* 1. 28. 102; *DL* 7, 135; cited Hengel, *Judaism*, 1.262.

drew on philosophical argument to support his interpretation of scripture. The God of the Bible was the *summum magnum*, than whom nothing could be greater. Justin passed through several philosophies before he came to the prophetic and Christian writings; in the words of Christ he found the only sure and profitable philosophy and the sole reason for being a philosopher. Clement speaks of the Bible as philosophy. In the story of Moses (*str.* 1.22.150–29.182), where he draws on Philo, Clement begins from Numenius' account of Plato as Moses in Attic dialect. 'This means that Moses was a theologian and prophet, and, as some say, an interpreter of sacred laws' (*str.* 1.22.150.4). Moses was educated in all Egyptian learning, including philosophy. He grew in wisdom and continued to learn when he was a shepherd. 'Moses stands before us as a prophet, a legislator, skilled in military tactics and strategy, a politician, a philosopher' (*str.* 1.24.158.1).[98] Moses, says Clement, teaches a philosophy which includes four parts: historical, legislative, liturgical and theological.

To this one move, the linking of the Bible and philosophy, Christian theology owes its first steps.

[98] Only the titles 'prophet' and 'legislator' are found in the Philonic parallel (vita Mos. 2.3).

CHAPTER 5

The unity of all things in Christ

In the account of God there was a constant stress on unity. God was the unknown, the first cause, the lord, the ruler of history, the father. In all these things he was unique: he was lord and there was no other. In the account of the word of God, there is an equal stress on unity and uniqueness; but the stress is made in a different way. The unity of the word includes rather than excludes.[1] The greatness of the son of God is that his power, presence, truth and reality are universal. There is nothing which can be added to him. Three ideas are used to develop this theme: fulfilment, recapitulation, salvation. These ideas and others describe the totality of the son of God. His work is to complete what commenced at creation, to restore what had fallen away, to redeem what was lost. In this way, Irenaeus challenges the claims of Gnostics to go beyond Jesus and his gospel. There is nothing left to be done after the totality of Christ. Answers to Marcion and to the Jews are also included: Jesus brings creation to its perfection and sums up the old dispensation.

FULFILMENT AND CONTINUITY

One should never begin to make a world unless one can complete it. Jesus finishes all that was partial and fulfils all that was expected of the one who was to come. Apart from his second advent which is already certain, there is nothing left which

---

[1] It is an inclusive rather than an exclusive unity. These are metaphors which cannot be used with precision. There are places where the father is described as enclosing and other places where the son is ineffable.

needs to be fulfilled. The prophets foretold all the details of Christ: his birth, his growth as a man, his miracles of healing, his rejection, his death and his ascension to be the son of God (1 *apol.* 31). Moses, the first prophet, spoke of him as the desire of nations who would bind the foal to the vine and wash his robe in the blood of the grape (1 *apol.* 32). Isaiah foretold that the gentiles, who had no expectation, would receive him, while the waiting Jews would not recognise, but reject him (1 *apol.* 49). Jacob spoke of his two advents, one in which he would suffer and one in which he would come in power and glory (*dial.* 52). Malachi spoke of the sacrifice offered throughout the world from men of every race. These sacrifices were the prayers and thanksgiving of Christians (*dial.* 117). Even Plato took from Moses the shape of the cross as the sign of salvation (1 *apol.* 60). There were many other prophecies of the king of glory (*dial.* 95), of Joshua who was a figure of Christ, and of Isaac, Jacob and Judah (*dial.* 113; *dial.* 120). All these were fulfilled in Christ (*haer.* 3.19.). He was born of a virgin, suffered, rode on an ass, drank vinegar and gall; he was despised among the people but remained the wonderful counsellor and the mighty God, who will come on the clouds of heaven as the judge of all (*haer.* 3.19.2). He fulfilled the ultimate prophecy that we should not be saved by man or angel but by the lord himself. He came as God from the South, fulfilling the words of Habakkuk (*haer.* 3.20.4).

The fulfilment of these prophecies may be understood by the careful reader of the scripture. Christ is the treasure hidden in the field and all who understand types and parables will find the fullness of the treasure. His coming and his humanity may now be understood (*haer.* 4.26.1); but all will not understand, says Justin, for grace is needed to perceive the truth (*dial.* 58).

Jews do not find fulfilment in Christ. Trypho rejects the Christian invention (*dial.* 8). If the Messiah has been born he is unknown, does not know himself and remains without power until Elijah anoints and announces him. Further, it is incredible and almost impossible 'that God endured to be born and become man'. Justin insists that he is not trying to prove this from his own resources but from the scriptures, and those who reject his interpretation will answer to God for the hardness of their hearts. Trypho agrees to look carefully at what Justin has learnt with great toil (*dial.* 68). One problem for the interpreter, says Justin, is that some passages, where the crucified man is proved to be God, have been cut out from the translation made by Seventy Elders (*dial.* 71). The king who reigns from the tree (Ps. 96:10) is not to be found in Jewish scripture.[2]

The richness of imagery, the mass of scriptural material which Justin and others put forward – these things point to the fullness of the Christ who has fulfilled the words concerning him and will fulfil them further when he returns in glory. For the prophets announced two advents (1 *apol.* 52 and *dial.* 32) and God has delayed the end because there are still some who will repent (1 *apol.* 28).

Trypho objects to the joining of the historical Jesus with past and future divine appearances. It is blasphemous to say that a crucified man had once been with Moses and Aaron, then later became a man, was crucified, rose and will return in glory. Any continuity of the work of the word was broken by the shame of Jesus on the cross (*dial.* 38). Trypho insists that Christ could not, without absurdity, exist as God before ages and then become first, a man, and then, more than a man (*dial.* 48). Justin argues to show the presence of Christ in many scriptures. The one God is forever active; there will be no inheritance in the mountain of God except through Christ (*dial.* 26). The God who appeared to Moses was not the father, but the word, angel or messenger of God (*dial.* 56). Irenaeus claims that if readers of scripture had believed Moses, they would have believed in Jesus, because he is found everywhere in the writings of Moses (*haer.* 4.10.1).

The God of creation came in Christ and all members of his new covenant declare one God and one Christ (*haer.* 3.12). Outside the family of the new covenant there are false disciples who speak of many gods and many Christs; but John insists on the unity of Christ with God. Every spirit which separates Jesus

---

[2] When Christians took over Psalms for liturgical use, they inserted such phrases as signs of appropriation; with the passing of generations, Christians assumed that their text was original. See J. M. Charlesworth, Christian and Jewish self-definition in light of the Christian additions to the Apocryphal Writings, in *Jewish and Christian Self-definition*, II ed. Sanders, 27–55. Also see Osborn, *Justin Martyr*, 103f.

is of the Antichrist. The one Christ, who entered the gates of heaven because he had taken flesh upon him, will return, in the flesh in which he suffered, and reveal the glory of the father. He is word of God, only-begotten of the father, Christ the lord (*haer.* 3.16). Against Marcion, who divided old and new dispensations, Irenaeus insists that Christ liberated Abraham and his seed; he fulfilled and did not destroy the law when he healed on the sabbath (*haer.* 4.8.2). Christ came for all who believed, who had believed and who would believe (*haer.* 4.22.2). Prophets and patriarchs pointed to him and thereby facilitated the work of the apostles, who entered into the work of others (*haer.* 4.23). Those who work to convert gentiles have a harder task, because no one has prepared the way (*haer.* 4.24).

The activity of the word has been concerned with right behaviour. The law of the sabbath was a temporary thing, made necessary by hardness of heart in ancient Israel (*dial.* 27). True righteousness comes only through Christ (*dial.* 28). He did not cancel the ten commandments, but reaffirmed and fulfilled them (*haer.* 4.16.4). Christians continue to commend the truth of God, although they are cursed in synagogues (*dial.* 96). There is no way to knowledge of God the father, except through the son who is true man and true God. The son administered all things from the father, receiving testimony from all, working from beginning to end (*haer.* 4.6.7). Through him, the word, Abraham knew the father and the coming son of God (*haer.* 4.7.1). There are many arguments against those who say that the prophets were inspired by a god other than the God who sent Jesus Christ (*haer.* 4.34.1). The parable of the vineyard speaks of one God who sent his prophets and then his son (*haer.* 4.36).

For Clement, there is the same continuity of the word in saving history. The word spoke through Moses, Isaiah and other prophets and then became man, so that man might learn to become God (*prot.* 1.8). Plato supports belief in the active, ever-present, avenger of evil (*prot.* 6.69f.). There are different ways of encouraging goodness and there is no peace to the wicked because of the constant activity of the word (*paed.* 1.10.94). There is one covenant of salvation from one God, one lord who gives one salvation (*str.* 6.6.44 and 6.13.106f.). His providence, like the ointment on Aaron, permeates the whole universe (*str.* 6.17.156).

Tertullian argues with equal force for the continuity of the work of Christ, whose two comings – the first in humility and the second in glory – were foretold from the beginning (*ap.* 21.15). The miracles, which he worked, proved that he was the word of God, for he did everything by his word as he had done of old (*ap.* 21.17). In the history of salvation, Christians provide a third race after the Jews and the Gentiles, because they worship God in a different way (*nat.* 1.8.1f.). The son of God was active from the beginning, administering his divine judgement (*Prax.* 16.2). Christ always acted in the name of the father, who rules every dispensation, and what seems the total disgrace of God is the sacrament of man's salvation (*Marc.* 2.27.7).

RECAPITULATION

From rose-windows to mosaics of the cosmic Christ, from parallel pictures and paired statues of the old and new covenants, the idea of recapitulation has penetrated European art. Yet it has sometimes seemed splendid poetry, bad logic and the road to millenarian madness. We shall therefore analyse it and show the logical structure of this persistent idea.[3] Its intricacy is one reason for the common neglect of its logic and the frequent flight into simple symbolism.

Elsewhere in patristic writings ἀνακεφαλαίωσις may mean a summary in words (Chrysostom, *hom.* 1.4 in *Eph.*), adding up

---

[3] Irenaeus certainly took over early material, as in what Bousset calls the 'Treatise on free-will' which is found in *haer.* 4.37–9. Like Clement of Alexandria (*str.* 2.16.72–5), he normally worked it into the structure of his own thinking. (See M. Widmann, Irenaeus und seine theologische Väter, *ZThK*, 54 (1957), 165.) However, in the so-called 'Presbyterpredigt' section (4.27–32), Loofs claimed there is no evidence of his own work. On the contrary, this section confirms Irenaeus' distinctive theological achievement: the universal economy of salvation and the theme of recapitulation (*ibid.*, 170). By this he brought together creation and redemption or the first and second articles of faith. His reproduction of earlier traditions was also part of his message. He wanted to show to the Gnostics the truth which had accumulated and to indicate that truth was simple, old, one, and not complicated or trendy and diverse (*ibid.*, 172f.).

accounts (Origen, *comm. in Eph.* 1.10), making a list (Euthalius *Diac. epp.* Paul, *Migne* 85, 716A) concentration in one person (*haer.* 5.29.2), presenting an anti-type (pseudo-Chrysostom, *mart.* 1), or renewal and restoration in Christ (Cyril, *glaph. Gen.* 1). The verb ἀνακεφαλαιόω is used also to designate the unity of the trinity (Athanasius, *ep. Serap.* 1.30 and Greg. Naz., *or.* 6.22).[4]

The key word is related in secular use[5] to the summing up of a speech (Dion. Hal., *Lys.* 9) or a mnemonic (Aristotle, frag. 133). κεφάλαιον is more frequently found, with various meanings: head, main point, headings of a play (Antiphanes, *Comicus* 113.5) or development, summing up, topic of argument, capital, sum total, crowning act, completion, chapter. The addition of ἀνά, brings the idea of increase and strengthening, repetition and improvement which distinguish the New Testament use of πληρόω, following the Hebrew מלא (mille) rather than הקים (heqim).[6] The past is not so much confirmed as completed. However no translation will save us from the long logical haul which an analysis of the concept requires. Against Marcion ἀνακεφαλαιόω indicates that a summing up adds no new material, and against the Gnostics it declares a finality which cannot be surpassed. After the gospel had claimed to fulfil Judaism, it was inevitable that Gnostics and others would try to fulfil the gospel. This enterprise is opposed by forceful use of the argument against infinite regress; Irenaeus points to the internal competition of those who wished to be more perfect than the perfect and more Gnostic than other Gnostics (*haer.* 1.11.5).[7] The same danger is first attacked in Ephesians, where the cross and the church are presented as the eschatological wonders, beyond which there can be nothing, because all has been

---

[4] G. W. H. Lampe, *Dictionary of patristic Greek, in loc.*

[5] H. G. Liddell and R. Scott, *A Greek–English lexicon, in loc.*

[6] C. F. D. Moule, Fulfilment-words in the New Testament: use and abuse, in *Essays in New Testament interpretation* (Cambridge, 1982), 3–36. Note especially, p. 31, with reference to Matt. 5:17, 'Are we not driven by the context to say that πληρῶσαι here implies something far deeper than mere prediction-verification?'

[7] N. Brox, *Offenbarung, Gnosis und gnostischer Mythos bei Irenäus von Lyon*, (Salzburg und München, 1966), 196–9, especially 197. 'Irenäus zeigt den Irrtum dieses Strebens in welchem er eine heillose Autonomie des Menschen erblickt.' See also A. Bengsch, *Heilsgeschichte und Heilswissen* (Leipzig, 1957), 11.

summed up in Christ.[8] Recapitulation declares the unity of God
and the unity of saving history. 'One therefore is God the father
and one is Christ Jesus our lord, who comes through the whole
dispensation and recapitulates all things in himself'
(*haer.* 3.16.6).

For Irenaeus the idea consists of three sets of concepts. First
there are *totality, perfection and correction*, secondly *history and
Christus Victor*, and finally the divine activity in *being, goodness and
truth*. These concepts combine with one another in all possible
ways, which is the reason why everything is joined to everything,
why many plausible accounts may be given of recapitulation,
and why there is no alternative to patient analysis of the idea.

The beginning of the idea is simpler than its exuberance
suggests. In God's world, correction of sin is the first priority;
this is done by going back to the first fault, setting it right and
then bringing all to a proper and perfect end. Perfection is the
proper goal for a world made by God. Totality, correction and
perfection come together in the completion by the son of the
work which the father has given him to do.[9] To recapitulate,
one must correct and perfect a totality.

There appears to be a conflict between the motifs of correction
and perfection, between the fall and judgement of Adam and
the infancy of Adam whose immaturity explains his failure. This
antithesis is solved by the grace of a God who is able to turn even
a serious fault into part of a total plan of salvation. The *felix culpa*
is no less a fault; its felicity is entirely of God who never lets man
leave his hands.

While *Against Heresies* remains the main source for the idea of
recapitulation, the *Demonstration* provides a fuller account of the

---

[8] Paul's theology of history is continued in the typology of Clement of Rome,
Barnabas, Justin, Melito. The ordering of all things under Christ is found in
Col. 1:15, the Johannine Prologue, the Apocalypse and Ignatius. Recapitulation as
repetition comes from Paul and is found in Ignatius' new humanity. Recapitulation
as perfection is found in Paul, John and Ignatius. Union with Christ and assimilation
to him are linked by Paul in cross and resurrection and are explicit in John and
Ignatius. The Apologists give cosmic dimensions to the Johannine Logos, who from
his cross draws all to himself. Irenaeus' account of recapitulation is itself a summing-
up of the theology and proclamation of the second century. E. Scharl, *Recapitulatio
Mundi* (Freiburg, 1941), 133.

[9] The importance of this idea in the Fourth Gospel has been noted above.

historical element, refers also to metaphysical (*dem.* 4, 12, 34, 43, 47) and ethical (*dem.* 87) issues, and points to participation in the communion of God and man (*dem.* 6).

We look first at Justin in whom the idea of recapitulation is clearly present, although the word is not to be found (apart from a fragment cited by Irenaeus, *haer.* 4.6.2). Jesus, who was wholly God and wholly man, taught for the conversion and restoration of the human race (1 *apol.* 23). His messengers went out to every nation on earth to tell his story (1 *apol.* 39). His cross is a universal symbol, visible on every side, the greatest symbol of his power and rule (1 *apol.* 55). The lord bares his arm to act in Christ. The suffering Messiah bears the sins of many and divides the spoil (*dial.* 13). He has many names, as he is called Jacob and Israel and son of man (*dial.* 100). His inheritance, says Isaiah, is the nations, and the covenant of God is the Christ (*dial.* 122). As one Jacob produced the race of Israel, so one Christ produces true sons of God (*dial.* 123), and this Christ unites all in his inheritance (*dial.* 139). All these references to the totality of Christ and his work are references to life and being, to the fullness which comes in Christ. His fullness is ontological; but there is more to be said.

The same word is the fullness of goodness. Christ is the eternal and final law and covenant which supersedes all previous laws and covenants; as a crucified Messiah he leads men to God. From him comes the true and spiritual Israel (*dial.* 11). Jesus kept the law in order to round off the dispensation of his father. At the same time he pointed to the new covenant which was to come and to endure for ever (*dial.* 67). There is only one universal righteousness for all men and this is summed up in the commands of Christ.

He is also the fullness of truth. Christ is the archetypal word in whom all men share. He is the perfect Logos who has sown seeds of reason in every man. Those who have lived according to reason were Christians before Christ. They included Socrates and Heraclitus as well as Abraham and Elijah. Those who lived without reason were hostile to Christ and his seed and killed those who lived according to the word (1 *apol.* 46).

Justin's account of fulfilment in being, goodness and truth, of the threefold totality brought by Christ, introduces the final clue to the meaning of this concept. Clement, we have seen, speaks of God as the first-principle of being, of ethics and of logic. As God is being, so he is the first-principle of physics. As he is goodness, so he is first-principle of ethics, and as he is reason, he is the first-principle of logic. This is the ultimate point where Hebrew and Greek thought come together. In his account of the good, Plato joins together three things: the cause of being, the reason or definition of things and final goodness.[10] For the student of early Christian thought, it is important to notice that these three ideas are also linked in the Hebrew heritage, where God is the source of life and being, the just and righteous one, and the giver of wisdom and truth.

These concepts are developed in Irenaeus. The summing-up of all things in Christ is not an abstract achievement, but is that in which each may find salvation, sharing in the reality of Christ, who is cause, purpose and explanation of his existence. Where Justin is fragmentary, Irenaeus is untidy and generous because he is competing with the many aeons of the Gnostics. He develops his parallels and his proofs without thought for the patience of his reader, as the main ideas return with remarkable persistence. We find them all in the following passage: 'As our lord alone is truly master, so the son of God is truly good and patient, the word of God the father, who became son of man. For he fought and conquered. As man he contended for the fathers and through obedience did away with disobedience entirely... For he is a most holy and merciful lord and loves the human race... Therefore he caused man to cleave to and become one with God... In what way could we share in the adoption of sons unless we had received from him through the son that fellowship which relates to God himself, unless his word had been made flesh and entered into communion with us?... God recapitulated in himself the ancient formation of man that he might slay sin, deprive death of its power and bring man to life. Because of this, his works are true' (*haer.* 3.18.6, 7). Here the lord of *being* deprives death of its power and brings man to life.

[10] See above, chapter 1.

The lord of *goodness* is pious and merciful, good and patient. He is truly master and his works are *true*. In this life of God man may share as he is called to cleave to and to be one with God (*haer.* 3.18. 7). The totality of the achievement of Christ and the particularity of Jesus are set together.

Recapitulation applies to being, goodness and truth, the concepts of totality, perfection and correction. It perfects and corrects the totality of being, goodness and truth.

The profusion and cohesion of several recent accounts produce an uncertain result.[11] First, it is evident that no one account is exhaustive. Second, several analyses present similar concepts in various logical structures, so that the same things are said in different ways. Third, all analyses are qualified by the insistence that the parts must be put together to make sense. Clement describes the son as ὡς πάντα ἕν, like the centre of a circle where the radii join. This is a more abstract statement of Iranaeus' account of recapitulation, for the son is 'neither one thing as one thing, nor many things as parts, but one thing as all things'. Clement goes on to the theme, that God, as being, goodness and reason, is the first-principle of physics, ethics and logic. If we look at Irenaeus on these lines we may achieve a clearer analysis and at the same time appreciate the richness of the concept.

Totality, perfection and correction define the life God gives in Christ, whose life passed through all the ages of man so as to destroy completely the power of sin and death, which, since Adam's fall, had kept mankind in slavery. The Law showed sin to be no king but a robber and murderer; yet the Law could only reveal and not remove the rule of sin.

Only a man could deliver humanity from death and that man must come from a virgin as he first came from the virgin earth. The Law pointed to the tree of testimony on which the son of God was lifted up, in the sight of all, to heal the serpent's wound, to draw men to himself and to give life to the dead (*haer.* 4.2.7). From bondage and death, man is delivered by the new man, who washes him from the stain of death and brings him to life in

---

[11] See Appendix 2.

God. Jesus washed the feet of his disciples, and gave them food while they were lying down, in order to declare his gift of life to those who lay in the earth; then he descended to them so that his gift might be for all (*haer.* 4.22.1). The life, which was breathed in Adam at his birth, is perfected by the word and spirit to life in the divine image and likeness (*haer.* 5.1.3). The lord suffered on the day Adam died, the sixth day of creation, so that he might begin a second creation (*haer.* 5.23.2) which ended the murderous fear and hatred of man for man (*haer.* 5.24.2).

Saving history points to the fulfilment of prophecies which perfect and correct the past (*haer.* 3.9). Four gospels follow from four covenants, which are summed up in the fourth, which is the fourfold source of the kingdom (*haer.* 3.11.8). History continues in the church which calls on the God who created heaven, earth and sea (*haer.* 3.12.5). Details of Adam's sin are corrected: disobedience with a tree by obedience on a tree, disobedience of Eve by obedience of Mary, the sin of the first-created man by the correction of the first-born of God, the crafty serpent by the harmless dove (*haer.* 5.19.1). At the return of Christ in glory, Antichrist will be destroyed and many from east and west will sit down with Abraham, Isaac and Jacob (*haer.* 5.30.4). All is the work of *Christus Victor* who ascended on high and led captivity captive. Had God's creature been forever lost to death, God would have been defeated; but the second man destroyed the strong man, plundering his goods and restoring life and liberty (*haer.* 3.23.1). The son of man, who keeps God's commands, overcomes the rebel angel and binds him with his own chains. In his temptation, the lord showed that Satan is a perverter of God's word, and a transgressor of God's law. He captured him and freed his prisoners, freely granting to them immortality (*haer.* 5.21.3).[12]

---

[12] It is clear that *Christus Victor* is not the sole theme of Irenaeus' account of salvation and that it has meaning only in relation to the other themes. Note criticism of G. Aulen on this point by W. P. Loewe, Irenaeus' soteriology: Christus Victor revisited, *AThR*, 67 (1985), 1–15 and J. P. Jossua, Le salut: incarnation ou mystère pascale (Paris, 1968), 1–7.

Being

All existence depends on the reality of Christ.[13] History and Christus Victor might have remained symbol and myth; but the account of life led to ontology and metaphysics. In *haer.* 3.21.10, Irenaeus begins from Paul's antithesis of the disobedience of one man which brought sin and death to the obedience of one man which brought righteousness and life.

Totality
THERE IS ONE CREATOR WHO MAKES AND REMAKES
ONE CREATURE

The word of God made Adam and then summed him up in himself, being born appropriately of no earthly father. 'But if the former was taken from the earth, and God was his maker, it was necessary that the latter also, making a recapitulation in himself, having been formed as man by God, should have the same likeness of origin.' (*haer.* 3.21.10). Humanity is united in the two Adams.[14]

THE UNIVERSAL CREATOR REMAINS THE SAME UNCHANGING
CAUSE AND THE CREATION REMAINS THE SAME CHANGEABLE
SUBSTANCE

The son, who works all things for the father from the beginning to the end, reveals the father to all. 'Therefore, in all things, and through all things, there is one God, the father, and one word, and one son, and one spirit, and one salvation to all who believe in him' (*haer.* 4.6.7). Dualism is excluded: 'All things therefore are one and the same substance, that is, they are from one and the same God' (*haer.* 4.9.1). While God makes, man is made. While God is always the same, the creature has a beginning, middle and end, and moves from one to another by a process of growth (*haer.* 4.11.2).

[13] See H. Lassiat, *Promotion de l'homme en Jésus Christ* (Tours, 1974), 59–146, 459f.
[14] *Ibid.*, 250–68.

MIND IS THE ONE CAUSE OF ALL

In the tradition of the *Geistmetaphysik*, God is defined as entirely perfect and homogeneous light, mind, and the fountain of all good. Man is the receptacle of his goodness and the instrument of his glory (*haer.* 4.11.2). The language of recapitulation is integrated with the language of metaphysics.

FATHER AND SON ARE ONE GOD

The one name of the lord is glorified among the gentiles. When a king paints a portrait of his son, he calls this likeness his own, both because he painted it and because it is of his son. The father confesses the name of Jesus Christ to be his own name because it is the name of his son and because he gave his son for the salvation of mankind. The name of the son belongs to the father (*haer.* 4.17.6).

ONE GOD COMMENCES AND COMPLETES HIS CREATION

God's word and wisdom, son and spirit were with him from the beginning; the substance and pattern of all that he made came from within him. Hermas' account of *creatio ex nihilo* is quoted as scripture, Malachi and Ephesians declare one God, and the words of Jesus, 'All things have been handed over to me by my father' prove that nothing has been kept back from Jesus. He alone can open the book of the father and he has received sovereignty over all that is in heaven, in earth and under the earth, so that all things might behold their king. Through his flesh we are clothed with the light of the father and attain immortality. The one God who created all things is unknowable in his magnitude, but knowable in his love, through his word who became man among men, so 'that he might join the end to the beginning, that is, join man to God (*haer.* 4.20.4).

Perfection

GOD CANNOT BE SURPASSED

It is quite proper for the earthly sacrifices of Moses to be types of heavenly, spiritual realities, since all earthly things are copies of invisible things above and the one God made them all. However the Gnostics claim that heavenly things are copies of still higher things and our God is a copy of another higher God. Their perpetual regress prevents them from ever finding God. God's greatness cannot be known or measured, nor can his glory in Christ ever be surpassed (*haer.* 4.19 and 20).

THE UNION OF THE CREATOR WITH HIS CREATURE IS
JUST AND EFFECTIVE

The domination of the devil was violent, unjust and unnatural. The word, despite his power, did not seize his own property but used persuasion to restore justice and prevent destruction. By giving his own blood, his soul for our souls, his flesh for our flesh, he imparted God to men through his spirit; by his incarnation he joined man to God, and in this communion immortality is surely and truly received (*haer.* 5.1.1).

Correction

FLESH AND EARTH WILL BE RESTORED

The flesh is capable of either corruption and death or incorruption and life; the two possibilities are not compatible with one another. The breath of man is temporal, but the spirit is eternal. The flesh is the sheep which was lost and then found by the shepherd. The same sheep is lost and found; the same flesh dies and is brought to life. The blind, who were healed, saw with the same eyes which had been blind. He who healed will also give life to the same flesh (*haer.* 5.12.6). If the flesh of the lord were not the same as ours, then he did not sum up the original work of the father and restore what had perished (*haer.* 5.14).

As the flesh, so the whole earth, will be renewed. Jerusalem

will be rebuilt on the pattern of the Jerusalem above and those
who are raised from the dead will live in it (*haer.* 5.35.2).

THE DIFFERENCE BETWEEN CREATOR AND CREATURE
CANNOT BE REMOVED

The story of Jonah shows that flesh must not glory in the
presence of God; man must gratefully acknowledge as a gift the
incorruption which he receives from God. Only God can confer
immortality on the mortal; man is the receptacle of his wisdom
and power. As a doctor is proved by his patients, so God is
proved through his healing of men. To overcome the separation
between God and man, the word of God dwelt in man to
accustom man to God and God to man (*haer.* 3.20.2). While
creator and creature are always distinct, their separation is
removed.

Ethics

All goodness, says Irenaeus, is summed up in Christ and all
virtue is assimilation to him. Natural law and the motif of
assimilation to God are joined to the concept of recapitulation.

Totality

RECAPITULATION CONFIRMS THE ONE LAW

God's goodness and moral law have never changed. The Law of
Moses pointed to Christian discipleship; for the lord set the
commandments before the young man and then told him to
leave all and follow, enforcing the law of the one God the father
(*haer.* 4.12.5). His antitheses were not those of a destroyer of the
Law 'but of one who fulfilled, extended and broadened it
among us'. The greater freedom of grace calls for greater
subjection and love, and greater love will bring greater glory
(*haer.* 4.13.3). God gave to Israel a most fitting law and brought
the whole race into harmony with salvation (*haer.* 4.14.2). All
his ordinances to Israel were types which taught them to fear

and serve him (*haer.* 4.14.3). Beginning from the universal precepts of natural law, God added the Law of Moses because of Israel's apostasy and hardness of heart (*haer.* 4.15). In Egypt they forgot the natural precepts of love which their fathers had kept; but the voice of God in his goodness led them out, gave his Law on Sinai, only to cancel it with his final covenant of freedom (*haer.* 4.16).

Perfection

THE WORD CALLS TO MORAL EXCELLENCE

Not the sacrifices of the law, which were secondary, but the hearing of his voice was the purpose of the delivery from Egypt (*haer.* 4.17.3). Man was called to righteousness not to the slavery of the Law (*haer.* 4.17.1). Free from the beginning, man followed the good counsels of God, without compulsion (*haer.* 4.37.1). Irenaeus consistently rejects the determinism of Gnostic teaching.[15]

LIKENESS TO GOD IS THE GOAL OF ETHICAL PROGRESS

Why was man not made perfect at the beginning? Created things are inferior to God, because they come to being later than he and are infantile, unused to perfect discipline. God could have made man perfect, but infant man could not have received perfection. Christ the pure bread of God was offered to us as milk. Every arrangement of God is directed to the restoration of his image and likeness in man. Stage by stage, man grows to glory and will see his God (*haer.* 4.38.2 and 3).

The incarnate word showed the image and re-established the likeness of God, by becoming like us and making us like him (*haer.* 5.16.2).

---

[15] See R. Berthouzoz, *Liberté et grâce suivant la théologie d'Irénée de Lyon* (Fribourg, 1980), especially pp. 246–53.

Correction

MAN HAS LEARNT SELF-KNOWLEDGE

Man had to learn, through the long journey from mortality to incorruption, that he was weak and powerless, merely a receptacle of wisdom, power and glory. God had declared man's unbelief and disobedience, and had cast him off, only to grant him by grace, adoption, likeness to himself and, indeed, his very self (*haer.* 3.20.2).

THE LOSS OF REASON PLACED MAN AMONG THE BEASTS-

Man has reason and the power of choice. As a rational creature he had the power to become wheat or chaff. He lived irrationally and opposed God's righteousness. Deserting honour and understanding, he became like a senseless beast (*haer.* 4.4.3). His rationality should lead him to logic and truth.

Logic

There is one truth which depends on the truth of the gospel.

Totality

TRUTH STARTS FROM ONE FAITH WHICH COMES FROM
SCRIPTURE AND TRADITION

Against the Gnostics, whose teachings are incredible, foolish, impossible and inconsistent (*haer.* 2.10.4), Irenaeus proposes what is credible, acceptable and consistent.[16] The first two books of *Against Heresies* reveal and refute by argument the claims of the heretics; the third proceeds to proofs of the one true faith which the lord gave to his apostles. From apostolic scriptures, we learn the plan of salvation by one God and one Christ, the whole of the gospel which they preached (*haer.* 3. *Pref. and* 1). The invisible God is known through the only son of God who gives the firm foundation of the Gospels (*haer.* 3.6f.).

---

[16] See Brox, *Offenbarung*, 202.

The whole church depends on the perfect teaching of the apostles concerning the father and the son (*haer.* 3.12.7). In this teaching the martyrs found their perfection. They preached to the Jews that the crucified Jesus was son of God, judge and king; to the Greeks hey proclaimed one God, creator of all and Jesus his son (*haer.* 3.12.13).

Perfection

TRUTH GOVERNS THE WHOLE WORK OF THE WORD

Every need of fallen man was rationally fulfilled by the total reconciliation achieved by the word. There was no pretence in his incarnation. 'Moreover, he was what he appeared to be... therefore his works are true' (*haer.* 3.18.7). Jesus was born of Mary, not made from dust; but God did not want a second formation, different from that of Adam, because he wanted to preserve the likeness and to sum up the original (*haer.* 3.21.10).

TRUTH IS HARMONIOUS WITH ITSELF

Daily study of scripture by a sound mind, which is dedicated in piety and love, progresses in knowledge of the plain truth. It does not study ambiguities but the harmonious unity of many parts. Everyone can grasp the coherence of the whole scripture and its account of creation. The system is for all to see and the lover of truth receives its certainty; the heretic goes from obscurity to obscurity until he has a god who is peculiarly his own (*haer.* 2.17). Irenaeus looks always to the agreement of scripture, not to the differences.[17] Yet his system is never closed and his account of recapitulation offers something new at every reading.

---

[17] 'Nicht Differenzen, sondern die grossen Zusammenhänge zu sehen – darauf kommt für Irenaeus alles an.' Brox, *Offenbarung*, 208.

Correction

HARMONIOUS TRUTH AND DIVISIVE ERROR ARE
TOTALLY OPPOSED

Error may borrow elements of truth and distort them, but it still
has no common ground with truth. On the one hand, truth is a
unity which draws all together and recapitulation requires that
Jesus be both God and man. 'For with him there is nothing out
of place, untimely or incongruent with the father.' He knew his
hour and fulfilled the wide and bountiful scope of his father's
will. At the opposite pole, dressed in sheep's clothing, wolves
destroy all homogeneity and harmony. 'For their opinion is a
murderous one, inventing indeed many gods and feigning many
fathers, but breaking into pieces and dividing into many parts
the son of God.' Error knows no harmony, divides God, and
draws distinctions between Jesus, Christ, only-begotten, word
and saviour (*haer.* 3.16.6–8).

TRUTH BRINGS ALL INTO COHERENCE

The true disciple will condemn those who have brought division
to the great and glorious body of Christ. They have no love of
God and think only of themselves. Dishonestly, they talk of
peace, but make war; inconsistently they strain at gnats, but
swallow camels. The disciple of truth will judge others, but will
not be judged. 'For to him all things are consistent; he has an
entire faith in one almighty God' (*haer.* 4.33.7). The ever-
diversifying variety of opinion among heretics provides its own
refutation. Their domestic pretence and solemn disagreements
convict them of falsehood, while the followers of the one true
God all say the same things because they have only one God and
one rule. This rule tells of one God, who created, sent prophets,
delivered his people from Egypt, revealed his own son, for the
fruit of righteousness and the confusion of unbelievers
(*haer.* 4.35.4). The devil has been a deceiver from the beginning
to the end, first lying to Adam and then falsely claiming the
sovereignty of the world in order to tempt Christ (*haer.* 5.24.1).

　　The idea of recapitulation, which began so simply, finishes in
a whole range of complex argument. The result calls for an

extraordinary degree of conceptual stamina. We are tempted to choose between two courses. We may grasp the central principles: perfection, correction and totality and apply them in turn to being, goodness and truth; or we may decline the exercise and fall back on the symbolism of *Christus Victor*. Neither of these alternatives is sufficient by itself.

Clement fights a similar battle against Gnostics, but his imagery is more restrained and his scope more concise. Clement speaks of the word himself as the mystery made known – God in man and man in God (*paed.* 3.1.2). God is beyond knowledge but the son is wisdom, knowledge and truth, and all else that has affinity to these things. He is the unity of all the powers of the spirit rolled into one. He is one thing as all things. To believe in him is to become a unit, to be made one by sharing in him (*str.* 4.25.157).

Clement shows an equal concern for the ethical content of the word. The final exhortation of his *Protrepticus* calls for the whole human race to come to one God and receive grace and immortality, to be brought into harmony with God and to be restored to the original likeness (*prot.* 12.120f.). In every part of his work, Clement finds a place for ethical exhortation and reproof. The whole of the *Paedagogus* is concerned with ethical instruction of a practical kind to guide the believer in the way of righteousness. This instruction is performed by the word himself, who is the totality of justice and goodness, for Marcion's separation of the just from the good is rejected. There is a new order of being. The drama of man's salvation has brought the dawn of a new day. The word is a fount of life and giver of universal peace (*prot.* 10.110). Finally, for Clement the word is shared by those who believe. He opens the eyes of the blind, brings knowledge, puts an end to corruption, death, and the disobedience which caused man's downfall (*prot.* 1.6). No one speaks with greater daring than Clement on the nearness of man to God. Faith joins man to the word in an indivisible unity. By knowledge and love the believer enters into God himself and lives his life as a festival of constant praise to God.

Tertullian maintains the same insistence on the totality of Christ, but has less place for the argument of Irenaeus and

Clement. Man recovered his salvation by a victory and entered through Christ into a paradise more glorious than that which Adam lost (*Marc.* 2.10.6). Christ takes the flesh of the ancient race of man and reforms it with new seed (*carn.* 17.3). He is the last Adam, and the first word: he is flesh and blood, the same in substance and form with us. At the last day, he will descend to those who once pierced him (*res.* 51).

The Christ of Marcion cannot bear the names which are given to him. He is a diminished being, whereas Tertullian insists 'I claim for myself Christ, I maintain for myself Jesus' (*Marc.* 3.16.7). All the nations call on Christ and find in him their help and salvation (*Marc.* 3.20.10). Tertullian saw, as clearly as any, that the heretics' claim to greater fullness was achieved through the reduction of Christ. The totality of Christ and his universal power remained essential. Why, asked Tertullian, halve Christ with a lie? He was the whole truth: God and man (*carn.* 5). To deny any part of his perfection is to diminish his reality and to place at risk the salvation which is only possible through the necessary dishonour of God (*Marc.* 2.27.7).

SALVATION THROUGH RECAPITULATION

The new song of salvation

Plainly, despite the recapitulation, the world is not yet subject to Christ. God has created and redeemed it; but it is not in harmony with his will. The totality of Christ requires that the work of salvation continue until God is all in all. The power of Christ may already be seen in the martyrs who confess faith in his saving name (2 *apol.* 10). The purpose of his incarnation and suffering was the healing of mankind (2 *apol.* 13); and by his stripes we are healed (*dial.* 137). His power is seen in Joshua who was able to stop the sun (*dial.* 132), and to reject Christ is to reject the God who sent him to save (*dial.* 136).

Irenaeus pursues the same theme of salvation. To follow light is to receive light (*haer.* 4.14.1). We see God through the spirit and the son, where God made himself visible and comprehensible to give life to those who believe (*haer.* 4.20.5). In love he became what we are to bring us to be what he is (*haer.* 5. *Pref.*). Paul tells of God's power present in our weakness, a power which leads to resurrection (*haer.* 5.3). We are redeemed by the flesh of our lord and re-established by his blood (*haer.* 5.14).

Clement speaks of the new song which soothes pain and anger, removes evil, frees man and recalls him to heaven (*prot.* 1.3). The same new song tames man, makes him a true child of God, and turns stones into men (*prot.* 1.4). Rescued from error and restored to truth (*prot.* 2.23), we follow the good monad, the one choir leader and teacher and unite in the chorus 'Abba father' (*prot.* 9.88). Faith in Christ means to seek God and live (*prot.* 10.107), sight for the blind (*prot.* 12.119) and an ordered place in the universe (*paed.* 1.2.6). The saviour gathers us as chickens under his wings, an image which points to our simplicity in Christ (*paed.* 1.5.14). The coming of Christ was not to isolated individuals, but rather to his community; the good shepherd was sent to save the flock of men (*prot.* 11.116). The church consists of members of a body held together by faith and hope (*paed.* 1.6.38); it is a city on earth doing God's heavenly will (*str.* 4.26.172), and an assembly of elect (*str.* 7.5.29).

Faith is the one universal salvation, the way by which all are saved (*paed.* 1.6.30). The Paedagogus guides, directs and leads (*paed.* 1.7.54). God wishes to save all creation, bringing it from mere existence to something better (*str.* 6.17.152). For Clement, salvation is the greatest gift, signified by the lively grain of mustard seed (*paed.* 1.11.96), and the most kingly work of God (*paed.* 1.12.100), for which nothing can be afforded in return (*str.* 7.3.15). The complete Christian seeks perfect salvation by every means (*str.* 7.7.48). The writer writes and the teacher talks for no other end than the salvation of his readers or hearers (*str.* 1.1.9). Indeed for Clement, 'salvation is all'.[18]

To prove this thesis, one writer has produced the longest (763 pages) study on Clement for all time. All the themes of Clement's soteriology which he finds – one God creates and saves, the

---

[18] A. Brontesi, *La soteria in Clemente d'Alessandria* (Rome, 1972), 237, 'la salvezza è tutto'.

salvific economy of one God in different times and places, the providence of one who always works for man's salvation and who sends Christ as saviour in the unity of the church – all declare the unity of God. All the roads of men run into the one royal road of the lord, with whom the believer is united and assimilated. Faith leads to knowledge and salvation; there is no division.[19]

In his account of salvation, a concern for unity turns Clement along Stoic rather than Platonic paths.[20] His logos doctrine has Stoic cosmic proportions, while his account of salvation, personal and cosmic, points both to humanity united by reason (τὸ ἡγεμονικόν) and to the world's coherence (συνέχεια) through the Logos. Man and the world, of which he is the centre, are joined by the agent of their common salvation. Body and soul are pointed to heaven. As ruler of the universe, man can, by his choice, bring the creation nearer to salvation. However, Stoicism gives way to the gospel: free will has become rational obedience to the father of the biblical message, and imitates a universal reason who is the person of the Logos who once became flesh.

The plan of salvation

For Tertullian, the church is central to the plan of salvation, for Christ is most plainly present in the penitent and in the daily life of the church (*bapt.* 2.1). Salvation is necessary, because we cannot prove that God is perfectly good, until we have been delivered or redeemed by him (*Marc.* 1.24.7). We have an eternal home in heaven, to which God will bring us (*Marc.* 5.12.1). The spirit, who through the spiritual man forgives sins, is God himself, so there is a sense in which church and spirit are identified.[21] The church as a *trium corpus* (*bapt.* 6.2), is identified with the spirit (*pud.* 21.16f.) or the substance of God, and certainly not with the bishops. The Christian must sanctify himself by the light of the spirit because

---

[19] *Ibid.*, 601. 'imitare Dio significa dunque *unificare* la propria realtà molteplice attorno al *logos*, facendo prevalere in se stessi l'attività logica'.

[20] *Ibid.*, 604, where Brontesi cites M. Pohlenz, *La Stoa: Storia di movimento spirituale*, translated from the German by V. E. Alfieri (Firenze, 1978), II, 291.

[21] E. Altendorf, *Der Kirchenbegriff Tertullians* (Berlin, 1932), 32.

there can be no compromise within a church which is *proprie et principaliter* the spirit. Tertullian already had this exalted idea of the church as spirit from his realist ontology, his belief that there was only one kind of reality.[22] The new prophecy subsequently brought him into conflict with the bishops on practical issues which indicated differences of ecclesiology.[23]

Unity marks the work of salvation at every point. There is one plan of salvation in both testaments (*haer.* 3.12; 4.15),[24] which derives its unity from its unique author, who may be understood either as father and son, since the father acts in the Old Testament and sends his son in the New, or as word and word incarnate, since the word is active from the beginning and incarnate at the end of time.[25] God does all things with measure and order (*haer.* 4.4.2). The immeasurable father is measured by the son, who is his measure because he knows the father. Christ as the end of the Law is also the beginning of the Law (*haer.* 4.12.4), for from the beginning the word of God was accustomed to descend and ascend for the saving of those in affliction.[26] In his incarnation, God is manifest that he may be seen. For to see God is, first, to see directly the face of his own word or son, then to see in him the face of the father, and finally, to see (as and with the son), the face of the father directly.[27] The incarnation of the son is a manifestation of God in the precise sense that it is the means by which man may see God and be led into his mystery. This contradicts the claim of the Ptolemaean Gnostics that the father remains unknowable and invisible; it gives a meaning to the enigmatic claim to see God. To see God is to find oneself in his effective presence. The purpose of Irenaeus is to let the divine glory shine and to lead others to it.[28]

The life of Christ is a divine parousia, not in the vague sense that there is glory everywhere, but as a direct manifestation of God. Irenaeus draws the full consequences of John's account of the word made flesh. There is a real appearance and not merely a plethora of signs of divine glory. The Hellenistic idea of a royal

---

[22] *carn.* 11.4: *omne quod est corpus est sui generis.*

[23] R. Braun, *Tertullien et le Montanisme: Église institutionelle et église spirituelle, RSLR*, 21 (1985), 257.

[24] R. Tremblay, *La manifestation et la vision de Dieu selon S. Irénée de Lyon* (Münster, 1978), 37. [25] *Ibid.*, 41. [26] *Ibid.* [27] *Ibid.*, 175. [28] *Ibid.*, 176f.

parousia is relevant to Irenaeus' account of the coming of the word in the history of Israel; but in his account of the incarnation, only the Fourth Gospel will make sense of what he says.[29] Novelty and immediacy are the key concepts.[30]

The renewal of the earth

Chiliasm, explicit in Rev. 20: 1–7 (cf. John 5.17; 9:4) has strong Jewish antecedents in Ezekiel 37–48, the Syrian Apocalypse of Baruch, the Testament of Isaac and elsewhere. In Justin it expands the account of the δευτέρα παρουσία which answers Jewish objections against the humiliation of Christ. The renewal of the earth begins in Jerusalem (*dial.* 40, 85, 113 and 138), and the restoration of the land to Abraham is fulfilled with the new and spiritual Israel (*dial.* 113, 119, 139). Justin's theology of history precludes a purely spiritual goal (*dial.* 80.4).

Irenaeus develops this anti-gnostic theme with firm insistence on physical resurrection (*haer.* 5.35.2), the inheritance of the actual land promised to Abraham (*haer.* 5.32.2) so that the new earth is centred on the new Jerusalem (*haer.* 5.34.1–4), and the need for further time to accustom man to God's glory (*haer.* 5.35.2; 5.36.2).[31]

How important was this theme to a Christian theology of salvation? Judaeo-Christian theology gives a restrained account in the *Ascension of Isaiah* (4.14–17) and Ebionism provides a materialist extreme.[32] Papias' enthusiasm for material plenitude[33] is developed by Irenaeus' account of the renewal of the earth (*haer.* 5.33.3) and fulfilment of promises in the times of the kingdom (*haer.* 5.33.2). They seem to stand between the physical abundance of Cerinthus and the austerity of Methodius.[34] However Irenaeus modifies the exuberance of his earlier account (*haer.* 5.33.3f.) in the *Demonstration*. Tertullian, for all his Montanist sympathy (*Marc.* 3.24), makes the flesh of Christ

---

[29] A. Houssiau, *La christologie de saint Irénée* (Louvain, Gembloux, 1955), 128.

[30] Montanism, with its enthusiasm, draws the sympathy of Irenaeus and the solid support of Tertullian.

[31] G. G. Blum, Chiliasmus II, Alte Kirche, *TRE* 7, p. 729.

[32] *Rec. clem.* 1.61; cf. Jerome *Comm. Jer.* 66.20. See J. Daniélou, *The theology of Jewish Christianity* (London, 1964), 379.   [33] Eusebius *h.e.* 3, 39:11f.

[34] Daniélou, *Jewish Christianity*, 396.

the new Jerusalem (*res.* 26.11–13) and claims that the universal kingdom of Christ is already established on earth (*Jud.* 7). Clement follows the chiliasm of Barnabas with seven millennia and an eighth day of rest and restoration (*str.* 4.25.159). More important is his transposition of chronology into cosmology, of time into space. The seven days become the world under the seven planets and the eighth day becomes the heavenly ogdoad.[35] Chiliasm is thereby delivered from the danger of material fantasies; but the dangers of docetism and rejection of the world emerge. The linear, historical approach, despite its hazards, preserves the divine economy and the progression of man towards final unity with God in immortality (*haer.* 4.38.3 and 4.20.5).[36]

The new creation

For Clement the new creation is the work of the word, who has brought light to the universe and who turns sunsets into sunrise (*prot.* 11.114). His new people live in newness of life (*prot.* 4.59). It is as word of God that the son is united to the father. The word of our teacher spreads out from Judaea, and, unlike philosophy which disappears when it is banned, it flourishes all the more, when it is proscribed (*str.* 6.18.167). Among the first-principles, the son is the timeless, unbegotten first-principle from whom we learn the remoter cause (*str.* 7.1.2). He is the highest excellence, the complete mind and word of the father (*str.* 7.2.5). He is saviour and lord of all and as divine word watches all and neglects nothing. The power of the holy spirit works like a magnet through steel rings, as men of different times are drawn towards him (*str.* 7.2.9). The eternal word is one saviour individually to each and in common to all. He is both the first and second cause (*str.* 7.3.16). The word spreads vision over all things, as the sun shines over all the earth sending light into the furthest recesses of each house (*str.* 7.3.21). As a faithful soldier the Christian does not desert the post which the word has given him, for the word is his guide in knowledge and in love (*str.* 7.16.100).

---

[35] *Ibid.*, 399. The same move is found in Valentinian myth; see *haer.* 1.5.3 and *Exc. Theod.* 63.   [36] Cf. Andia, *Homo vivens*, 322.

The account of Christ as word points back to the prologue of
the Fourth Gospel. For Justin, the earlier pattern of cross and
resurrection has been subsumed within the threefold scheme:
pre-existence, incarnation, exaltation.[37] He speaks of Jesus'
birth 'through' rather than 'from' a virgin, of the fullness
(2 *apol.* 10.1) of his humanity, and he presents the first integrated statement of both patterns (1 *apol.* 21.1). As in the
Fourth Gospel, the power of the cross obliterates the folly
(1 *apol.* 55). 'Christ did not become κύριος καὶ θεός after the
resurrection. He was always κύριος καὶ θεός.'[38] Justin's main
contribution to early christology is the emphasis which he places
on the pre-existence of Christ within three contexts: prior to
creation when he is numerically distinct from the father, in the
Old Testament theophanies which hint of an incarnation, and
in the pagan world where he is both nomos and logos, as well as
the formidable destroyer of demons.[39] Because of the sharp
antithesis between the eternal unbegotten God and the world
(*dial.* 5.4), the word proceeds as God from God, fire from fire,
light from light, (*dial.* 128) to do God's work in the world.

Unity remains the theme, for the word governs all (*verbum dei
gubernans et disponens omnia* (*haer.* 5.18.3)). Creation, salvation,
knowledge of God, freedom, resurrection of the body, beatific
vision – whatever is the question for Irenaeus – everything is
understood by reference to the word.[40] Renewal of man and
revelation of God proceed through the activity of the word, so
that his incarnation brings all that is new, in him who has been
foretold (*haer.* 4.34.1). The power of God is revealed in all things
(*haer.* 4.20.4).

Justin speaks frequently of the word as the power of God.[41] In
history, all are created and indwelt by the word. Philosophers
shared in logos (2 *apol.* 10) and Plato spoke of the power of the
cross (1 *apol.* 60). The prophets, moved by logos (1 *apol.* 36.2)
announced Christ (1 *apol.* 31.7f.) who is the κύριος τῶν δυνάμεων
(*dial.* 85.1). The word who appeared to Moses as man and angel

---

[37] D. C. Trakatellis, *The pre-existence of Christ in the writings of Justin Martyr* (Ann Arbor,
1976), 174–6.   [38] *Ibid.*, 179.   [39] *Ibid.*, 179–83.
[40] L. Escoula, Le verbe sauveur et illuminateur chez S. Irénée, *NRTh.*, 66 (1939), 385f.
[41] E. Rodriguez, *La dunamis de Dios en San Justino* (Santiago, 1982).

(*dial.* 128) was rejected by the Jewish people (1 *apol.* 38.2).
Grace, as opposed to human capacity (2 *apol.* 13), is divine
power (*dial.* 87.5). That Jesus is the Christ is proved by his
power. The power of God is the cause of his birth (*dial.* 105;
1 *apol.* 32.9–13) and of his blood in particular (1 *apol.* 32). His
words have power (*dial.* 102; 1 *apol.* 15) as do his cross (1 *apol.* 35
and 55; *dial.* 13.1; *dial.* 138) and his name (*dial.* 115; *dial.* 132;
dial. 30). Jesus derives his name from the saving power he
exhibits in his conquest of the devil (*dial.* 125).

Through him, the power of God is evident in Christian
people. The twelve apostles depended on the power of Christ,
the eternal priest, and by this power they went out to all nations
(*dial.* 42; 1 *apol.* 50). Today, by his power, his people leave the
worship of idols (*dial.* 11.4) and exorcise demons (2 *apol.* 6). At
his second coming they will be saved as he destroys all sin and
death (*dial.* 45).

The Logos is the first power after the father and lord of all
(1 *apol.* 32.10). His activity in history continues from the
moment of creation to the present time.[42] For human power is
not enough (2 *apol.* 13.6); grace is a necessity. Trypho is
scandalised by Justin putting his hope in a man (*dial.* 8.3) and
God's power is hidden in the cross (*dial.* 49.8). Jesus is saviour,
greater than demons, lord of the powers by his resurrection from
the dead, the whole word, now active in his people.

Participation

We may acknowledge[43] that the theme of unity dominates
Irenaeus whether he speaks of the one father or the one Jesus
Christ or of both together (*haer.* 1.3.6; 3.1.2; 3.4.1f.; 3.16.6). As
well as the twofold formulae there are threefold formulae which
make the same point (*haer.* 1.10.1; 4.33). Salvation is through
participation, for human development goes together with divine
dispensation.[44] Union with God intensifies humanity. The end
of recapitulation is the perfection of the human creature, *plasma*

---

[42] *Ibid.*, 85.
[43] With A. Benoit, *Saint Irénée, introduction à l'étude de sa théologie* (Paris, 1960), 204.
[44] See K. Prümm, *Göttliche Planung und menschliche Entwicklung nach Irenäus' Adversus
haereses*, Schol. (1938), 206–24, 342–66.

eius conformatum et concorporatum Filio (*haer.* 5.36.3). The perception of God, which has drawn much attention recently,[45] does not negate humanity (*haer.* 4.20.7). The unity of the church follows with equal emphasis (*haer.* 4.26.2; 4.33.7).

Where unity is central to salvation, the theme of participation or communion becomes prominent.[46] Gnosticism thrived on incommunicability or dissociation. God was at the limit of remoteness. Salvation was not reconciliation of man with God, but the reconstitution of the divine fullness from the divine sparks scattered in the world. There was a thorough dissociation between matter and spirit, between time and eternity, with no place for history and eschatology. Man was estranged from man by his material, psychic or spiritual nature. Knowledge rendered morality redundant.

In sharp contrast, Irenaeus took his theme (*haer.* 5.1.1) from 1 John 1:3, 'that you might have *communion* with us and our communion is with the father and with his son Jesus Christ'. (My emphasis). Communication, exchange, or openness to others is commonly expressed by the word: κοινωνία or *communio*.[47] This communion exists within God between father, son and holy spirit as well as between God and others. There is communion between flesh and spirit, between time and eternity. The exchange-formulae underline this process of salvation: 'the glory of God is the living man and the life of man is the vision of God' (*haer.* 4.20.7). The purpose of history is to accustom God to man and man to God so that their communion might be without division. All races of men are joined by the spirit in common praise of God. The church witnesses to this communion as it sends sons on to their father. Within the body, members are joined to the only God by his word, who is the head of the body (*haer.* 4.32.1). The prayers and pleas of believers invite and urge all Gnostics to join this fellowship (*haer.* 3.25.7). The focus of unity is in the eucharist where the church proclaims the κοινωνίαν καὶ ἕνωσιν of flesh and spirit, of earthly and heavenly,

---

[45] *Ibid.*, 218 f.

[46] See E. Osborn, The logic of recapitulation, in *FS Antonio Orbe*, ed., E. Romero-Pose (Rome, 1990), 327–39, and P. Lebeau, Koinonia, la signification du salut selon S. Irénée, in *EPEKTASIS, FS J. Daniélou*, eds. J. Fontaine et C. Kannengiesser (Paris, 1972), 121–7.   [47] Which occurs eighty times in *Against heresies*.

so that the bodies of believers share in incorruption and hope of resurrection (*haer.* 4.18.5). While the heretics speak of God as if he were not alive and present, the eucharist proclaims Jesus by whom both God and man are glorified (*haer.* 4.17.6). The word is joined to the ancient substance of Adam, so that man, restored to life and perfection, becomes able to grasp the perfection of the father (*haer.* 5.1.3).

CONCLUSION

The account of God has fallen into two parts, father and son, Alpha and Omega, cause and consummation, monarchy and summing up, with many interconnections. For the first part, we have the monad, father, cause and lord, spirit, lord of history and active goodness. These claims were supported as much from Plato as from scripture. To them has now been added a second half: continuity of divine activity, recapitulation, salvation and participation. This draws on prophecy and apocalyptic, also finding good allies in Platonism and Stoicism. There is similarity between Irenaeus' cosmic reconciliation and the Hymn of Cleanthes, where Zeus knows how to make the odd even:

ἀλλὰ σὺ καὶ τὰ περισσά (τ') ἐπίστασαι ἄρτια θεῖναι
καὶ κοσμεῖν τἄκοσμα καὶ οὐ φίλα σοὶ φίλα ἐστίν.

In Clement the twofold hope of Paul is the same as the twofold end of Plato (*str.* 2.22) and the powers of the spirit come together in the son, fulfilling prophecy, expounding Paul and Plato (*str.* 4.25.156). Apocalyptic and philosophy share common ground. For Clement the prophetic and Pauline unity of the powers of the spirit answers to the second hypothesis of Plato's *Parmenides*. The circle of Plotinus (*Enn.* 5.1.7) and the Alpha and Omega of the Apocalypse (Rev. 1:8; 21:6) sit side by side.

Irenaeus is our major source. Art (Michelangelo), music (Bach and Handel) declare the wonder of recapitulation. So we commonly conclude its substance to be aesthetic. Now we have discovered that it holds within it a mass of tightly woven argument, which wearies the most energetic mind. Who is right – the artists or the logicians? The plea by von Balthasar for a theological aesthetic offers relief from extended theological reasoning. It is supremely important that we should learn the necessity of both. Long chains of argument need myth or symbol to hold them together. Plato's *Republic* is sufficient proof of such a claim. Few can understand either recapitulation or Plato's world of forms without *Christus Victor* on the one hand or the Myth of the Cave on the other. Without vision, the logician perishes, not because the logic has gaps but because it needs to be grasped as a whole and not as a series. No other theologian displays this truth as clearly as Irenaeus.

The second achievement of Irenaeus is, despite all the argument, one of simplification. He reduces the complexity of Paul and John to one motif. *Ephesians* was a simplification of Paul, and Irenaeus follows in the Ephesian tradition, with an even wider Pauline and Johannine base. Irenaeus' presentation is so exuberant that the fragile reader may well be dismayed, for like Plato, Irenaeus wants to show that the form of the good cannot be reached in a single step. The kingdom of heaven may come suddenly and plainly; but it brings a treasure store of things old and new. Simplicity remains his genius; for had he presented to his readers the detail of Romans, or 2 Corinthians or John, we should fervently desire that short word which was sent to replace the long-windedness of the Law (*dem.* 87). This word, 'when he was incarnate and became man, summed up in himself the long line (*longam expositionem*) of men, providing for us a brief compendium of salvation, so that what we had lost in Adam, the image and likeness of God, we might regain in Christ Jesus' (*haer.* 3.18.1).

CHAPTER 6

One God in a new way: by the son and spirit

THE PROBLEM CHANGES

The question of the unity of God had, from the beginning, two answers. The first answer, we have seen in preceding chapters, had to do with saving history and the unity of father, son and spirit in a *Geistmetaphysik*. The son was in the father and the father was in the son. All the powers of the spirit were united in the son.[1] The metaphysic of mind gave to Middle Platonism and earliest Christian thought the concepts of νοῦς, λόγος, πνεῦμα which were able to express the unity of the divine first-principle. The divine simplicity was declared by God the νοῦς, God the λόγος, and God the πνεῦμα, without division.[2] The second answer, which was to play an increasing role, was the doctrine of the trinity. There were trinitarian formulae from the earliest times, when they sought to express the unity of the *Geistmetaphysik*. Formulae preceded doctrine, but they were never remote from argument.

It was once thought, by analytic philosophers, that problems remained the same, while answers changed. Most now recognise that problems change and the purpose of any history of ideas is to show when and why they changed.[3] Because the first account of one God was so convincing, Gnostic and Marcionite dualism lost ground. The success produced its own exaggeration and turned the problem around. (Successful theologians and philosophers should always consider what new mistake they have

---

[1] Osborn, Word, spirit and Geistmetaphysik, 61–72. See above, chapter 2.
[2] *Ibid.*, 72.   [3] *Philosophy in history*, eds. Rorty, Schneewind and Skinner, 12.

facilitated.) Instead of asking how three gods could be one, the Monarchians now asked how one God could possibly be two or three. 'They praise the monarchy at the expense of the economy' (*Prax.* 9). There was now a different problem. For if God were to be one God in the whole history of salvation, it was necessary that he be father, son and holy spirit, not successively, but indivisibly and distinctly.

The Monarchians pushed the arguments for unity to extremes and rejected any plurality within the Godhead. Son and father were, for Praxeas, ever identical; to deny this was to deny the unity of God. Tertullian replied to Praxeas that the monarchy of God is not compromised by the existence of consubstantial son and spirit, and that the evidence of scripture points to the son, word or wisdom of God as a second person beside the father; further, Tertullian had found in the paraclete one who sanctified the faith of those who believe (*Prax.* 2). Praxeas' fault was twofold: he had driven away the paraclete and crucified the father (*Prax.* 1).

ARGUMENT, ANGELS AND FORMULAE

The divine unity was the chief concern of the first Christian theologians since their opponents (Marcion and Gnostics) were concerned to divide God or to deny the divinity of the son. Only when unity became a fault in Monarchianism, did a sustained account of the trinity appear; yet the trinitarian tradition had been there. It included argument, formulae and the angels of apocalyptic, and when the need arose Tertullian was able to give an extended account of trinitarian belief.

Argument

If one takes the first centuries as a preparation for Nicaea, it is easy to claim too little for early argument and too much for tradition or liturgy which was passed on without question.[4] Hermas begins from the faith that God is one, that he created

---

[4] The importance of liturgy remains, for it is in worship, baptism and eucharist that the divine Triad is most frequently mentioned.

and established all things, bringing them into existence out of nothing (*Mand.* 1.1). The father and maker of the whole cosmos (*Clem. Rom.* 1 *Cor.* 19.2) is the lord almighty (*Did.* 10.3) who governs the universe (*Barn.* 21.5). Aristides argues for one God as an Aristotelian first mover and declares (*Apol.* 15.3) that Christians 'acknowledge God as creator and demiurge of all things... and apart from him worship no other God'. Justin's monotheism is emphatic, whether he talks to pagan Romans or to Trypho the Jew.

How, we are asked, may this belief be joined to the Christian revelation of father, son and spirit in the church? The move is made by argument, angels and formulae. There are plenty of formulae concerning divine dyads and triads in the New Testament and these are followed by Ignatius (*Eph.* 18.2, *Trall.* 9, *Smyrn.* 1.1) and Justin (1 *apol.* 13; *dial.* 126.1).[5]

A succinct account is given by Athenagoras, using philosophy and the Bible. The relation to the transcendent father (*leg.* 10.1) of the son is (in philosophical terms) 'ideal form and energising power' and (in scriptural terms) unity with the father for 'through him all things came into existence; since the Father and the Son are one' (John 1:3 and 10:30). The prophetic spirit flows out from God (Wisd. 7:25), like a ray of the sun, streaming out and returning to its source. Christians therefore 'set forward God the father and God the son and the holy spirit and proclaim both their power in unity and their diversity in rank' (*leg.* 10.5).[6] Athenagoras' use of philosophy and the Bible goes beyond mere conjunction to creative thought. 'Now since the son is in the father and the father is in the son by a powerful unity of spirit, the son of God is the nous and the logos of the father' (*leg.* 10.2).

---

[5] Yet it is insisted, 'No steps had been taken so far, however, to work all these complex elements into a coherent whole. The Church had to wait for more than three hundred years for a final synthesis, for not until the council of Constantinople (381) was the formula of one God existing in three co-equal Persons formally ratified. Tentative theories, however, some more and some less satisfactory, were propounded in the preceding centuries' (J. N. D. Kelly, *Early Christian Doctrines* (London, 1958), 87f.

[6] R. M. Grant, *Gods and the one God* (Philadelphia, 1986), 157f. This is an excellent brief treatment of our problem. An earlier assessment by the same writer gave emphasis to the biblical rather than the philosophical background.

Athenagoras answers the accusation that Christians are atheists in what has been hailed as the first 'carefully worked out doctrine of the Trinity'.[7] The three persons 'correspond to the experience and thought of Christians...that the three are somehow one'.[8] Belief in one God does not make Christians atheists (*leg.* 10), and the charge of atheism appears even more absurd when the trinity and angels are considered. Justin had made the same point (1 *apol.* 6). This is hardly 'incipient polytheism';[9] perhaps, the term 'pluralistic monotheism' could be considered.[10]

All early accounts can be linked with the metaphysic of mind we noted in an earlier chapter. Another example is found in Theophilus of Antioch. The word was immanent in God from the beginning. When God wished to create, he begot and brought forth his λόγος (speech), without emptying himself of λόγος (thought). Here the Stoic bond between λόγος in thought and speech, between λόγος ἐνδιάθετος and the λόγος προφορικός is yet another useful element within the *Geistmetaphysik*.[11]

Argument is found in Irenaeus (*dem.* 6) who shows *why* God must be father, son and spirit. It is not enough for God to make a world; he must complete it by salvation and send a paraclete who will lead his children into all truth. 'This, then, is the order of the rule of our faith... God the father, not made, not material, invisible; one God, the creator of all things: this is the first point of our faith. The second point is this, the word of God, son of God, Jesus Christ our lord, who was manifested to the prophets according to the form of their prophesying and according to the method of the father's dispensation; through whom all things were made; who also, at the end of the age, to complete and gather up all things, was made man among men, visible and tangible, in order to abolish death and show forth life, and to

---

[7] R. M. Grant, *The Early Christian Doctrine of God* (Charlottesville, 1966), 91.

[8] *Ibid.*, 100.

[9] Nevertheless one writer concludes with four qualifiers and a double negative. 'But against the pagan background that we have sketched, we can understand why Christian monotheists engaged in the apologetic task would not find a kind of pluralism in the doctrine of God totally unacceptable'. Schoedel, Neglected motive, 356–67.   [10] Schoedel, *ibid.*, 367, cites Loofs, *Leitfaden zum Studium* I, 95.

[11] *Autol.* 2.22.

produce perfect reconciliation between God and man. And the third point is the holy spirit, through whom the prophets prophesied, and the fathers learned the things of God, and the righteous were led into the way of righteousness; who at the end of the age was poured out in a new way upon mankind in all the earth, renewing man to God.'

In the same way, the threefold baptismal formula (Matt. 28:19; *Did.* 7; Justin, 1 *apol.* 61) has a rational basis. One God required one baptism (Eph. 4:5); but there was a distinction in the Gospels between water baptism and fire (or spirit) baptism. Acts showed confusion and controversy over the one baptism and the gift of the spirit. Paul insisted that if any did not have the spirit of Christ, he did not belong to Christ (Rom. 8:9). There was no way in which one baptism could neglect father, son or holy spirit; in time a theological necessity became a liturgical habit, so that all might be explicit to the new initiate.[12] Argument and formulae went together.

The New Testament, we have seen, provides evidence of theological reflection. Paul gives an account of plurality and unity in God, when he links christology with pneumatology in Romans 8 and 1 Corinthians 12. The controversies over baptism in Acts show the importance of the spirit. The Fourth Gospel at two places stresses the unity of three persons. In the Farewell Discourses (chapter 14) the same predicates are applied to father, son and spirit, so that the works of the three are indivisible. In the closed room (chapter 20), the risen Jesus commits his disciples to their task. He gives the spirit and identifies himself with the father.

It is reasonable to consider the Apostolic Fathers as 'witnesses to the traditional faith rather than interpreters striving to understand it'.[13] Yet, when Clement of Rome uses the threefold name in an oath (58.2), the meaning is backed by his experience: 'Have we not one God and one Christ and one spirit of grace poured upon us?' There is community between

---

[12] It is therefore unwise to insist that the early formulae 'represent a pre-reflective, pre-theological phase of Christian belief' and that the more sophisticated accounts of the theologians were constructed out of such 'raw material' (Kelly, *Early Christian Doctrines*), 90.   [13] *Ibid.*

word and spirit, since Christ spoke through the spirit in the
Psalms and the holy spirit has inspired God's prophets in every
age. Of course there are limitations. Ignatius, despite his use of
triadic formulae (*Eph.* 9.1. *Magn.* 13.1 and 2) thinks of one
divine monad and different modes of revelation.[14]

Angels

In the historical development, apocalyptic sources again
contribute the imagery which holds argument together. Angels
and triads interact with the trinitarian content of the New
Testament.[15] The Apologists frequently identify the Logos with
the angel of the lord, who appears in the Old Testament at the
burning bush and elsewhere. Hermas refers to the Logos as the
glorious (*Vis.* 1.3) and most venerable angel (*Vis.* 5.2). Apocalyptic appeals to the eye rather than to the mind, so the angel
is always of enormous size, taller than a tower (*Sim.* 9.6.1).
He may be accompanied by the six first-created angels
(*Sim.* 9.12.7f.), and is sometimes identified with Michael
(*Sim.* 8.3.3), who is captain of the host, a title widely given to
Christ.[16] The same link is found in other Jewish Christian texts
(2 *Enoch* 22.4–9; *Test. Dan.* 6.2) and in Ebionite texts
(*Clem. Recog.* 2.42; *Clem. Hom.* 18.4). Gabriel is sometimes assimilated to the holy spirit; Isaiah is called to worship the angel
of the holy spirit who stands on the left of the lord, while the
glorious angel stands on the right (*Asc. Is.* 9.27–36). Elsewhere
(2 *Enoch* 21f.) Gabriel performs the functions of the holy spirit,
and is linked with the word who says: 'I took the form of the
angel Gabriel' (*Epist. Apost.* 14 and *Sib.* 8.456–61). The angel
who wrestled with Jacob is called 'Israel' and is identified by
Justin with the Logos (*dial.* 75.2. and 125).[17]

Jewish Hekhalot literature (mystical writings at the time of
the Talmud) tells of heavenly ascents into cosmic secrets and of

[14] Cf. F. Loofs, *Leitfaden zum Studium* 76.
[15] See J. Barbel, *Christos Angelos* (Bonn, 1941), and Daniélou, *Jewish Christianity*,
117–46.
[16] Jewish Christianity made use of the angelology of later Judaism where a whole world
of intermediaries filled the gap between God and man.
[17] Daniélou, *Jewish Christianity*, 143f.

angelic descents to reveal secrets on earth. Prayer, fasting and ritual baths prepare the mystic for revelatory Merkabah (throne or chariot) experiences.[18] There was some interaction between Merkabah mysticism and Gnosticism but neither can be reduced to the other.[19] The dominant figure is the Metatron (σύνθρονος) who shares the throne of God.[20] The concept of the Gnostic demiurge was anticipated by Jewish ideas about the creative agency of the divine name and the angel of the lord.[21]

Investigation into angelogy reveals variety and confusion, yet establishes without doubt the presence of divine intermediaries. They were of historical relevance to the doctrine of the trinity; but they provided in logic a contradiction, an alternative or, at best, a supplement to trinitarian belief. One could believe in the trinity and in angels, only if one recognised their fundamental difference. Where they were confused, subordinationism replaced trinity. Old Testament theophanies were taken as manifestations of the Logos by the fathers, but not by the New Testament where they were regarded as angelic. The angels are part of the world view of the New Testament environment rather than a part of its own theology.[22] In the New Testament Christ is never given the title of 'angel' and never described in such terms.[23]

Formulae

After angels come trinitarian formulae.[24] Eusebius (*P.E.* 11.20) claims that there are oracles of the Hebrews which speak of the father, son, holy spirit or the trinity; but he generally claims that knowledge of the trinity came with Christ. Clement and Justin saw the idea in Plato (*str.* 5.14.102f. and 1 *apol.* 60.7).

---

[18] Gruenwald, *Apocalyptic and Merkavah mysticism*, 98–109. See also P. Schäfer, *Hekhalot-Studien* (Tübingen, 1988).   [19] *Ibid.*, 118f.

[20] The meaning of the name is still subject to debate and to uncertainty. See above, chapter 1.

[21] See Fossum, *The name of God*. Gnosticism owed much to pre-Christian Jewish sources, and most to Dositheism, a Samaritan lay movement.

[22] Barbel, *Christos Angelos*, 347.   [23] *Ibid.*, 352.

[24] The following account is indebted to the detailed work of G. Kretchmar, *Studien zur frühchristlichen Trinitätstheologie* (Tübingen, 1956). It is anachronistic to call this material a theology of the trinity.

Theophilus of Antioch is the first to speak of a triad. The three
days before the making of the stars point to the threeness of God,
word and wisdom (*Aut.* 2.15). Irenaeus speaks four times of the
same triad and on three occasions identifies word and wisdom,
with son and holy spirit, who are the hands of God. Irenaeus
may depend on Theophilus, whose account of God, word and
wisdom had been influenced by hellenistic Judaism. The
Ethiopian *Book of Enoch* speaks of the son of man and wisdom as
heavenly powers, now hidden, but to be revealed at the last day.
The ideas of wisdom as divine creative will, Christ as divine
word, and church as divine bride, were common in the first two
centuries. Through Theophilus the triad of God, wisdom and
word spread widely in east and west.[25]

In Alexandria there is trinitarian tradition which mixes
apocalyptic with metaphysics. Clement knows threefold formulae and speaks of the triad of father, son and holy spirit
(*str.* 5.14.103.1); but the Logos, rather than the trinity, dominates his thought. When Celsus accuses Christians (*Cels.* 6.18)
of stealing the idea of a trinity from Plato (*Ep.* 2.312e), Origen
replies that the Seraphim of Isaiah and the Cherubim of Ezekiel
are sufficient sources. This same hierarchy of heavenly beings is
found in the Ascension of Isaiah, Philo and the Odes of
Habakkuk (3:2 'in the middle of two living creatures you will
be known').

From the tradition of Asia Minor, Irenaeus (*dem.* 10) speaks
of God as glorified by his Logos or eternal son, and by the holy
spirit or wisdom of the father of all. The powers of word and
wisdom are cherubim and seraphim who praise God continually. The Rabbis spoke of the two measures (Dan. 7) of
God: justice and mercy. Two highest powers were also found in
teaching concerning the Messiah and the angels.[26] The threefold
Sanctus of Isaiah's vision was connected with the trinity even in
the West by the end of the fourth century.[27] In the liturgy of
Alexandria, the trinitarian *Sanctus* had, by the third century,
become the place where the church joined the chorus of angelic
powers in praise of father, son and holy spirit.[28] The distinctive

[25] *Ibid.*, 59–61.   [26] *Ibid.*, 120.   [27] *Ibid.*, 148.   [28] *Ibid.*, 158.

object of Christian faith is threefold: God the father, Christ and the spirit at work in the churches. From this belief comes the liturgical practice.[29]

A tradition which sees Christ and the holy spirit as the two highest heavenly powers goes back to the first century. Another tradition links three heavenly witnesses to baptism. In the earliest trinitarian thought, the two highest heavenly paracletes of late Jewish thought are replaced by Christ and the holy spirit. The movement is from apocalyptic to metaphysics; but the son and holy spirit remain present realities as in apocalyptic.

While the earliest Christian baptism had no fixed formula, the trinitarian formula soon came into general use. There is evidence of its presence[30] from Matthew (Matt. 28.19b) to the Didache (7.1) to Justin (1 *apol.* 61) to Irenaeus (*dem.* 7.1) to Clement (*str.* 2.11.2; 5.73.2; *paed.* 1.42.1) and finally to Tertullian (*bapt.* 6.1; *Prax.* 26). Justin shows the importance of trinity for baptism (1 *apol.* 61), eucharist (1 *apol.* 65) and confession at martyrdom (*Acts of Justin* 2.5f.). He joins trinity and christology in a confession of faith which has clear definitions. The father is the father of Jesus and of the universe which he has created and now preserves (1 *apol.* 13.2). The son comes from the father so that adoptianism is excluded. The holy spirit is not a gift, but a divine power equal to the father and the son.[31]

For Irenaeus, just as eucharist declares the unity of God with Christ and the integrity of man's salvation (*haer.* 4.18.4f.), so baptism declares the truth of one God, who is father, son and holy spirit (*haer.* 3.17.1), the creator who renews the whole man (*dem.* 7). The unity of the father, incarnate son and the spirit given to all believers, is declared in baptismal act and confession.[32]

A recent investigation of baptism 'in the name of the lord' and of 'naming the name', argues that the threefold Aaronic

---

[29] *Ibid.*, 216, 'Auch für die Trinitätslehre gilt, dass die lex credendi zur lex orandi wurde und nicht umgekehrt, aber im Gottesdienst lebt dieser Glaube der Kirche, die Liturgie bewahrt und entfaltet hin.'

[30] H. von Campenhausen, Taufen auf den Namen Jesu? *VC*, 25 (1971), 1–16.

[31] W. Rordorf, La trinité dans les écrits de Justin Martyr, *Aug.*, 12 (1980), 293.

[32] A. Houssiau, Le baptème selon Irénée de Lyon, *EThL*, 60 (1984), 50.

blessing (Num. 6:22–7) and imposition of the name explain the threefold baptismal formula.[33] The baptismal candidate would see the parallel with Jewish liturgy. The invocation of the three names in the rite, presupposes the presence of father, son and holy spirit, and admits a new Christian into their presence.[34]

The sonship received by Jesus at baptism complements the sonship of the word made flesh. The union of the spirit and man makes possible the mediation of Jesus for his brothers. Irenaeus stresses the unity and unifying force of the sonship of Jesus.[35]

CHRISTOLOGY AND CONTINUITY

Unity and plurality

Justin speaks of Jesus as the son of God in a proper sense (2 *apol.* 6). Christ is the God and lord of hosts of whom the psalms (Pss. 24, 26) speak (*dial.* 36). The Old Testament appearances of God, or theophanies, point to plurality in the godhead, for the father could not be present in this way (*dial.* 56 and *dial.* 60). The word is called wisdom, glory, son, angel, god, lord, word, captain. He proceeds as logos from logos or fire from fire and is one with the father (*dial.* 61). Jesus is the promised Christ of God (*dial.* 142).

The theme of unity continues. Christ is the son in the father and father in the son (*leg.* 10). He, who suffered as Jesus, calls his disciples to suffer (*haer.* 3.18.4). For Irenaeus, Adam is the type of the one to come (*haer.* 3.22.3; Rom. 5:14) and our flesh is included in him as it is taken by the son of man who demonstrates the particular care which God takes of his creature. While the Valentinians are forever trying to 'super-transcend' God (*haer.* 2.25.4), 'the main concern of Irenaeus is the unity of the Creator God and the God and father of Jesus

[33] L. Abramowski, Die Entstehung der dreigliedrigen Taufformel, *ZThK*, 81 (1984), 417–46.
[34] *Ibid.*, 440. 'Der durch die Taufe in die Gemeinde aufgenommene Christ erhält damit Zugang zum Bereich der kultischen Gegenwärtigkeit von Vater, Sohn und Geist, die sich in jedem Gottesdienst erneuert.'
[35] A. Orbe, San Ireneo adopcionista? En torna a adv.haer. 3.19.1, *Greg.*, 65 (1984), 5–52.

Christ (*haer.* 3.1–15), the unity of Jesus Christ himself (*haer.* 3.16–25) and the unity between the Old Testament and the New Testament (*haer.* 4.9)'.[36]

Yet some plurality persists, for son and spirit are God's two hands to whom he said 'let us make man' (*haer.* 4. *Pref.* 4).[37] There is no division for 'God created man with his own hands' (*dem.* 11). Justin had spoken of the hidden hand of the lord who fought against Amalek and identified this power with the crucified Jesus (*dial.* 49.8). Against the Gnostics, Irenaeus affirms vigorously that the creator is the supreme God. 'Ipse fabricator, ipse conditor...Hic conditor, hic factor, hic fabricator, qui fecit ea per semetipsum, hoc est per verbum et per sapientiam' (*haer.* 2.30.9). He who created, modelled, gave the breath of life and nourishes us, is an ultimate and immediate presence in creation and redemption. Drawing on Isa. 40:12 and Jer. 22:23 Irenaeus uses the 'hands of God' to describe the spiritual and intimate relation of God to man. God's hands learned to handle, hold, carry and place his creation where they wished (*haer.* 5.5.1). Adam never left the hands of God (*haer.* 5.1.3) who allowed no gap in his long chain of theophanies, miracles and prophecies. Man's image and likeness pointed to the longing for intimacy between creator and creature. The hands show also the simultaneity and immediacy of the trinity; Irenaeus refuses to affirm anything of one divine person which he does not affirm of another (*haer.* 2.13.8; 2.28.4; 2.28.5).[38] The hands show the interrelation of every part of divine activity in creation, redemption and sacrament.[39] The holy spirit, as the hand and wisdom of God at creation, reveals his presence in both testaments as life-giving spirit and revealer of the father, and helps man to recognise that God and his spirit are always the same (*haer.* 4.33.15).

---

[36] J. T. Nielsen, *Adam and Christ in the theology of Irenaeus of Lyon* (Assen, 1968), 56.

[37] J. Mambrino, Les deux mains de Dieu chez S. Irénée, *NRTh*, 79 (1957), 355. See also *haer.* 4.20.1, 5.1.3, 5.5.1, 5.15.3–4, 5.16.1, 5.28.4.   [38] *Ibid.*, 366.

[39] *Ibid.*, 369, 'Mais Irénée par son image des mains de Dieu a rendu comme sensible cette proximité ineffable et terrible, et n'a pas diminué la sainteté de Dieu en montrant presque comme familière. Nul intermédiaire entre le Créateur et sa créature: il ne cesse pas de la travailler, de la faire et de la refaire, depuis la création initiale jusqu'à la résurrection des morts.'

Justin's account of the divine theophanies is important for both Judaism and Christianity, presenting a common front against the super-celestial tendencies of Gnosticism. Jew and Christian declared that in love God had descended from heaven to his people, finding the lowest spot on earth, confining in narrow limits his own infinity. Poor, humble, in the form of a servant, he shared the deepest suffering of his people.[40] While Judaism rejected Christian theology, Christians might draw on Jewish accounts of divine condescension to present the mystery of the incarnation. Differences remained at the significant extremes: the ultimate humiliation of Christ's passion and his ascent which drew his followers above.[41]

In Irenaeus, three citations of the beatitude, 'Blessed are the meek' (*haer.* 3.22.1; 5.9.4; 5.32.2) point to the flesh, the word at his incarnation and the spirit at the resurrection. God's two hands receive and transform the flesh, so that the church, as the children of Abraham, may receive the promised earth. The beatitude points to the end of history when Christ returns in glory to earth.[42]

Clement speaks similarly of the unity of God in Christ, the son in the father and the father in the son. God in form of man, and man in form of God is Jesus (*paed.* 1.2.4). The word is the face of God (*paed.* 1.7.57). He is one with the father (*paed.* 1.8.71) and called lord, son, father, teacher and charioteer. The father, son and spirit are all in one and one in all, with perfection of goodness, beauty and wisdom (*paed.* 3.12.101). The word is seen as teacher (*str.* 4.25.162). Plato refers to father and son (*str.* 5.14.102). The voice of the lord, the word, has no shape but has power in truth (*str.* 6.3.34). He is the only source of truth. Plato said truth could come only from God or from an offspring of God (*str.* 6.15.123). Clement's account of co-operating causes is important for his understanding of the relation between father and son (*str.* 8.9.25). Like the Fourth Gospel (John 14:28),[43] he includes subordination in his account of unity (*str.* 7.3.16).

---

[40] P. Kuhn, *Gottes Selbsterniedrigung in der Theologie der Rabbinen* (München, 1968), 104f.
[41] *Ibid.*, 109. Cf. Augustine, *Serm.* 337, *PL* 38, 1477.
[42] Y. de Andia, Matt. 5:5, La beatitudine dei miti nell'interpretazione di San Ireneo, *RSLR*, 30 (1984), 275–86.   [43] Barrett, *Gospel according to John*, 71.

Tertullian's apologetic work is strongly monotheist while his work against Praxeas is more pluralistic. There is no incoherence here, but an awareness of different audiences and different problems. Tertullian develops his christology in opposition to Praxeas who has made a heresy out of the divine unity (*Prax.* 1). The distinction between person and substance needs to be maintained (*Prax.* 5), and the names of the father and son point to this difference (*Prax.* 10f.). As the rays of the sun are inseparable from the sun, so the son cannot be separated from the father (*Prax.* 18f.). Nor can the son be divided in himself. He is the word made flesh and, unlike an alloy, remains both divine and human (*Prax.* 27). The flesh of Christ proves that he was man and son of man (*carn.* 5); spirit, word, reason, Jesus Christ and lord are properly his titles (*or.* 1).

Two natures

Tertullian will continue to attract attention for his striking statement: 'We see a twofold state, not confused but joined in one person, God and man, Jesus' (*Prax.* 27).[44] There is an identity of essence between father and son. The word of the Gospel, 'I and the father are one' is absolute.[45] However the two-nature formulae are equally striking: *caro–spiritus, sermo–caro, filius Dei – filius hominis, Deus–homo, condicio humana – condicio divina, substantia interior – substantia exterior, substantia carnis – substantia spiritus, substantia humana – substantia divina, utraque substantia.* There are *duae substantiae, duplex status, duae naturae.*[46]

The insistence on unity (*duplex status...coniunctus in una persona...caro et spiritus in uno esse possunt*) is intelligible through a Stoic concept of interpenetration of physical bodies, by which each retains its specific qualities and is not replaced by a third thing. For Tertullian, as for other Stoics, the technical phrase 'two in one' means the interpenetration of two bodies, their

---

[44] 'videmus duplicem statum, non confusum, sed coniunctum in una persona, Deum et hominem Jesum.' This formula has been regarded as a theological miracle, by Cantalamessa, *La cristologia* 168, who quotes Harnack, Tixeront, Altaner, Bardy, Grillmeier, Quasten in support of his claim.

[45] *Ibid.*, 26f.   [46] *Ibid.*, 94f.

physical union in κρᾶσις δι᾽ ὅλων.[47] His understanding of two
natures comes direct from scripture (in particular Rom. 1:3f.
and John 1:14), to underline his reaction against Gnostic
dualism and Marcion's docetism.[48] Tertullian also used
Phil. 2:6–8 against the docetism of Marcion and Apelles and
against the modalism of Praxeas. On the one hand, he insists on
the unity of the plan of salvation, in which pre-existence and
incarnation are joined, and, on the other hand, he maintains a
real distinction between father and son.[49]

TRINITY: ONE GOD IN A NEW WAY—BY THE SON
AND THE SPIRIT

A new way

Irenaeus says that, to give an account of God, we must begin
from God, and not, as do the Gnostics, from his works
(*haer.* 2.25.1). Son, spirit, word, wisdom, all share in the creation
of the world (*haer.* 4.20.1; 2.30.9; 2.2.4), for the word is always
with his creature (*haer.* 3.16.6; 3.18.1; 4.6.2; 5.16.1). At the
same time, Irenaeus declares the economy by which the persons
of the trinity are clearly one. The father anoints the son with the
spirit (*haer.* 3.6.1).[50] Yet the divinity and personality of each of
the three is preserved.[51]

Tertullian's attack on Praxeas is remarkable in two ways.
First, he is much more restrained in his abuse than in most of his
other polemics. Secondly, he is much more lucid and matter-of-
fact than his interpreters allow. Trinity goes beyond the mere
existence of three heavenly beings. It requires that they be one

[47] 'Ma per Tertulliano, come del resto per gli stoici in genere, *duo in uno esse* è espressione
tecnica per designare la compenetrazione dei corpi, cioé l'unione fisica secondo la
κρᾶσις δι᾽ ὅλων' *Ibid.*, 148.
[48] His limited but genuine achievement was to fortify the West against any monophysite
tendency. *Ibid.*, 196.
[49] A. Verwilgher, Phil. 2.6–8 dans l'œuvre de Tertullien, *Sal.*, 47 (1985), 433–65.
[50] 'Et unxit quidem Pater, unctus est vero Filius, in spiritu, qui est unctio.' J. Kunze,
Die Gotteslehre des Irenaeus (Leipzig, 1891), 62, comments, 'Dieser Konstruction
scheint das amans, amatus, amor Augustins und der Viktoriner nachgebildet.'
[51] *Ibid.*, 62.

God, 'God is believed as one in a new way – by the son and the spirit.' The three are the object of the same faith and adoration which is directed to one, only, identical and original divinity. This is that of the father, revealed in and by the others, in so far as they are one with their first-principle (*prax.* 18.5; 19.5; 22.11).[52]

God is unique and of three divine persons.[53] Because the three are of one *status, substantia, potestas,* God remains unique although three in *gradus, forma* and *species.* The dominant concept is that of *monarchia,* the insistence that one God creates and rules the world as its only lord. When Praxeas (3.2), and his followers insist 'we hold to the monarchy', Tertullian responds that the devil pretends to defend truth so that he may destroy it. The lord is he who rules all, God the father, and his son who has received from his father the rule over all creation (*Prax.* 4; 16.1).

The rule of faith had pointed unambiguously to one God and the divinity of father, son and holy spirit.[54] The father was one God, creator of all, father of men and father of Jesus Christ.[55] The background to the concept of *monarchia* was threefold: the philosophical religion of the Greeks, the theology of the Bible and the ideas of Alexandrian Judaism.[56]

One God has sovereign rule, while many beings have different offices (*ap.* 24.3). God is the great Most-high (*summum magnum*) established in eternity (*Marc.* 1.3.5). His greatness is known only to himself (*ap.* 17.2f.; *Marc.* 1.9.2). Within the trinity, the father, as the origin and proprietor of power is the greatest (*Prax.* 9.2; 14.10); yet the three possess in different ways the same greatness. There is no delegation of authority, as with God and the angels; but there is a community where each possesses without limit the family property.[57] The father communicates all that he has to son and spirit, so that they too are omnipotent (*Prax.* 7.3). A legal account of the free sharing of property points to the unity of God where the son and spirit share in the substance of the father. Finally, every kind is referred back to its

---

[52] J. Moingt, Le problème du dieu unique chez Tertullien, *RevSR*, 44 (1970).
[53] *Ibid.,* 337–62.   [54] 1 *apol.* 6.
[55] 1 *apol.* 21; *dial.* 7f. *haer.* 1.10.1; *praescr.* 36.5.   [56] Philo, *opif.* 61, 171.
[57] Moingt, Le problème, 356.

origin (*nat.* 1.12.12). Unity of origin implies unity of substance and identity of nature.

Substance

What did Tertullian mean by substance? There are several possibilities: God's substance might mean God himself, his mode of existence, his rank or character, his divinity or eternity. Probably it has a straightforward meaning and signifies 'the unique stuff which is, or composes, the divine *corpus*, and which Tertullian denotes *spiritus*'.[58] Spirit may describe the whole trinity (*pud.* 21.16), or what issues from God the father (*Prax.* 26.3–4), namely the word (*ap.* 21.11). The metaphors of either the sun with its rays, or the spring, brook and river, show that *spiritus* can be used either of the whole trinity or of each person. The substance of the divine word does not change at incarnation. Tertullian's account suggests 'a certain tension between the simple Monarchian teaching traditional at Rome and the pluralistic theology which he adopted from the earlier Apologists and developed for the purposes of controversy'.[59] It is unlikely that he normally regarded as a πρώτη οὐσία a 'One who is identical with each of the persons taken singly, although these three persons are not identical with one another'.[60]

Substance for Tertullian means 'stuff' or 'material'. One substance was òne physical thing.[61] The soul, as well as God, logos and holy spirit were all corporeal realities. '*omne quod est corpus est sui generis*' (*carn.* 11.4; cf. *Prax.* 7.8). So Tertullian's view of substance sprang from his very refined materialism. He thought of one substance divided into three parts which remained together (*coniunctae...cohaerentes*); each part was the embodiment of one of the three members of the trinity. This meant that his language had to be reinvested with a different meaning. The variety of possible meanings has provided work for subsequent theologians who have to make something out of non-material material or *stoffloser Stoff*.[62] In the end the only

[58] Stead, Divine substance in Tertullian, 62.   [59] *Ibid.*, 65.
[60] This is the view of Evans, as given by Stead, *ibid.*, 65f.
[61] S. Schlossmann, Tertullian im Lichte der Jurisprudenz, *ZKG*, 27 (1906), 407.
[62] *Ibid.*, 430.

guides to his plain meaning are the metaphors which he uses 'of *substantiae*, which admit of a kind of distribution, and equality, which does not constitute a division'.[63]

Person

Tertullian attributes to the divine spirit a representation which is corporeal enough to make the divine persons distinct from one another. While he does not talk literally of the hands and face of God and allows a vast difference between a human and a divine body,[64] he insists that it is vital that God be the kind of reality which can be shown and not an abstraction which leads the heretics to deny the flesh of Christ. A substance is *aliquid* as opposed to *nihil*. The body of spirit is the thing itself, a unity of being and action. Tertullian, like others, never quite succeeds in defining his concept of being.[65] A quick reading of *Against Praxeas* suggests that Tertullian has not avoided a division of the divine substance, and a closer reading indicates that he may not have given the son and the spirit a totality of divine substance.[66]

Tertullian finds in 'word' (*sermo*) the substantiality of a 'body' (*corpus*) with a 'form' (*effigies*), of a 'thing' (*res substantiva*) which exists individually, and he affirms the unity of this substance in father, son and holy spirit. Particularity is achieved by *species, gradus, forma, proprietas* and above all, *persona*. His most diligent interpreter struggles. 'There are in God several things (*res*) which have each the determination of substance, which all have together the condition of the same substance, which are therefore identical in physical constitution and nature: that is the first aim of Tertullian's argument... The second aim is to understand and to express the particularity and the individuality of these things... Tertullian calls these things *personae*.'[67] *Gradus* is a term which Tertullian takes from Valentinians and applies in his own way. He wants to avoid the dreaded word *alius* for the distinction between father and son, and he finds *gradus* useful against modalists,[68] despite its

[63] Stead, *Tertullian*, 66.
[64] J. Moingt, *Théologie trinitaire de Tertullien* II (Paris 1966), 333.   [65] *Ibid.*, 337.
[66] *Ibid.*, 338.   [67] *Ibid.*, 431.   [68] *Ibid.*, 477.

openness to subordinationist interpretation; it shows the link with one origin, the cohesion of monarchy and the unity of divine substance. *Species* and *gradus* distinguish parts of a whole when considered from outside. *Forma* and *proprietas* point to intrinsic and reciprocal difference. *Forma* goes to the root of individuality, while *proprietas* often indicates no more than particularity and numerical distinction.[69] *Persona*, the keyword, may be considered as part of an economy or as a metaphysical term in its own right. As member of the Godhead, the *persona* of Christ may mean individual, personage, mouthpiece or representative. The son makes the father evident by his teaching, his incarnation or his theophanies in human flesh. In legal terms, the son represents the father by revealing the disposition, and inaugurating the discipline of the creator, as well as by speaking and acting with the authority of God.

In Tertullian there is development in the concept of *persona* from his *Against Marcion* to his *Against Praxeas*; but the development is only possible because of the detailed exegesis of the earlier work. In this development, *persona* moves beyond the incarnate Christ to divine being as in father, son and holy spirit, and also from the notion of 'representative person' to 'distinct individual existence (or existing individual)'. The concept is still economic or concerned with an external manifestation rather than a metaphysical entity.[70] Tertullian draws on the ideas of the Apologists and even on recollections of Valentinian controversy. He outlines the contours of the two key terms. 'Person' designates the distinctive elements in the inner life of God, while 'substance' refers to the unitive element.[71] Because *persona* refers to the manifestation of the distinctive being of God, it cannot end either in modalism or in tritheism.[72] So Tertullian manages to find a way between these two extremes. To prove the reality of word (*sermo*), he indicates the rational substance of God; but to prove the distinction, he considers the son in relation to the other divine persons according to scripture. When arguing philosophically he will express the trinitarian

---

[69] *Ibid.*, 549.   [70] *Ibid.*, 615.
[71] *Ibid.*, 669, citing R. Braun, *Deus Christianorum* (2nd edn, Paris, 1977), 237f.
[72] *Ibid.*

distinctions by *res, species, forma, gradus*, but when he wants to show what these indicate in the story of divine revelation he uses *persona*. 'This word designates exactly what the other words mean, but it does not by itself signify what is formally expressed by the others.'[73]

In all this, Tertullian handed on a logical language, not just a number of new words.[74] Since philosophy in this century has rediscovered the flexibility of definitions and the importance of usage, that would be achievement enough. We may add that, with the new language, he opened the way to future developments which linked trinity and christology, *persona* and ὑπόστα-σις, proving just how fertile language may be in the *sermo per quem loquens cogitas (Prax. 5.6)*.[75] Fourth-century developments, however, were directed against a quite different target. Praxeas had joined father and son in too close a unity; Arius divided father and son with too wide a distinction.

Persons in dialogue

By translating πρόσωπον (Lam. 4:20; Prov. 8:30 and 2 Cor. 4:6) as *persona*, Tertullian was able to provide the formula 'three persons, one substance'.[76] However, in Justin (1 *apol.* 62.2f.) as in Tertullian (*Prax.* 12) the idea of person is derived from the dialogue character of the text, not from an explicit reference. This has been called 'prosopographical' or person-related exegesis and is explained from Justin (1 *apol.* 36.1f.) who frequently employs the appropriate formula ὡς ἀπὸ προσώπου.

The concept of Christ as one of three persons, comes from prosopographical (person-related) exegesis in Justin, Irenaeus, Hippolytus and Tertullian. Each takes the verb, 'let us make' to

---

[73] *Ibid.*, 670.

[74] *Ibid.*, 673. 'Pas seulement un nombre de mots, mais un discours construit au moyen de liaisons conceptuelles, qui rassemble les mots dans des structures rationnelles, fermes et claires.' [75] *Ibid.*, 673f.

[76] Harnack considered Tertullian's legal knowledge was also part of the development. But Schlossmann (Tertullian im Lichte der Jurisprudenz, 251–75, 407–30) argued convincingly that Tertullian's lack of legal knowledge was essential to the formulation of the idea. Tertullian's theory was rhetorical not legal. Much has been written on the relation to Hippolytus on this point.

indicate a plurality of persons.[77] This argument sets out, for
Tertullian, the distinction of the trinity. 'For there is the spirit
who himself speaks and the father to whom he speaks and the
son concerning whom he speaks. Similarly there are other
passages which establish each person in his specific character,
spoken here by the father to the son, here by the son concerning
the father or to the father, here by the spirit' (*Prax.* 11.9f.). The
argument does not indicate the origin of the term *persona*, nor
does the formula mean what it later meant for Augustine.
Tertullian uses 'person' in a more philosophical sense to mean
'particular individual' or 'personal substance' (*Val.* 4.2).[78]
This tradition of exegesis was also to influence western theology
independently of Tertullian. Because of its excesses the defenders
of the *homoousia* had to sort out *ousia* and *hypostasis*; their success
was partly due to their neglect of mythological or angelic
elements. The concept of person was rationally based on the
logic of prosopographical exegesis.[79]

This is the way in which (*Prax.* 20–6) Tertullian proves his
case. The trinity is three 'not by diversity but by distribution,
not by division but by distinction'. God appeared to the
patriarchs; but the father cannot be seen, therefore it was the
son who appeared. The Monarchian case had rested on three
texts: (Isa. 45:5, 'I am God and beside me there is none else',
John 10:30, 'I and the father are one' and John 14:9f.),
whereas there are hundreds of texts which require a distinction
between father and son. Clearly the cross ('Why hast thou
forsaken me?' 'Into thy hands I commend my spirit'),
resurrection, sitting at the right hand of the father, all make a
distinction between father and son necessary.

Can the personal analogy be pushed so that a social theory of
the trinity emerges? This is the argument of some recent

---

[77] Prosopographical exegesis is 'una esegesi che tien conto, in particolari testi biblici e
mette in rilievo l'esistenza di un "dialogo" e la presenza di vari "interlocutori"
(Gesprächspartner)', Cantalamessa, *La cristologia*, 156 and Andresen, Zur Entstehung, 1–39. Cantalamessa summarises: 'L'idea centrale del suo lungo articolo è la
seguente: l'introduzione del concetto di "persona" nella dottrina trinitaria non è
l'opera esclusiva di Tertulliano, né di altro singolo autore, ma è il risultato di una
esegesi prosopografica praticata fin da Giustino.'   [78] *Ibid.*, 195.
[79] Andresen, Zur Entstehung, 1–39.

exposition, which claims that monotheism must be rejected because it was based on political motives. In the second century, we have seen, nothing could be further from the truth. Tertullian (*ap.* 24.4) uses the political analogy, participation in rule, although he knows it is a standard defence of polytheism. It may indeed seem strange that Tertullian should so play into the hands of his opponents;[80] but the argument is concerned to indicate the possibility of shared *imperium*, and to meet a particular objection at a particular point. Tertullian is certainly not concerned with the elaboration of a political theology. Nor is he concerned to transfer 'the secular monarchy concept of pagan theology to the trinity'. An examination of his total argument leaves no doubt on this point. Most apologetic argument works with a logic of objection and rebuttal; individual rebuttals, directed against different objections, sometimes conflict, and need not be related to the total argument of the apologist.

It must be admitted, despite the imagination behind the political application, that 'monotheism is not in itself a political problem'.[81] Yet, although the older thesis has been shown to be untenable on historical, logical and theological grounds, it remains a magic formula which is still respected.[82] It was formulated at a time (1935) when its political relevance was so acute, that its deficiencies were overlooked.[83] However even the Cappadocian position was not of political use; it harmonised the three and the one by making all three of equal rank without robbing the triune God of his *monarchia*.[84]

Divine economy

For one recent writer, the key notion is freedom through the trinitarian history of God. God is the inexhaustible freedom of those whom he has created.[85] Where another wrongly defines 'the threefold God as transcendent primal ground of salvation

[80] E. Peterson, *Der Monotheismus als politisches Problem* (Leipzig, 1935), 50f.
[81] A. Schindler (ed.) *Monotheismus als ein politisches Problem* (Gütersloh, 1978), 70.
[82] e.g. Schoedel, Neglected motive, 362.   [83] Schindler, *Monotheismus*, 9.
[84] *Ibid.*, 60.
[85] J. Moltmann, *The trinity and the kingdom of God* (London, 1981), 218.

history', it is argued that he has abandoned the 'interpersonal relations of the triune God'.[86] There has to be a social relation between three divine persons, an eternal *perichoresis*.[87]

The main argument is set out elsewhere.[88] If perfect societies show multiplicity in unity and the unity is more complete as the society is more perfect, 'then there is nothing contrary to reason in supposing the divine Nature to exhibit these characteristics in the most complete manner'. Here there are too many ambiguities to make the argument worthy of consideration: 'perfect' 'more perfect' 'multiplicity in unity' 'nothing contrary to reason' 'more complete unity' 'most complete manner'. Any analogy is useless without careful definition. Against this account must be set the criticism of all 'social' theories of the trinity that 'to appropriate such philosophical advantages as the conception of a plural Deity would offer, involves an unconscious desertion of the catholic faith'.[89]

Is Tertullian's doctrine of the trinity consistent with the unity of God as he had defended it against Marcion? His use of οἰκονομία provides an answer; he does not apply this term, as the Gnostics had done, to explain the disposition of the Godhead, but uses it to connect the reality of the triune God to the history of salvation. The Montanist account is no more acceptable than the Monarchian; the triune God is active in all the dispensations of saving history.[90]

The grounds for Christian monotheism were not found in politics, but in fidelity to the God of Israel; Marcion had made the choice inevitable. The explanation of monotheism could be philosophical, salvation-history, or trinitarian. The last could centre on the father or on the Godhead.

Tertullian shows a way of talking about a God who is three and one. Later a choice is made between two sorts of analogies – psychological which preserve the unity and imperil the trinity, or social which imperil the unity and preserve the trinity. The former have been favoured in the west since Augustine, and the

---

[86] *Ibid.*, 156.   [87] *Ibid.*, 157.
[88] W. R. Matthews, *God in Christian thought and experience* (London, 1930), 193.
[89] F. R. Tennant, *Philosophical Theology*, II (Cambridge, 1930), 268f.
[90] Braun, *Deus Christianorum*, 158–67.

latter have been favoured in the east. Social theories can be combined with the psychological analogy. All our experiences of unity fall short of the degree of unification and 'the intensity of that unifying power...which constitutes the unity of the Blessed Trinity'.[91] The only thing in favour of a committee God, is that it would solve the problem of evil automatically. The frustrations and perils of human history require no further explanation if the universe be governed by a divine committee.

The economy of the divine persons, faces more profound difficulties than the economy of salvation-history. Tertullian did as much as anyone to find a way through the difficulties; he could not abandon either unity or plurality in God. From Tertullian onwards, trinitarian theologians are looking for something between a noun and an adjective, between a substantival existent and an adjectival subsistent. A 'person' has to be 'neither an individual nor an attribute of an individual'; it is 'the ground or basis of a special function rather than a special function and yet stops short of being an individual subject'.[92]

CONCLUSION

While social trinitarians are denounced as tritheist and psychological trinitarians are pronounced to be modalist, it is wise to remember that from the beginning of Christian thought, there has been tension between μοναρχία and ἀνακεφαλαίωσις, or between a first cause and a cosmic mind. The first cause will incline to a social trinity and the *Geistmetaphysik* to a psychological trinity. The problem has survived in ever changing forms; but all could give thanks to the only father and son, son and father, with the holy spirit, τῷ μόνῳ πατρὶ καὶ υἱῷ, υἱῷ καὶ πατρί, παιδαγωγῷ καὶ διδασκάλῳ υἱῷ, σὺν καὶ τῷ ἁγίῳ πνεύματι. πάντα τῷ ἑνί, ἐν ᾧ τὰ πάντα, δι᾽ ὃν τὰ πάντα ἕν, δι᾽ ὃν τὸ ἀεί, οὗ μέλη πάντες, οὗ δόξα, αἰῶνες, πάντα τῷ ἀγαθῷ, πάντα τῷ καλῷ, πάντα

---

[91] L. Hodgson, *The doctrine of the trinity* (London, and New York, 1944), 95f. Cited Moltmann, *Trinity*, 250. Moltmann has referred elsewhere to a royal committee analogy used by Hodgson. I cannot find this but am intrigued by the possibility, and its illumination of the problem of evil.

[92] Tennant, *Philosophical Theology*, II, 268.

τῷ σοφῷ, τῷ δικαίῳ τὰ πάντα. ᾧ ἡ δόξα καὶ νῦν καὶ εἰς τοὺς αἰῶνας (*paed.* 3.12.101).

Clement's 'and with the holy spirit' reminds us that Tertullian's advance towards a full doctrine of the trinity, by its developed account of the spirit, goes beyond earlier writers and indeed beyond the Creed of Nicaea, 'and in the holy spirit'. Nicaea, like Irenaeus and Clement, was concerned with the unity of father and son. Tertullian, like the Creed of Constantinople, declared one God in a new way, by the son and the spirit. The fourth-century thinkers did not copy Tertullian, but worked out their theology in relation to later problems.

CHAPTER 7

One good

The one God, who has spoken in one word, the one son of God, has given one law, one commandment and one way of life that all may follow. As there is one good God so there is one goodness.[1] The good life consists in becoming like God who has made man free to follow his law and regain his likeness. Clement writes: 'For those who serve *one God* must ensure that their goods and possessions also exhibit the signs of *a life that is one and good*, and each individual must be seen to practise, with unwavering faith, other things which conform to this *uniform plan* and are in harmony with this *one disposition*' (*paed.* 2.3.38. My emphasis).

ONE GOD, ONE LAW

Antithesis of law

Three of the groups hostile to Christianity (Romans, philosophers and Jews) are concerned with law and the Christian lack of it. For Celsus, Christians represented the antithesis of law.[2] They hid in the dark, like criminals, bats, ants, frogs, or indeed worms in a dung heap, as they argued and competed for the place of first sinner (*Cels.* 4.23). A religion must be visible if it is to be acceptable and the obscurity of Jesus' birth is matched by the secrecy of his followers. They transgress both the hidden law of reason and the public laws of the state. Jesus collected ten or

---

[1] Osborn, Origen and justification, 18–29.
[2] Andresen, *Logos und Nomos* 225–38.

197

eleven taxmen or sailors, with whom he travelled and indulged in dirty tricks (*Cels.* 1.62). They offered the kingdom of God to knaves as well as fools, so that any clear-thinking criminal knew he would be welcome (*Cels.* 3.59). Jesus was an underworld boss who collected fellow criminals (*Cels.* 2.12 and 44). All of which shows that Christians are as hostile to νόμος as they are to λόγος.

The gospel had been presented, we have seen, as a form of universal history, with a beginning in creation, a middle in Christ and an end in apocalypse. Celsus simply reverses the Christian argument, which had, since Paul, made the story of man's salvation an upward climb, from good to better and to best. Celsus starts from an original word of truth (*Cels.* 1.14) and the conviction that things will get worse rather than better. Christianity stands then, not at the peak, but at the bottom of the darkest descent of all. The claim that Celsus worked out a philosophy of history in answer to Justin's theology of history may seem to go beyond the evidence, until one considers the total argument.[3] When this is placed together with the literary evidence, the grounds for the hypothesis are strong.

For Justin, the seminal word was the same word who, having spoken through the prophets, became man in Christ (2 *apol.* 10). For Celsus, the wisdom of the ancients provided the only way (through analysis, synthesis or analogy) to an understanding of the unknown God (*Cels.* 7.42). But Justin had claimed the priority of Moses over the ancient Greeks and shown how Plato took his account of creation and of three principles from Moses (1 *apol.* 59f.). For Celsus, the borrowing went in the opposite direction (*Cels.* 1.21 *et passim*), since Moses stole from earlier sages. Justin's whole position, of love for truth, of rejection of falsehood however ancient (1 *apol.* 2), is challenged by the identification of the ancient with the true.

Origen will reply that Christians live by the moral law, which is king of all, and have rejected any law which runs contrary to this. Origen uses the same philosophical tradition as Celsus but reverses his conclusions. Origen opposes the divine law to the laws of the state (*Cels.* 8.26) and speaks of the spiritual law

---

[3] *Ibid.*, 344–72. See above, pp. 21f.

which Isaiah foretold (Isa. 2:3f., *Cels.* 5.33). All this repeats the earlier claim of Justin that Christ was law and logos of all things.

How can God judge justly when laws differ from country to country? Justin admits that evil demons have perverted laws, but claims that the true word has shown the difference between bad and good (*2 apol.* 9.4). Despite evil efforts of demons, the true word has achieved what human laws could not (*1 apol.* 10). Now, there is point to man's judgement because the word has shown what is right and what is wrong. Now, too, the word leads men away from demons to the only God; their moral transformation is evident to all (*1 apol.* 14). Indeed, contrary to the common criticism, the Christian was sometimes seen by the Jew and gentile to have a stronger devotion to law than others. The Christian is depicted in popular cartoon as a donkey dressed in a toga and holding a book (*nat.* 1.14.1). Trypho could admire the gospel but insist that its precepts were too hard for practice (*dial.* 10).

Natural law

Christians accepted a natural law which derived from creation. In contrast, the Mosaic cult was a temporary and punitive measure, prescribed because Jewish hearts were hard or perverse (*dial.* 18.2; 21f.; 46.5). While the Law could not be despised, it came later than the natural law which was written on the hearts of the patriarchs (*Jud.* 2.7) and it flourished for a limited time (*Jud.* 2.7f.). Adam and Abel lived without sabbaths or circumcision (*Jud.* 2.11f.). The law given to Adam included the love command and the ten commandments (*Jud.* 2.3).

In contrast to the temporary Law of Moses there is an eternal, universal law of God. For God implants the knowledge that certain acts are wrong (*dial.* 93); his universal justice is summed up in the teaching of Jesus, the love of God and the love of neighbour (*ibid.*), and is linked with the gift of reason. God gave man freedom, reason and a law (*dial.* 141).

The Christian offers to God, says Athenagoras, the rational worship of which Paul spoke (*leg.* 13). For Clement, too, rationality is linked to the law which comprises the ten

commandments and the love commands of the Lord Jesus
(*prot.* 10). The way to divine perfection is through the law
written in the heart (*prot.* 11). Such virtue is the same in man
and woman, who share one God and master, one church, one
pattern of virtue and an equal yoke in marriage (*paed.* 1.4.10).

Scripture, nature and discipline all play a part in the law
which derives its foundation from scripture, its support from
nature and its demand from discipline. These three belong to
God and indicate ways in which he confronts man (*virg.* 16.1f.).
The unwritten natural law existed before the Law of Moses and
was understood and kept by patriarchs habitually (*Jud.* 2.7).
The link with creation is clear. Man is the image of the creator
and Christ is the head of man (*Marc.* 5.8.1). Tertullian saw the
complexities of natural law and by his own errors indicated
some of its difficulties. A man should not cover his head; he has
an excess of hair and therefore may shave or cut his hair. His
true head is Christ. Women on the other hand should cover
their heads (*virg.* 8.1f.). God could have produced purple and
blue wool on sheep; since he did not wish to do so, it is wrong
to dye wool to an unnatural colour (*cult.* 1.8.2).

Ethics in Irenaeus owes its place to natural law. Because the
gospel recapitulates the beginning it restores the laws of nature.
Since the one logos is the source of all law, a levelling of
distinctions might be expected. But Clement makes it clear that
philosophy and Mosaic Law are but preparations for Christ.
With all the subsequent nomism and moralism, some might
expect a diminution of the place of Jesus; this is not the case.
The link between Jesus and right action becomes stronger than
ever.[4] For Irenaeus as for Clement, all ethical obedience is
crowned with the vision of God.

A remarkable thing about Marcion is that, despite his
rejection of the creator, he believed that the twofold love
command was a summary of the Law, and was a spiritual law,
inscribed by the good, most-high God, on human hearts. The
gospel was a new law (*Marc.* 4.12) and Marcion was legalist in

---

[4] V. E. Hasler, *Gesetz und Evangelium in der alten Kirche bis Origenes* (Zürich and
Frankfurt, 1953), 103–5, 108.

orientation.[5] Irenaeus takes the Stoic account of natural law and is able to explain that the Pharisees transgress the law of God because they do not have the love of God (*haer.* 4.12.4). Jesus did not annul the natural law but extended it (*haer.* 4.13.1). Decalogue, law of nature and love command all coincide (*haer.* 4.16.3).

Mosaic Law

The view that the Mosaic Law was incomplete provides the starting point. It was part of the divine economy (*dial.* 19.3–6; 20.1; 23.3) and the education of man for ultimate salvation (*paed.* 3.12.94; *str.* 7.14.86; 2.7.35 and 18.91). It kept the Jews from worshipping idols (*haer.* 4.15.2), ruling by a fear which the gospel has replaced by faith. Yet the Law was good because it showed God's special concern for man (*Marc.* 2.4.5) and guaranteed man's freedom to choose (*Marc.* 2.5.6–7.3).

Justin further distinguishes, within the Mosaic law, what is valid (but incomplete), firstly, from what is invalid and out of date because it concerned the hardness of Israel's heart, and secondly, from what points as a type to the mystery of the Messiah (*dial.* 44.3).

The Law is beautiful and good despite its punitive and corrective aspects, for it heals and delivers the soul from sin (*str.* 1.27.171). Indeed all ethical teaching is derived from the Law of Moses, where justice and wisdom draw men from visible shapes to the father and maker of all things. Fixed on one God, this Law shows the connection of virtues and the good of the soul. Man grows like God in obedience to the Law (*str.* 2.18.80).

Critical interpretation of the Mosaic Law was no problem to Marcion who rejected it all. For Ptolemaeus, disciple of Valentinus, it was a different matter, and his Letter to Flora shows an intellectual subtlety rare among Gnostics. God was responsible for some of the Law, Moses for some and the traditions of the elders for the rest (4.5–12). God's part was further divisible into what was good but incomplete (like the decalogue), what was wrong and needed to be corrected and

[5] *Ibid.*, 46, 120.

what pointed in symbols and types beyond ritual to a higher
world (5.1–9). The paschal lamb and the unleavened bread had
been shown by Paul to be images of Christ (5.10–15). Such a
mixture could not come from one ἀρχή who was simple and
entirely good, nor could it come from the devil, but only from
the mixed-up demiurge who stood between them. The question
of the Law was again inescapable for Christian protagonists of
one God.

Justin confronts the problems of Law which divide Jews from
Christians.[6] His controversy with heretics is also relevant, for
the Law was the first point of division for Marcion and the
Gnostics. On one occasion, he even employs a Marcionite
criticism of the Law against the Jews (*dial.* 94.1–2). The variety
of divine dispensations in saving history provides the chief
Christian defence. Justin distinguishes three epochs (*dial.* 46):
that of the patriarchs who lived without the law of Moses, that
under the Mosaic Law and that of the final, eternal law of
Christ (*dial.* 11.2).

The law of God points to what he requires and declares his
reason or wisdom. Christians do not reject the one God who
gave the Law but they insist that what Moses received was
incomplete and temporary. Jews should now look beyond the
Law of Moses. They should hear the words of the prophet and
circumcise their hearts (*dial.* 16). The Law was only necessary
because of the wickedness of the Jews. The sabbath law was
given, like other laws, because the people had not lived righteous
lives (*dial.* 21) and sacrifices were also given to keep them from
idolatry and sin (*dial.* 22).

Justin describes (*dial.* 95f.) the double curse of Deut. 27:26
and 21:23, which embodies the Jewish objection to Christian
faith. Paul argues (Gal. 3) that the curse on all who have not
kept the whole Law has been assumed by Christ in his accursed
death on the cross. Paul had persecuted those who did not keep
the whole Law until he saw that Christ, by his death on the tree,
had taken on himself the curse of all (Gal. 3.13). Then he saw
that he was persecuting, indeed crucifying Christ, and joined

---

[6] T. Stylianopoulos, *Justin Martyr and the Mosaic Law* (Montana, 1975), 165–8.

Christ on the cross (Gal. 2:19f.). Paul is concerned with the ultimate mystery of the atonement; from a belief that the two curses (failure to keep the whole Law and crucifixion) were cumulative, he moves to the belief that the second cancelled the first. For this reason he neither needed nor desired to know anything but Christ and him crucified (1 Cor. 2:2).

Neglect of the Mosaic Law is not trivial (*dial.* 95f.), for the cursing of Christians in synagogues bears fruit, according to their enemies, in the persecution which Christians suffer. The curse on the crucified Jesus intensifies the curse on those who follow him. Justin is dependent on Galatians for these texts;[7] but his use of them is different and their relevance is due to their continuing place in Jewish polemic more than to Justin's appropriation of Paul. The Galatian problem was more complex than that of Justin; those who had begun in spirit, were moving backwards to the flesh. Justin's Jews, he believed, had begun in the flesh, and were not prepared to move anywhere.

Tertullian's enthusiasm for the old dispensation provides a more complex picture; parts of the Law were plainly temporary but parts had permanent value. The observance of the sabbath was not a permanent requirement (*Jud.* 4.1). On the other hand the command to love one's enemies is in the Old as in the New Testament; even the law of retaliation can be consistent with the kindness of Jesus (*Marc.* 4.16.1f.). The ceremonial law was abrogated by the creator himself (*Marc.* 5.4.6), who preferred the circumcision of the heart because spirit took precedence over letter (*Marc.* 5.13.7). The limits of the Mosaic Law became evident when the thunder of the gospel shook the old foundations. The apostle insisted that the only parts which had a claim on Christians were those which concerned sacrifice, fornication and blood (*pud.* 12.3f.). All sex outside marriage is forbidden by both Testaments, Old and New, and adultery is linked with idolatry as a form of disloyalty (*pud.* 5.1f.).

There were differences of opinion over whether food offered to idols could be eaten by Christians. Some followed Paul in arguing that an idol was nothing and therefore sacrificial food

---

[7] *Ibid.*, 103–8.

was not contaminated. Others saw food offered to idols as part of a confession of allegiance to those idols. To eat such food was to confess the idol to whom it had been dedicated. Justin insists that true Christians do not eat food offered to idols; but he acknowledges that some dubious Christians commit this error (*dial.* 35). Yet, on general observation of the Law, he takes a more tolerant line than Paul: if a Christian keeps the Law for the sake of his own conscience and does not seek to impose its requirements on others, then he does no wrong.

New law

Law is, in the Bible, the way which God enables and requires. In the Old Testament, law begins from Sinai, is confirmed and developed by Deuteronomic and priestly writers until it is finally linked with the order of creation. At the same time there is a growing awareness of Israel's fallibility and need for renewal. The prophets Isaiah, Micah, Jeremiah and Ezekiel point to a new revelation which will go out from Zion, first to Israel, and then to the whole world. The Zion Torah is the eschatological fulfilment of the Sinai Torah. The two are never reconciled and, despite the transmission of the traditions of Zion Torah, Jewish legal theology is tied firmly to Sinai as the basis of life and faith. From this tension within the Old Testament, we may proceed to the New Testament theology of law.

Jesus teaches the twofold love command with the dialectic of the great antitheses (Matt. 5:21–48); he challenges ritual purity and the sabbath command. As Messiah and son of man, he fulfils the Sinai Torah and brings the Zion Torah. His gift of God's righteousness brings a new order, which threatens the law of Moses by which he is cursed and crucified. God confirms his work by the resurrection, and his community proclaims the end of the Mosaic Law. Matthew and James show that some Christians are still able to promote a synthesis of Mosaic Law and faith in Christ, under the theme of the love command. But other Christians (followers of Stephen and the writer to the Hebrews) see the eschatological law of Jesus as a new beginning, which supersedes the limits and claim of the old law. Paul stands in the tradition of Stephen and sees his apostolate tied to the end of the Mosaic Law. His theology may be summarised under four headings:

1 The Christian community lives, through the death and resurrection of Jesus, already under the new covenant of Jer. 31:31–4.
2 A new age of freedom from the Law of Moses has begun.
3 This freedom must be defended in the holy spirit under the law of Christ (Gal. 6:2).
4 The messianic Torah of Christ, with the love command and decalogue, fulfils the intention of the Sinai Torah.

By his sacrifice on the cross, Jesus ends the Mosaic Law and inaugurates his law of Zion; the creative wisdom of God is to be found in the new spiritual law of Christ (Rom. 8:2). Quite independently, John declares the new commandment of Jesus (John 13:34) which offers the same dialectic as was found in Paul.[8]

Irenaeus and Tertullian reflect the New Testament account of a new law. The prophets pointed to something new (*haer.* 4.17.1–5), to a new universal law which went outside one nation (*haer.* 4.9.2). The antitheses of the Sermon on the Mount go, in the presence of God, beyond an overt action to the desire which is its spring (*haer.* 4.13.1). The new law is a law of freedom surpassing the servitude of the old (*haer.* 4.13.2). The prophets foretold (*Jud.* 3.7) and Jesus brought (*Jud.* 6.2f.) a new and spiritual law.

The success of the case for continuity between law and gospel is developed in a recent study.[9] The Apostolic Fathers continue the strong nomism of the synoptic Gospels. In the face of coming judgement, demands are heightened, inward motives judged and ascetic rules required. Ethics gains ground and Jesus becomes a Greek moral teacher rather than a Rabbi.[10] This new element depends on the realised fulfilment of prophecy, so that

---

[8] Here we stand closer to the teaching of Jesus and we should not try to harmonise Matthew and James with John and Paul, but use the former as moderating influences. See P. Stuhlmacher, Das Gesetz als Thema biblischer Theologie, in *Versöhnung, Gesetz und Gerechtigkeit* (Göttingen, 1981), 136–65.
[9] Hasler, *Gesetz und Evangelium*.　　　　　　　　[10] *Ibid.*, 42.

the old scheme of promise and fulfilment loses one part of its structure.[11] Consequent legalism in Hermas (*sim.* 5.2.7 and 5.3.3) may be deplored, but the reasons for it must be respected.

The new law, which is Christ, stands under the necessity of one God and is universal. As Torah from Zion, it is new in fulfilment of what was promised of old. Justin (*dial.* 11) begins from the necessity of one God who replaced the law of Horeb with the 'eternal and final law which is Christ'. This law goes out from the same God (Isa. 51:4f.) and is the new covenant which he promised (Jer. 31:31f.). As Christ is the new law, covenant and hope, so his faithful followers are the true and spiritual Israel, who have been led to the one God by the crucified Messiah.

The newness of the covenant, says Clement, points to the 'one and only God', who has been known by Greeks, Jews and Christians in three different ways (*str.* 6.5.39). The Christian way is new and spiritual. A 'new' covenant requires one God whereas a different covenant would point to a different God. Tertullian makes the same point against Marcion (*Marc.* 1.20f.). There is one God because the same creator said he would do a new thing (Isa. 43:19) and would make a new covenant (Jer. 31:31f.). The God of the law is the God of Christ. Christians disagree on many points of discipline but there is never any dispute about God (*Marc.* 1.21.4). There are plainly differences in documents, precepts and law; but these do not compromise the 'one and same God' who arranged and foretold the Torah from Zion (*Marc.* 4.1.3).

The new law is universal. Justin tells of God's word, the Zion Torah which goes out to all by its own power, through twelve illiterate apostles, to every human race (1 *apol.* 39; Isa. 2:3). Clement calls on the Greeks (*prot.* 1) to leave Helicon and Cithaeron, and come to Zion where truth, wisdom and the holy choir of the prophets now radiate light and salvation. The word and athlete from heaven, having run his race, has been crowned as champion of the universe. Tertullian tells Marcion of the mountain or eminence of the lord and the house of God which

---

[11] *Ibid.*, 48.

is Christ and which will tower over all other powers (Isa. 2:3). To it shall come all nations to walk in his 'way' which is 'the new law and word in Christ', and to show peace and moderation instead of hostility (*Marc.* 3.21.3). The power of the new law is invincible and superior to all philosophy. God's teaching went out from Judaea, not from Greece, and was preached by fishermen, not by Sophists; its truth and heavenly wisdom can shatter the falsehood of philosophy (*an.* 3.3).

The fulfilment of Isaiah 2 and Micah 4 may be observed in the lives of Christians under the law which was dispersed by the apostles. Swords have become ploughshares for those who once were warlike, but now live in peaceful piety; they suffer in the hope of Messiah's second coming when the rest of the prophecy will be fulfilled (*dial.* 109f.). The new covenant is fulfilled (*haer.* 4.33.14) by the new heart and spirit, by the freedom and the new wine of the gospel. The way in the desert and streams in dry land (Isa. 43:19f.) point to faith in Christ which brings the way of righteousness and streams of the holy spirit. Tertullian explains to Marcion the logic of fulfilment. The end of time belonged to God as much as did the beginning. So he was able to wait until the fullness of time to send his son, to make the crooked straight and to begin the new law from Zion (*Marc.* 5.4.3). To the Jews, Tertullian explains that the new law, foretold by Isaiah, has been fulfilled in Christ, and in his followers who replace war with peace (*Jud.* 3.10).

ONE GOD, ONE COMMAND

Summing-up

The one commandment of one God sums up the whole law, the command to love God and neighbour. In Mark (12:29–33), the scribe who asks the question, repeats the words of Jesus with their insistence that there is one lord.[12] It is an emphatic confession of one God, in opposition to pagan polytheism.[13] In

---

[12] E. Osborn, The love command in second-century Christian writing, *The Second Century*, 1981, 223–43.

[13] G. Bornkamm, Das Doppelgebot der Liebe, in *Geschichte und Glaube*, 1 (München, 1968), 39.

Matthew 22:35–40 and Luke 10:25–8, the setting is con-
troversial and eschatological: the kingdom of God brings the
royal command of love and forgiveness and the new age is love
itself, powerfully present and creative in history. The love
command sums up the whole law. Justin argues, against the
background of a universal sense of justice, that Jesus properly
brought all righteousness and piety together, 'For he who loves
God with all his heart and might, being full of a mind that is
turned to God will honour no other as God... He who loves his
neighbour as himself will desire for him the good that he desires
for himself... Now a man's neighbour is none other than man,
that living rational creature with similar feelings to himself'
(*dial.* 93).

Clement of Alexandria quotes a saying, 'You have seen your
brother, you have seen your God' as a pointer to the love
command (*str.* 2.15.71). Law is defended with the help of
Heraclitus and Socrates, because all law is summed up in the
love of God and neighbour (*str.* 4.3.10). The love command
describes the good life which the philosophers have sought
(*prot.* 11.115), and produces the heavenly feast which is the
kingdom of God (*paed.* 2.1.6). There is nothing higher than love
and there is no other way to ascend to the highest truth
(*str.* 4.18.111). In the second century the love command
continues the claims of the New Testament for the summing up
of all commands in one. From Stoicism and Platonism, the
command is shown to be universal and rational. Paul's concern
for the unity of God is joined to the Platonic vision at the summit
of love.[14]

Universal law

Tertullian argues against the Jews (*Jud.* 2.1f.) that the
universal law which commands the love of God could not
possibly belong to Israel alone. This primordial law, the source
of all the commandments, was given to Adam and Eve, and
would have been quite adequate had it been kept. If Adam and
Eve had loved God, they would not have disobeyed; if they had

---

[14] Osborn, The love command, 237.

loved their neighbour they would not have brought death upon themselves. For Tertullian, again, the love command is a proof against Marcion, of the continuous action of one God, from Moses, to Christ and the apostles (*Marc.* 5.8.9f.).

Identity of commands

For Irenaeus, the unity of God is proved from the identity of the commands given by Moses and Jesus. Paul saw love as the eternal perfection of the law, 'He who loves God is perfect both in this age and in that to come. For we never cease from loving God, but the more we continue to gaze upon him, the more we love him' (*haer.* 4.12.2). Christ is the end of the law, 'and how could he be the end of the law if he were not also its beginning?' When Jesus came, he declared neither another God the father, nor another son or mother, nor a pleroma. He taught his disciples to obey the precepts which God had commanded from the beginning (*haer.* 4.12.4, 5).

The love command clarifies the claim of the philosophers that there is only one good. Plato saw that the brotherhood of men could only be realised through acceptance of one God and teacher. Within God's family, brotherly love points beyond itself to love of God (*str.* 5.14.97f.). The change from old to new covenant is a change from fear to love, brought about by the incarnation. The same teacher who once said, 'You shall fear the Lord your God', now says, 'You shall love the Lord your God' (*paed.* 1.7.59). The new commandment fulfils all divine commands, is written on the heart and therefore cures sin at its source (*prot.* 10.108f.). Love of neighbour excludes the wearing of jewels, for God gave all things to all men and it is an outrage for some to live in luxury when others live in poverty (*paed.* 2.12.120). The rich young man, who came to Jesus, had kept all the commands except that of love to neighbour. Perfection required that he should share his possessions in love (*str.* 3.6.55).[15] Clement answers the objection that he expects too much and that not all can be philosophers: how can anyone

---

[15] This does not involve sexual promiscuity as the followers of Carpocrates claim (*str.* 3.4.29). See E. Osborn, *Ethical patterns in early Christian thought* (Cambridge, 1976), 46–9.

love God and neighbour and not be a philosopher? It is not a
matter of reading and study but of living and loving. Faith, love
and following God are open to all (*paed.* 3.11.78).

Love and the body

Tertullian saw danger in the love command where it might be
used to evade fasting, and serve as a specious argument to
protect the appetites of carnal Christians (*iei.* 2.7f.). On the
other hand, flesh is the neighbour who must be loved;
resurrection is certain because God could never abandon the
flesh which is his image, the work of his hands, and the sister of
Christ, to destruction (*res.* 9.1f.). A woman's clothing is important because immodesty can harm the lustful observer. 'Are
we then to exhibit ourselves so that others might perish, when it
is said on this account: you shall love your neighbour as
yourself. It is surely wrong to pay so much attention to one's
own affairs and not to care for the other' (*cult.* 2.2.5). Mutual
practical love is the distinctive mark of Christians (*ap.* 39.7).
While the human race is a unity, 'with how much more reason
are they called and considered brothers, who recognize one God
as their common father' (*ap.* 39.9).

Love of enemies

Grace is most clear in the love of enemies which, for Justin, is
proof that the day of the lord has already joined lion and lamb
in peace (*dial.* 85.7). The command reveals the truth about God
that he is good, just and creator, and the truth about men that
they are his children and brothers to one another (*dial.* 96.2, 3).
Christians pray for their persecutors, with the goodness of the
God who sends sunshine and rain on saint and sinner alike
(*dial.* 96.2). Clement speaks of the new creation in Christ, who
turns sunset into sunrise, who reflects the father's goodness
which sends rain and sprinkles the dew of truth on all
(*prot.* 11.114). A miracle of the last days is the life of the true
Christian, who does good to others independently of their
deserts and their response; he never acts for human or divine
reward (*str.* 4.22.137).

Tertullian is ruefully aware that God commands that enemies should always be loved and never cursed (*spect.* 16.6). This is part of his apocalyptic Christianity.[16] Love of enemies is distinctively Christian and derives from the one God. 'For this is our perfect and proper form of goodness, not something which is shared in common with others. For all love their friends, but only Christians love their enemies. So they who know the future and see the signs of things to come much preach unwelcome truths out of love, and for the salvation of enemies' (*scap.* 1.3). As Justin had pointed to the newness of love for enemies in contrast to harlots who love and tax-collectors who give for the sake of reward (1 *apol.* 15), so when we pray, 'Hallowed be thy name', we pray for all, including our enemies, in simple obedience to our lord (*or.* 3.4).

To summarise: One God means one law, which completes and corrects the law of Horeb. This law is summed up in the command to love one God, to love neighbour and to love enemy. The new law which is Christ comes from the same and only God.

ONE GOD AND THE SOVEREIGNTY OF GOOD

Because God is one and God is good, the only path to goodness is that of becoming like God.

Clement begins his account of *assimilation to God* with an exposition of Plato's twofold end and Paul's twofold hope (*str.* 2.22).[17] Elsewhere, Apuleius distinguished between the good or God and the virtues which flow from this source[18] and Justin distinguished carefully between what is participated and what participates (*dial.* 6.1).[19] This distinction does for Clement what eschatology did for Paul: it limits man's present salvation and contradicts the Gnostics for whom God and elect man were

---

[16] M. Spanneut, *Tertullien et les premiers moralistes africains* (Gembloux, 1969), 55.

[17] See Osborn, *The philosophy of Clement of Alexandria* (Cambridge, 1957), 84–94, and *Ethical patterns*, 67.

[18] Apuleius, *De Platone*, 2.1.220: 'prima bona esse deum summum mentemque illam, quam νοῦν idem vocat; secundum ea, quae ex priorum fonte profluerent, esse animi virtutes, prudentiam, iustitiam, iustitiam, fortitudinem'.

[19] See also on this point Plutarch, *Adv. Colotem* 15, *mor.* 1115D.

of the same substance. Clement pursues the theme of the twofold
hope in scripture, finding the finest statement at Prov. 1:33, 'he
shall dwell trusting in hope'.[20]

Doxography and exposition

Clement uses a widespread tradition concerning assimilation, in
his own way, without losing a mass of earlier development.[21] His
doxographical material, though based on other works, is so
arranged as to anticipate later references to Paul. He acknowledges a variety of opinion on the meaning of image and
likeness. Here he indicates two places in Plato (*Laws* 715f. and
Theaet. 176f.) and later (*str.* 5.14.94) he will give an account of
Timaeus 90. Other references in Plato might be found; Arius
Didymus cites *Republic* 613 while Alcinous points to *Phaedo* 82
and *Phaedrus* 248. It seems that the main doxographical tradition
on this theme comes through Eudorus of Alexandria. Plato had
left different directions within his diverse account. *Theaetetus*
points to religion and ethics, *Timaeus* to astronomy and *Laws* to
honouring the gods of the underworld after the gods of Olympus
(717). The first speaks of flight to God as becoming righteous
and holy with discernment. There is a proper limit to man's
divine assimilation.[22] *Laws* speaks of following the God who
holds the beginning, end and middle of all things, and who
exercises justice and measure. Clement begins from the relevant
texts, comments on particular points and produces his own
statement. Plato's 'ancient saying' indicates a debt to the Old
Testament. Clement's justification of humility rebuts the
accusation of Celsus that Christians had misunderstood Plato
on this point. Clement handles the text of *Laws* and *Theaetetus*
with greater attention to detail than did Middle Platonic
writers. He introduces eschatology and uses the Stoic distinction
between σκοπός and τέλος. The goal is to be just and pious with

---

[20] The 'trusting' is supplied by Clement and is not found in LXX.
[21] See the excellent account of D. Wyrwa, *Die christliche Platonaneignung in den Stromateis
des Clemens von Alexandrien* (Berlin, 1983), 173–89, and also E. Osborn, Paul and Plato
in second-century ethics, *St Patr.* (Berlin, 1984), 474–85.
[22] This anticipates a problem which Plotinus dealt with at some length: how can
human virtue consist in growing like God whose virtues are different from ours?

discernment, while the end is the fulfilment of the promises. Clement shows common ground between Plato and Paul. The twofold end of Plato (the good life and the goodness in which it shares) is like the twofold hope of Paul (present hope which is not ashamed because it has received God's love, and the future object of that hope).[23]

The next theme of Clement is the priority of the ethical demand, as expressed in the *Theaetetus*. This is abundantly supported from scripture. Clement is able to blend Paul with Plato because he faces antinomian problems with heretical Gnostics which are similar to those faced by Paul with Corinthian enthusiasts. For this reason he qualifies the *Theaetetus* reference to ὁμοίωσις by a reference to ταπεινοφροσύνη which is explicit for Plato in *Laws* 4.

Assimilation is, for Clement, plainly ethical and its chief virtue is ἀπάθεια which means for him the exclusion of sinful passion (*str.* 2.20.103; *str.* 4.23.147; *str.* 7.3.13; *str.* 7.11.64; *str.* 2.19.97). Freedom from passion produces unity, so that the believer becomes one like God (*str.* 4.23.152; μοναδικός). κάθαρσις and ἐποπτεία also play their part. In *str.* 4.23.151, Clement speaks of ἀπάθεια but moves closer to Plotinus' religious (rather than ethical) interpretation when he speaks of θεωρία (*str.* 4.23.151). God is seen only by those who are like him (*str.* 5.1.13).[24]

Assimilation means that the aim of Clement's ethic is the ever closer restoration of the divine image which has been renewed in Christ, free from the scars and distortions of sin.[25] Imitation or following of God means obedience to his commands and the recovery of his likeness. Plato and the Old Testament had already been joined by Philo and one section of Clement draws on Philo.[26] The Pythagorean call for man to become one is taken up by Clement in the call to ἀπάθεια. Other qualities

[23] Rom. 5:5 and 8:24.
[24] H. Merki, ΟΜΟΙΩΣΙΣ ΘΕΩΙ. *Von der platonischen Angleichung an Gott zur Gottähnlichkeit bei Gregor von Nyssa* (Freiburg CH, 1952).
[25] W. Völker, *Der wahre Gnostiker nach Clemens Alexandrinus*, *TU* 57 (Berlin, 1952), 580–97.
[26] *str.* 2.19.97 follows *virt.* 168. Indeed there are Philonic parallels from *str.* 2.18.78 to *str.* 2.19.100.

which produce likeness to God are ἀγάπη (*str.* 6.12.102), χρηστότης (*str.* 4.14.95), ἀμνησικακία (*str.* 7.14.86 and *str.* 4.22.137), εὐποιΐα as ἕξις (*str.* 6.7.60), γνῶσις (*ecl.* 33.1f.) and ἀγάπη (*q.d.s.* 7.3). The soul of the righteous man becomes a third divine image (*str.* 7.3.16).[27] The life of the sinless perfect Lord is the pattern, indeed the mirror in which we look to adorn (κοσμοῦντα) ourselves (*q.d.s.* 21.7). Assimilation is also the way to adoption, deification and immortality.[28]

Perfection

If there is one God, and he alone is good, then the one way should aim at perfection. So the Christian claim for moral excellence is supported by ever more radical moral demands. The teaching of Jesus shows the rigour and lack of compromise which perfection requires. Eye is to be plucked out, or hand is to be cut off; love of enemies, giving to those who are in need, kindness and mercy are all part of the Christian way. Adultery in the heart is condemned, marriage of divorced people is not allowed (1 *apol.* 15). The continence of Christians is well known and any accusations of promiscuity are without grounds. Justin tells of a Christian in Alexandria who sought permission to be made a eunuch (1 *apol.* 29). Justin's so-called second apology is occasioned by the drastic effect which the new morality of a Christian woman had upon her pagan husband (2 *apol.* 2).

To be a 'Christian' is Justin's boast and chief endeavour (2 *apol.* 13). The only criticism to be levelled against Christians is that they do not follow the Law of Moses. Apart from this there is nothing that can be objected against their behaviour. The accusations of cannibalism and promiscuity cannot be taken seriously. The demands of Christian perfection are recognised by outsiders. The precepts of the gospel, says Trypho, are too difficult (*dial.* 10). The claim of the Sermon on the Mount is a call to perfection. Perfection comes from a sense of the universal presence of God. God rules the whole of the life of the believer (*leg.* 31). Because of this sense of the presence of

---

[27] A similar idea is found in Paul: 1 Cor. 11:1; see *str.* 2.22.136.
[28] Völker, *Der wahre Gnostiker*, 597.

God, Christian moral performance is far beyond that of other
persuasions; this is achieved by careful observance of teaching
and also by scrupulous avoidance of any occasion for sin
(*leg.* 32). Why, then, are Christians slandered and accused of
immorality? Their moral excellence invites criticism from their
inferiors. Yet how absurd it is, to claim that Christians eat
human flesh, when Christians believe that bodies will rise again!
Christians stay away from gladiatorial fights because they
believe that it is wrong to kill (*leg.* 34f.).

The free response of Christians is a total dedication to their
lord. They do not merely give a tenth of what they have, but
freely offer all (*haer.* 4.18.2).[29] This total giving is the purity of
heart by which man sees God and finds life. The sight of God
brings life (*haer.* 4.20.2), and man passes into God because God
has first passed into man (*haer.* 4.20.5). We receive now, says
Irenaeus, a portion of the spirit. To prepare ourselves for the
incorruption of eternity we become used to carrying God within
us (*haer.* 5.8.1). The temple must be cleansed and pleasures be
replaced by self-control so that the friend of Christ may become
worthy of God's kingdom (*prot.* 11).

Perfection is not a distant goal but begins now. In growing
towards it, we remain gentle with the simplicity of the young, an
eternal simplicity which lives in perpetual springtime. We have
joy as the children of Christ; our king looks down, from above,
to our laughter and thanksgiving (*paed.* 1.5.22f.). Christ, who is
our pattern, gives us illumination at baptism and brings us to
become sons of God. From sonship we move to perfection and
immortality. Salvation is life and light. There is no half-way
house between light and darkness and the end belongs to those
who believe and who will rise again. To reach the end means
receiving the promise that has already been made (*paed.* 1.6.28).

---

[29] The one God guarantees the validity of certain prescriptions of the Mosaic Law. Just
as Israel brought offerings, so the church brings offerings; but the former were servile
while the latter are free. While God is one and the same, the gifts may differ. Those
who have received freedom, give all (*haer.* 4.18). Hence there were two dangers
attached to Christian tithing: the total demand was limited and the limit was fixed
by Mosaic Law. The freedom of the disciple was no longer dominant. Hence tithing
was linked specifically to the humanitarian activities of the community and seen as
a protection from servitude to Mammon. L. Vischer, Die Zehntforderung in der
alten Kirche, *ZKG* 8, 70 (1959), 217.

The Christian moves on to perfection in the way of Christ (*paed.* 1.6.52). His instructor guides the child through the storms of life, both steering his ship and sending the right wind to blow him in the true direction (*paed.* 1.7.54).

The unique perfection of the way is matched by the variety of the methods used to train the soul. There are thousands of instructions and thousands of warnings to keep the soul from wickedness (*paed.* 1.10.94). Simplicity remains, for we are stripped of pride and ostentation; we hold on to what is good and what is truly ours. We follow God in faith by confessing him who suffered, and doing good to men. Just as Jesus showed nothing extravagant, so our lives must always be simple. Simplicity or singleness should mark the servants of one God. Perfection is the path of oneness (*paed.* 2.3.38).

Sin must decrease in the life of the believer, for the continual repetition of penitence is not a Christian trait (*str.* 2.13.57). Blessedness comes to those whose sins are forgiven, and love hides a multitude of sins. There are three kinds of sin which are described in David and in Moses: walking in the council of the ungodly, standing in the way of sinners and sitting in the seat of pestilence. Sin is also understood in animal terms (*str.* 2.15.67f.), and, while all are called to perfection, the vision of truth is given only to the few. This is the conclusion of Plato and of Moses (*str.* 5.1.7).

Within the unity of the good life there are different degrees of achievement. It is better to know than to believe, and to be honoured after being saved is better than being saved. The many heavenly mansions indicate the upward path. He who has sinned after baptism, will be tormented when he sees the heights which others have attained; his punishments may cease, but grief at his lower level remains (*str.* 6.14.109). The different mansions are indicated by the numbers in the Gospel: thirty, sixty and a hundred. The perfect man is according to the image of the lord, not in shape or even in virtue, but, as a friend of God, he shares in the perfection of the gods, if he has reached the fullness of the gospel (*str.* 6.14.114).

The life of the true gnostic is marked by unity in all time. Always and in every place he prays and lives as king and priest,

aloof from worldly things and temptations, firm in the presence
of God. Fixed hours of prayer are wrong because the whole of
life belongs to God as a festival of prayer, praise and reading
(*str.* 7.7.35). Such a man is never caught off balance, but
possesses goodness firmly and without change. Eating, drinking,
marrying are necessary, but not the chief end of such a life
(*str.* 7.12.70). The lord's commands are fulfilled day and night
with joy and thanksgiving (*str.* 7.12.80). The Christian forgives
and forgets those who have sinned against him, and does good
deeds, as an instrument of God's goodness (*str.* 7.13.81).

Tertullian does not see perfection as a process of growth but
rather as a way of doing more than might be expected, going
beyond what has been asked. We must love our enemy, the
stranger, so that we may love our neighbour better. This
requirement, of what is not due, produces increase in the
benevolence which is due (*Marc.* 1.23.4). Perfection is linked
with love. Justin speaks about the care of Christians for one
another, in need, sickness or other distress (1 *apol.* 67). They
fulfil the law of God, loving their neighbours as themselves
(*dial.* 133).

Image and likeness

It is only possible for man to become like the one God, because
his soul is made in God's image. The soul is not unbegotten and
immortal in its own right as the Platonists claim (*dial.* 5); but it
can come to share in life as it becomes like God. The true and
spiritual disciple confesses one God, seeing the unity of the two
testaments (*haer.* 4.33.1f.). Made in God's image, man knows
good and evil. Obedience is good and disobedience is evil. God
made man. Man did not make God; but he may attain to
sharing in the glory of God. Yet, if man does not believe, and
flees from the hand of God, then he will not find perfection
(*haer.* 4.39.3). We are all sons of God by nature; but when it
comes to obedience and doctrine, only those are sons who
believe and do God's will. They alone receive God's inheritance
(*haer.* 4.41.2f.). Man is perfected by the outpouring of the spirit
and this is what it means to be in both the image and likeness of
God (*haer.* 5.6.1). As Christ rose in the flesh, so we also shall be

raised, our face will see his face, and we shall rejoice with joy unspeakable (*haer.* 5.7.1). From the beginning of time man has been shaped by the hands of God, the son and the spirit, that he might become the image and likeness of God (*haer.* 5.28.4). Godliness is knowledge of the truth and makes man like God, who is his only teacher (*prot.* 9). Man, who has received his soul from God, should belong entirely to him. He is made by him and he should not serve another master. So he should move from ignorance to knowledge, from folly to wisdom, from licence to self-restraint, from wickedness to righteousness and from godlessness to God. The alternatives are clear: God or the evil one, wisdom or idolatry, life or death. There is only one question: whether we should worship God and follow Christ (*prot.* 10.92f.).

The image of the divine word is a true man. This image becomes like the divine word, so that truth and purity are found (*prot.* 10.98). Following true knowledge, Christians draw themselves to God as to an anchor. They seem to draw God to themselves, but it is God who holds them firmly and draws them to himself (*str.* 4.23.152). The Greeks knew about man's relation to one God. The saying 'Know thyself' has many explanations. It shows man that he is mortal and that wealth, fame and honour do not matter; his essence concerns his relationship to God (*str.* 5.4.23). So the true Christian is a divine image which enshrines the eternal word of God, one saviour individually to each and in common to all (*str.* 7.3.16). Such a man is prudent and righteous, wise and courageous. He is the true athlete who overcomes his passions and receives his prize from the son of God (*str.* 7.3.20). Another interpretation sees, in the claim 'Know thyself', an awareness of why we were born. God may be obeyed through his commandments which declare his salvation, and confessed in faithfulness and love. The saviour receives kind acts done to men as personal favours and feels any injury inflicted on his believers (*str.* 7.3.20f.). How can man be a living image of the lord? He does not have the outward form, but he is a symbol of power and he preaches the same message as does the lord, giving testimony to the truth by what he does and what he says. He does always what is right, in word, action and thought. So his life becomes a total offering to one God (*str.* 7.9.52f.). The word has given to us a post which we may not desert, for he is the guide of knowledge and of life. Many men have not even asked whether there was someone who should be followed, who he might be, and how he is to be followed; but this is the true word, and the life of the believer consists in following a God who brings all things to an end in his righteousness (*str.* 7.16.100).

It is important to remember the ambiguity of the concepts of assimilation and perfection in Clement. He is careful to distance himself from 'some of our people' who distinguish and define carefully the image and likeness of Gen. 1:26. His own position is much more open. On the one hand he may divide clearly likeness from image; on the other hand he may identify them as either innate human reason or as a higher gift of grace. Ambiguity is also to be found in Irenaeus.[30]

Assimilation and one God

Assimilation to God becomes, in Christian hands, a wider and richer concept. All are made in the image of God and all, not just a few, can achieve his likeness. This likeness is more than the flight of a solitary soul to a solitary God; to become one with God is to be the disciple of Jesus and to find in him the divine fullness. For Irenaeus, the way to perfection may be freely chosen by all; this is his polemic against Gnosticism. The grace of God is ever present to aid in the recovery of the divine likeness.[31] Irenaeus has confronted philosophy chiefly in its 'bastardized Gnostic form';[32] but Clement knows the philosophers and uses them readily. Assimilation to God means overthrowing plurality and passions through the intense unity of divine love. Clement's account of the true gnostic sounds philosophical at a first reading; in the end the philosophy is

---

[30] See, on Clement, A. Mayer, *Das Gottesbild im Menschen nach Clemens von Alexandrien* (Rome, 1942), 5–32, and Wyrwa, *Platonaneignung*, 175; on Irenaeus see Daniélou, *Message*, 398–407.

[31] See J. M. Rist, *Human value* (Leiden, 1982), 157f., where the philosophical consciousness of Irenaeus and Tertullian is underestimated. Sagnard and Fredouille have shown the influence of classical thought on these two writers.

[32] *Ibid.*, 158.

swallowed up in a festival of Christian love in the home, in the
fields or on the sea. All of this gives value to human life in a way
no philosopher has done. Despite the limitations of a new
concept which leaves some unreformed pockets, the path to
perfection is open to all, men and women alike.[33] Differences
remain, for women are to cook and not to wrestle (*paed.* 3.10);
but these differences are overcome in the divine likeness which
is neither male nor female. Faith and knowledge are as
inseparable as the father and the son. Faith has opened the door
to all, the son has revealed the divine likeness in a wealth of
glory.

One recent account links Clement's concern for wisdom to his
competence as a teacher and the dominance of the παίδευσις
motif. He was, it is claimed, the first Christian teacher to write
about a Christian view of teaching and was chiefly concerned
with the growth of Christian wisdom.[34] There is nothing esoteric
in his 'true philosopher' or 'true gnostic'; he is thinking of the
full development of each Christian. Avoiding other ideals of
perfection like intellectualism, asceticism and enthusiasm, he
presents an ideal which, by the grace of the one God, is open to
all Christians. Christ is the pattern and following Christ means
education and training. It is by learning, not by nature, that
goodness is achieved (*str.* 1.6.34). Wisdom means to know what
to fear and what not to fear (*str.* 2.18.79). Wealth is a gift of
God (*q.d.s.* 13; 15; 14); but true wealth is righteousness
(*paed.* 3.4.36), excess of virtuous deeds (*str.* 6.12.99) and above
all, wisdom (*str.* 5.4.23). All the virtues unite with faith and
knowledge to produce wisdom.[35] The basis of faith and
knowledge illuminates the later problem of tradition and
reason. Long ago, it was argued on the basis of Clement's
thought that the only basis for European culture must be
classical παιδεία and Christianity.[36] Clement was praised widely
during and after the Enlightenment, when his ideas on wisdom
were distorted to fit the contemporary debate. Clement's ideal

[33] For inconsistencies see *paed.* 2.2.33 and 2.11.117; cf. *str.* 4.8. See Rist, *Human value.*
[34] A. Koffas, *Die Sophia-Lehre bei Klemens von Alexandreia* (Frankfurt, 1982).
[35] *Ibid.*, 211.
[36] By A. Korais (1748–1833); see A. Papaderos, METAKENOSIS, *Das kulturelle
Zentralproblem des neuen Griechenlands bei Korais und Oikonomos* (Mainz, 1962).

of the true gnostic springs solely from belief in, nearness and likeness to, one God. 'If he then possesses wisdom and wisdom is something divine, he participates in the ἀνενδεής and is himself ἀνενδεής' (*str.* 7.7.47). He takes the uniqueness of God seriously, and, by adoption, forms his life in God's likeness (*str.* 2.19.97). Wisdom, for Clement, is an account of man as God made him and as God intends him to be (*str.* 7.14.86). Only by the divine instruction (ἡ κατὰ τὸν θεὸν παιδαγωγία) can the end be reached (*paed.* 1.7.54).

Finally, hope guides the whole enterprise to perfection. For Clement, to live was to hope, since those who had no hope were dead (*str.* 4.22.144). Hope is like blood to faith and without it, faith cannot live (*paed.* 1.6.38). Yet the perfection of love goes beyond hope for there is nothing left to be fulfilled (*str.* 6.9.73f.). The divine word leads safely from fear and hope to the promised haven of rest.[37]

Tertullian points the martyrs to the holy spirit who has led them into prison. This same spirit will lead them to their lord (*mart.* 1.3). The opposite to righteousness is idolatry which can be practised without a visible idol and is the summing up of all unrighteousness (*idol.* 2.5). God has condemned the making and worship of idols (*idol.* 4.1). To make an idol is to sacrifice one's ability or ingenuity, and to offer the sweat of one's body to the idol; this is a form of worship (*idol.* 6.3). It is wrong to come, from the work of making idols, into the church and there to give to God the hands which have made idols (*idol.* 7.1). Idolatry is the opposite to assimilation, for it finds the likeness of God in the wrong way: it reverses the true direction by making God in the image of fallen man instead of restoring man to the likeness of God. Yet wayward Christians compromise with idolatry, lighting lamps and placing wreaths on their doors (*idol.* 15.1). The worship of pagan gods has been forbidden and will be punished, for idolatry is the worst sin of all (*scorp.* 4.1); it is wrong to accompany the birth of a soul with pagan rites because their influence is evil (*an.* 39.2). A Christian cannot be a soldier because no one can serve two masters (*idol.* 19.2). Patience

[37] L. Padovese, La speranza 'del vero gnostico' secondo Clemente di Alessandria, *Laur.* 25 (1984), 131–51.

keeps all the decrees of God and strengthens faith, peace, charity and humility. Patience rules the flesh, preserves the spirit and bridles the tongue (*pat.* 15.2).

The passions are the strongest challenge to the Christian life because they present a multiple threat to the single love of God. One God requires one love (*str.* 4.23.148; 5.4.19). To free the soul from the claims of the body (*str.* 4.3.12), Clement's mature Christian follows the ascetic way and lives in the city as if he were solitary in the desert (*str.* 7.7.36). He despises the things of the world, because he serves his lord alone (*str.* 7.12.78) and because he grows like the God who needs nothing and is free from passion (*str.* 2.18.81). Freedom from passion is all; the presence or absence of earthly goods is a secondary matter.

The issues are clear. There is one gospel and one Jesus who will, at the last day, deny every one who has denied him and acknowledge everyone who has acknowledged him (*cor.* 11.5). God's property should be kept clean, and fit for him who will crown it as he chooses (*cor.* 15.1). The soul contains some of that original divine goodness with which God made it. What is derived from God is not extinguished but merely obscured. Some men are very bad and others are very good. God remains without sin and the only man without sin is Christ, since Christ is also God (*an.* 41.3).

Growing like God means holding to unity. We come from one marriage, in the case of Adam according to the flesh, or in the case of Christ according to the spirit. One God implies one wife, one Christ and one church (*cast.* 5.3). Leviticus insists on one marriage. Such unity is opposed to plurality and this places an obligation on both priests and laity (*cast.* 7.1f.). We admit one marriage as we do one God (*mon.* 1.2). We have one father, God, and one mother, the church. We are called priests by Christ and are called to one marriage in accordance with the first law of God (*mon.* 7.9); when we turn from law to gospel we find the same requirements of monogamy and continence (*mon.* 8.1). The first Adam had one wife; the second Adam had none. If second marriage is ever to be justified, we should need to find a third Adam who had two wives (*mon.* 17.5). So likeness to the only God remains the ground for a mass of ethical injunctions which are held together by the revelation of the perfect likeness in Christ.

Martyrdom

Two tendencies

There were two main tendencies in early Christian ethics: the way of becoming like Christ through cross and martyrdom, and the way of life in God's world by a positive defence of creation against heretics. Both were governed by obedience or assimilation to one God. The stronger tendency was the drive to martyrdom; only as Christians reacted against the extremes of dualists like Marcion and the Gnostics, was an adequate account given of the goodness of creation.

Christians, argued Justin, did no wrong; but because of the name of Christ they were punished, as if criminals, by death (1 *apol.* 24). In the Jewish war, Bar Cochba gave orders that Christians should be punished, unless they denied Christ and uttered blasphemy (1 *apol.* 31). A Christian faces death without fear because he knows that all must die and that he will be free from suffering and need to all eternity (1 *apol.* 57). The behaviour of Christians in the face of death convinced Justin that they were not immoral people and that he should become one of them (2 *apol.* 12). The restraint and self-control of Christians was well known and therefore it was foolish to accuse them of promiscuity (1 *apol.* 29).[38]

The martyr and Jesus

Early Christian martyrdom cannot be assimilated to other forms, because it is tied so closely to Jesus.[39] His charge to his disciples points to total dependence on the holy spirit (Matt. 10:19f. *par*), to unconditional fear of God (Matt. 10:32f.

---

[38] Justin uses much Stoic terminology without a real acceptance of Stoic values; against the rational fatalism of the Stoics, Justin defends the oppressed, poor and insecure. P. Montini, Elementi di filosofia stoica in S. Giustino, *Aquinas*, 28 (1985), 475.

[39] 'Jesu Auftreten, Predigt und Tod sind die entscheidende Voraussetzung für die Idee und Wirklichkeit des Martyriums', H. von Campenhausen, *Die Idee des Martyriums in der alten Kirche* (Göttingen, 1964), 5.

par) and to unity in confession and suffering with the lord who
sends them. Paul sees the matter as Christ's apostle, who is not
concerned to please men, and who must suffer because of what
he preaches. Sharing in the suffering of Christ is a special
compulsion for Paul, the former persecutor, and becomes the
basis of virtue.

Ignatius of Antioch intensifies the longing of the martyr for
his goal, and develops the notions of sacrifice and imitation.
Through suffering, the martyr is united with Christ and
immediately joined to God. He is θεοφόρος as well as χριστοφόρος.
His goal is not merely to be in Christ but to gain God,[40] having
boldness to enter the divine presence,[41] and to mediate between
ordinary believers and Christ.

By the middle of the second century, the solidarity of the
martyr with Christ goes further (*Acta Perp. et al.* 15.3), when the
miraculous presence of Christ turns the religious meaning of
martyrdom in a new direction.[42] In answer to the accusation of
Basilides that, if God be just, martyrs must suffer for their own
sins, Clement argues that as Christ himself drank the cup, so do
the martyrs, not just for their sins but for the sins of others.
Origen develops the idea of sacrifice and applies it as Clement
does: the death of Christ has universal application while some
particular churches have been entrusted to particular martyrs.

Different views

In *Stromateis* 4, Clement speaks of the martyr as the perfect
Christian, who follows the way of faithfulness and loyalty to
God, reaching perfection in the complete work of love. True
martyrdom is knowledge of the only true God (*str.* 4.4.13); all
may earn its glorious crown, whether they be men or women,
slaves or free (*str.* 4.8.58). The martyrs show the patience, love
and perseverance which are commended in scriptures
(*str.* 4.16.99f.). The struggle of the martyr is part of the spiritual
warfare which Paul describes: heaven is filled with good angels

[40] Cf. Paul, Phil. 1:23; 2 Cor. 5:8, with Ignatius, *Eph.* 12:2; *Magn.* 14; *Trall.* 12:2;
13.3 *et passim.* See Campenhausen, *Idee Martyriums*, 78 and 69.
[41] E. Peterson, Zur Bedeutungsgeschichte von ΠΑΡΡΗΣΙΑ, in *FS R. Seeberg*, (1929),
283–97.   [42] Campenhausen, *Idee Martyriums*, 91.

and the opposing forces of the devil. So the battle goes on and the contest requires constant vigilance (*str.* 5.14.93).

Tertullian gives a more rigorous account. His exhortation to martyrs assures them of the noble struggle and eternal prize for which they have been chosen. The holy spirit trains them for citizenship in heaven and everlasting glory. God directs them closely and their one concern must be the discipline of their minds and bodies (*mart.* 3.4). A Christian welcomes martyrdom because of the corruptness of the world; his only regret is that he has not been a Christian for a longer period. He glories in the confession of Christ, offers no defence when he is accused and gives thanks to God when condemned (*ap.* 1.12). Christians are wrongly accused, for they have committed no crime; there should be joy rather than surprise when a wise man becomes a Christian, for Christians live in a new and better way (*ap.* 3.1f.). Only bad emperors like Nero and Domitian have crucified Christians (*ap.* 5.3f.). Christians pray with their hands stretched out as on a cross, prepared to suffer unjust punishment for their name (*ap.* 50.1f.).

Persecution should never be a cause for flight or for evasion through bribery (*fug.* 12.1). He who fears, is not perfect in the love of God and he who flees from persecution, has fear not love (*fug.* 9.3f.). Peter and Paul share the common glory of martyrdom (*praescr.* 24.4). Martyrdom considers it good to be absent from the body and present with the lord; but this does not devalue the flesh (*res.* 43.3f.). The flesh of the martyr will wear his crown (*res.* 56.1).

Unlike Clement, Tertullian begins his account of the martyr from the sovereign will of God (*fug.* 1.2) and not from a portrait of the perfect Christian. The martyr is a soldier under God's command,[43] and has no immunity from fear and pain. Obedience to and dependence on God are his only strength (*fug.* 3.2). He does not choose, but is chosen for martyrdom (*fug.* 1–4), which is his happiness and profit (*scorp.* 2.1) for he gains eternity as a bargain (*mart.* 2), thanks to God who rewards him for his light affliction (*scorp.* 5.10). The better rooms in the

---

[43] *Ibid.*, 119. See also A. von Harnack, *Militia Christi* (Berlin, 1905), 32–40.

father's house go to those who have paid more in earthly pains
(*scorp.* 6.7). Only when death is for God, when the disciple bears
his cross after his lord, can it be the key to paradise (*res.* 43.4).

Yet the very selflessness of the martyr's act became a proof of
God's reward and a ground for veneration. Martyrs were visited
in prison (*mart.* 1.1) and their chains were kissed (*ux.* 2.4.2).[44]
Clement celebrates the heroism of martyrdom while Tertullian
works with promise and command.[45] Whether for courage or
reward, the martyr is concerned to serve one God. With similar
simplicity, the martyr sees his judges to be under the higher
judgement of God. The destruction of persecutors is a necessary
verdict at the end of history, if God's righteousness is to triumph.
Tertullian's rejection (*cor.* 13.4) of this world in favour of
citizenship in heaven found its natural conclusion in martyrdom.[46] At the same time his positive attitude to the world
balances his rejection of earthly values, for salvation is at work,
not in heaven, but in the world.[47]

Objection to God

While few issues show more clearly the difference between
Tertullian and Clement than their attitude to martyrdom,[48]
both take account of the heretical attack on a God who requires
the death of his own people. The objections are: the martyr's
death is pointless because it takes the command to confess Christ
(Matt. 10:32) as relevant on earth and not in heaven, and it is
wrong because it denies the unique efficacy of the death of
Christ and indicates an avenging God. No sacrifice of any
creature is pleasing to God who wills the repentance, not the
death of the sinner (*scorp.* 1.8). These objections are substantiated from the Gnostic *Testimony of Truth* (31f.).[49] Clement adds

---

[44] Campenhausen, *Idee Martyriums*, 128, insists that Tertullian does not want Christian heroes but only God's will. Yet the overtones of heroism are strong.

[45] *Ibid.*, 128.

[46] M. Schoepflin, Servizio militare e culto imperiale: il "de corona" di Tertulliano, *Apoll.*, 58 (1985), 207.

[47] See R. Bélanger, Le plaidoyer de Tertullien pour la liberté religieuse, *SR*, 14 (1985), 291 and J. M. Hornus, Étude sur la pensée politique de Tertullien, *RHPhR*, 38 (1958), 38.

[48] D. van Damme, Gott und die Märtyrer, *FZPhTh.*, 27 (1980), 107–13.

[49] See Koschorke, *Die Polemik*, 127–37.

other objections (*str.* 4.4.16) and cites Basilides' claim that, to preserve the goodness of providence, all martyrs either must be guilty in act or intent, or must suffer as children (*str.* 4.12.81f.).

Tertullian can see nothing in martyrdom which might challenge the goodness of God, whose will should never be questioned (*scorp.* 2–4). God has, by his law against idolatry, provided that some should die (*scorp.* 6.1f.). The Christian, who has sinned, receives in martyrdom a final opportunity to cleanse himself with blood (*scorp.* 6.9). Yet martyrdom is not so much good as a matter of necessity.[50] The authority of God, who has frequently forbidden the worship of idols, is at stake. Martyrdom fulfils the divine law and declares the authority of God (*scorp.* 3f.). 'Le martyre est le terme normal du voyage.'[51]

Clement treats the objections more seriously and more rationally (*str.* 4.9.70–4.13.88). Persecution is not a good thing. Flight is good because it avoids the double evil of persecution, where the actor perpetrates, and the sufferer endures, what is wrong. Jesus did not suffer by the will of God; persecutions take place because God does not prevent them. Man is free to choose and the persecutor is responsible for his evil choice. As for those who suffer, God turns their suffering to good account, as correction either for their sins or for the sins of others (86f.). For Clement as for Tertullian, the unity of God is central to the argument. Tertullian takes the straightforward and unconvincing position, that the sovereign God actually wills the persecution of his people. For Clement, the sovereign God allows persecution and turns it to good effect.

Confession of faith
Irenaeus is closer to Clement than to Tertullian. He considers that martyrdom or testimony could refer to confession of faith (*haer.* 3.12.10; 3.12.13; 3.18.5), but should normally be sealed by death as was the case with Polycarp (*haer.* 3.3.4). God and the love of God are the sole concerns of the martyr. He witnesses

---

[50] It is not in the first place a question of the goodness and utility of martyrdom, but rather a question of necessity (*debitum, necessitas*).
[51] Spanneut, *Tertullien*, 191.

for God (*haer.* 3.12.13) and for love of the true God and his
Christ (*haer.* 4.33.9f.). In this he receives, in a new way, the
same spirit which was given to the persecuted prophets
(*haer.* 4.33.9). Such testimony is marked not by weakness of the
flesh, but by readiness of spirit which absorbs flesh. A living man
of flesh lives by sharing in the spirit (*haer.* 5.9.2).

The readiness of the martyr declares the presence of the spirit.
That is why the Gnostics should accept the testimony of
Stephen to the oneness of God. Stephen's authority is proved by
his apostolic appointment as first deacon and by his following in
the steps of his lord who confessed and died (*haer.* 3.12.10). In
contrast, the Gnostics have rejected the apostolic teaching
concerning the one true God and have preferred human
opinions (*haer.* 3.12.12). Their call to the perfection of martyrdom proved that the apostles and their disciples were perfect
in teaching the oneness of God. Stephen saw the glory of God
with Jesus at his right hand; the perfection of his teaching was
marked by the imitation of his master who prayed for those who
killed him. The martyr is perfect in his imitation of the crucified
lord and in his teaching of one God; nothing can surpass the
peak of this perfection. When Peter (Matt. 16:16) confessed to
the son of the living God, the lord spoke of the necessity of
suffering and death (*haer.* 3.18.4). The Gnostics claim that
following the way of the cross (Matt. 16:24) is the heavenly
function of Horos; but Irenaeus insists that the next verse
(Matt. 16:25) means losing one's life (*haer.* 3.18.4f.). Their
docetist view is absurd, for if Jesus had not suffered what he calls
us to suffer, he would surely be false (*haer.* 3.18.6). He shows
himself to be our one true master by suffering as the word of
God.

The martyrs hold their place in the history of salvation by
carrying the cross after their lord (*haer.* 3.18.5). The church as
the salt of the earth is like Lot's wife, a pillar of salt, and sends
her sons on to the father (*haer.* 4.31.3). Gnostic communities
cannot do this. Only the church supports and is known by the
members who suffer (*haer.* 4.33.9). The martyrs are sent on
(*haer.* 4.31.3; 4.33.9) to prepare for the kingdom of the son and
to reign with him when he returns in glory (*haer.* 5.32.1). It is

right that they should live again in the same world where they died for love of God (*haer.* 5.32.1).

To sum up, the martyrs have attained to the likeness of God, they reveal God's continuing love as shown first on the cross of Jesus, and they declare the wisdom of God which is human folly. They are offered as sons to the father, whose only son is the lamb eternally sacrificed. Loyalty to one God explains martyrdom and ascetic practice.

Askesis

The work of Clement's Paidagogos is to cure the passions of the soul so that, like the word, the Christian becomes free from sin, guilt and passion. He who orders the heavens and the movements of the sun, concentrates upon man as his greatest work. He regulates the soul with wisdom and temperance and the body with beauty and proportion. Whatever order there is in man's action comes from the word (*paed.* 1.2.5). Luxury has no place, because it destroys order. We follow God, stripped of all that is superfluous, bearing the cross which gives us life (*paed.* 3.3.21–5). Cosmetic embellishment contradicts the divine simplicity which needs nothing (*paed.* 3.3).

For Tertullian modesty comes before moderation. The lusts of the world are linked with idolatry, drunkenness, vanity and falsehood; that is why idolatry and a life of lust must be avoided (*idol.* 1.1f.). Pleasures of ear and eye are not an offence in their own time and place (*spect.* 1.3). Not the world itself, but the sin of the world, takes us from God. We break with our divine maker if we go to the Capitol, the temple of Serapis or the theatre (*spect.* 8.10). Modesty in clothing is appropriate for women as they remember how sin came into the world through a woman (*cult.* 1.1.1f.). Gold and silver can be occasions of foolish indulgence when they are used for toilet vessels (*cult.* 1.5.2). Precious stones have no value other than their rarity (*cult.* 1.7.1). Perfect modesty abstains from whatever tends to sin as well as from the sin itself (*cult.* 2.2.1). Superfluity is to be rejected (*cult.* 2.3.3) and elaborate clothing should be avoided (*cult.* 2.9.1). A Christian may wear poorer clothing, because she has become wealthy in Christ (*cult.* 2.11.3), and

must both be and seem to be modest (*cult.* 2.13.3). It is right for
the soldier, who earns a crown from Christ, to refuse to wear an
earthly crown, even if he be accused of being too eager to die
(*cor.* 1.4).

The property of God must be kept clean and untainted for
him, who will crown it when he chooses (*cor.* 15.1). Beauty
adorns the mind and plucks out lusts. Licence and luxury insult
the apostle and do not blush when his teachings are read
(*mon.* 12.3). Paul's teaching on the subject is set out (*mon.* 10.1f.).
Modesty is the flower of manners, the honour of bodies and the
grace of the sexes. It indicates every good disposition and
endures in spite of all obstacles. Modesty is now challenged, but
its discipline revives in true teaching and its rigour responds to
both testaments (*pud.* 1.1f.).

Gluttony and lust are connected in disposition and practice.
Fasting is important for faith and love of God, rather than for
the emptiness of lungs and intestines. There are many pretexts
which are used to avoid fasting (*iei.* 1.3f.); but fasting began in
the law against eating given to Adam who yielded to his belly
rather than to God (*iei.* 3.2). After the flood there was a new
limit to lawful food and a greater opportunity for abstinence
(*iei.* 4.4). Moses and Elijah saw God's glory and heard his voice
when they fasted. In the New Testament there are similar
examples in Anna and the lord himself (*iei.* 6.5; 8.1). Fasting
prepares the soul for times of hardship in prison and builds
powers of endurance. Heretics put kitchens in prisons to feed
their so-called martyrs and one such martyr was so drugged
with wine that instead of confessing his lord, he could do
nothing but hiccup (*iei.* 12.3). Even the heathen practise forms
of denial, at special seasons and in times of drought (*iei.* 16.5).
In contrast, there are Christians who eat too much, and an
overfed Christian is an edible Christian, better placed among
the lions than in the service of God (*iei.* 16f.).

Tertullian's attitude to marriage is both positive and negative.[52] Nature should be venerated. God blessed marriage by his
command, 'Be fruitful and multiply' (*an.* 27.4). 'We do not

[52] R. Uglione, Il matrimonio in Tertulliano tra esaltazione e disprezzo, *EL* 93 (1979),
479–94.

deny that the joining of man and wife has been blessed by God'
(*ux.* 1.2.1). For Tertullian, marriage between man and woman
is a symbol of the mystical union between Christ and the
church. Worldly desire and fleshly lust may lead to marriage;
yet marriage remains lawful (*ux.* 1.2.1f.). In all religions and
nations, priesthood requires some form of celibacy. A king or
chief priest does not marry a second time; even the enemy of
God may affect to follow the way of holiness (*ux.* 2.7.5).

Marriage is governed by chastity and self-denial. Faculties
are dulled by a first marriage and more so by a second marriage.
Marriage helps the carnal nature to dominate over the spiritual
(*cast.* 11.1). There are many excuses offered for second marriage; but all of them would be met by a housekeeper instead of
a second wife (*cast.* 12.1). The gospel moves beyond the Law to
continence and monogamy (*mon.* 8.1).

Tertullian's account of spiritual marriage is governed by the
theme *nubere deo* and declares a passionate dedication to God,[53]
which seeks and desires him in intimate prayer and the company
of angels. Contemplation comes through virginity and continence rather than through rational inquiry, because continence prepares the body for incorruption (*ux.* 1.7.1).
Tertullian speaks of the spiritual affection of those who are
married to Christ or God (*ux.* 1.4.4f.) and the beauty (*speciosae
puellae*) of those who belong to him (*ux.* 1.4.4). This beauty is
known spiritually (*cast.* 10.2). The rule of continence derives
from the last days when he who has a wife should be as one who
has not and when the nearness of God brings a divine intimacy.
Life is dominated by the one God.[54]

Epicurus links the word μοναχός with simplicity while Plotinus
uses it to designate the uniqueness of the One (*Enn.* 5.8.7). In
Syria it designates the highest rank of ascetic and refers to the
unique or μονογενής.[55] It is hard to fix the extent of philosophical

---

[53] C. Tibiletti, Vita contemplativa in Tertulliano, *Orph.*, NS 2 (1981), 332.

[54] *Ibid.*, 339, 'La visione cristiana della vita risulta in Tertulliano unitaria, pur tra
contingenti fluttuazione. Lo anclito escatalogico, che associa celibato e vita
contemplativa, pervade e anima il suo pensiero, dalla conversione alle ultime opere
a noi note.'

[55] A. Adam, Grundbegriffe des Mönchtums in sprachlicher Sicht, *ZKG*, 65 (1953/4),
209–39. See also E. A. Judge, The earliest use of the word 'monachos' for monk (P.

influence on early Christian asceticism. Cynics and Stoics had
practised asceticism. The Cynic saw himself as the messenger of
Zeus and the Stoic lived as a member of the city of God.[56]

In summary, the motives for early ascetic practice were
various. The example of Jesus in poverty, celibacy and with-
drawal from the world, presented a pattern to the disciple.[57] The
nearness of the end (ὁ καιρὸς συνεσταλμένος ἐστίν, 1 Cor. 7:29)
is taken up by Tertullian (*ux.* 1.3.2) and developed with
Montanist zeal (*ux.* 2.2.4). The world to come is anticipated by
the life of angels (Matt. 22:30), the preparation of Adam for his
return to paradise (*iei.* 3–7; *mon.* 4f.), citizenship in heaven
(*Diogn.* 5) and promised rewards for works of supererogation
(*sim.* 5.3.3; *mand.* 4.4.2). Care for the poor was a sufficient
ground for fasting (*Aristides, apol.* 15.9). Apologetic rebutted
charges of immorality with proofs of austerity. Chastity stood
high among Justin's claims for Christian practice. He tells of a
young man who sought castration and of a woman who divorced
her dissolute husband (2 *apol.* 1f.) and then successfully peti-
tioned the emperor for relief from his reprisals.[58] Finally,
asceticism was governed by following God, stripped of all
superfluity in divine simplicity, or by marriage to the only God.

THE WORLD, THE FLESH AND RIGHT REASON

The tendency to the ascetic way, so strong in Tertullian,[59] is
balanced, by him and his contemporaries, with a strong
affirmation that the world belongs to God and has been ordered
by God. Clement's enthusiasm for the world, like his flight from

Coll. Youtie 77), *JAC* 20 (1977), 72–89; the fullest account is found in F.-E. Morard,
Monachos, Moine, Histoire du terme grec jusqu'au 4e siècle, *FZPhTh.* 20 (1973),
332–411.

[56] J. Leipoldt, *Griechische Philosophie und frühchristliche Askese* (Berlin, 1961), 6of.; see
opposite view of K. Heussi, *Der Ursprung des Mönchtums* (Jena, 1936).

[57] P. Nagel, *Die Motivierung der Askese in der alten Kirche und der Ursprung des Mönchtums*
(Berlin, 1966), 5–19.

[58] That this woman was the Gnostic Flora and her teacher Ptolemaeus has been
proposed by G. Lüdemann, Zur Geschichte des ältesten Christentums in Rom,
ZNW, 70 (1979), 97–114 and elaborated by R. M. Grant, A woman of Rome, *ChH,*
54 (1985), 461–72.

[59] For recent criticism of Tertullian's asceticism see C. Rambaux, *Tertullien face aux
morales des trois premiers siècles* (Paris, 1979).

the world, stems from his dependence on one God who made all things which are needful and profitable for life (*str.* 6.8.67). Thankfulness is a theme which traces all good things, whether they be spiritual or physical (*str.* 5.10.61), back to God (*str.* 3.6.52f.). The creator is an object of wonder (*str.* 7.11.60). The right use of the world is found in the pursuit of the mean (*paed.* 2.1.16; 3.10.51) between excesses which produce passions. The value of marriage is measured by the degree to which those who are married are better able to serve God (*str.* 3.12.88; 7.9.64). While virginity can bring freedom from passion and assimilation to God (*str.* 4.23.147), there is great value in marriage. Clement's position is marked by tension (*str.* 7.12.70).[60]

Wealth, which Clement also defends, may deflect its possessor from God and proliferate passions (*q.d.s.* 17). It must always be seen as a gift from God (*q.d.s.* 16) and never as private property (*q.d.s.* 31). One God determines all values; he who follows God should despise wealth (*paed.* 3.2.12; *paed.* 2.3.39), yet the proper enjoyment of all things, including food and drink, leads on to God, who gives all (*str.* 7.7.36).

For Tertullian, the Stoic concepts of nature and reason unite God with his world. God is *sermo ratione consistens* and his creation is a *rationale opus* (*Prax.* 5.3; *an.* 43.7). He is the God of rational order which is traced back to him, for he has made all things well (*spect.* 2.4). Trust only in nature! Neither God nor nature lie; but, to be able to believe in God, trust the witness of the soul! (*test.* 6.1). Creation and goodness belong to God. Sin is irrational and the work of the devil.[61] God is body and spirit (*Prax.* 7.8), but is unlike all created beings (*carn.* 3). Goodness (*test.* 2) and rationality (*Prax.* 5) are shown in his creation (*spect.* 2f.) and his plan of salvation. These provide a sound framework for ethics; to live according to nature is, for the Stoic, to choose, freely and rationally, the end of likeness to God. For

---

[60] Clement's positive attitude to marriage is supported by a reading of 1 Cor. 7:32–4 which indicates a division, not within married men, but between married woman and virgin. C. Tibiletti, Un passo de Clemente Alessandrino su verginità e matrimonio, *Orph.*, NS 5 (1984), 438f.

[61] S. Otto, '*Natura*' und '*Dispositio*', *Untersuchung zum Naturbegriff und zur Denkform Tertullians* (München, 1960), 37.

Tertullian, however, while free will reflects the image of God in man, there is also an active force of evil, a second adulterous nature (*an.* 16.1f.) which may be traced back to the devil.

What teeth will you gnash?

The resurrection of the body is essential. It will be easier for God to raise man from the dead than it was, in the beginning, to make him out of the dust of the earth (*haer.* 5.3). Tertullian, who is so fierce in his renunciation of the world, defends the goodness of the flesh and creation with the strongest claims. This goes beyond Stoicism, to a Christian, anti-Marcionite position. For Seneca, our little body (*corpusculum*) is necessary but no great thing (*Ep.* 23.6), and the flesh is the bearer of death (*Ep.* 122). The heretics, says Tertullian, despise the flesh and think only of the resurrection of the soul; in this they despise the lord of the flesh (*res.* 2.2). The chief concern of the heretic is to attack the flesh, denigrating its origin, substance and end; for him it is always unclean, worthless, weak, guilty, miserable and full of trouble (*res.* 4.2). In response, Tertullian praises the flesh. It was created by God and the body was prior to the soul (*res.* 5.8). God has mixed the breath of his own spirit with flesh, and the union is so intimate, that one cannot say whether flesh carries soul or soul carries flesh (*res.* 7.9). The flesh fights for the name of Christ and is exposed to the hatred of men. It goes to prison, suffers every privation and in the end offers itself in death for Christ. The flesh must be most blessed and glorious when it can fully repay its Master so vast a debt (*res.* 8.6). Do men have to die permanently when birds, like the phoenix in Arabia, are sure of resurrection (*res.* 13.4)? The soul is physical, perceives, suffers and will need flesh in order to perceive after death (*res.* 17.1). Heretics see the resurrection as something present, removing the soul from the body and escaping from the world (*res.* 19.7); but Paul often mentions the resurrection of the flesh for final judgement (*res.* 24.1f.). The prophets of hope described the resurrection in a literal, physical way (*res.* 28–32). What teeth will you gnash? There must be flesh at the resurrection to provide for weeping and gnashing of teeth (*res.* 35.12). The whole of faith is acted out by the flesh. The mouth utters holy words, the tongue refrains from blasphemy, the heart avoids irritation and the hands both give and work (*res.* 45.15). We are never told to put off the flesh, but to change the manner of our life to a way of holiness, righteousness and truth (*res.* 49.7). God has given to every seed its own body; what is sown in death will emerge full and perfect (*res.* 52.10). The usefulness of the resurrected flesh is certain because, in the presence of God, there will be no idleness (*res.* 60.9). Flesh and spirit are united in Christ as bride and bridegroom (*res.* 63.1). Marcion is the only man who has so hated his own flesh as to rob it of resurrection; he hates the church too, because Christ loves both flesh and church (*Marc.* 5.18.9).

Breath of God

Tertullian agrees with the Stoics that the soul is physical and argues, against Plato, that the soul is created and originates at birth (*an.* 4.1). The soul is both a spiritual essence and a physical substance (*an.* 5.1f.). Soul must be physical, so that its image can have bodily substance, and so that it can suffer in hell (*an.* 7.1). The arguments from Plato for a non-physical soul are considered and rejected (*an.* 8.1). A religious sister saw visions of a soul in bodily shape (*an.* 9.4). Soul and body are together conceived, formed and perfected, to be objects of reverence and not of shame, which comes from lust not nature (*an.* 27.4). The soul could not live a human life without a body. As student, soldier, judge, merchant, farmer or sailor, the soul must have a body (*an.* 56.6). The soul is the breath, but not the spirit of God; it is a gentle breeze blown by the spirit but it is not the spirit. It was improper, but still possible, for the breath of God to disobey him (*Marc.* 2.9.1f.).

God, truth and reason

The whole of morality comes under the theme of word and law, of λόγος and νόμος. Justin's apology depends upon his imperial reader being a guardian of justice and learning. Love of truth is more important than life itself (1 *apol.* 2). Both those who rule

and those who are ruled must follow piety and philosophy.
Unless both rulers and ruled are philosophers no happy state
will ever arise (1 *apol.* 3). Truth is all important. It would be
easy for Christians to deny their faith; 'but we would not live by
telling a lie' (1 *apol.* 8). Christian lives are open for all to see
their integrity and truth. Immorality, magic and the pursuit of
wealth are abandoned in favour of chastity, obedience to God
and sharing. Those who hated and destroyed one another, now
live in friendship and pray for their enemies. The truth declares
them to be right (1 *apol.* 14). The case for Christians can be
stated simply and Justin asks 'Do not decree death against those
who have done no wrong' (1 *apol.* 68). For Irenaeus the true
and spiritual disciple confesses one God because he understands
what prophets have said about Christ and the New Testament
(*haer.* 4.33.1). The heavenly word controls the actions and
habits of men.

   The *Paedagogus* is concerned with practice and the training of
the soul in virtue (*paed.* 1.1.1). Reason connects law with God
who is reason. Sin is whatever goes against right reason. The
passions of lust, fear and pleasure are forms of disobedience to
reason. Virtue is a state of soul harmonious, through reason,
with the whole of life. The whole life of a Christian is a system
of reasonable actions which are taught by the word and
governed by the energy of faith. This rational system follows the
commandments of the lord which have been written down for us
(*paed.* 1.13). Rationality is inconsistent with gluttony; what we
should eat is a banquet of reason. In contrast, cattle are
irrational and prepared for death. We do not have to abstain
from food but we are not to be ruled by it. We must avoid excess
and eat in a way that is becoming and proper (*paed.* 2.1.1).
Drunkenness and love of wine are not compatible with love of
the word; the heart is drowned by drunkenness just as if it were
drowned at sea. The cup of friendship makes for peace and
lawful enjoyment. Whatever is disgraceful is not proper for man
because he is rational. It is much less proper for women whose
nature should be an object of reverence (*paed.* 2.2). Clothing
should be simple and reasonable. It is foolish to chase after what
is rare and costly instead of using what is handy and inexpensive.

He who knows what is really beautiful and good, does not worry about show or appearance (*paed.* 3.1f.). God gave his Logos to all men and he made all things for all men. Things should therefore be held in common and the inward beauty of the soul should be placed before any external beauty (*paed.* 2.12.120). Knowledge of self leads to the knowledge and likeness of God, doing good and requiring little because God needs nothing (*paed.* 3.1). It is rational to have a bath for a useful end, not for pleasure nor as a social occasion. It is best to wash the soul in the cleansing word (*paed.* 3.9).

All sin is irrational, and therefore comes from the devil and is foreign to God (*an.* 16.2). The mind is always part of the soul (*an.* 19.1f.). Seneca, who is often one of us, says 'There are implanted in us the seeds of all the arts and all the periods of life, and God our master secretly produces our mental dispositions' (*an.* 20.1).

God's righteous order

Our whole life derives from one God and one teacher, and man's righteousness is an ordered unity. Plato calls us brothers because we come from one God and have one teacher; we are brothers in the God who formed us in different ways (*str.* 5.14.98). This means that one righteous man differs in no way from another; whether we follow the law of the Jews or Greeks, we live rationally according to the law. Reason and order come from one God who joins us with our fellow man (*str.* 6.6.47).

Righteousness is good in itself and not because it produces virtue. The word is our great commander who brings us to liberty (*paed.* 1.8). The only righteousness of God comes by faith in the one Christ who justifies the believer (*paed.* 1.8.73). Righteousness is marked by order. Everything should be kept in place. Licence and luxury are wrong because they bring disorder (*paed.* 3.3). Just as a horse is guided by a bit and a bull by a yoke, man is tamed and brought to order by the word who tames wild beasts. As ruler and creator of the world, he teaches man to follow in his way (*paed.* 3.12.99). The order of righteousness is received by faith. Most men have a stormy and unstable disposition which is the result of their lack of faith (*str.* 4.3.8).

The concern of Christians for one another indicates the corporate nature of Christian morals. Christians show special concern for those in need, sickness or other distress (1 *apol.* 67). The church alone sustains the reproach of those who suffer for righteousness' sake and becomes strong again soon after it has suffered persecution (*haer.* 4.33.9).

Did God's righteous order require Christians to withdraw from the secular community?[62] It seems that, for Tertullian, all commerce is linked with idolatry (*idol.* 11.1f.). Yet he claims in his apology that Christians trade with others. There is no evidence that the church required its members to withdraw from commerce, for the life of a provincial citizen was tied to his city which was his true *patria*. Nor was there an embargo on the teaching of the schools, despite all its pagan myths. Without secular studies, the divine pursuits could not survive (*idol.* 10.4f.). Christians were still bad for business since they were not interested in sacrifice and they sometimes listened to Tertullian's warnings against luxury. Did Christians take part in public office? Tertullian did not consider it possible. The office of magistrate was tied too closely to the cult of idols and belonged to the *pompa diaboli*. While Tertullian truly represents a Christian position, the number of people affected was small. More evident was the failure of Christians to participate in pagan festivals. Yet even here there were solid exceptions, who rendered to Caesar what they thought was his due (*idol.* 15). Tertullian's attack on public spectacles was continued and confirmed by the opposition of the church through its bishops, long after the accession of Constantine. Together with the rejection of idolatry and its related shows, there was considerable compromise and coexistence. One could live without political office (a parallel system of honours arose within the church), and perhaps without pagan festivals and pagan games; but trade, work and family were essential to living.

---

[62] See G. Schöllgen, Die Teilnahme der Christen am städtischen Leben in vorkonstantinischer Zeit, *RQ* 77 (1982), 1–29.

One fascination of Tertullian is that for all his disdain of the world, no one could have been more firmly marked by his environment. His rhetoric was Carthaginian, designed to outdo that of Rome, and his vitality of style expressed the lively resurrection which Carthage, after its many catastrophes, always enjoyed. The strength of the paganism which he attacked came from Punic roots; public and private observances were signs of community life. Doubt remains over his relation to Montanism. Here again his strong sense of God is the best explanation. He could not tolerate laxity in the church because he identified the church with the spirit, who was bound together with the father and the son.[63]

CONCLUSION

One God defines the ethics of one law, one commandment, assimilation to one good, martyrdom for the only God and right use of his world. This is tidy and predictable. The scheme is enlarged by the incarnation. It is a new thing to obey and love a God who died and to love those united by his cross. 'You have seen your brother, you have seen your God', quotes Clement. To follow and to become like the son who is in the father, to drink the cup which he drank and to wear a common flesh in his world, all this enriches the one obedience to one God. Both ascetic and secular discipleship were governed by the order of the word of one God. 'Order' said Augustine, 'is that which, if we hold it in our lives, will lead to God'.[64]

At the same time, the first theologians produce a simplification of the New Testament. The tension between law and gospel, letter and spirit, rule and discipleship, nomism and participation is sustained and resolved. Under one God, a simple, clearly intelligible, line runs from Mosaic Law to natural law to one commandment to Christ, who is the law, and finally to participation in him or assimilation to God.

---

[63] A. Quacquarelli, *La cultura indigena di Tertulliano e i tertullianisti di Carthagine*, *VetChr.*, 15 (1978), 218.   [64] *de ordine* 1.9.27.

CHAPTER 8

One mind, truth and logic

It is easy to see why, and even how, God should be the source of being and goodness. His existence has been proved from time to time by cosmological and moral arguments, which claim the need for a cause of being and goodness. But why and how is God mind, reason or the first-principle of logic? Because John writes that the word (not the son or saviour) was in the beginning, this is an important question for Christian thought. Clement has been seen as the forerunner of the tradition of open conversation between faith and reason.[1] This confidence in reason was to reappear in Origen and Augustine and to dominate medieval thought. For the first theologians, the unity of truth was as important as the unity of being and of goodness. Truth came from one God through one word, one scripture and one tradition. Truth was one, both in the sense that it excluded error, and in the sense that it included partial statements which qualified and defined one another.[2]

One truth is exalted as God himself, abbreviated as the rule or canon of faith, accessible to all in scripture, the sole object of faith and knowledge, grasped in part by philosophy, and denied by heresy.

ONE GOD, ONE TRUTH

God is truth and the criterion of truth: 'Love truth, and let nothing but truth proceed out of your mouth, that the spirit which God made to dwell in this flesh, may be found true in the sight of all men; and thus shall the lord, who dwells in you, be

---

[1] M. W. Strasser, Faith and reason revisited in Clement of Alexandria, in *Proceedings of PMR Conference*, 7 (1982), 58.   [2] Osborn, *Philosophy of Clement*, 113–26.

glorified; for the lord is true in every word, and with him there is no falsehood.'[3] Truth was not known to the Greeks, says Clement, but has now descended from heaven and gone out as the word from Jerusalem (*prot.* 1.2). Christ gave himself the name of truth and not the name of custom. The rule of faith, one and unchanging, points to one God, the creator, and his son Jesus, born of Mary, crucified, raised, ascended into heaven, sitting on the right hand of God and destined to come to judge the living and the dead at the resurrection (*virg.* 1.3). The word has disclosed the one truth.

Truth is entirely different from error. There is one royal road that leads to salvation, while the other roads lead to destruction (*str.* 7.15.91). Truth is sure and certain and belongs to God. Enquiry has its place, provided it leads to discovery and not to pointless strife. Those who truly seek will find (*str.* 5.1.12). Truth is seen with the mind, not with the eyes, as Plato said in the *Phaedrus* (*str.* 5.3.16). While man is helpless, God can give wisdom and is known by his power; our life was hung on the tree so that we might believe (*str.* 5.11.72). Appearances are misleading, so truth seems new and falsehood seems old (*prot.* 1.6). While some people prefer custom or convention, any ruler knows that truth is essential to authority (1 *apol.* 12). Truth is hated in proportion to its greatness (*an.* 1.6) and Socrates showed that truth was always disliked (*an.* 1.5f.). Falsehood loves to masquerade as truth, so Irenaeus exposes Gnostic pretension (*haer.* 1. *Pref.* 1). Error and magic stand in clear contrast to truth (*haer.* 2.31).

Truth is stronger than error. The limbs of the body of truth have been torn apart; but the power of Christ's truth brings them together again (*str.* 1.13.57). The truth of Greek philosophy is partial, a limb torn from the body. Real truth shows up the plausibility of Sophists and false teachers with the clarity of black and white (*str.* 6.10.83). If the objection is raised that Christians have many sects, then it should be remembered that there are many sects in Judaism and in philosophy; divisions alone do not discredit a claim to truth (*str.* 7.15.89). By acting

---

[3] *mand.* 3.

out the law, promises and powers of the creator and only God, Christ presented a coherent account of truth (*Marc.* 4.6.4). The whole of Christ must be perceived if his truth is to be grasped; the powers of the spirit prove that he was the Christ of God and his suffering proved his human flesh: 'Why halve Christ with a lie? He was wholly the truth.' (*carn.* 5) The law and the prophets are united by the church into one volume with apostolic writings, because they are seen to be consistent with one another (*praescr.* 36.5). Hermogenes, in his heresy, has described matter as incoherent, confused or turbulent, and he himself is aptly described by these adjectives (*Herm.* 45.6). Heretics make free use of parables and find strange interpretations because they ignore the rule of truth, and seize on what is accidental (*pud.* 8).

For Justin truth is unique, unchanging, universal, and the ground of human dignity.[4] Scripture gives the mystery of revelation (*dial.* 44) and is grasped by grace and inquiry. It makes manifest what is always true. God not only reveals, but is the truth; the end of all inquiry is the being of God (*dial.* 3; *dem.* 2).[5]

Truth is marked by God's own simplicity.[6] Philo had written, (*Leg. all.* 2.1–3): ὁ θεὸς μόνος ἐστὶ καὶ ἕν, οὐ σύγκριμα φύσις ἁπλῆ. In contrast with the plurality of the creature, the creator is not mixed with anything. We might say that God has been ordered in accordance with the one and the monad, or rather that the monad has been ordered κατὰ τὸν ἕνα θεόν. Abraham found simplicity by looking to the one and only God, avoiding the plurality and passions of those who follow many things (*migr.* 153). Within the New Testament and Hermas, simplicity points to truth. It applies to the pure being of God, simple speech, plain truth, lack of ambiguity, simple praying, simple giving, integrity of heart and the rejection of passions.[7]

For Clement, tenderness and simplicity set the lambs at the right hand of their judge (*paed.* 1.5.14f.). Truth and simplicity go together τὸ δέ ἐστιν ἁπλότητος καὶ ἀληθείας ὑπόστασις (*paed.* 1.5.19). Faith leads from what is above proof to the

---

[4] L. Dattrino, La dignità dell'uomo in Giustino Martirio e Ireneo di Lione, *Lat.*, 46 (1980), 233f.

[5] *Ibid.*, 237.   [6] Amstutz, Ἁπλότης.   [7] *Ibid.*, 155–7.

universal, simple, ultimate, and immaterial essence (*str.* 2.4.14). Dialectic leads to what is first and simple (*str.* 6.9.80) and salvation was revealed by the word who had simplified the truth ἁπλώσας δὲ ὁ λόγος τὴν ἀλήθειαν (*prot.* 11.116).

The claim that God is truth is possible through the Christian transformation of metaphysical and biblical ideas of truth.[8] The Greek and the barbarian philosophy prepare for the true philosophy which is in Christ. For Plato truth is that which is, is rational, able to be known and linked with real events.[9] The truth of things that are (*Meno* 86b) is joined by consistency with what has been received (*Phaedo* 99e). Truth and being are combined in what is τὸ ἀληθινὸν ὄντως ὄν (*Soph.* 240). Truth is clear, pure, genuine, and allied to mind, good sense and knowledge. The barbarian philosophy of the Old Testament points to truth, אֱמֶת, which is sure and faithful. The lord is a faithful God (Deut. 7:9). In time and history, faithfulness is found in the one who is (ἐγὼ εἰμι ὁ ὤν). Finally the Fourth Gospel adds the extraordinary claim that Jesus is the truth himself, present now in history. Truth is in the word who is the self-expression of God and who has become incarnate. In the beginning was the word... the word became flesh... full of grace and truth.

ONE TRUTH CONTRACTED IN ONE CANON

Canon and criterion dominated four hundred years of Hellenistic philosophy as it faced the questions: is there an objective truth? if there is, how can it be known? Stoics and Epicureans affirmed truth and found it by following a criterion or canon. Sceptics denied truth and attacked any canon. *Regula* (κανών), as a summarising principle, also had a common legal application which has wrongly drawn more interest than the philosophical use.[10]

The emergence of a rule of faith in the second century has been regarded either as a restriction on reason (by Celsus) or as

---

[8] W. Beierwaltes, Deus est veritas, in *Pietas, FSB. Kötting*, ed. E. Dassmann and K. S. Frank, *JAC* (Münster, 1980), 15–29, traces the concept through to Gregory of Nyssa and Augustine.   [9] It is an ontological, logical and epistemological unity.
[10] P. Stein, *Regulae iuris* (Edinburgh, 1966), 66f. cites Paul, *Ad Plautium* xvi. Interest in the legal meaning of *regula* was encouraged by the belief that Tertullian was a jurist; this view has been discredited by Barnes and Fredouille.

a decline into intellectualism (by nineteenth-century liberals). Tertullian uses it to limit and guide inquiry: argument from scripture alone is useless. Only the rule is decisive and apostolic. Whoever has the rule does not need to go further, for after Christ there is no place for disputation (*praescr.* 7f.). Clement also claims that argument needs the rule as a starting-point, but insists on the need for inquiry, while Irenaeus regards the apostolic preaching, on which the rule is based, as capable of proof from Scripture. Clement and Tertullian agree on the place of reason in their polemic against Gnostics.

Plato uses κριτήριον to explain the claim of Protagoras that man is the measure of all things 'having in himself the criterion for these things' (*Theaet.* 178b; cf. *Rep.* 582a).[11] The *Canon* of Epicurus is devoted to the theory of criteria.[12] Elsewhere, in a fragment from *On Nature*, Epicurus insists that without a canon which discriminates opinions, no inquiry is possible and foolishness will be encouraged.[13]

A canon is, literally, a straight stick, which can be used for testing straightness or measuring length. Aristotle explains its value: 'by means of the straight line we know both itself and the curved – the carpenter's rule enables us to test both – but what is curved does not enable us to distinguish either itself or the straight'.[14] The Epicureans saw that without a rule no foundation was secure.[15] Three words (*regula, norma, libella*) explain the importance of the canon for laying good foundations. Without a canon nothing is firm.[16]

---

[11] See E. F. Osborn, Reason and the rule of faith in the second century AD, in *The making of orthodoxy, FS Henry Chadwick*, ed. R. Williams, (Cambridge, 1989), 40–61. In this discussion I am indebted to G. Striker, Κριτήριον τῆς ἀληθείας, *NAWG*, 1974, 1, 47–110 and to Robin Jackson, Studies in the epistemology of Greek atomists, (Dissertation, Princeton, 1982), especially 238–49.   [12] περὶ κριτηρίου ἢ κανών

[13] Arrighetti, frag. (34) 31, 11–27.   [14] *de anima* 1.5.411a4, cited Jackson, 247

[15] Lucretius wrote:

> denique et in fabrica, si pravast regula prima,
> normaque si fallax rectis regionibus exit
> et libella aliqua si ex parti claudicat hilum,
> omnia mendosa fieri atque obstipa necesse est.
>
>					(*de rerum natura*, 4.518–21)

[16] *de rerum natura*, 4.505–6:

> et violare fidem primam et convellere tota
> fundamenta quibus nixatur vita salusque.

Since a canon is a means of judging, legal terms are frequently found in philosophy. We judge what is true and false and assess testimony for and against a proposition. A dispute is to be settled by the sensations whose testimony is sure. The *Canon* of Epicurus is described by Seneca as concerned with judgement and rule,[17] and by Cicero as if the rule, by which all things are to be judged, had fallen from heaven![18]

In his canon and criteria, Epicurus is concerned with a theory which can move to fresh knowledge. Epictetus talks about preconceptions and common notions, and makes much use of the canon (*Diss.* I. 28, 28–30; II. 11, 13–25; II.20, 21; III.3, 14–15; IV. 12,12; *Ench.* 1.5). The purpose of philosophy is to find the rule which distinguishes truth from appearance, or to establish rules which will require rational application[19] The permanence of the theme is evident in Alcinous who begins his account of Platonic dialectic with a discussion of the criterion *Did.* 4).

It has been argued that the emergence of the church universal was governed by three standards, one of which was the rule of faith as it developed out of the baptismal confession. The claim has been overstated because the three standards are treated in close proximity by Tertullian (*praescr.* 21, 32 and 36), from which, 'it directly follows that three standards are to be kept in view, viz., the apostolic doctrine, the apostolic canon of scripture, and the guarantee of apostolic authority, afforded by the organisation of the Church, that is, by the episcopate, and traced back to apostolic institution. It will be seen that the Church always adopted these three standards together, that is simultaneously.'[20] While the mutual dependence of the ideas is clear, their relation cannot be defined with such precision. The 'baptismal hypothesis' once confidently declared that, by the middle of the second century the Roman church had a fixed

---

[17] *Ep. Mor.* 89.11.
[18] *de finibus* 1.63.
[19] An examination of Epicurus and the Stoics reveals three distinct ways of understanding canon and criteria. Striker, Κριτήριον, 90.
[20] A. von Harnack, *History of Dogma*, II, (London, 1896), translated from the third German edition, 19.

baptismal creed which was the source of the rule of faith.[21] This
theory was based on two false premisses – that the rule of faith
was identical with the creed and that declaratory creeds were
always used in baptism; but baptismal liturgy cannot be used as
a source for declaratory creeds at this time.[22]

With the rejection of documentary theories, several other
approaches have emerged. One account takes the church as the
fundamental reality.[23] Irenaeus includes, in the rule, the plain
teaching of scripture, the doctrine preached by the apostles,
transmitted by their succession and taught in the churches. The
rule is a body of which the different doctrines are members, and
the formula for the interpretation of scripture.[24] In Clement, the
rule governs the distinction between true believer and heretic,
dividing truth of church from error of heretics. The norm, it is
claimed, is the church itself, which handles sources of truth and
preserves them.[25] Other questions are subordinate to the
unchanging doctrines of one God, one revelation and one
economy of salvation.[26]

A variant on this view looks to the catechumenate to explain
the rule. Tertullian's rule of faith is identifiable, verbal, twofold
and verbally variable. It is an oral composition, performed by
catechists, and 'chosen from among old and familiar elements
of Christian teaching' to combat the heresies of the second
century.[27] All of which sounds reasonable, in spite of the variety
of old and familiar elements in early Christian teaching.

The rule may also be identified with the whole truth as found
in holy scripture.[28] For Irenaeus, the rule is the original truth
which the church preserves. With God's open testimony, there
is no excuse for wandering into other opinions (*haer.* 2.28.1).
Truth stands in the centre of all theology, one and absolute,
over against the different 'truths' of the Gnostics. This is what

---

[21] See F. Kattenbusch, *Das apostolische Symbol*, II, Verbreitung und Bedeutung des
Taufsymbols (Leipzig, 1900 and Hildesheim, 1967).

[22] J. N. D. Kelly, *Early Christian Creeds*, (London, 1952), 63f.

[23] D. van den Eynde, *Les normes de l'enseignement chrétien, dans la littérature patristique des
trois premiers siècles* (Gembloux et Paris, 1933).   [24] *Ibid.*, 291.

[25] *Ibid.*, 314.   [26] *Ibid.*, 319.

[27] L. W. Countryman, Tertullian and the Regula Fidei, *The Second Century* (1982), 226.

[28] This is the thesis of B. Hägglund, Die Bedeutung der 'regula fidei' als Grundlage
theologischer Aussagen', *StTh.* 12 (1958), 1–44, whose argument is here set out.

Irenaeus means when he speaks of the *corpus* of truth (*haer.* 1.9.4), in contrast to the fabrications of the heretics which fail tests of internal coherence and correspondence with the canon (*haer.* 1.8.1).[29] The one teaching and message of salvation declares the reconciliation wrought in Christ incarnate. Truth is the harmony of different parts of scripture (*haer.* 1.9.4). Irenaeus often refers to individual texts or books of the Bible as a 'rule of truth', making scripture and rule coincide.[30]

For Tertullian the rule is fixed, unshakeable, irreformable, identical with the totality of revelation, prior to all heresy, running straight back to the apostles and Christ. Heresy is secondary; truth is primary, complete and always the same. Clement describes the rule of the church as truth in contrast to philosophy or heresy, and as the first-principle of doctrine which leads back to the words and works of Jesus, and forward to true knowledge. As saving revelation of Christ and as ultimate reality, it declares Christ himself who speaks through the agreement and harmony of law, prophets and gospel (*str.* 6.15.125).[31]

To sum up, the rule is an objective truth which stands over against the mutability of human opinion. Truth imposes its rule, for the 'power of the tradition' (*haer.* 1.10.2) is universal and those who receive and hand it on, do not change it. The early teachers were concerned to guard the truth of the preaching (Eusebius, *h.e.* 5.28.3). It is remarkable how creative Irenaeus is, when one remembers his determination not to be original, but to hand on the canon of truth.

All of which is confirmed by another recent study which sees the canon of truth as the ground of all particular doctrines, and as the fullness of right belief found in scripture and tradition.[32] As for Clement, so for Irenaeus, it is the true knowledge: Γνῶσις ἀληθής, ἡ τῶν ἀποστόλων διδαχή (*haer.* 4.33.8).[33]

---

[29] The mosaic of a king, which the Gnostics have turned into a fox, shows the need for these tests.

[30] *Ibid.*, 14.   [31] *Ibid.*   [32] Brox, *Offenbarung*, 105f.

[33] There is a widespread and erroneous belief that Irenaeus was too cautious to recommend a 'true knowledge'.

ONE TRUTH IN ONE BIBLE LOGIC AND SYMBOL

There is no knowledge of God apart from the incarnate word, for it is necessary to see and hear out teacher, if we are to imitate his works and words. He was first, the source of all truth, existing before all created things (*haer.* 5.1.1), a creative word who now gives freedom from corruption and a share in eternity (*paed.* 1.5.20). This word is now accessible in scripture which is understood by logic and symbolism.

Logic

(i) Scripture is interpreted by the principle of coherence. Interpretation is not a matter of repeating texts, but of understanding the argument behind them (*dial.* 92). When attention is paid to argument, then heresy will be avoided. Heretics distort the prologue of John and change its meaning. They twist expressions of scripture into an unnatural sense, like those who combine odd verses of Homer to make a new concoction (*haer.* 1.9.4).[34] When the verses of scripture are kept in their order, truth will be perceived. The rule of truth will indicate the way in which scripture may be understood and make it clear that the heretics have upset the order (*haer.* 1.9.4). Tertullian also compares the misuse of scripture to the practice of those who jumble lines of Virgil or Homer to make stories of their own (*praescr.* 39.5).

The understanding of scripture requires a sound, pious mind and a love of truth which grows in understanding through daily meditation. Scripture has its own clarity, so parables should not be left ambiguous. The body of truth is found when the whole scripture is taken in harmony, without ambiguity and without contradiction. Scripture is coherent, because it declares one God who formed all things coherently by his word. While parables may be taken in different ways, it is necessary to hold to what is certain and true against what is uncertain and a matter of conjecture (*haer.* 2.27). The unity of the scriptures, old and new, is shown by the lord who used the law against the devil

---

[34] See above, chapter 3, note 2.

to resist temptation (*haer.* 5.21.2). Since the totality of scripture is intelligible we must not subtract from or add to it (*haer.* 5.30.1). Clement uses the metaphor of birth – the scriptures give birth to truth, but remain virgin, concealing the mystery of the truth. So the true gnostics are born from scripture, while heretics deny conception (*str.* 7.16.94). Scripture can give clear answers to the questions about God and the world (*haer.* 2.27).

(ii) The one tradition of scripture goes back to the apostles who all agreed in their teaching. Luke cannot be separated from Paul. Both were governed by the truth and Paul taught so simply that there is no excuse for misusing him (*haer.* 3.14.2). The Marcionites claim that only Paul knew the truth, but Paul insisted that he and Peter served the same God (*haer.* 3.13.2). The presbyters, who have succeeded the apostles, received with the episcopate a certain gift of truth, so that they might guide others in truth, peace and righteousness (*haer.* 4.26.2). Paul was not shunned but was received by the brethren; Peter and Paul were explicitly joined together (*praescr.* 23.6). Tertullian explains why Paul rebuked the apostles and how Marcion went wrong (*Marc.* 4.3.2f.). The catholic Gospels pass the test of antiquity (*Marc.* 4.5.1f.), for John and Matthew were apostles who received truth from the lord himself while Luke and Mark were apostolic men who received truth from the apostles (*Marc.* 4.2.2). The one teaching of all good things goes back to the lord who taught true philosophy, wisdom, gnostic tradition and sure knowledge (*str.* 6.7.59). Such teaching glorifies God as creator, sees his providence in particular events and regards physical elements as changeable and uncertain (*str.* 1.11.52).

(iii) The formation of a Christian Bible is governed by the concept of one God who is the first-principle of one truth.[35] Gnostics and Marcion denied this unity. The perfect God could not have given an imperfect law which needed someone else to fulfil it;[36] unworthy parts of scripture must come from another god. In reply, the one Bible rejected Marcion's dualism as it rejected polytheism.[37]

---

[35] H. von Campenhausen, *Christian Bible*, 98, 206f.
[36] Ptolemy, *Letter to Flora*, 3.4.   [37] von Campenhausen, *Christian Bible*, 87.

Justin begins from philosophers who talk about God, but know nothing of him. Human doctrines are not enough; 'I choose not to follow men and human doctrines, but God and what he has taught' (*dial.* 80.3). Every word of scripture conveys God's power and presence. The fulfilment of prophecies proves the truth of scripture. In salvation-history, the Mosaic law is made obsolete by the eternal law of Christ (*dial.* 11.2). In contrast to the Gnostic Ptolemaeus, 'Justin holds unshakeably to the old belief in one God. This gives his anti-Gnostic polemic an inner affinity with the Old Testament which Ptolemaeus lacks; but at the same time it compels him to lay on this one God the whole heavy burden of a historically dead revelation and an obsolete law.'[38] Justin holds to the saving history 'of a single God. This allows him to incorporate the scriptures *en bloc* and to explain the varying statements which they contain in terms of different eras without losing hold on the sovereignty of God. This is a decisive victory.'[39] The absolute unity of scripture was a Jewish idea which Justin turned into a principle of Christian theology. He was successful because he showed more sympathy than his Jewish opponent for the imaginative unity of scripture. Scripture is truth itself. For Irenaeus too, scripture conveys the life-giving presence of the one, saving God of both testaments.[40] The Old Testament proofs of Christ and the gospel explain the suffering and death of Christ and balance them by an account of his exaltation and lordship.[41] From the New Testament onwards there is no change in this tradition,[42] which continues until Augustine's *City of God.*[43]

Justin's interesting account of the Gospels as the 'memoirs of the apostles' is concerned in his Dialogue to establish the real suffering of the Christ. The memoirs of the apostles prove to Gnostics and others that docetism is not tenable and that the suffering foretold by the prophets really happened.[44] Hege-

---

[38] *Ibid.*, 100.   [39] *Ibid.*   [40] L. Dattrino, *La dignità*, 239f.
[41] A. von Ungern-Sternberg, *Der traditionelle alttestamentliche Schriftbeweis 'de Christo' und 'de evangelio'* (Halle, 1913), 284.   [42] *Ibid.*, 297.   [43] *Ibid.*, 304.
[44] 'Die hauptsächliche Funktion der Erinnerungen der Apostel in der Auslegung des 21 Psalms besteht darin, dass sie als *geschehen* dokumentieren, wovon im Psalm verheissen wird, das es in Zukunft geschehen wird, so *Dial.* 101,3; 102,5; 103,8; 104; 105,1;

sippus shows that notes and memoirs may share an apologetic concern.[45] It is hardly possible, however, to restrict the liturgical use of the memoirs (1 *apol.* 67) to this concern.

It might appear that, since Marcion had already established a Christian Bible, Justin was simply following his example. The situation is more complex. Because of Marcion and other dualist or polytheist positions, Justin could not appropriate the scriptures without first dealing with heresy; the argument of his lost *Syntagma* is the basis of his *Dialogue* and *Apology*. In it he dealt with the themes of recapitulation by Christ as new Adam, his victory, final judgement, divine being, transcendence, and fulfilment of prophecy, through birth, pre-existence, passion, resurrection, rejection by Jews and salvation of gentiles. Justin added a call to individual decision.[46] On this basis of universal salvation, he could claim for Christ the totality of scripture.

Irenaeus begins from the same apologetic principle, with '*his feeling for the essential and unitary*: the one God, the one Christ and the one salvation, which God has given to mankind, and which the Church, in accordance with the "canon of truth", has taught and guarded'.[47] With the Apocalypse of John, scripture is able to include the beginning, middle and end of saving history which has its centre in Christ and his true disciples. This new concept, of a normative scripture which comes from Christ and his true disciples, is the work of Irenaeus. The Bible is the book of Christ, who speaks in it, and to whom both testaments bear witness. Clement can use διαθήκη to mean both covenant and scripture (*str.* 4.12.85).[48]

Some plurality continues in the free citation of scripture for

---

106,1.2.4., L. Abramowski, Die 'Erinnerungen der Apostel' bei Justin, Das Evangelium und die Evangelien, ed. P. Stuhlmacher, *WUNT* 28 (Tübingen, 1982), 350.

[45] Much written of Hegesippus can be shown to be improbable; but some affinity with Justin's memoirs is clear. See N. Hyldahl, Hegesipps Hypomnemata, *StTh.* 14 (1960), 70–113.   [46] Prigent, *Justin*, 335f.

[47] von Campenhausen, *Christian Bible*, 206f. My emphasis. He continues, 'It rests on a broad foundation and a rich experience, which allows it to grasp the One in the Many and again and again to bring it out forcefully and afresh. The spaciousness which Marcion's dogmatism had obstructed has, thanks to Irenaeus, become a basic feature of the New Testament, never to be lost again.'

[48] See discussion, *ibid.*, 260f.

pastoral and catechetical use.[49] Allegorical interpretation, despite its freedom, supports the unity of the two testaments. Tertullian, for all his bigotry, sees a continuity between Jews and Christians (*test.* 5.6), between law and gospel (*scorp.* 2.2; *Marc.* 4.11.11; *ap.* 45.4; *orat.* 7.3; *ux.* 1.2.2); the difference between Jews and Christians is simply that the former think that Christ was a mere man and are still waiting for the Messiah (*ap.* 21.15; *Marc.* 3.16.1).[50] Scripture controls Tertullian's enthusiasm for the spirit and, indeed, his legalism is evident at several points.[51]

Clement is the first writer to use vigorously the whole range of scripture to prove theological and ethical propositions.[52] It is therefore remarkable that his hermeneutical principles have seemed elusive and problematic.[53] He has seemed to reverence without comprehension the clearly defined corpus of scripture, and yet to regard it with the eyes of a philosopher.[54] Logic and symbolism play equally important roles in his use of scripture. (iv) God, as reason, is the first principle of logic. Logic and exegesis are mutually dependent for Clement; without a base in scripture, logic remains in the realm of opinion, and without the resources of logic, scripture can be twisted to mean anything. Yet there is much in Clement that does not seem logical, for he has inherited from Philo and others the ways of allegorical exegesis: scripture says nothing superfluous, its repetitions are significant, and its silences are full of meaning; everything is connected to everything, so that meaning can be transferred from one point to another; words may be taken in all possible senses. Numbers, objects and names have symbolic meaning. These rules were common to the Hellenistic world and are even

---

[49] G. Zaphiris, *Le texte de l'Évangile selon saint Matthieu d'après les citations de Clément d'Alexandrie comparées aux citations des Pères et des Théologiens grecs du IIe au XVe siècle* (Gembloux, 1970), 935.

[50] T. P. O'Malley, *Tertullian and the Bible* (Nijmegen, 1967), 123f.

[51] H. Karpp, *Schrift und Geist bei Tertullian* (Gütersloh, 1955), 71.

[52] There are roughly 3,200 references to the Old Testament and 5,000 references to New Testament. See E. Osborn, La Bible inspiratrice d'une morale chrétienne d'après Clément d'Alexandrie, in *Le monde grec ancien et la Bible*, ed. Mondésert, 127.

[53] H. Kutter, *Clemens Alexandrinus und das Neue Testament* (Giessen, 1897), 17, 45.

[54] *Ibid.*, 45. Also see p. 18f. for the claim that Clement approaches scripture always as a philosopher. Cf. above, chapter 3.

found in the Stoic treatment of Homer.[55] They were too loose;
anything could mean anything when it moved from its physical
to its spiritual meaning. Philo had the constraints of Judaism.
Clement had the looser constraints of Christian tradition; but
he could not readily answer those who, in the name of a higher
spirituality, rejected both history and church tradition. Argument was the only possibility, so he used it negatively against
heretics and positively for the exploration of the Bible. He saw
that the Gnostic theosophists were wrong in their history and in
their imagination; the way to discredit them lay in the logic
which they claimed to transcend.

Some Christians hesitated about logic. Irenaeus commended
the simplicity of Christ, and warned against the impiety of
minutiloquium (*haer.* 2.26.1); Aristotle, he said, had provided an
impetus to trivial and needless questions (*haer.* 2.14.5). Tertullian claimed an apostolic ban on endless questions (*an.* 2.7). By
contrast, Clement saw positive value in inquiry, which led faith
by way of demonstration to knowledge. There was no other
path to knowledge and those who ignored logic were like
farmers who tried to harvest grapes without cultivating and
caring for the vines (*str.* 1.9.43). Knowledge came from the
demonstration of the logical implications of a passage of
scripture (*str.* 2.11.49).

Logic and exegesis interact within the totality of the logos.
There are no breaks. Scripture and secular writings may be
quoted together (*str.* 1.8). Our lord used logical ambiguity to
defeat the devil in exegetical combat (*str.* 1.9.44). The prophets
are not immediately intelligible, but call for skilful teachers
(Prov. 22:20). While prophets and apostles had no philosophical techniques, the mind of the prophetic spirit in them
calls for these skills in interpretation. In logic, one must stand for
or against the logos, without whom nothing was made
(*str.* 1.9.45).

Hermas shows the difference between reading letter by letter
and reading whole syllables. The true gnostic explains the
scripture in its syllables (*str.* 6.15.115–32); he looks for and

[55] C. Siegfried, *Philon von Alexandrien als Ausleger des Alten Testaments* (Jena, 1875), 337–9.

expounds connections and sequences, tracking them as a hunter follows his quarry. Clement uses the metaphor of the hunter when he talks about scripture and about the disorder of the *Stromateis* (*str.* 1.28.179). Jerome and others were to follow his lead in this account of the exegetical pursuit.

(v) The use of logic is negative as well as positive. In *Stromateis* 3 Clement uses argument against the tenets of the Carpocratians, discrediting their exegesis and disputing their claims. Righteousness is not to be rocketed into the heavens so that it may mean a universal sharing of all things, including marital relations. There are specific commands against lust, adultery and covetousness, which the heretics insist were meant as a joke (*str.* 3.2). Against the case for promiscuity, Clement argues, 'This is an insult to the name of communion. To do something wrong is called an action, just as also to do right is likewise called an action. Similarly communion is good when the word refers to sharing of money and food and clothing. But they have impiously given the name of communion to common sexual intercourse.' The misuse of Luke 6:30: 'Give to every one that asks you' is countered by Eph. 4:20–24 and 5:1–4, 5–11: 'But you have not so learned Christ…But fornication and all impurity and covetousness and shamefulness and foolish talk, let them not be mentioned among you as is fitting for the saints'. Those who reject the law as given by an inferior creator god, are inconsistent in their opposition. They break the command against adultery, but keep the commands to increase and multiply, to eat and enjoy, to take an eye for an eye. If they are set on disobeying the creator, they should not keep any of his words nor use any of his products. There is a short passage in which Clement summarises his plea for logos as scripture and as reason (*str.* 3.5.42.4–6). 'We must follow where the word leads (Plato, *Rep.* 394d); and if we depart from it we must fall into endless evil (Homer, *Odyssey* 12.118). And by following the divine scripture, the path by which believers travel, we are to be made like the lord as far as possible (Plato, *Theaet.* 176b). We must not live as if there were no difference between right and wrong (Plato, *Theaet.* 176e – 177a), but to the best of our power we must purify ourselves from indulgence and lust and take care for our soul (Plato, *Phaedo* 107c), which must continually be devoted to the deity alone. For when it is pure and set free from all evil, the mind is somehow capable of receiving the power of God and the divine image is set up in it. "And everyone who has this hope in the Lord purifies himself" says the scripture "even as he is pure"'. Here, as elsewhere, we see the remarkable synthesis in Clement of all that he took to be logos.

(vi) Logical demonstration, as Clement understands it, ends as a method of biblical interpretation.[56] Aristotle's logic becomes Clement's hermeneutic. Whereas rhetoric and dialectic, by themselves, lead to opinion, faith leads to true knowledge which expounds revelation with the precision of Greek logic (*str.* 6.9.78; *str.* 7.15.91; cf. *anal. post.* 87a 31–5).

From the beginning of the *Stromateis*, Clement is concerned with logos. In writing as in teaching, he puts the word at the disposal of others, who will either test and reject or choose and use it with profit. From the word come the gift of salvation and the way to heaven (*str.* 1.1.4). The need for testing is paramount and this requires faith which grows into wisdom and knowledge (*str.* 1.1.5). For on the believer alone, the word, the head of the universe, rests (*str.* 1.3.23), and Plato who loved the truth seems to have been inspired by God, when he urged us to follow the best word (*str.* 1.8.42).

The true dialectic (*str.* 1.28) is described within the philosophy of Moses, which includes ethics (history and law), physics (sacrifice) and theology (the vision of the greatest mysteries). Plato describes dialectics as the science which discovers the reasons of things and this science is acquired by the wise man so that he may please God in what he says and does. Plato's discussion in the *Statesman* is concerned with the question of what makes a good argument. Suitability is not enough; brevity, however welcome, will not do for the 'ability to divide according to real forms' may need more or less time to fulfil its task. When anyone complains at the length of an argument, he must be required to prove 'that a briefer statement of the case would have left him and his fellow disputants better philosophers,

---

[56] G. Apostolopoulou, *Die Dialektik bei Klemens von Alexandria* (Frankfurt, 1977), 113.

more able to demonstrate real truth by reasoned argument'. Nothing else matters.[57] Similarly in *Philebus* 22c, Plato distinguishes between his own reason and the 'true, divine reason' against which common objections fail.

There is, says Clement, a true dialectic which mixes philosophy and truth, tests powers as it climbs to the highest essence and goes beyond to God. The knowledge, which follows, governs the speech and action of those who achieve it, the skilful money-changers who test all things and keep only what is good. An apocryphal saying of Jesus and a Pauline reference (1 Thess. 5:21) support this crucial command. Dialectic descends to show the nature of every individual thing. True wisdom deals with things as they are and is untroubled by passion. The saviour removes ignorance and brings true knowledge of God and of ourselves. Only the son knows and can reveal the father. This is the mystery of Christ by which we may judge between the different senses of the law, which may be symbolic, prescriptive, or prophetic. For scripture must be taken as a complex whole and not as a single bald-headed Myconos, and therefore 'those who hunt after the sequence of the divine teaching must approach it with the utmost perfection of the logical faculty' (*str.* 1.28.179).

All of this is developed later in the account of the true gnostic or savant (*str.* 6.9f.), who is able to talk about the good and to follow heavenly archetypes. His knowledge is based on a wide range of preliminary studies and culminates in dialectic, which enables him to distinguish and divide genera and species, to know simple and primary existences (*str.* 6.10.80); he is well able to stand up to the Sophists because the cause of all error and falsehood is the inability to distinguish between universal and particular (*str.* 6.10.82). Dialectic is chiefly concerned with this distinction which is as important in scripture as elsewhere; for in scripture one expression may have many meanings and many expressions may have one meaning. Dialectic enables the gnostic to avoid what is irrelevant, to discern and to test.

For Clement dialectic was not merely a wall of defence

---

[57] *Pol.* 286e–287a, trans. J. B. Skemp.

against Sophists and heretics (*str.* 6.10.81; 1.20.100), but a path to spiritual vision, the way into the ἀκολουθία of scripture and the guide to life (*str.* 5.3.17). Logical sequence may be the first meaning of ἀκολουθία;[58] the rules of logic are concerned to govern valid inference from premisses to conclusion and all forms of logical implication (*str.* 8.3.8; 7.15.91; 5.13.87). These correspond to the order of nature, which depends on an omnipotent providence (*str.* 6.3.34). Then ἀκολουθία is also the structure of a passage of scripture (*Ecl.* 56) and the coherence of law and gospel (*str.* 3.12.86). The intellectual formation of the true gnostic must follow an ordered sequence. His mind must be ordered so that he will see the order which governs all (*str.* 7.10.59). The unity of the virtues, their ἀκολουθία, springs from the fact that one virtue implies another; it is proclaimed widely by Clement and the Platonic tradition. Following God brings coherence to moral life (*str.* 2.19.110).

So the concept runs through the whole of Clement and merits continual attention. Gregory of Nyssa wrote in similar terms: ἀκολουθία began as logical sequence, the coherence of truth with the principles of faith; it included the order of the cosmos as exhibited in the sequence of natural phenomena and the sequence of history in the plan of salvation. One last meaning pointed to the structure of a text of scripture and the pattern of events within a narrative.[59]

As Clement draws his account of the true gnostic to a close, he returns to scripture as the source of truth; for the scriptures, in all their variety, come from one lord through prophets, gospels and apostles, and they guide from beginning to end. He who turns to the truth in scripture, becomes in a sense divine (*str.* 7.16.95). The truth of scripture burns away falsehood. The true gnostic grows old in the scriptures, maintains the teachings of the apostles, and lives by the gospel which he finds to be demonstrated in the law and the prophets (*str.* 7.16.104). Scripture commands investigation. Those who seek will find. Those who knock will find an open door and will be given that

---

[58] R. Mortley, *Connaissance religieuse et herméneutique chez Clément d'Alexandrie* (Leiden, 1973), 103.

[59] J. Daniélou, 'Ἀκολουθία chez Grégoire de Nysse, *RevSR* 27 (1953), 219–49.

for which they have asked. God gives to those, who ask questions in the scriptures, the gift of his divine knowledge and illumination in logical investigation (*str.* 8.1.1). Just as all demonstration is traced back to indemonstrable faith, so all logic is dependent on the true dialectic which hangs on God.

Symbol and allegory

Logic is not all. The unity of the Bible draws on the power of its centripetal images. Metaphor goes with metonymy and description.[60] The woodenness of some modern historical and theological exegesis cannot do justice to biblical symbolism and the need for imagination. Clement faced opponents whose imagination was prolific but frequently trivial. His own use of symbolism has rightly attracted interest, since he gives as much space to its exposition (*str.* 5.4–10), and to its practice, as he does to logic.[61]

Much of Clement's exegesis is concerned with allegorical transposition from this world to a world above; but because of his concern with logic, Clement is never far from true dialectic and the coherence of reason. We may see this most clearly (*str.* 6.16) where he gives a strange exposition of the decalogue. For one thing, he omits two of the ten commandments and treats others out of the biblical order, in order to show their logical sequence. The first commandment means that there exists only one sovereign God and the second means that we should not give the name of God to created things. He-who-is is absolutely unique. The fourth commandment does not mean that God needed a rest, or indeed that God ever stops doing good. It points rather to our true rest which is Christ, who is light, truth, the ordering of created things and the first day. The fifth commandment tells us to honour God as our father and wisdom as our mother. The seventh commandment forbids the adultery which abandons true knowledge as found within the tradition of the church. Adultery is false opinion about God and

---

[60] See Northrop Frye, *The great code* (London, 1982), 7f.
[61] See C. Mondésert, Le symbolisme chez Clément d'Alexandrie, *RSR*, 26 (1936), 158–80 and also D. Wyrwa, *Platonaneignung*, 265f.

deifies created objects in the idolatry which Paul denounced as fornication. The sixth commandment forbids murder, which is the destruction of the true doctrine of God and the immortality which it brings. The eighth commandment forbids stealing what is another's, giving divine honour to a statue, attributing growth and other natural phenomena to the stars as causes and assuming for oneself anything which belongs to the sole creator. The tenth commandment forbids all lusts, the desire of false things, the belief that animate things have a power of their own, or that inanimate things can save or hurt without an agent. For there is one first cause, one providence which works through many intermediate causes. The true dialectic links separate truths to produce universal precepts.

For Clement, as for Justin, the scriptures are the mind and will of God (*dial.* 68). Spirit and word are identical ways to the divine truth which is above all opinion (*dial.* 7). Study of scripture is immediate encounter with the divine ideas, in an effort to find their ἀκολουθία. This is all that esoterism means for Clement: there is nothing which cannot be made clear with the help of the profound concepts of scripture and the Platonic dialectic.[62] Mystery and symbol are accessible through the Logos who is the key which unlocks and the light which shines from the centre of all scripture. Allegory can easily forget history; but Clement resists this danger more effectively than Philo and Barnabas.[63] He finds in scripture at least five senses: historical, doctrinal (moral, religious or theological), prophetic, philosophical (cosmic or personal), and mystical.[64]

Justin, Irenaeus, Clement and Tertullian all show constant sensitivity to the imagery of the Bible. Clement justifies the secrecy of symbols in four ways.[65] Truth is too precious a pearl to cast before swine; it must be hidden from the unworthy and remain open to those who have proved themselves in faith. Concealment also makes a teacher indispensable, and teachers preserve the tradition with integrity. Symbols make a more vivid impression on those who perceive them. 'Moreover all things that shine through a veil show forth the truth in a grander

[62] Mondésert, *Clément d'Alexandrie*, 61.   [63] *Ibid.*, 148.   [64] *Ibid.*, 153–62.
[65] Osborn, *Philosophy of Clement*, 169–71.

and more venerable form, like fruits which are seen through water and forms which are seen through veils' (*str.* 5.9.56). Some of the power of symbols is due to their ability to say many things at once. While 'clear things can be understood in one way only, it is possible to receive several meanings at once from sayings with a hidden meaning. In such circumstances the inexperienced and unlearned man falls into error; but the knower understands' (*ibid.*).

In symbolism as in logic, unity is revealed. 'At the basis of symbolism, as Clement understands it, there is a profound idea which in their own way the very excesses of the method of interpretation underline. This idea is the relatedness of all things among themselves, the intelligible bond which sets them in order, and brings them together again, which makes them *one* beneath their multiplicity, *one* by their cohesion and their unity.'[66]

Numbers and proportions form part of the dialectic of scripture. Some examples of this are fantastic, like the 318 servants of Abraham and the name of Jesus; but the construction of tabernacle and ark points to regular proportion of a kind which leads from objects of sense to objects of intellect. In later Platonism the forms were frequently replaced by numbers (*str.* 6.11); the development begins in Aristotle's account of the 'unwritten doctrines' and continues in Speusippus, Philo and Nicomachus of Gerasa.[67] It represents a bridge between logic and symbolism which has carried much traffic in the wrong direction.

When we consider him anachronistically, in our own terms, Clement may not seem as logical as he tries to be, nor as lucid as one might expect from his handbook of logic. Nevertheless, within the context of his time, his ideas are rationally acceptable and his competence in argument is clear.[68] He insists that the cause of most errors is the failure to distinguish between the universal and the particular. This is clear in his rejection of the

---

[66] Mondésert, *Clément d'Alexandrie*, 151f.

[67] See Dillon, *Middle Platonists*, 4f., 17, 159, 355.

[68] Quentin Skinner has developed the important distinction between what is rational and what is, in a given context, rationally acceptable. Neglect of the distinction results in conceptual parochialism.

libertine exegesis of 'Give to him who asks'; but much of his exegesis, especially his true dialectic, finds a universal meaning in a particular statement. This is because dialectic works in two directions. It rejects the false inference from a proposition which is not universal. On the other hand, by dividing and joining, it works towards a more ultimate and universal principle.

Here symbol and allegory played a powerful role. The quickest way from particular to universal was to allegorise. The Old Testament must be freed from its crudities by allegory. When attention was paid to symbolism, all the hidden links emerged. The more connections one saw, the closer was the coherence of the whole. Clement grasped ideas in synthesis, seeing every aspect in one glance.[69] This does not mean, as has been claimed,[70] that he lacked the power to analyse. His criticism of Gnostic royal freedom, his distinction between free will and freedom, his eclectic philosophy, his account of faith, all indicate powers of analysis. But his synthesising imagination is the reason why he returns to an earlier topic to add a fresh connection which had been omitted; the loose plan of the *Stromateis* shows the profusion of his ideas. Allegory works by analogy and Clement is concerned to indicate every analogy. This is why a work which appears disparate and incoherent springs from a mind which saw everything together; because the λόγος is ever active, because truth can pick up its scattered seeds, it is neither necessary nor desirable to tidy up. Regrettably for us, in the untidiness, some superficial and false analogies are mixed with those which are subtle and illuminating; but Clement has explicitly requested hard work from his readers. The word does not do it all. There is much labour, he says, between seed and harvest, between plant and fruit.

[69] E. de Faye, *Clément d'Alexandrie, Etude sur les rapports du Christianisme et la philosophie grècque au IIe siècle*, (Paris, 1898), 123. 'Clément a l'esprit foncièrement synthétique; il embrasse les idées dans leur ensemble et comme en bloc; il en aperçoit du premier coup et d'un seul regard tous les aspects.' [70] *Ibid.*

GOD AS ONE TRUTH, THE OBJECT OF FAITH AND KNOWLEDGE

Faith as the road to reality

Clement joins with Paul in his account of faith as the way to reality. As Abraham showed, righteousness is by faith, not by works (*str.* 1.7.38). Guessing at truth is one thing, truth itself is another: ἄλλο ὁμοίωσις, ἄλλο αὐτὸ τὸ ὄν, καὶ ἦ μὲν μαθήσει καὶ ἀσκήσει περιγίνεται, ἦ δὲ δυνάμει καὶ πίστει. Reality is reached, not by learning and training, but by power and faith. The one good God brings all by different paths to the one gate of faith. Clement takes the Pauline antithesis between faith and works, between the wisdom of this world and Christ, who is the power and wisdom of God, and joins it to the antithesis in Plato between opinion and truth. The Sophist is to be rejected for his φανταστικὴ τέχνη and ψευδὴς δόξα.[71]

Faith is both exclusive and inclusive, exclusive in that it is uniquely necessary for salvation, inclusive in that other things may be built upon it (*str.* 5.1.2). Faith is the key to the intellectual gates of the word (*prot.* 1.10). It is a free choice and not, as Basilides claims, a natural advantage with which some people are born (*str.* 2.3.10). Faith requires co-operation between subject and object: just as a ball is thrown from one person to another and both thrower and catcher are necessary (*str.* 2.6.25).[72] Faith grows, by investigation, into knowledge (*str.* 5.1.5). Philosophy is a slow track to truth whereas faith is rapid in its route to perfection (*str.* 7.2.11).

Arguments for faith

Since a major objection was that Christians were believers and not thinkers, it was necessary to offer a philosophical justification of faith. This Clement did, as no other had done. To summarise, in anticipation, faith is justified because it is the

[71] *Sophist* 236c and 240d. See Osborn, *Paul and Plato*, 475.
[72] Cf. R. M. Rilke, 'erst wenn du plötzlich Fänger wirst des Balles, den eine ewige Mitspielerin dir zuwarf', cited at beginning of H.-G. Gadamer, *Wahrheit und Methode* (Tübingen, 1960).

acceptance of an indemonstrable first-principle (*str.* 8.3.6f.), which it receives from God and not from man (*str.* 2.4.13). It is the judgement of a soul which has been trained by God to distinguish true from false (*str.* 2.4.15). It is a preconception which gives meaning to words like 'God' (*str.* 2.4.16) and an assent of the mind (*str.* 2.12.54). Faith obeys God's commands and learns from his scripture (*str.* 2.11.48). It is the one alternative left when other logical means of inquiry are useless (*str.* 5.1.5).[73] The act of faith is directed to what is ultimate and primary, on which all else depends. The only proper object is the one God. As we now examine them in extended form, we shall find that all the arguments point this way.

The argument for the indemonstrable first principle is like the argument against infinite regress, which Justin uses to prove the existence of God. Plato had used the argument to indicate the form of the good in the *Republic* and to prove the first cause in the *Laws*. All knowledge is based on what is known before. Accounts of first-principles are not based on what is known before, therefore accounts of first-principles are not knowledge. This is confirmed by the ignorance of philosophers concerning first-principles, an ignorance which had pointed Justin along the road to faith. Since first-principles can only be reached by faith, 'call no man your teacher on earth' (*str.* 2.4.14). Knowledge comes by demonstration, but faith 'is a grace which leads on from indemonstrable things to that which is absolutely simple, which neither is with matter, nor is matter, nor is dependent on matter'. Faith sees ultimate things, whereas materialists like those in Plato's *Sophist* cannot see. Only the prophets, said Justin, saw God and were able to speak accurately. Clement concludes that 'with a new eye, new ear, new heart, all things can be seen, heard, and apprehended by faith and under-standing when the lord's disciples speak and hear and act in a spiritual way' (*ibid.*). Elsewhere Clement links this perception to the principle that 'like perceives like' and to the need for the moral transformation which faith brings. The loving and faithful God is known by those who love and have faith. 'We

---

[73] See Osborn, *Philosophy of Clement*, 131–40.

must be joined to him by divine love, so that by like we may see like, hearing and obeying the word of truth, guilelessly and purely in the manner of children who obey us' (*str.* 5.1.13). On the other hand, the impure cannot perceive the pure, and the unbeliever is blind and deaf to spiritual things (*str.* 5.4.19). With a divine teacher and saviour, faith leads to the vision of God.

Clement goes on to speak of faith as a trained perception which judges critically between true and false. It is, as for Aristotle, a decision which follows knowledge. This makes it higher than knowledge and only God can train the soul in this way. 'To obey the Logos, whom we call teacher, is to believe in him and not to go against him in anything' (*str.* 2.4.16). Faith, which must come from God, goes together with knowledge, 'by a kind of divine reciprocity' (*ibid.*).

Faith, as a preconception, is equally dependent on its divine object. From Epicurus, we move to Ben Sirach (25:9) and the blessedness of speaking to ears that hear and to Isaiah, 'except you believe, you will in no way understand' (Isa. 7:9). Plato claimed that knowledge of the true king made the knower kingly. So those who believe in Christ are good (χρηστοί) and kingly because they have cared for the king. He, who fulfilled the law and did the will of his father, was a living law, a pattern of divine virtue for those who see the mystery of the cross. He is the law which is king of all (*str.* 2.4.19).

Faith in scripture produces a demonstration which confirms and strengthens faith (*str.* 2.11.48f.). It is the wisdom taught by God. Here again, the crux of the argument is the power of God. The strength of the proof is the strength of the scripture which is the strength of God. Faith in God, which learns scriptures and obeys commandments, is strengthened by the power of God.

Faith is the assent which, according to Stoics and Platonists, provides the basis of human knowledge and common life (*str.* 2.12.54). The prevalence of human error shows that, without God's help, all is precarious; but the elect of God are saved by faith which surrounds them. Obedience to God's commandments must be fulfilled with love. Fear of God and repentance are the ways to understanding.

Faith is the only alternative left when other logical means of inquiry are useless. This argument for faith would be singularly strange if it were not for 'the indisputable consideration that it is God who speaks and who gives in writing information concerning every single point I want to know. Who then would be so impious as to disbelieve God and to ask for proofs from him as from men?' (*str.* 5.1.5).

In all these arguments for faith and elsewhere, faith is dependent on its divine object. Apart from the one God, faith, which is the first and last step along the way to truth, cannot move. For Aristotle, knowledge must come partly from previous knowledge and proof comes from prior and immediate premisses.[74] There must be indemonstrable first-principles to avoid an infinite regress[75] and these are grasped by νοῦς not by ἐπιστήμη.[76] In Aristotle faith is a conviction or ὑπόληψις, a term which Clement uses.[77]

Philo had already done much for the meaning of faith which directed trust to God, away from self and earthly things, τὴν πρὸς τὸν θεὸν πίστιν καὶ τὴν πρὸς τὸ γενητὸν ἀπιστίαν.[78] It was the opposite of οἴησις, τῦφος, μεγαλαυχεῖν.[79] Faith is not just intellectual, but a movement from creature to God and a final detachment from self.[80] The opposite to faith is not sense-perception. Nor is faith merely a beginning, but goes on to ecstasy in the self-transcendence of the highest part of the soul, to assimilation with God and perfection.[81]

---

[74] *Metaph.* 992*b*; *Post. Anal.* 71ab; *Prior Anal.* 64b. See E. A. Clark, *Clement's use of Aristotle* (New York, 1977), 17.

[75] *Magna moralia* 1197a22. This work is no longer considered to be by Aristotle.

[76] *Post. anal.* ii.19.100 b 9–17.

[77] *Top.* iv.5.125b37 and 126b18. *str.* 5.28.1. Clark (*Clement's use*, 26) claims that 'in Clement's rehabilitation of faith as a mode of perception not to be disparaged, he was aided more than he acknowledged by Aristotelian definitions'. But Clement could not be trusted as an interpreter of Aristotle, without much more exact investigation and assessment of the intermediaries through whom he received his knowledge.

[78] *mut.* 201. See also *heres* 93, and *Abr.* 268. For comment see W. Völker, *Fortschritt und Vollendung bei Philo von Alexandrien* (Leipzig, 1938), 240, and 248–50.

[79] *heres* 93; *mut.* 155.

[80] E. Bréhier, *Les idées philosophiques et religieuses de Philon d'Alexandrie* (3rd edn Paris, 1950), 219–21.   [81] *Ibid.*, 248.

Knowledge: logic and prayer

Knowledge, like faith, looks to one God. It both excludes and includes, for there is one distinctive form of knowledge which embraces many fragments of truth. True knowledge and true philosophy come through faith (*str.* 2.11.48f.). Truth includes knowledge of the true and a mental habit of truth (*str.* 2.17.76). Of the kinds of knowledge which are commonly discussed, there is, first, that of physical objects, second, that of reasoned argument, and third, the saviour himself. Physical things can hardly be proper objects of knowledge, reason is a valid kind of knowledge, but the highest kind is that of the saviour (*str.* 6.1.2f.). God may be worshipped in the ways of Jews or Greeks or in the third, new and spiritual way of the Christians (*str.* 6.5.41). Just as there are different methods of grafting into a tree, so there are different kinds of knowledge and conversion; but the highest form of knowledge is the gnostic[82] teaching which looks into the realities of things themselves (*str.* 6.15.119–21). This depends on the unique wisdom which is taught by God and is the basis for all other wisdom. Even with this God-given wisdom, man can only reach a limited concept of God (*str.* 6.18.166). Yet it is strong enough to unite the knowledge of things, to perform what λόγος suggests and to handle secret truth (*str.* 7.1.4). The movement to knowledge is the movement from essentials to certitude, science and comprehension (*str.* 7.10.57).

At every stage of the journey, there is dependence on the one God who gives wisdom. 'The lord is allegorically called the vine from which, with care and logical husbandry, the fruit is to be gathered' (*str.* 1.9.43). The true dialectic goes to the highest being, the God of all things, by the grace of the saviour who removes ignorance and gives knowledge (*str.* 1.28.177). The saviour into whom we are transplanted is the spiritual garden in which knowledge grows until we see God face to face. Continual prayer keeps the gnostic in the company of God, until he is joined to him in divine love. 'For he lacks none of the things that

---

[82] Clement depicts his true gnostic in opposition to the heretical Gnostic. To avoid confusion, I have spelt the heretic with a capital letter.

he thinks are good, being already sufficient for himself through the grace of God and knowledge. But having become self-sufficient he wants for no other things. Knowing the will of the Almighty, and having a thing at the same time as he prays for it, he is come close to almighty power, and striving to be spiritual through infinite love, he is made one with the spirit' (*str.* 7.7.44).

Some interpreters have had difficulty with the logical element in Clement's true dialectic, but recent work has shown its importance.[83] In Irenaeus too, there has been fresh appreciation of logic and vision.[84] Plain logical inconsistency is noted in the teachings of Gnostics (*haer.* 2.12.3; 2.13.1; cf. *haer.* 2.18.1) and their theories are shown to be void.[85] Irenaeus claims for the doctrine of the salvation of the flesh both logical consistency and coherence with the eucharist (*haer.* 4.18.5).[86] The vision of God enters, participates, communes in the divine mystery, gazing directly on the face of the son of God. Against the Gnostics, Irenaeus finds in the incarnation the final meaning of God, for by it, man is accustomed to receive God and God is accustomed to dwell in man (*haer.* 3.20.2). Life is participation in God, seeing God and enjoying his bounty.[87]

Tertullian discusses other aspects of knowledge. He tells of Plato's ambivalence with regard to the body – does the body help or hinder knowledge? There are, for Plato, invisible substances which are divine and eternal and these are the patterns and causes of the objects of nature (*an.* 18.1). Yet for Tertullian, God may be known through his creation and through his revelation in both covenants (*Marc.* 1.18.2). There is also the universal testimony of the soul, which is simple and true. The soul which is naturally Christian is conscious of God (*test.* 5.1), from whom all knowledge comes.

Clement may seem confused in his call to knowledge and his reluctance to leave faith behind. Yet he is trying to offer an

---

[83] See above for discussion of true dialectic, and below for the logic which has been set out by Apostolopoulou, *Die Dialektik.* For a more theosophical approach, see J. Pépin, La vraie dialectique selon Clément d'Alexandrie, in *EPEKTASIS FS J. Daniélou* eds. J. Fontaine and C. Kannengiesser (Paris, 1972), 375–83.

[84] Tremblay, *La manifestation.*   [85] *Ibid.*, 32f.   [86] *Ibid.*, 34.

[87] *Ibid.*, 175.

important insight, so we must think carefully. Faith and knowledge are not separate stages of a journey where one may be discarded for the other. There is never faith without knowledge, nor knowledge without faith. They exist in what he calls a 'divine reciprocity'. No one ever leaves the beginners' class. No one is denied the vision of mysteries.

PHILOSOPHY AS THE FRIEND OF TRUTH

We have seen (chapter 4) that the Christian account of God depended on the union of philosophical and biblical ideas which in turn depended on the acceptance of the Bible as the barbarian or true philosophy. The continuity of the gospel and philosophy is evident at many points.

The true philosophy

Justin makes his way through different schools of philosophy with some misgiving. While philosophy is the greatest possession because it leads to God, it should not have different schools because knowledge is one (*dial.* 2). The knowledge of reality and human happiness is not acquired like the knowledge of music, arithmetic and astronomy, but requires a different dedication (*dial.* 3). Justin goes to Platonism because it offers a vision of God, and then moves on to the prophets who alone had that vision. His concerns are God and truth (*dial.* 6.1; 1 *apol.* 23.1; *dial.* 3.7 and 7.1).[88] In the words of the prophets and of the friends of Christ, Justin finds the true philosophy, which speaks of God, his unity and his providence.

Seeds of reason

The seminal logos or reason is spread through all the human race. Those who have lived with logos are Christians (1 *apol.* 46). This, however, is only part of the Logos, whereas Christians know Christ, who is the whole Logos (2 *apol.* 8 and 10).

[88] See Osborn, *Justin Martyr*, 78.

Heraclitus and Socrates stand to Christ as the part to the whole, as copy to reality. From the context it would seem that Justin is optimistic, not pessimistic about human reason, even if it bring but an obscure perception of reality.[89] There is one truth, which is perceived dimly through a copy by the pagan, and clearly and directly by the Christian.

How good are the seeds of reason? The relation of Justin to philosophy has been keenly discussed.[90] The older liberal view, that 'the Church appears as the great insurance society for the ideas of Plato and Zeno' and produces the future dogmatic 'which presupposes the Platonic and Stoic conception of the world long ago overthrown by science', is disproved by the dominance of Christian ideas.[91] Later interpretation claimed that it could identify the school of Middle Platonism to which Justin belonged, and that Justin provoked the attack of Celsus.[92] In the opinion of some, philosophy was given only a minor place in Justin's thought,[93] because of the distinction between the logos-Christ and the logos-seed; however, radical discontinuity between the two is improbable, so optimism survives.

Justin's confidence in reason springs from his belief in its divine origin and illumination;[94] he separates religion from culture and opposes all pagan religious philosophy with a more coherent alternative.[95] The ordered plan of the *Apology* indicates Justin's rhetorical and logical skill. The presentation develops through association of ideas, keywords, synonyms, parts of a phrase, or a new phrase which announces a theme in cryptic form; the main stages of the argument are clear. As in Plato,

[89] *Ibid.*, 140–45, where the disagreement between Chadwick and Holte is discussed.

[90] J. Morales, La investigacion sobre San Justino y sus escritos, *ScrTh.* 16 (1984), 869–96.

[91] von Harnack, *History of Dogma*, II, 228f. This account remains valuable and important.

[92] C. Andresen, Justin und der mittlere Platonismus, *ZNW* 44 (1952/3), 157–95. A convincing criticism of Andresen's link between Justin and Celsus is found in Burke, Celsus and Justin, 107–16.

[93] R. Holte, Logos Spermatikos, Christianity and ancient philosophy according to St Justin's Apologies. *StTh.* 12 (1958), 109–68. N. Hyldahl, *Philosophie und Christentum* (Copenhagen, 1966). J. C. M. van Winden, An early Christian philosopher: Justin Martyr's dialogue with Trypho, chapters 1 to 9, *PhP* 1 (Leiden, 1971).

[94] J. Morales, Fe y demostracion en el metodo teologico de San Justino, *ScrTh.* 17 (1985), 219.   [95] *Ibid.*, 223–5.

270 *One mind, truth and logic*

progressive exposition is concealed under apparent disorder.[96]
Dialogue 1–7 has a simple linear structure while the rest of the
Dialogue has a radial logic which keeps returning to central
arguments. A frustrated Justin objects to Trypho's lack of
method in argument. Instead of arguing to and from agreed
propositions, Trypho cuts back to deny what he has earlier
accepted. So Justin repeats the same things in several contexts.
The order of truth, like the stars in the heavens, is fixed, and
repetition is inevitable. It will take time for many to see the
connections.

Irrationality was the major peril of the human race; that is
why Justin defines his neighbour as a λογικὸν ζῷον, why
Tertullian describes Marcion as a body without a mind, why
Clement prepares his hand-book of logic and why Irenaeus
ridicules the irrationality of the Gnostic schemes. With rationality goes freedom of choice. Enforced legalism is not just bad
theology; it is ethically bad because it denies freedom.[97] Justin,
like Paul (Gal. 2:14), insisted that compulsion (ἀναγκάζειν) was
wrong; but he took the argument further. If a Christian wants
to practise the Law, he may do so, provided he does not seek to
impose his views on others (*dial.* 47).

It has been argued, on literary grounds, that Clement does
not depend on Justin for his account of the seeds of truth.[98] Yet
continuity is clear at two points. First, the seed, which is the
word, points to the parable of the sower, which has an effective-
history (*Wirkungsgeschichte*) in Justin, Clement, John Chrysostom and Augustine.[99] Secondly, there is the common claim
that whatever has been well said belongs to Christians and
philosophy.[100] Literary dependence may be unproved, for

[96] See C. Munier, La structure littéraire de l'Apologie de Justin, *RevSR*, 60 (1986), 37f.
and H. H. Holfelder, Εὐσέβεια καὶ φιλοσοφία, Literarische Einheit und politischer
Kontext von Justins Apologie, *ZNW*, 68 (1977), 48–66. See also the valuable analysis
of the rhetorical structure of Tertullian's *praescr.* provided by C. Munier, Analyse du
traité de Tertullien, de praescriptione haereticorum, *RevSR*, 59 (1985), 12–33.
[97] For the conflict between birth dogma and philosophic faith see chapter one above
and the discussion by A. J. Reines, Birth dogma and philosophic religious faith,
HUCA, 46 (1975), 298.
[98] F. Weissengruber, 'Samenkörner der Wahrheit' bei Clemens Alexandrinus, in
Ecclesia peregrinans, FS J. Lenzenberger, ed. K. Amon (Wien, 1986), 5–16.
[99] E. Osborn, Parable and Exposition, *ABR*, 22 (1974), 11–22.
[100] 2 *apol.* 13.4; *str.* 1.37 and 38.

Clement claims to preserve spoken rather than written tradition; but the continuity of an idea, which never returns in identical form from one moment to another, is the stuff of the history of ideas. 'But only what has already been thought prepares what has not yet been thought, which enters ever anew into its abundance.'[101]

The necessary preparation

For Clement philosophy is a preparation, under the providence of one God, for the truth of Christ. It is a tutor for the Greeks, as the Law, in Paul's eyes, was for the Jews (*str.* 1.5.28). Philosophy consists of whatever has been rightly said by any sect; but truth itself, found in scripture, stands over these attempts (*str.* 1.7.38). Greek philosophy does not cover all truth, but prepares the learner to receive the truth of the gospel (*str.* 1.16.80). Philosophy is a co-operating cause in the search for truth. A ship is pulled to the water by many hands and not by one particular man. Philosophy does not bring understanding, but works with other things for a good result (*str.* 1.20.97). Philosophy and logic are needed to understand the complexity of scripture (*str.* 1.9.48). Whatever co-operates in the discovery of truth is to be received (*str.* 6.15.123). Philosophy knocks, that doors of truth might be opened. Plato speaks of a true philosophy and the way of both philosopher and Christian is described in the *Theaetetus*. Pythagoras, Socrates and Plato say that they hear God's voice when they contemplate the structure of the universe. They learned from Moses of the word of God and his creative act (*str.* 5.14.99). A true dialectic distinguishes the objects of thought, dividing things into their different kinds, and leads to wisdom with the help of the saviour who removes the dark veil of ignorance (*str.* 1.28.177).

Clement, Philo and Justin offer at least three theories of the origin of philosophy: philosophy was inspired by God, stolen by the Greeks or stolen by heavenly powers. Clement uses different theories for different parts of philosophy (*str.* 1.17.87); but the

---

[101] M. Heidegger, *Identity and Difference*, trans. J. Stambaugh (New York, 1974), 48.

theme of the Greeks and the great truth robbery dominates.[102] The Greeks stole from the Bible, the barbarians and from one another; doubt has been thrown[103] on the claim that these sections of the *Stromateis* were an independent entity.[104]

Logic as a discipline

Clement was the first Christian writer to value logic as a discipline, and to produce a small handbook on the subject. Clement names Chrysippus as the supreme dialectician (*str.* 7.16.101) and Aristotelian logic is present everywhere in his work. *Stromateis* 8 is a handbook of the logic which Clement has used in earlier parts of his work.[105] It mixes Aristotle and Stoicism.[106] To bold spirits, some elements have suggested Antiochus of Askalon as the chief source, pointing to the rough harmony of Aristotle and Stoicism, the refutation of scepticism, seeking and finding, common notions, the use of demonstration and its relation to syllogism, the accounts of definition, faith, division and causes. A more interesting probability is the school of Galen, whose Εἰσαγωγὴ διαλεκτική blends Stoic and Aristotelian logic. We know that Galen wrote small compendia and that there is more biology than theology in *Stromateis* 8. The definition of the foetus as an animal is discussed, and man is placed among the different species of animal. The surgeon's book and scalpel, fever and spleen, not to mention the whole discussion of causes, have obvious medical relevance. We can be sure that logic and medicine went together in Clement's world and that Stoicism and Aristotelianism were the chief ingredients of that logic.[107]

Clement discussed the many advantages of logic. λόγος was not for inflated tricksters who argued in order to deceive

---

[102]　*str.* 5.13.89 – 6.4.38, with anticipations in *str.* 1.16.80 – 1.20.100 and elsewhere. See Wyrwa, *Platonaneignung*, 298–316.

[103]　J. Munck, *Untersuchungen über Klemens von Alexandria* (Stuttgart, 1933), 127–51.

[104]　W. Bousset, *Jüdisch-christlicher Schulbetrieb in Alexandria und Rom* (Göttingen, 1915), 205–29. The question is not closed.

[105]　H. von Arnim, *De octavo Clementis Stromateorum libro* (Rostock, 1894), 16.

[106]　R. E. Witt, *Albinus and the history of Middle Platonism* (Cambridge, 1937), 31.

[107]　M. Spanneut, *Permanence du Stoïcisme* (Gembloux, 1973), 145. See especially *str.* 8.4.9f. The connection with Galen was first suggested by Dr H. A. S. Tarrant.

(*str.* 1.1.8–1.3.24). Life according to λόγος meant not worrying about words (*str.* 1.10.48; cf. Plato, *Pol.* 261, *Theaet.* 184). Philosophy could not make the truth more powerful, but it could protect it from the Sophists (*str.* 1.8.39). Yet the philosopher steals his knowledge by logic and guesswork; only the Christian can know with true intelligence (*str.* 1.20.100); for whereas the philosopher has torn off a limb from the body of truth, the Christian grasps the one whole truth which is Christ (*str.* 1.13). He who has ears may hear. He will see both what is clear and what is dark, 'hailstones and coals of fire' (*str.* 6.15.116). The instruction of the lord opens his mouth (Isa. 50:5). Philosophy may be grafted into Christ, the good olive tree. Whoever is transplanted into Christ and into faith receives the holy spirit who is transplanted in return (*str.* 6.15.117). The purpose of the lord's coming was to lead to the objects of thought and into a new world (*str.* 6.15.126). There is one law as Proverbs (6:23), Pindar, Hesiod and Plato declare. 'The word is one and God is one' (*str.* 1.29.181).

Clement uses demonstration as a way of understanding the Bible and dialectic as a preparation for the vision of God.[108] Elements of Clement's work have been traced to Alcinous who credited Plato with the logic of Aristotle as developed by Theophrastus and Eudemus. Dialectic is concerned with finding first, the substance and then, the accidents of a thing. To elucidate substance it may descend a priori in division and definition or it may ascend a posteriori by analysis. Analysis climbs from sense objects to intellectual objects, from demonstrable to indemonstrable propositions and from hypotheses to principles.[109] So Clement may use a variety of logical tools for different tasks.

Clement finds syllogisms in the Bible (*str.* 6.15.121). It is necessary that the conclusion of a syllogism be a complex and not a simple proposition, that premiss and conclusion have the same reference and that the conclusion follow from the premisses. Dialectic has the positive function (*str.* 6.17.156) of putting truth in a correct logical form. All deduction depends

[108] Apostolopoulou, *Dialektik* 113. There is ample evidence to support this conclusion which needs further development. [109] See Dillon, *Middle Platonists*, 276f.

on an indemonstrable first-principle, which for Aristotle is known by intuition (*Metaph.* 100a), and for Clement by faith. He wants Platonic support for faith (*str.* 2.5.23) and omits Plato's negative comments on the topic. Propositions may be taken as true through their acceptance by the wise or by common consent. Eristic and sophistry work with premisses which are not in this category (*Top.* 100b.26). Knowledge in the strictest sense covers the principles and causes of things (*Analecta post.* 71b.9–11). Opinion, for Aristotle, has a purely subjective grounding in faith (*de anima* 22a.20–22). Dialectic may show, negatively, that an argument is not valid, or positively, that proof has been rationally demonstrated.

Being and salvation

Clement goes respectfully to Plato at many points. He takes from Plato the hostility of philosophers to Sophists, whom he identifies with heretics. Heretics and Sophists do not go behind words to the world of ideas which is the eschatological reality (*str.* 5.3.16). Why is all this important to a study of one God as first-principle? 'Clement is the first Christian philosopher who wants to join, in one ontology, both being and salvation. The realm of being is for him not just the realm of the divine, as it is in Greek ontology, but also the realm of saving power.'[110]

Despite one reference which links Marcion's rejection of the world with Plato (*str.* 4.4.18), Clement turns to Plato for argument that there is one law, one word, one God (*str.* 1.1.82) who is both just and good (*paed.* 1.8.67) and who governs the world in goodness (*str.* 3.3.19). Heretics were philosophers in appearance only (*str.* 7.16.98).[111]

Heraclitus is Justin's first philosophical Christian and Clement finds truth in his account of piety, eschatology and ethics.[112]

---

[110] Apostolopoulou, *Dialektik*, 64.

[111] Clement's philosophical Christianity is governed by one God clearly. His defence of baptism against the Valentinian attack shows his concern for the life of the church and for its rule of faith. M. Mees, Die frühe Christusgemeinde von Alexandrien und die Theologie des Klemens von Alexandrien, *Lat.*, 50 (1984), 124.

[112] Clement quotes him 126 times. See H. Wiese, Heraklit bei Klemens von Alexandrien (Dissertation, Kiel, 1963), 294–99 and P. Valentin, Héraclite et Clément d'Alexandrie, *RSR*, 46 (1958), 27–59.

There is much of value in his view of man's relation to God; 'gods are men, men are gods' is Clement's version of Heraclitus' (frag. 62; Diels 28) 'immortals are mortals, mortals are immortals' (*paed.* 3.1.2). While we may hesitate to claim too wide an influence for Heraclitus, there is a great affinity between the two writers for whom the ever-present word was supreme and the truth no easy task.

Irenaeus' philosophy has attracted less attention, but his insistence on the freedom of the divine will points clearly to the *Timaeus*.[113] He begins his attack on the Gnostics with an account of the unique omnipotence of God (*haer.* 2.1.1), whose self-determining will must not be subject to necessity (*haer.* 2.5.4) and whose goodness is the cause of creation (*haer.* 3.25.5); there can be no higher cause (*haer.* 5.4.2). Creation and the divine revelation in history follow God's plan (*haer.* 3.23.1). With clear echoes of Xenophanes, he asserts the identity of God's will and thought (*haer.* 1.12.2): ὅλος ἔννοια ὤν,ὅλος θέλημα, ὅλος νοῦς, ὅλος ὀφθαλμός, ὅλος ἀκοή, ὅλος πηγὴ πάντων τῶν ἀγαθῶν. In Platonism, he found arguments for free will and arguments about God.

Jerusalem and Athens

While Clement had criticised Sophists because of their trivial objections to Christian teaching (*str.* 1.3.22f.), Tertullian is more widely critical and insists that the heresies have come from philosophy (*an.* 3.1) and that God-given intelligence has been falsely inflated (*an.* 2). The Academy is insolent because it subverts the order of nature. The good providence of God is not seen although John points to what eyes have seen and hands have handled of the word of life (*an.* 17.14). Christians meet with opposition because they possess the truth and are opposed by those who falsely claim it (*nat.* 1.4.5). The various opinions among the philosophers point to their ignorance of the truth and lack of the godly fear which is the beginning of wisdom (*nat.* 2.2.3). Philosophy brings heresy. Plato's forms produced the aeons of Valentinus, and the heretics and philosophers

[113] E. P. Meijering, Irenaeus' relation to philosophy in the light of his concept of free will, in *Romanitas et Christianitas, FS J. H. Waszink* ed. W. den Boer (Amsterdam, 1973), 221–7.

continually discuss the same questions concerning evil and man. But Athens has nothing to do with Jerusalem – there can be no agreement between academy and church, or between heretics and Christians. Therefore it is wrong to try for a Christian philosophy which joins Stoic and Platonic elements. After Christ, there is no need for anything; after faith there is nothing more (*praescr.* 7.13).

Yet Tertullian owes much to philosophy.[114] The mantle joyfully assumes a better and Christian philosophy (*pall.* 6.2). Philosophy is proper to the Christian because it owes no duty outside itself; the better life is to be found in seclusion rather than in public behaviour (*pall.* 5.4).[115] Soranus teaches the truth about the soul (*an.* 6.6) and Seneca is often one of us. Tertullian's reading of Plato can be documented precisely.[116] Anyone who adopts the *pallium* should become a Christian, for the Christian can take his intellectual inheritance into his new faith. This means that 'The antithesis between Athens and Jerusalem, between the Academy and the Church, has been resolved.'[117] While Tertullian distrusts philosophy because of its part in division and heresy (*ap.* 47.9), there is ample evidence for his use of it and other elements of classical culture. His mind is marked by classicism, a wide culture as well as his own distinctive way of thinking.[118]

HERESY AS THE ENEMY OF ONE TRUTH

There is much scattered truth which may be brought together; but there can be no coherence between truth and heresy. Heresies try to subvert faith, yet they point to an ultimate truth which judges them (*praescr.* 1). Truth is one in origin, com-

---

[114] C. de L. Shortt, *The influence of philosophy on the mind of Tertullian* (London, 1932), 11, criticises the view of Bethune-Baker (*JThS*, 4 (1902), 440), that Tertullian was a jurist first and a philosopher second. See also the recent discussions by Barnes and Fredouille.

[115] He argues for the replacement of toga by *pallium* on Cynic (indifference to public life) or Stoic (according to nature) grounds or both (preference for education over materialism).   [116] D'Alès, Tertullien helléniste, *REG*, 50 (1937), 334–42.

[117] T. D. Barnes, *Tertullian* (Oxford, 1971), 231.

[118] Fredouille, *Tertullien*, 481–5. 'L'unité profonde d'une vie et d'une œuvre, l'une et l'autre plus complexes, plus inquiètes, mais aussi plus cohérentes qu'on ne le soupçonne généralement.'

munity and logic. It comes from and declares one God. It has been transmitted by apostles and is found in one church. It declares one God in a coherent logic, within a continuous community.

Truth and misrepresentation

In Justin, Athenagoras and their successors, the unique reality of one God is the reason for the rejection of heresy. For God gave, by Moses and the prophets, the true philosophy from which the different schools have deviated (*dial.* 2.1). Indeed, the truth which God gave at the beginning has been subject to constant falsification, so that there is now 'no truth free from misrepresentation, neither the nature of God, nor his knowledge, nor his activity, nor all that logically flows from these and traces the outline of our religious teaching' (*de res.* 1).[119]

Dualism and division

Irenaeus sets out the claims of orthodoxy: unity of faith in contrast with plurality of heresy, truth against error, total scripture and total church in face of the divisions of heretics. Unity, truth and totality are mutilated by heresy.[120] Heretics blaspheme the creator, deny the salvation of the flesh and the incarnation of the word. Blasphemy against God springs from pride, while blasphemy against scripture springs from falsehood.[121] The rule of truth declares the unity of God (*haer.* 1.22.1; 2.28.1; 3.11.1) and functions as a principle of interpretation which ensures a common understanding of texts (*haer.* 4.35.4; cf. 2.27.1). The consistency of the different parts of scripture reflects the harmony of creation (*haer.* 2.26.3). There is agreement between the four Gospels and the four living creatures of the Apocalypse (*haer.* 3.11.8), between Paul and Luke (*haer.* 3.13.3), and between the two testaments (*haer.* 3.12.12). Heretics break κοινωνία in every form and shut themselves in a

---

[119] J. C. M. van Winden, The origin of falsehood, Some comments on the introductory passage of the treatise 'On the resurrection of the dead' attributed to Athenagoras, *VC*, 30 (1976), 306.

[120] Y. de Andía, L'hérésie et sa réfutation selon Irénée de Lyon, *Aug.*, 25, 3 (1985), 631–44.   [121] *Ibid.*

'universe of incommunicability'.[122] In his attack, Irenaeus reduces heresy to a dualist interpretation of scripture and tradition, which denies that flesh is either made by God or assumed by the word or saved by resurrection. Therefore if he can refute these doctrines he has refuted the conclusions of heresy. He further reduces heresy to the Valentinian heresy, so that a refutation of Valentinianism covers all.[123]

One truth, health and consistency

The preaching of the apostles declared one God and one Christ; to deny their preaching is to deny their lord. One truth starts from one God (*haer.* 3.1). Law and prophets insist on the first point of the rule: that there is one God (*haer.* 3.6). Paul begins with the same claim.[124] There is no arguable ground for a second God anywhere in scripture. Many passages from the Gospels prove the unique God and father (*haer.* 3.10), and when the lord took bread and wine from creation to make more of each, he showed the unity of the creator and redeemer (*haer.* 3.11.5). Other apostolic writings confirm the uniqueness of God (*haer.* 3.12). Irenaeus prays that heretics might be rescued from the pit which they have dug for themselves, and that they might abandon empty shadows for a knowledge of the only true God (*haer.* 3.25.7).

One truth must be primitive, handed down from the apostles. Heretics claim a secret, higher and exclusive tradition (*haer.* 3.2.2); but the apostles would not have kept secrets from those to whom they gave the care of churches. The succession of the church of Rome, for example, proves the one life-giving faith and apostolic truth (*haer.* 3.3). The believer who accepts this tradition finds the highest wisdom and rejects the novelties of heretics who arrived too late for the original truth (*haer.* 3.4.2).

The coherent truth of Christ can be proved from scripture. His disciples were determined to pass on truth and not to send

---

[122] *Ibid.*, 644, where the phrase is taken from Lebeau, Koinonia, 1972, 121–7.

[123] A. Benoit, Irénée et l'hérésie, *Aug.*, 20 (1980), 67.

[124] Heretical objections which start from 2 Cor. 4:5 and Matt. 6:24, receive a reasoned answer.

blind men along false paths (*haer.* 3.5.2). Refutation of heretics is possible even from their selected parts of the Gospels (*haer.* 3.11.7). In summing up the argument of Book 3, Irenaeus returns to the theme of coherence. Heretics have been destroyed by their own arguments which point to conclusions which deny their opinions. The preaching of the church is consistent with itself and with scripture. While saving faith is founded on a sound system of proof, heretics wallow in error, playing with words instead of following argument (*haer.* 3.24.1f.).

Heresies, says Tertullian, were predicted and they now provide a test for the proving of faith (*praescr.* 1). As a sick fever which can overpower the weak, they should be an object of loathing (*praescr.* 2). In the face of apostasy, every Christian must persevere, as the son of God persevered, sinless to the end (*praescr.* 4). The church displays consistent belief (*praescr.* 5). Paul explains that a heretic is a self-condemned man, because he chooses his error (*praescr.* 6). Philosophy and heresy keep turning over questions of evil and human origins, churning out fictitious tales, endless genealogies, futile questions and cancerous words. Therefore philosophy must not be connected with Christ, whose gospel lacks nothing (*praescr.* 7).

Primitive origin and logical content confirm the same unity

Tertullian links logical and ecclesial coherence; the true church is proved by its unity, communion, brotherhood and hospitality, signs which spring from its common rule. From the present existence of a universal church Tertullian assumes the former existence of one primitive faith (*praescr.* 21).[125] Two objections (Jesus did not tell the apostles everything, and the apostles did not pass on all they knew to everyone) are proved false from the text of scripture (*praescr.* 22–5). To a further objection – that the churches have wandered from truth which the apostles taught their fathers – it is answered that all could not have deviated

[125] 'It remains that we should demonstrate whether this our teaching, the rule of which we have given above, may be attributed to the tradition of the apostles, and for this reason, whether all other doctrines do not come from falsehood. We hold communion with apostolic churches because our doctrines do not differ: this is the attestation of our truth.'

into uniformity (*praescr.* 28). The lateness of the heresies is
evidence against their claim to primitive truth (*praescr.* 31).
Those who walk according to the rule can claim the inheritance
of the earliest churches; but heretics have no right to the
scriptures (*praescr.* 37), which they misuse either by addition,
subtraction or rearrangement. They turn to magicians, mounte-
banks, astrologers and philosophers, because, without fear of
God, they have no check on their curiosity. The wisdom that
begins with the fear of God is marked by serious, thoughtful
diligence, by fear and modesty. God and logic come together
before the judgement seat of Christ to the confusion of any who
deny both truth and final judgement (*praescr.* 43f.).

Clement, too, is critical of heretics on the grounds of origin
and content, of God and logic, of church and coherence. The
lord gives all truth through prophets, gospel and apostles, in
different ways and times. If a more ultimate source be sought,
then infinite regress sets in. The only first-principle and criterion
is the voice of the lord (*str.* 7.16.97). The true gnostic holds to
right belief, grows old in scripture, lives according to the gospel
and discovers proofs in the law and the prophets. He never
corrupts the canon of the church, but always teaches his
neighbour the truth. Heretics (*str.* 7.17.106) do not enter the
church by the main door of Christ, but cut a side door to install
their own evil mysteries. The church must be one, because its
God and lord are one; without this unity there can be no true
church (*str.* 7.17.106).

CONCLUSION

One God is the first-principle of things logical and faith is the
simplicity of all knowledge. Truth is marked by simplicity and
faithfulness because the only God never fails. Jesus is this one
truth. God has given one rule or criterion to test all claims to
truth. He has spoken in the scriptures which, by joining
beginning, middle and end, declare the saving history of a single
God. The true dialectic ascends to the highest essence and goes
beyond to God; scripture replaces the forms of Plato as the mind
and will of God. Logic is supported by symbolism in the

distinction of the universal from the particular; it is essential to the understanding of scripture. Faith remains the one way and it is not discarded by the knowledge which is subject to its criterion (*str.* 2.4.15). Philosophy is best seen as a preparation for the one truth of the gospel; it may also be seen as the mother of heresies, which by their plurality deny the truth of God.

The priority of reason is decisive for the separation of the one truth from heresy. The accusation of incoherence has been taken as part of standard polemic against heresy.[126] Indeed, if there were no agreement on the nature of logic, the accusation might simply mean that heretics are different.[127] However in the second century there seems to be some agreement on the nature of argument, but little agreement on whether it is a good thing. Clement has to argue for the necessity of philosophy or argument.[128] People were not called irrational because they were heretics. They were called heretics, partly because they were irrational, and this was part of a total account of one truth as seen in rule, scripture and philosophy.

There are three reasons why this innovation has been overlooked. First, it is not a theme of the New Testament although Paul (Rom. 12:2) speaks of the renewing of the mind. Secondly, faith remains the rule or criterion which reason uses. It is never discarded. Thirdly, there is much in the writers of the second century which seems irrational to us, even if it was rationally acceptable in their day. The study of the history of ideas should free us from conceptual parochialism through 'the distinction between what is necessary and what is the product merely of our own contingent arrangements'.[129] Here we may learn that our concepts are not specially privileged and that the alien character of other beliefs may provide their relevance.[130]

---

[126] In his work, *La notion d'hérésie dans la littérature grecque IIe–IIIe siècles*, A. le Boulluec recognises the various issues at stake. 'Comme l'hérésie cependant est aussi pour Clément une erreur de la raison qui procède d'une faute du jugement moral, le débat s'était déplacé plus d'une fois vers la psychologie et l'éthique', II, 416.

[127] *Ibid.*, 555.

[128] Both simple believers and heretical Gnostics did not want argument or reason.

[129] Quentin Skinner, Meaning and understanding in the history of ideas, *HTh.*, 8 (1969), 52f.

[130] Quentin Skinner, A reply to my critics, in *Meaning and context*, ed. J. Tully (Cambridge, 1988), 287.

In order to recover the historical identity of past thinkers we are
obliged to discuss the rational acceptability of their claims, to
ask whether, against the background of beliefs of the time, their
ideas provide evidence of critical thought.[131]

Within their own world, the writers, whom we have discussed,
exhibit a high degree of consistency and reasonableness. This
was because their one God was νοῦς and the first-principle of
logic. Because he was truth, the one God had given a rule of
truth, scriptures which were governed by logic, and philosophy
which, although imperfect, could harmonise with truth. So it
was the church as academy rather than the church as institution,
which rejected Gnosticism and much other irrationality.[132]

[131] One interesting suggestion goes further. In practice we should always separate our
logical and our historical reconstruction of a past writer's ideas. In the former, we
make our subject a conversational partner, and in the latter, we put him in the
context of his own time. 'We should do both of these things but do them separately',
R. Rorty, The history of philosophy: four genres, in *Philosophy in history*, eds. Rorty,
Schneewind and Skinner, 49.
[132] To use a valuable distinction of Williams, *Arius*, 82–91.

Conclusion

'All philosophers, then, even if unwillingly, reach complete agreement about the unity of God when they come to inquire into the first-principles of the universe' (*leg.* 7). Belief in one God, who is the first-principle of being, goodness and reason defines the shape of early Christian thought.[1] This is the emergence of Christian theology. Unity may be seen as both simple and complex. As being, God is one lord, universal word and trinity. As good, one God gives one law and provides one end and resource for ethical endeavour, whether by martyrdom or by the right use of his world. As reason, one God leads to one truth of faith and knowledge. Faith leads to and grows with knowledge; there can be no separation. True philosophy is all that has been well said, while heresy is a separate limb, torn from the one body of truth. Christian theology must include physics (i.e. metaphysics), ethics and logic.

(i) How did Christian theology emerge? Theology was a response to diverse objections from four complex sources. However, rebuttals of objections do not by themselves produce coherent statements. For the objections commonly come from different, even contradictory positions. Therefore we may expect inconsistencies like those in Clement's account of marriage. Marriage is a good thing, and children make one less selfish, he argues against Marcionites and other dualists. Yet the true Christian is a passionless philosopher, pleads Clement to others. Therefore he lives with his wife as a sister, a practice which will limit the growth of his family.[2]

---

[1] A first-principle, for Aristotle, is 'the first point from which a thing either is or comes to be or is known' (*Metaph.* 1013a).   [2] Osborn, *Ethical patterns*, 64f., 76f.

Two things enable apologetic to produce coherence among its responses. First, there are new concepts which rebut several objections at once. These include, for Justin, the spermatic logos, for Irenaeus, the recapitulation of all things and for Clement, the divine unity. Secondly, within the framework of such universal concepts, there are intelligent and new connections. Through the fusion of former incompatibles, progress in human thought can occur. Some of the moves in early Christian theology are quickly identified. In the account of God, philosophy and the Bible are joined, when the latter becomes the barbarian or the true philosophy.[3] The account of recapitulation links logic and apocalyptic, argument and vision. Ethics join law with discipleship and participation in the good. Logic links faith and reason, for faith is the rule which reason applies so that faith might grow in knowledge.

(ii) Much is unresolved. While the concept of divine unity provides a key to the mass of ideas which have been examined, it offers no closed system. Middle Platonism is not an ordered doctrine, but a succession of teachers who gave different accounts of the One and the world. While Middle Platonism is now easier to map,[4] it remains philosophy and the variety of interpretations will not diminish, for to write about philosophy, one must do philosophy. The disagreements of those who discuss ancient Platonism are more commonly philosophical than historical, for the preferred meaning involves concepts, like cause, which cannot be simply described. To explain what ancients thought about causation, the historian must think about it now. Given the historicality of understanding, meanings will change, however slightly, when each thinker thinks.[5] This does not mean that everything is infinitely ambiguous, but

---

[3] Some Christians, then and now, have been distressed by this move.

[4] Thanks to the work of John Dillon, *Middle Platonists*.

[5] H.-G. Gadamer, *Truth and method* (London, 1975), 235–341. It is not the case however, that anything goes. The only valid interpretations will take account of the problems an ancient writer was trying to solve and the ways in which those problems have changed for him and for us. There will be diversity of interpretations or no interpretation, different ways of understanding or no understanding. Our understanding will be better because we have worked through the complexity and forsaken the quest for unambiguous formulae.

that the effective history (*Wirkungsgeschichte*) of an idea goes on. Nor is Platonism the only secular story in early Christian theology. Stoicism enters time and time again.

In each of the three areas studied there were surviving questions. The ambiguity of the One made it possible to explain how father and son could be one God; just as the One was simple and complex, so God was father and son. Does this offer an adequate account of the distinction between father and son? Tertullian's account of the God, who was one in a new way, went further; for he was clever enough to argue that God's unity came through, and not in spite of, the son and the spirit. Questions of trinity and incarnation remained as a challenge to the future.

In the area of ethics, how was the one commandment to be fulfilled? Militant monotheism can be a basis for cruelty and barbarism. Assimilation to God needed the humanity of the Jesus of the Gospels and the safeguards of natural law. Further, was God to be loved in separation from, or through, his creation? There was no plain answer to the choice between asceticism and the right use of the world. Neither the Bible nor philosophy could indicate how all things were given to those who, by the cross, were Christ's.

In logic and epistemology, tension remained between rule and reason and between faith and knowledge. Gnostic heresy rejected both rule and reason; much heresy would reject rule but not reason. Reason could not be used to the constant advantage of faith, which was marked by an openness which could lead to its own destruction. Happily, second-century Christians, for all their fixed canon, came down on the side of reason. Neither was faith to be separated from knowledge nor the father from the son. The alternative to unity was dualism, Marcionite or Gnostic. The first was argued; the second was not. Clement saw all this, as did Irenaeus. Tertullian, despite his sharp perception on many points, did not choose to grasp the antithesis between argued discourse and theosophy. He linked philosophy and heresy because both were always discussing the nature of man and the problem of evil. Yet he himself was deeply influenced by the philosophical and cultural background of his day. Incompleteness marked the other writers in different ways. Justin leaves ambiguities on the nature of logos. Irenaeus and Clement are repetitive and disorderly in the arrangement of their ideas.

(iii) Our study has elucidated the first (one cause) and third problems (one first-principle of physics, ethics and logic). Yet at every point, the second problem (God in Christ) has intervened. Justin, already a Platonist, finds safe and useful philosophy in the words of Christ and acknowledges the cross of Christ as the greatest symbol of divine power. Irenaeus only believes in a God who became what we are to bring us to be what he is. For Clement, the unknown God is declared in Christ and is approached from abstract unity through the dimension of Christ. Tertullian, so strongly monotheist, pleads above all for that total dishonour of his God, which is the sacrament of man's salvation.

Recapitulation, by which Christ makes all things one, enters the history of the Platonic tradition. By apocalyptic, it links Heraclitean conflict, Platonic dialectic, and Stoic cosmic harmony. Indeed, it provides a missing apex for Greek thought. Kant claimed that Greek philosophy could not give an account of man's supreme good. Epicurean happiness was insufficient. Stoic virtue was too optimistic, but the kingdom of God was able to join virtue and happiness, law and mercy. The human will could not, of itself, supply the chief end of man.[6] Plato did not bring the form of the good within human reach.[7]

Unity was rational as well as ethical. The chief division between Gnostic and Christian was not in result but in method. The Gnostics abandoned the rational process at the beginning of their investigation, rather than at the end. This does not mean that they are without interest. It would be easy to react against contemporary enthusiasm for the occult[8] and to reject it

[6] *Critique of practical reason*, 1.ii.2.5. Kant's account of the kingdom of God was not as strong a claim as recapitulation.
[7] Besides this claim must be set much argument that Platonism and Christianity do not fuse readily. See Appendix 3.
[8] See Layton, *The Gnostic Scriptures*. xviii. A useful analysis has been given by G. C. Stead, The Valentinian myth of Sophia, *JThS*, 20 (1969), 75–104 and, In search of Valentinus, in *The rediscovery of Gnosticism, I: The school of Valentinus*, ed. B. Layton

all as mediocre mumbo-jumbo. No movement is without
diversity, and reason is not enough to cope with the problem of
evil. However, had the rejection of reason triumphed permanently, we should have no tradition of Christian theology or
European humanism. Luther drew on Augustine and Erasmus
on Origen.

In contrast to Gnostic alienation, Christian theology followed
a policy of openness and rationality. The scriptures of Judaism
were fulfilled. It was even possible for Christians to practise the
Jewish Law, said Justin, provided they did not try to impose
their way on others. Clement used Philo freely, if not always
significantly. Philosophy was accepted where it seemed sound,
for God had spoken to Greeks as well as to Jews. Clement was
prepared to use Valentinianism, where it could be consistent
with the rule and reason it rejected. The rule was always a
rational criterion. Even Tertullian is dominated by a belief that
reason and rule suffice. Christian openness sprang from a
formidable sense of the immediacy of God and of union with
him. No forms or powers fixed a barrier between man and God,
for all were included in the son of God. The Christian entered by
prayer into God. Separation and alienation were past. To
believe was to be indivisibly made one in the son of God. There
was no gulf between faith and knowledge nor between the father
and the son.

(iv) In an earlier work, it was found that the second century
faced different problems from the fourth-century councils which
had dictated the shape of many histories of doctrine.[9] Second-
century problems were closer to the twentieth century because
they dealt with issues which challenged Christian belief within
a non-Christian world. After investigation of the second-century
account of one God as first cause, son and father, first-principle
of physics, ethics and logic, there is ground for the further claim
that in logical scope the second century surpasses and supplies
the framework of fourth-century Christian thought.[10] While the

(Leiden, 1980). Both articles are reprinted in G. C. Stead, *Substance and Illusion in the Christian Fathers* (*London*, 1985). [9] Osborn, *Christian philosophy.*
[10] This view has been expressed in the past by two important theologians: Charles Raven and Geoffrey Lampe.

fourth century reaffirmed and built on the achievement of the second century, it gave its councils and controversies to the problem of son and father, or christology and trinity.

By itself, the fourth-century discussion of trinity and christ-ology obscures the development of Christian thought. Seen as central within the threefold claim of the second century, it is illuminating. For the second century had to begin from the first and third questions (one cause, one first-principle of physics, logic and ethics), and find its answers in the second problem (father and son). While in the fourth and fifth centuries, christology and trinity were handled far more adequately, these doctrines only make sense within the context of the other two claims concerning one God. Augustine reaffirms the wider framework of the second century: God is *causa subsistendi, ratio intelligendi, ordo vivendi.* 'For if man was created, so that his most excellent part might attain to that which excels all things, that is, to the one, true, supremely good God, without whom no nature subsists, no teaching teaches, no good has use, then let him be sought, in whom for us is all that is sure, let him be discerned in whom for us is all that is true, let him be loved in whom for us is all that is right' (*civ. dei* 8.4). Christology is a part and not the whole of Christian theology, even if it be the part on which the whole will turn.

Is it, then, desirable to choose between the Christian literature of the second and fourth centuries as the decisive literature or canon[11] for Christian theology? The test would be whether one of them 'has degenerated in respect of coherence or sterility'.[12] To be rationally superior, one account must be relatively coherent (yet not so coherent as to stultify intellectual progress) and fruitful in the solving of problems.[13]

A case for the second century has been established. A case against the fourth-century councils might rest upon incoherence and sterility. Over the last twenty years, incoherence has erupted on all sides. The common account of this period

[11] The term is used here, in the sense common to historians of ideas, to designate the decisive literature by which other literature in a field is judged.
[12] A. McIntyre, The relationship of philosophy to its past, in *Philosophy in history*, eds. Rorty, Schneewind, Skinner, 44.   [13] *Ibid.*

'neither corresponds to the facts nor accounts for the evidence'.[14] Controversy occurred without a common understanding of the key terms. It is difficult therefore to see it as the permanent solution of the problems which had vexed the church.[15] If the story be as intricate as has been shown recently (in nine hundred pages),[16] should it be seen as such a solution? One writer turns to Matthew Arnold for the description, 'where ignorant armies clash by night'.[17] Another uses a near contemporary account from the historian Socrates (*hist. eccl.* 1.23): 'The situation was exactly like a battle by night, for both parties seemed to be in the dark about the grounds on which they were hurling abuse at each other.'[18]

Further, the apparent primacy of soteriology in these conflicts raises difficulty.[19] For contemporary exegesis has claimed that in the New Testament, christology takes precedence over soteriology, and to reverse this order lands us in the *Nabelschau* which Paul's Corinthians and all pietists have enjoyed. 'Christ has freed us from concern for our own salvation.'[20] Among the Corinthians, soteriology had 'obscured the glory of Christ'.[21]

Equally important is the charge of sterility. Some good attempts to do justice to Arius and the controversy which he provoked, have found him and his followers to be wooden and unimaginative. This is evident in his submission to the bureaucratic fallacy[22] and his boy-scout ethics.[23]

[14] R. P. C. Hanson, The achievement of orthodoxy in the fourth century AD, in R. Williams (ed.), *The Making of orthodoxy* (Cambridge, 1989), 143.
[15] *Ibid.*, 156.
[16] R. P. C. Hanson, *The search for the Christian doctrine of God* (Edinburgh, 1988).
[17] *Ibid.*, xviii.   [18] Kelly, *Early Christian doctrines*, 239.
[19] M. F. Wiles, Eunomius: hair-splitting dialectician or defender of the accessibility of salvation? in Williams (ed.), *The making of orthodoxy*, 157.
[20] Käsemann, *Perspectives on Paul*, 30; see also p. 165 *et passim*.
[21] E. Käsemann, *Jesus means freedom* (London, 1969), 65.
[22] Williams, *Arius*, 195 and 230–2. Note that Arius uses the centrifugal rather than the centripetal mode of the fallacy. Intermediaries separate rather than join. Fallacy remains in that if x is needed to separate a and b, then y will be needed to separate a and x and z to separate x from b. Proclus falls into the fallacy of the 'Third Man' argument of the *Parmenides*, through his impartibles, although they are meant to separate rather than join.
[23] E. Osborn, Arian obedience: scouting for theologians, *Prudentia*, 16 (1984), 51–6, review article on R. C. Gregg and D. E. Groh, *Early Arianism, a view of salvation*

However councils and controversies are not the whole of the fourth century. The charge of sterility cannot be sustained against writers such as Athanasius and the Cappadocians, who provide a wealth of argument which illuminates the doctrines of christology and trinity, showing them to be central to Christian thought. Even the councils may be defended. Evidence against the charge of incoherence has already appeared[24] and older work[25] will find its defenders. Further, the creeds and declarations of the fourth and fifth centuries remain the creeds of Christendom. Nothing emerged in the second century which might ever challenge their place.

It is clear that there is little point in a competition between the writers of the second century and those of the fourth century. Each group can enrich the ideas of the other, provided there is clear analysis of each and no confusion between them. From Irenaeus to Gregory of Nazianzus the problem of οἰκονομία changes. In a word, because the Gnostics wanted to go ever higher (*supergredi*), the economy in Irenaeus is dominated by the unsurpassable summing up of all things in Christ. In Gregory, because Arians reduced the son to humanity, the economy is dominated by the theology of the trinity, which is a summing up of the godhead (*or.* 6.22.35.749 cf. *or.* 33.17.36.236). Again, Clement's account of the divine simplicity gives ground for questioning Gregory, for whom nothing is more simple and free from complexity than the godhead (*or.* 31.3.36.585); yet, in some sense, trinity and unity place Christians between the Jews and the pagans (*or.* 38.8.36.320), between one God and many.

Improverishment has commonly come through the retrospective method by which fourth-century creeds, councils and controversies have shaped standard introductions to early Christian doctrine and provided a deterrent against its study. Such histories of dogma, like 'the most honest and conscientious and exhaustive books called "A History of Philosophy" – especially these, indeed – seem to decorticate the thinkers they

(London, 1981). There is enough variety within Arius and his followers to make most generalisations insecure.

[24] T. F. Torrance, *The trinitarian faith* (Edinburgh, 1989).

[25] By Kelly, Prestige and Gwatkin. Kelly's history of doctrine is a masterpiece of composition.

discuss'.[26] By looking at the conclusions of each council and thinker, they neglect logic and problems of thought. This, however, is the fault of the method and not of the fourth century, when there were lively thinkers, several of whom were involved in the making of creeds.

The retrospective method, which views earlier ideas from the position of the fourth-century councils, had been used in many textbooks because it is necessary to understand creeds and controversies against the background of earlier thought. This method is not useless but it is inferior to that of problematic elucidation, which analyses each writer in terms of the problems he faced and the answers he gave. This second method has made it possible, here and elsewhere, I think, to give a more accurate account of second-century Christian thought.[27] For in this respect, theology resembles philosophy and 'the philosopher – unless he be a very bad philosopher – does not set out to construct a system; what he is trying to do is to solve problems'.[28]

The study of early Christian thought will be best pursued when the problems which concerned each writer are elucidated. The problems may change and the historical setting can illuminate this process. We are on the verge of rediscovering the richness of patristic thought, provided we sustain a concern for problems. The first benefit will be our liberation from conceptual parochialism by being forced to look at questions in different ways. The second benefit is that there is always something in this creative period which will stimulate our thinking. For example, a first analysis of Clement's account of faith, looks in turn at the moral and then at the logical elements of faith.[29] Then it becomes clear that these two elements cannot be separated; logical arguments, like the Stoic 'grasping impressions', will not work apart from the spiritual depth of a saving faith.

---

[26] R. Rorty, The historiography of philosophy; four genres, in *Philosophy in history*, eds. Rorty, Schneewind, Skinner, 62. Ryle describes these doxographical efforts as 'calamity itself and not merely the risk of it' *ibid.*

[27] Osborn, *Christian philosophy*, 10–17 and 273–88.

[28] John Passmore, The idea of a history of philosophy, HThS 5 (1965), 27.

[29] Osborn, *Philosophy of Clement*, 127–45.

(v) The elucidation of the most persistent second-century problem declares God to be the first-principle of physics, ethics and logic, and shows the threefold scope of Christian theology.[30] God was the ἀρχή of all being, because of the saving act of Jesus Christ. Certainly he was the creator; but the chaos of sin had perverted the original design. The Platonic world of the divine mind existed in the saving work of God in Christ. His new creation was the ultimate reality. What lies behind the visible world is the cross and resurrection, the kingdom which is Christ.[31] Creation and redemption are joined because the maker is also the remaker, and all is summed up in Christ.

The scope of ethics is also universal and christological. Christian theology was concerned with human values because the image of God had been known in human form.[32] From the barbarities of war and amphitheatre, to the detailed duties of family and community, divine values condemned and guided. Theology could not retreat from the challenge of human confusion and misery, without ceasing to be Christian.

Logic extends over all discourse. In the beginning was the word. In claiming reason for God, Christians made a dangerous choice. Logic opened up an area of conflict, in which there could be no assurance of victory. Gnostics claimed a higher way than argument, while Marcion used logical disputation, with antitheses which destroyed the unity of God. Yet this way was chosen and with it came a theology and indeed a whole culture.

---

[30] The present ecumenical movement is, as I write (Canberra, 1991), challenged by Orthodox participants who want only to establish common dogmatic beliefs (physics) and by Liberationists who want only to discuss ethics. A failure to accept the threefold diversity of the problems of theology leads to the common neglect of logic or apologetics.

[31] It is the same with Origen. 'Les réalités spirituelles signifiées en dernier ressort dans l'Ancien Testament et dans le Nouveau lui-même ne sont donc ni des sortes d'essences platoniciennes ni des drames ou des liturgies transcendantes, telles qu'en imaginait la Gnose. Elles sont en dépendance de la Croix, en dépendance de la mort et de la résurrection de Jésus. Elles sont, comme le dit Origène, "la réalité même des choses qui concernent le Fils de Dieu" telles que nous sommes appelés à en vivre. C'est toute la sphère du "royaume des cieux" tout entière dans Celui qui est lui-même ce royaume en personne: αὐτοβασιλεία.' H. de Lubac, *Histoire et esprit* (Paris, 1950), 294. This is why Clement's dependence on Philo is so limited.

[32] See Hans Küng, *The Christian challenge* (London, 1979), 272; *idem, Christ sein* (München, 1974), 535; ET (New York, 1976), 544.

Philosophy was not an optional extra for the theologian, but a part of his enterprise.

(vi) In each of the second-century claims, there was an attempt to answer changing questions by reference to God in Christ. Christian theology emerged as a christocentric monotheism.

The importance of rationality remains the chief surprise and the major offering to subsequent history and indeed to the twentieth century which has been so easily enticed away from reason. While the arguments of the second century were soon to produce, through Origen against Celsus, a powerful apology, none of them is unanswerable.[33] Origen would not have needed to write, if Celsus' attacks had been completely smashed by our five writers. Further, there are parts of the second-century claims (like exorcism and the defeat of demons) which cannot be transposed to modern times. What is rationally acceptable at one time may prove unacceptable in another climate of knowledge; but the commitment to reason, in the discussion of the main arguments, should endure. It is a happy risk, says Clement, to take one's way to God. Argument is enlivened by a sense of adventure and of progress in faith and knowledge. Belief in one God means that nothing in the world is indifferent to the gospel, that there is no discharge from the war against evil or the argued pursuit of truth.

This combination of Greek philosophy and Christian gospel was a turning point for European culture. Following it, and such later development as has reaffirmed it, we now do science, think and read books instead of casting spells and playing magic. Gnostic nonsense and fideist narrowness will return from time to time, to provide relief from the trauma of thought. For all their interest, they cannot present a serious option, unless the issues and decision of the second century be ignored. Why was this decision so momentous? At first sight, it seems that Jerusalem owed everything to Athens. It was Greek metaphysics which provided the concepts of unity and dialectic to make

---

[33] It can always be asked: why, if God is like Jesus, the world is as it is; how asceticism and the right use of the world fit together; why, in order to avoid infinite regress, faith needs to start with a Christian God.

Christian monism possible. What did the gospel add to these ideas? The answer lies in the summing up of all things by Christ, that powerful mixture of symbolism and logic, which gave the one first-principle a chance of being true. For no one can believe that all existence is good and rational. Being, virtue and reason are deeply flawed by death, sin and the irrational. To believe in one God was to be indissolubly united in Christ. Christians claimed that the first-principle had entered and transformed human history, turning sunset to sunrise. The problem of one God exercised the thoughts of the first Christian theologians, because they were confronted by a divine initiative, without which monotheism would be unacceptable. Within European art, the themes of nativity and crucifixion fill the field; they represent Tertullian's unique hope for the world, the necessary dishonour of faith. When we shall come to the end and gaze on the face of Irenaeus' God, he will be no other than the one who was born of Mary, who suffered and died. According to Plato, inquiry concerning divine mysteries should begin with a great and difficult sacrifice, and, said Clement, that demand has been met, not by theurgy, but by the son of God, Christ our passover, consecrated for us ἄπορον ὡς ἀληθῶς θῦμα, υἱὸς θεοῦ ὑπὲρ ἡμῶν ἁγιαζόμενος (*str.* 5.10.66; *Rep.* 378a).

APPENDIX I

Scripture and philosophy

In one brief and impressive work[1] it is argued that New Testament ideas find in the early fathers a natural, if not final interpretation which relates them to the philosophy of the time. The father of Jesus is the God of Abraham, Isaac and Jacob, transcends man's understanding, but embraces all with his goodness and love. Paul's account of God (1 Cor. 8:6) is not far from that of Maximus of Tyre (*Diss.* 17.5) for whom there is one God, who is king and father of all and many gods or sons of God. Paul insists that 'for us there is one God the father from whom are all things and for whom we are and one lord Jesus Christ, through whom are all things and through whom we are'. The prepositions (from, for, through) may be translated into causal relations – first, final and efficient (or instrumental).[2] In Rom. 11:36, God is described as all three causes, so that Paul maintains the unity of God and expresses his diversity in terms of causation; like other New Testament writers, he sees some knowledge of God as possible through creation, but all true knowledge coming through Christ.

Ignatius expresses the important paradoxes that the eternal, invisible, intangible, impassible became visible and passible for us (*Polycarp.* 3.2), to confound the Docetists who by their error point to the identification of father and son. The Preaching of Peter develops the negative theology of popular philosophy. God is invisible, uncontained, without need, incomprehensible, eternal, imperishable, unmade; but the same God sees, contains

---

[1] R. M. Grant, *The early Christian doctrine of God* (Charlottesville, 1966).
[2] *Ibid.*, 6.

all and is needed by all for their very existence (*str.* 6.4.39.). Aristides describes God as the unmoved mover of all things, the first cause who is beyond man's understanding, eternal, unbegun and without end; he then proceeds to attack pagan gods. Hermas begins his very unphilosophical work with the basic belief in which he has been instructed – one God, who alone created all things out of nothing. Justin in his search for truth, learns from Platonism of the transcendent God, but is reduced by Aristotelian arguments to a dependence on scripture where alone the eternal cause of all things has been perceived. God is above all names and description. There is little difference between his account and that of Alcinous (*Did.* 10), or that of the Stoics (Diog. Laert. 7.147; *SVF* 2.1021). Athenagoras and Iren-aeus make similar points and Clement's account, as we shall see, is clear and comprehensive on all these matters.

The account of Jesus as son of God found final form in the Logos of the Fourth Gospel, who was God and was with God. Origen's Dialogue with Heraclides insists that in one sense there are two Gods and in another sense there is one. The son is distinct from the father but the two Gods become one. What of the spirit? In Rom. 8 and 1 Cor. 12, it is clear that spirit, lord and God have identical functions. Justin misquotes Plato's second epistle on the king of the universe, the second and the third; for him the second is the Logos and the third is the spirit (1 *apol.* 60). Clement also links Plato with 'the holy triad' as does Justin who, it is recognised, does not have a doctrine of the trinity.[3] The 'Christian idea' came directly or indirectly from Numenius, but none of Numenius' interpretation was carried on. The optimism of this claim is evident from the fact that there is no evidence that Numenius used this passage let alone passed it on. Philosophy and Gnosticism provide frameworks 'in which speculation about the triad as Trinity could have been set'.[4] What triggered off the statement of Athenagoras was the accusation that Christians were atheists. His concise response is assessed as 'a carefully worked out doctrine of the Trinity'.[5] Athenagoras has based his statement on scripture and not on philosophy. The three persons' correspond to the experience and thought of Christians not only in the apostolic age but also after it, and these Christians recognised that the three are somehow one'.[6]

All this is salutary and indicates the following points. First, talk of a triad and the doctrine of the trinity are different things. Second, to deny the latter to Justin and attribute it to Athenagoras requires specific argument. Third, Athenagoras is concerned primarily with the unity of father and son, devoting far more exposition to this truth than to the separate accounts of father and spirit. Fourth, the holy spirit is an unexpanded postscript, as he is in the creed of Nicaea. Was it improper to describe the spirit who was leading into all truth and to whom belonged the present and the future, who revealed and was to reveal the end? Fifth, the threefold formula was liturgical in use and raises the question of the priority of doctrine over liturgy.[7] Sixth, Athenagoras himself sees more importance in his argument for the unity of God (*leg.* 8) which he describes as a λογισμός of the Christian faith. This argument has Stoic (Plutarch *Orac.* 23–30) and Aristotelian (*Metaph.* 10) antecedents but its presence in Plutarch, a recipient but less frequently a thinker, shows it to be common place.[8]

This brief and informative account provokes useful questions.[9] Is the complexity and apparent indecision really in the texts or is it the result of looking for later things? Why do such expositions, however long or short, look like chapter one, when early Christian writers saw their work as the conclusion? They were not writing the first draft of a report to be sent on to another committee. Finally does any one, who is worth reading, write without a deep concern for one or two problems? What made these writers take the dangerous step (*str.* 1.1) of putting ideas down in writing instead of just talking?

Another useful way to investigate the early account of divine unity is to consider the christological terms and the binitarian or trinitarian definitions. Recently a fresh examination has shown how christology and pneumatology relate to the unity of God.

---

[6] *Ibid.*, 100.   [7] *Ibid.*, 101.   [8] *Ibid.*, 105–10.
[9] See also Grant, *Gods and the one God* for further valuable discussion.

The subtlety of Justin, Athenagoras and Theophilus rewards investigation.[10]

[10]	See the lucid and comprehensive accounts of M. Simonetti: Il problema dell'unità di Dio da Giustino a Ireneo, *RSLR*, 22 (1986), 201–40; Il problema dell'unità di Dio a Roma da Clemente a Dionigi, *RSLR*, 22 (1986), 439–74.

Recent recapitulation

Of the many investigations of this concept we begin with two nineteenth-century works. The first finds these themes: the necessity of the divine advent through love for an imperfect creature, the freedom of man, and the work of Christ in restoration and perfection.[1] The advent was needed because the world, although made by God in pure love, was γενητός and not perfect (*haer.* 4.38.1). It had to grow and increase that man might pass through adolescence and beyond imperfection. Further, man's freedom had produced negative effects, which made the advent necessary. Made free from the beginning (*haer.* 4.4.3), man had lost the image of God and the first-fruits of the spirit; he followed the devil into depravity and bondage (*haer.* 5.21.1; 3.23.2; 4.41.3). Disobedience led, in turn, to alienation from God, then to the loss of all good things, including immortality.

The work of Christ was twofold: restoration and perfection. Under the first, man must be redeemed from the power of the devil, purified from sin, reconciled to God and saved from death. When Christ recapitulated the ancient formation of Adam in himself, he comprehended, repeated and emended it (*haer.* 5.1.2). He had to vanquish the devil and he did this by an obedience which broke the power, and a defeat which showed up the defection, of the enemy. He sanctified man in himself, from infancy to old age (*haer.* 2.22.4), and gave his present self to mankind (*haer.* 4.9.2), with all the benefits of forgiveness, justification and atonement (*haer.* 4.8.2).

[1] C. Hackenschmidt, *S. Irenai de opere et beneficiis domini nostri Jesu Christi sententia* (Strasbourg, 1869).

The consummation wrought by Christ signified, on the human side, that man had reached his final perfection through temptation and glorification (*haer.* 3.19.3); by his incarnation Christ accustomed man to perceive God and God to dwell in man (*haer.* 3.20.2).

On God's side the consummation meant that the vastness of God was 'measured' in Christ (*haer.* 4.4.2). Father and son differ only in that one is invisible and the other is visible (*haer.* 4.6.6). This means that the father can be known through the son alone (*haer.* 4.5.1; 4.6.3; 4.6.4; 3.6.2; 5.1.1). On man's side the consummation was needed because the weakness of the creature meant that he could not receive the fullness of the divine glory. The father remained invisible, so that man should not despise God and so that man might still have a goal to achieve (*haer.* 4.20.7). Man moves to perfection in three ways. First, the spirit in Jesus becomes accustomed to the human race (*haer.* 3.17.1) and in man brings life and renewal (*haer.* 4.20.10). Second, man's flesh makes necessary the physical renewal of all things for a thousand years. Third, man leaves the body behind, and in heaven is handed over to the father that God might be all in all (*haer.* 4.20.5).

A second work relies on a different set of concepts. First there is a threefold distinction between recapitulation in Christ, in Antichrist and in man.[2] The two elements in recapitulation are κεφάλαιον, ἀνά. The first means *capitulum, caput, summum*, or that 'in which many parts are joined by participation or necessity to produce a certain unity'.[3] The second means repetition or reintegration. Taken together the two elements mean 'to collect again, to comprehend again in a sum, to reduce to unity, to gather again'. Christ both recapitulates and is recapitulated, or better, recapitulates himself, for the middle voice is more appropriate than the passive as a translation of *recapitulatus est* (*haer.* 5.21.1). He recapitulated in himself the *longam hominum expositionem* (*haer.* 3.18.1) as though mankind were the extension of Adam. Therefore recapitulation may be defined as 'the repetition of Adam, through agreement and difference, consum-

---

[2] G. Molwitz, *de ἀνακεφαλαιώσεως in Irenaei theologia potestate* (Dresden, 1874).
[3] *Ibid.*, 2.

mated by Christ with the purpose that he might subject all things to himself'.[4] The two ideas of repetition and bringing to a head may be applied to Christ, Antichrist and man. Christ draws all things in subjection to himself as head and lord (*haer.* 4.20.6). The Antichrist will recapitulate all diabolical error (*haer.* 5.25.5) as his number 666 indicates (*haer.* 5.30.3). Finally, man will experience recapitulation, when he is renewed in the image and likeness of God (*haer.* 5.12.4). The consequences of recapitulation may be listed: for God, the unknown is known through his word; for the angels, the son of God becomes prince and the devil is overthrown; for man, there is perfection of spirit, soul and body; for Christ, there is a new dispensation, a second Adam and a victory over the devil; for salvation, man is brought to life (*haer.* 3.22); and for the end-time, there is advent and reign of Antichrist, the millennium, the general resurrection and judgement, and life eternal.

Another brief account insists that however much we analyse, we may not separate logical and cosmic significance.[5] For the logical meaning declared is the cosmic reality of the new Adam (*haer.* 3.16.6) whose obedience to death (*haer.* 3.16.9; 5.2.1f.; 5.14.1–4; 5.16.3; 5.17.1–4; 5.18.1, 3) cancels out the ancient disobedience (*haer.* 5.19.1) and restores the divine likeness. The work of Christ not merely contradicts, but is the antithesis to the sum of all apostasy in the devil (*haer.* 3.23.3, 5, 8; 4. *pref.* 4; 4.40.1). While Irenaeus develops a physical redemption theory, all is done according to reason (*haer.* 5.18.3 and 4.4.3), justice and persuasion (*haer.* 5.1.1).

Recapitulation, in a recent account, has three main elements.[6] The first is the rhetorical *summary* or κεφάλαιον which modulates into a theological summary. Christ summarises mankind in himself and at the same time gives a compendium of salvation (*haer.* 3.18.1). All the types and figures of the past are fulfilled in him. The second significance of recapitulation is the *inauguration* of a new humanity under Christ as κεφαλή. This depends on the first meaning, for it is as head of creation and

---

[4] *Ibid.*, 11.
[5] A. D'Alès, La doctrine de la recapitulation en Irénée, *RSR*, 60 (1916), 1–9.
[6] Daniélou, *Message*, 166–83.

head of the church, with primacy and power, that he brings together all things in heaven and in earth (*haer.* 3.16.6). The third main point is that the incarnation is *redemptive* or corrective. What was lost in Adam is regained in Christ (*haer.* 3.18.1) who as victor overthrew the powers of sin and death (*haer.* 3.18.7 and 5.21.1). Further, the life which was lost by disobedient Eve is regained by obedient Mary (*haer.* 5.19.1).

The most extended account divides recapitulation into two parts: intention and event.[7]

(i) Recapitulation gives the meaning of the whole history of salvation in the one Christ 'veniens per universam dispositionem et omnia in semetipsum recapitulans' (*haer.* 3.16.6). The proof of the apostolic preaching consists of the demonstration that all previous history is fulfilled in Christ, who at the same time brings all that is new (*haer.* 4.34.1). For all the vast scope of the οἰκονομία, it finds a concise summary in Christ.[8] The same meaning is present at the creation of the world where the eternal word is *exemplum factorum* (*haer.* 4.20.1) and especially the pattern from which and for which[9] man is made (*haer.* 5.16.2); the saviour precedes the saved (*haer.* 3.22.3).[10] So the beginning and the course of all history is to be understood in Christ.

(ii) Now there is a real recapitulation as the event of Christ takes effect in man. True God and true man, as mediator, he joins man to God (*haer.* 4.20.4). Here as in Ephesians, recapitulation is a joining of members to Christ as head (κεφαλή) not a subsuming under a heading (κεφάλαιον). In him as head they find perfection and renewal. The first Adam is the type of the future, while the second Adam acts on fallen humanity to renew, restore, reintegrate, recall, refashion and reform.[11] Adam reappears with his mortality swallowed up in immortality (*dem.* 32f.).

The new presentation of man destroys his sin, nullifies death and gives life (*haer.* 3.18.7). The good shepherd carries his sheep

[7] E. Scharl, Der Rekapitulationsbegriff des heiligen Irenaeus, *OrChrP*, 6 (1940), 376–416. [8] *Ibid.*, 387. [9] *Ibid.*, 391; *causa exemplaris, causa finalis.*
[10] See J. A. Aldama, Adam, typus futuri, *SE*, 13 (1962), 266–80.
[11] *renovare, restaurare, rursus redintegrare, revocare, replasmare, reformare.*

on his shoulder, back to the fold of life (*haer.* 5.15.2). Not only men, but the whole creation will find pristine splendour in Christ (*haer.* 5.32.1; 5.33.4). The disobedience of Adam (*haer.* 5.19.1), the hostility of the serpent (*haer.* 5.21.2), and the debt of death (*haer.* 5.23.2) are all done away.

Continuity with creation is essential, since the beginning is as relevant as the end to recapitulation. Fulfilment and restoration would point in opposite directions were it not for God's hand (his word), 'who forms us from beginning to end, adapts us to life, is present to his creation and perfects it according to the image and likeness of God' (*haer.* 5.16.1). Renewal and progress to perfection would also look in opposite directions unless there be one person, who is beginning and end, Alpha and Omega, head of creation and head of the church (*haer.* 5.36.3 and 3.16.6). Even the heavens find their head in him (*haer.* 5.20.2). He is the eternal king who recapitulates all things in himself (*haer.* 3.21.9),[12] because he is the beginning (*haer.* 1.10.3) and joins man, the end, to God who is the beginning (*haer.* 4.20.4). He makes all things new, rejuvenating and enlivening man.[13]

The question 'what is recapitulation?' runs into the question 'who recapitulates?'[14] and the answer is 'the word made flesh'. 'Recapitulation is thus an exclusive property and exclusive activity of the incarnate word.'[15] It consists in summarising or making a statement and he is the statement, which covers every age from childhood to maturity (*haer.* 2.22.4). Our new birth follows his mysterious birth from a virgin (*haer.* 4.34.4). Through him man enters God and God enters man (*haer.* 4.33.4) so that the detail of his life is important as a moral example (*haer.* 2.22.4) and as the means by which we may share in his likeness (*haer.* 3.22.1).

The incarnate word makes his statement through what he is and does in obedience and victory on the cross (*haer.* 5.21.2). This final act is the decisive recapitulation (*haer.* 5.16.3;

---

[12] Scharl, Rekapitulationsbegriff, 405. 'Das ganz Weltall ist vom Kyrios in Ihn hinein (in semetipsum) rekapituliert. Er ist Haupt der Kirche, diese Ihm eingekörpert. Er ist der Schlussstein im Bau des Universums, dieses in Ihm gehalten, geeint, gekrönt. Das ist der Kerngedanke des Rekapitulationsbegriffes bei Irenäus.'
[13] *haer.* 4.34.1; *omnem novitatem, innovatura et vivificatura hominem.*
[14] Scharl, Rekapitulationsbegriff, 407.   [15] *Ibid.,* 408.

5.17.3f.; 5.19.1; *dem.* 34). His death perfected our salvation (*haer.* 3.18.2). 'With his own blood he redeemed us, giving his soul for our soul and his flesh for our flesh. The spirit of the father flowed out to bring the inner union of man and God' (*haer.* 5.1.1). On the cross his two hands stretched out to bring together Jew and gentile to one God. The cross declares the unity of God for while there are two hands there is one head between them 'for there is one God over all and through all and in us all' (*haer.* 5.17.4). Indeed, the cross includes all the symbolism of recapitulation; it sums up what God has to say. All that remains is for Christ to return in glory (*haer.* 1.10) and to give universal effect to cross and incarnation.[16]

The most recent account focuses on the central aspect of life eternal and incorruptible.[17] ἀφθαρσία is regained by the re-capitulation which takes place at the cross (*haer.* 5.18.3) where our life hangs on the tree (Deut. 28.66; *haer.* 5.18.3) and whence flows the spirit who is living water (*haer.* 5.18.2).[18] The recovery of the divine image includes the recovery of incorruptibility (cf. Wisd. 2.23). Restoration and union with Christ as head brings life since he is the source of life and divine likeness (*haer.* 3.18.1), while the joining of the end to the beginning connects man to God.[19] The temptations of Adam and Christ are similar in form but opposite in outcome. Adam's disobedience produces sin and death, while Christ's obedience produces life and immortality for those whom he restores (*haer.* 5.21.3). The incarnation of the word (John 1:14) and the recapitulation of all things in Christ (Eph. 1:10) are the two poles of Irenaeus' theology.[20] In this way the two aspects of recapitulation – reunion of God with man and subjection to Christ as head – are preserved. Union is possible only because Christ took flesh, becoming what we are, so that he might make us what he is. The mixture of the word with the flesh of his πλάσμα is the union of man with God which in turn restores to man ἀφθαρσία.[21]

Two recent accounts of reconciliation show how deeply this theme is embedded in Christian thought. The first is an

---

[16] *Ibid.*, 416.   [17] de Andia, *Homo vivens.*   [18] *Ibid.*, 343.   [19] *Ibid.*, 6of.
[20] *Ibid.*, 155.   [21] *Ibid.*, 157.

exposition of the Adam–Christ parallel.[22] From the thesis of Rom. 1:16f., there develop two sets of parallel statements which describe on the one hand the wrath of God and on the other hand his righteousness, on the one hand the sin of man and on the other hand justification, on the one hand works and on the other faith, on the one hand law and on the other grace. Paul brings these themes together in chapter 5 through the concept of reconciliation. Here he speaks of the love of God as having the character of righteousness and of the work of this love as reconciliation or the removal of hostility between man and God. The removal of this opposition is the negation of negation (Rom. 5:12–21).

The dialectic of the Christ event is the dialectic of God's activity. The opposition between God and sin is affirmed as real and then removed through the opposition between God's wrath and God's love. This dialectic understands negation as a productive force. Hegel saw this in his account of the incarnation: 'the unity of the divine and human nature, God has become man.'[23]

Reconciliation is a negation of negation, which denies human striving for salvation and offers something new. Atonement is real salvation because in the midst of sin there is forgiveness and in the midst of death there is resurrection. The reconciliation in Christ removes the estrangement which sprang from Adam by a process of concrete negation, 'Where sin abounded, grace did much more abound'.

A second account is concerned to set out a biblical theology which will correspond with historical reality, preserve links between Old and New Testaments, show the unity of the New, relate proclamation to faith, and be accessible to all. Such a theology is to be found in the gospel of reconciliation,[24] which runs through the whole of the New Testament and connects the New with the Old. The Gospels portray Jesus as the Messianic son of man and reconciler, whose work brings man and God

[22] U. Wilckens, *Der Brief an die Römer* (Zürich, Einsiedeln, Köln, 1978), I, 330–7.
[23] G. W. F. Hegel, *Vorlesungen über die Philosophie der Religion* (Theorie-Werk-Ausgabe, Bd. 17, Frankfurt, 1969), 203f. and 294f. Cited Wilckens, *Römer*, I, 334f.
[24] P. Stuhlmacher and H. Class, *Das Evangelium von der Versöhnung in Christus* (Stuttgart, 1979), 17.

together in peace. Jesus looked towards his death, as an offering for many, to establish community between man and God. This reconciliation is the historical substance of the gospel and the essence of the work of Jesus. In Paul the same message (Rom. 3:25 and 1 Cor. 15:1f.) points to the central tradition which Paul received. Faith in Jesus Christ the reconciler coincides with obedience to Jesus Christ the lord and judge of the world.[25] Paul's gospel of justification points to the cross, where Jesus died for all, as the climax of his messianic work of reconciliation. In the letters to Colossae and Ephesus the theme of reconciliation is stated more strongly, and in the Pastoral Epistles the reconciling Christ reveals the goodness of God to men. The letter to the Hebrews speaks of the reconciliation which God has brought through sending Jesus Christ.[26] The same theme may be traced through each of the Gospels. From this saving act comes the reality which is the first-principle of physics.

[25] *Ibid.*, 29.

[26] *Ibid.*, 33.

Christianity and Platonism

DÖRRIE'S DILEMMA

The relation of Christianity to Platonism will be described variously according to the different definitions currently given to these two terms. In a desire to show that there was continuing disparity between the two traditions, one modern scholar has defined Christianity as that clear teaching which produced symbols and expositions of faith or decisions of councils and Platonism as an equally clear ontology which is entirely foreign to and incommensurable with Christianity.[1] Yet something commonly called 'Platonism' was used effectively as a means of propaganda directed to heathen. Philo had already used the philosophical language and concepts of Hellenism to attract outsiders; but orthodox Jews were not prepared to accept his compromise. (On the contrary, while every thinker carries something of his environment upon him there is more than propaganda in this instance. Most of Clement's Platonism is to be found in the *Stromateis*, not in the *Protreptikos*, in his development of the mystery of faith, not in his invitation to the Greeks.) Further, it is claimed that Platonism had become a religion and its philosophical side could not be split off from a religion which was incompatible with Christianity. (Indeed, Platonism had shown itself to be compatible with religion. Christians argued, rightly, that it was more compatible with

---

[1] H. Dörrie, Die andere Theologie, *ThPh*. 56, 1 (1971), 4. These definitions are inappropriate because symbols and expositions of the faith were, as we have seen, only a part in Christian truth. Similarly Platonism never was the clear ontology but rather a way of thinking. See also Dörrie, Was ist spätantiker Platonismus?, 285–301.

their monotheism than with pagan polytheism. Proclus' later
pluralism confirmed their judgement.)[2]

Platonism was a philosophy in the ancient sense of leading to
knowledge of θεῖα πράγματα. The claim has been made, that for
Christians, it was the 'other theology' of one impersonal God,
which could never be fused with their beliefs.[3] (Rather,
Christians found the transcendent account of God necessary to
purge persistent polytheism and any anthropomorphism which
incarnation could suggest.) Both had a longing for salvation, a
life beyond death, the necessary ordering of present life
according to the will of God, rejection of pleasure and
conversion out of the world. Peculiar to Platonism were a
rational world order, the absence of a saving event or new
revelation, man's rational autonomy and the impersonality of
the divine.

At this point, our critic struggles to find the rationale behind
Christian theology which rejected Greek polytheism with vigour
but treated Platonic theology with patience and apparent
tolerance. He resorts to history and propounds two phases, a
polemical phase which attacked Greek contradictions (Pseudo-
Justin, Hippolytus, Athenagoras, Tertullian) and a harmon-
ising phase (Clement of Alexandria) which covered up contradictions and invented the fiction that, because Greek philosophy
and the gospel were so close, Christian converts did not need to
give up any of their old ideas or to begin a new life![4] However
the slender basis for this sleight-of-hand hypothesis has little
place in early Christian literature and is incompatible with the
great difficulties which attended conversion.

Some results of this theory seem ludicrous. So effective was
the proposed fiction, that the partiality of Christian theologians
to Platonism did not affect the substance of their teaching.
Their pretended Platonism did no harm. Neither was it of any
help in solving the problems of faith, nor in enabling the two
parties to talk. It was rather a form of arguing which

---

[2] See Proclus, *Elements of Theology*, propositions 162–5, and R. Wallis, *Neoplatonism*,
(London, 1972), 152, for an outline of the complex argument needed to move from
the One to divine body.   [3] Dörrie, Die andere Theologie, 19.
[4] *Ibid.*, 30.

disappeared when its audience ceased to exist, and gave way to medieval Platonism, Proclus and Aristotle. There were positive features. Christians were able to talk the language of their targets; they put 'Christian substance in Platonic clothing' rather inadequately because they lacked Platonic subtlety and were not prepared to change anything substantial. Christian Platonism was not a hermeneutic[5] but a device to keep Platonism out, a slick manoeuvre to resist an opponent who could not be tackled openly; it had no real place in the development of Christian thought which followed very different lines.

The only value of this account lies in its challenge to simple acceptance or denial of Numenius' thesis that Plato is Moses in Attic dialect.[6] Its own solutions are quite inadequate. The Christian confidence man is a familiar figure; but he will not, like Justin, with his eye on Socrates, die for love of truth. He will be no help with problems of faith. Yet Platonism did help with the Christian problems of one God, divine transcendence, faith and reason, free will and determinism, spiritual perception, and the unity of virtues.[7] The failure of the modern critic to handle the history of ideas is due to his concentration on conclusions rather than problems. His treatment of philosophy is that which Wittgenstein disowned as the kind of thing that could be learned from a book.

PANNENBERG'S PROBLEM

From Ritschl, Harnack, Loofs to Pannenberg, there have been those who have seen in the theology of the second century a disastrous compromise with Hellenism. This early theology degraded faith to the level of philosophy, replaced God with a metaphysical idol, allowing metaphysics to interfere with revelation.[8] Most dogmatic theologians in the first half of the

---

[5] This contradicts the earlier claim on p. 26 that the Christian position was a 'hermeneutic'.   [6] Moses was best known in LXX Greek.

[7] Other grounds for rejecting Dörrie's position are summarised by C. J. De Vogel, Platonism and Christianity, *VC* 39 (1985), 1–62.

[8] W. Pannenberg, The appropriation of the philosophical concept as a dogmatic problem of early Christian theology, 119–83 in *Basic questions in theology*, II (London, 1971).

twentieth century took a similar position. Pannenberg examines
and reconsiders this opinion; despite some divergence he ends
with a similar negative assessment.

Greeks saw their gods as the ultimate origin of the world. The
philosophers, who believed in one beginning, differed in their
account of the divine nature. Eventually God was seen as non-
material, one, unknowable, simple. In contrast, the Hebrews
saw God as one in the course of history;[9] but the Jewish and
then the Christian mission presented this God as the one true
God whom the philosophers sought. Paul first makes the
Christian claim to satisfy the description of the philosophers;
but Christian theology should radically change any philosophy
which it appropriates. There is no basic agreement between the
Christian and the philosophical accounts of one God; even
among Christians, creation *ex nihilo* is only gradually clarified.
Pannenberg sees the concept of the divine will to be threatened
by divine incomprehensibility. God's spirituality, unchange-
ability, simplicity, absence of properties are all discussed with
limited reference to the early fathers. The discussion is inadequate because it is unable to recognise the meaning of
patristic sources from isolated citations and unreliable secondary literature.[10]

The conclusion is that, while Christian theology did not
entirely err in its assimilation of Greek philosophy, it failed to
state clearly the biblical account of the God who acts in
history.[11] The nineteenth-century assessment may be rejected;
but 'neither Irenaeus nor Alexandrian theology, nor early
Christian theology as a whole succeeded in carrying out a
definitive critical revision of the encounter of the Judaeo-
Christian testimony to God with philosophy'.

The weakness of this account lies in the question it asks and
the answer it desires. The question, 'Did early Christian
theology completely assimilate the Greek position?' fails because it simplifies the accounts of theology, philosophy and the

---

[9] *Ibid.*, 135. G. von Rad, *Old testament theology*, ET (1962), 1, 210f.
[10] As for example, H. A. Wolfson, *Philo: Foundations of religious philosophy in Judaism, Christianity and Islam*, 2 vols. (Cambridge, Mass., 1947)
[11] Pannenberg, *Basic questions*, II, 175.

relation between them. It does not recognise the contingent
nature of theology, its limitation through its own setting. The
claim that 'in the recasting of the philosophical concept of God
by early Christian theology considerable remnants were left
out' is foolish.[12] Because there is only one cosmic mind, some
things will always be left out. To believe that theology's task is
'to rework every remnant that has not been recast',[13] one must
ignore the episodic nature of all theology from the beginning
until now, the way in which all theologians have but a short
spell on the stage before they are replaced.

Equally unhappy is the assessment of Greek philosophy. The
opponents of metaphysics in the nineteenth century understood
Greek philosophy in terms of their own idealism. Pannenberg
also understands metaphysics in this way and this makes his
contemporary value uncertain. Further there is no recognition
that later Platonism, as in Maximus of Tyre, Numenius and
Plotinus, had a religious tendency. Proclus later writes on the
elements of theology.

The treatment of Greek philosophy and of Christian theology
is doxographical and critical, listing propositions and examining
their truth. The weakness of such a method, as against
philosophical analysis and problematic elucidation, is evident.
The account of a divine mind fails to observe the complexity in
the development of this theme which has been established.[14]
Isolated propositions do not provide an accurate account; the
ambiguity of the divine attributes is much richer and more
elusive. Heterogeneous elements cannot be juxtaposed without
inaccuracy in both biblical and philosophical exposition. There
is need to consider a larger text of at least one philosopher and
one early Christian writer. The tautological conclusion points
to this need: 'As self-enclosed wholes, neither permits of being
treated as a mutually complementary part.'[15]

Equally unsatisfactory is the answer which is required. God
must be seen as a God who acts in history and whose
transcendence is that of the irrational freedom of his acts. 'The

[12] *Ibid.*, 182.   [13] *Ibid.*, 183.   [14] See Krämer, *Geistmetaphysik*.
[15] Pannenberg, *Basic questions*, II, 180.

otherness of the author of the world is radically exhibited only where expectations and world pictures are overturned by concrete, contingent events.'[16] Here Irenaeus is wrongly claimed as an ally, for Irenaeus did see history as compatible with metaphysical transcendence.[17] For him history was the revelation of the divine οἰκονομία, not of radical surprise. Where has Pannenberg found his divine irrational freedom and why is it attractive? It has some affinity with a modern view of man which is behaviourist, existentialist and utilitarian, 'a happy and fruitful marriage of Kantian liberalism with Wittgensteinian logic solemnized by Freud'.[18] Kant found the sublime in the contemplation of natural contingency, human fate and rational power,[19] so the parallel is close if not exact. Yet this will not represent Pannenburg accurately, for the transcendent divine freedom which 'is the origin of contingency in the world, is also the ground of the unity which comprises the contingencies as history'.[20]

We may conclude that the reconsideration of early Christian thought by Pannenberg, however well intentioned, fails because of its inadequate treatment of theology and philosophy and its untenable account of God. In a more recent work he speaks of the patristic failure to revise critically its philosophical borrowings, and the subsequent sad excess and crudity of its presentation, the very qualities which seem to be found in his own account of both Greek philosophy and the fathers.[21]

PHILOSOPHICAL OBJECTIONS

The criticism of Dörrie and Pannenberg does not mean that there are no difficulties in joining Platonism and Christianity. It can be argued that the good does not need God. If objective value explains and creates, there is no place for God as the first-

---

[16] *Ibid.*, 181. [17] *Ibid.*, 180.

[18] Iris Murdoch, *The sovereignty of Good* (London, 1970), 9. [19] *Ibid.*, 82.

[20] W. Pannenberg, *Basic questions in theology* (Philadelphia, 1970), I, 75. I am grateful to Professor G. H. Kehm for correction on this point.

[21] W. Pannenberg, *Systematische Theologie* (Göttingen, 1988), I, 90.

principle of being, ethics and logic.[22] The distinctive claim of the second century was that God in Christ was a more credible first-principle than the Platonic good.

[22] See John Leslie, *Value and existence* (Oxford, 1979) and J. L. Mackie, *The miracle of theism* (Oxford, 1981), 230–9.

Bibliography

TEXTS AND TRANSLATIONS

Albinus, *Platonis Dialogi*, ed. D. F. Hermann, 6 vols. (Leipzig, 1921–36), vi
  Epitomé, ed. P. Louis (Paris, 1945)
Die ältesten Apologeten, ed. E. J. Goodspeed (Göttingen, 1914)
Apuleius, *De philosophia libri*, ed. P. Thomas (Leipzig, 1908)
Aristotle, ed. W. D. Ross
  Physics (Oxford, 1936)
  Metaphysics 2 vols. (Oxford, 1924)
  De Anima (Oxford, 1961)
Aristotle, *Works*, translated under editorship of J. A. Smith and W. D. Ross, 12 vols. (Oxford, 1908–52)
Aristotle, *The complete works of Aristotle: the revised Oxford translation*, ed. Jonathan Barnes (Princeton, 1984)
Atticus, *Fragments*, in Eusebius, *Praeparatio evangelica*, xi: 1–2; xv: 4–12, ed. J. Baudry (Paris, 1931)
Clemens Alexandrinus, ed. O. Stählin *GCS*, 4 vols. (Leipzig, 1905–36). Revision by Ursula Treu: 1, 3 *Aufl.*, 1972; 2, 4 *Aufl.*, (L. Früchtel), 1985; 3,2 *Aufl.*, (L. Früchtel), 1970; 4, 1, 2 *Aufl.*, 1980)
Clemens von Alexandreia, trans., O. Stählin 5 vols. (*BKV*, 1933–38)
Clément d'Alexandrie, text and trans. *Sources Chrétiennes*, ed. C. Mondésert
  Le Pédagogue: 70 (1960), 108 (1965), 158 (1970)
  Protreptique: 2 (1949)
  Stromate i: 30 (1951)
  Stromate ii: 38 (1954)
  Stromate v: 278, 279 (1981)
  Extraits de Théodote: 23 (1948)
Clement of Alexandria, selections from text with translation, G. W. Butterworth (*LCL*, London, 1919)
Clement of Alexandria, *Stromateis 3 and 7*, translated with notes by H. Chadwick (*LCC*, London, 1954)

314

Clement of Alexandria, trans. W. Wilson (*ANCL*, 4, 12, 22, 24, 1882–4)

Clement of Alexandria, text and trans. *Miscellanies, book 7*, F. J. A. Hort and J. B. Mayor (London, 1902)

To Diognetus, A Diognète, text and trans. H. I. Marrou (SC, 1951)

Irenaeus, *Against heresies*, text, R. Massuet (Paris, 1710), *PG* 7 (Paris, 1882)

Irenaeus, *Against heresies*, text, W. D. Harvey, 2 vols. (Cambridge, 1857)

Irenaeus, *Against heresies*, text and trans., *Sources Chrétiennes* ed. C. Mondésert

Contre les Hérésies:

    I: 263, 264 (1979)

    II: 293, 294 (1982)

    III: 210, 211 (1974)

    IV: 100 (1965)

    V: 152, 153 (1969)

Démonstration, trans. 62 (1959)

Irenaeus, *Against heresies*, trans. A. Roberts and W. H. Rambaut (*ANCL*, 5, 9; 1883–4)

Irenaeus, *Démonstration de la prédication apostolique*, trans. (*SC*, 62; 1959)

Irenaeus, *The demonstration of the apostolic preaching*, trans. J. Armitage Robinson (London, 1920)

Irenaeus, *Des heiligen Irenäus Schrift zum Erweis der apostolischen Verkündigung in armenischer Version entdeckt herausgegeben und ins Deutsch übersetzt von K. Ter-Mekerttschian and E. Ter-Mekerttschian and E. Ter-Minassiantz* (*TU* 31, 1; Berlin, 1907)

Justin, *Apologies*, text, A. W. F. Blunt (Cambridge, 1911)

Justin, *The dialogue with Trypho*, trans. A. Lukyn Williams (London, 1930)

Justin, *First Apology*, trans. E. R. Hardy (*LCC*, 1; London, 1953)

Justin, *Opera*, text, J. C. T. Otto (3rd edn Jena, 1876–9)

Justin and Athenagoras, trans. M. Dods, G. Reith and B. P. Pratten (*ANCL*, 2; Edinburgh, 1879)

Justin, Aristides, Tatian, Melito, Athenagoras, *Die ältesten Apologeten*, text, E. J. Goodspeed (Göttingen, 1914)

Maximus of Tyre, text, ed. H. Hobein (Leipzig, 1910)

Numénius, text and trans. E. des Places (Paris, 1973)

Oracles Chaldaïques, text and trans. E. des Places (Paris, 1971)

Origen, *Contra Celsum*, trans. H. Chadwick (Cambridge, 1953)

Origen, text (*GCS* 2, 3, 6, 10, 22, 29, 30, 33, 35, 38, 40, 41 (Leipzig, 1899–1941)

Philo, text, eds. L. Cohn and P. Wendland, 6 vols. (Berlin, 1896–1915)

Philo, text and trans. F. H. Colson, G. H. Whitaker, R. A. Markus *LCL* 12 vols. (London, 1929–62)

Plato, text, J. Burnet, 5 vols. (Oxford, 1900–7)

Plotinus, text, P. Henry and H. R. Schwyzer, 3 vols. (Paris and Brussels, 1951–9)

Plotinus, text, P. Henry and H. R. Schwyzer (edn minor) 3 vols. (Oxford, 1966, 1977, 1988)

Plotinus, text and trans., A. H. Armstrong, *LCL*, 7 vols. (1966–88)

Plotinus, text and trans., E. Bréhier, 7 vols. (Paris, 1924–38)

Plotinus, text and trans., R. Harder, R. Beutler, W. Theiler, 12 vols. in 8 (Hamburg, 1956–71)

Plotinus, trans., S. Mackenna (2nd edn, London, 1956)

Plutarch, *Moralia*, text and trans., F. C. Babbitt, W. C. Helmbold, P. H. de Lacy. *LCL*, 15 vols. (London, 1927–8)

Plutarch, *Moralia*, text, C. Hubert, M. Pohlenz, W. R. Paton, 2nd edn (Teubner, Leipzig, 1925–74)

Posidonius, text, E. Bake (Leyden, 1820)

Procli commentarius in Parmenidem, eds. Klibansky, Labowsky, Anscombe (London, 1953)

Proclus' Commentary on Plato's Parmenides, trans. G. R. Morrow, J. M. Dillon (Princeton, 1987)

Proclus, *Elements of Theology*, text and trans. E. R. Dodds, 2nd edn (Oxford, 1963)

Pseudo-Aristotle, *de mundo*, text and trans., D. J. Furley (*LCL*, London, 1955)

Tertullian, *de anima*, text, J. H. Waszinck (Amsterdam, 1947)

Tertullian, *Works*, text, *CChr* (*SL*1 and 2, Brepols, 1954)

Tertullian, text and trans. E. Evans:
  Treatise against Praxeas (London, 1948)
  Treatise on the incarnation (London, 1956)
  Treatise on the resurrection (London, 1960)
  Homily on baptism (London, 1964)
  Adversus Marcionem, 2 vols. (Oxford, 1972)

Tertullian, text and trans. *Sources Chrétiennes*, ed. C. Mondésert,
  A son épouse: 273 (1980)
  Contre les Valentiniens: 280, 281 (1980, 1981)
  De la patience: 310 (1984)
  De la prescription contre les hérétiques: 46 (1957)
  Exhortation à la chasteté: 319 (1985)
  La chair du Christ: 216, 217 (1975)
  Le mariage unique: 343 (1988)
  La pénitence: 316 (1984)
  Les spectacles: 332 (1986)
  La toilette des femmes: 173 (1971)

Tertullian, trans. Peter Holmes and S. Thelwall, *ANCL*, 7 (1878), 11 (1881), 15 (1800), 18 (1884)
Tertullian, trans. W. P. Le Saint, *Treatises on Marriage and remarriage* (ACW13, London, 1951); *Treatises on penance* (*ACW* London, 1958)
Tertullian, trans. J. H. Waszinck, *Treatise against Hermogenes* (*ACW* London, 1956)
Xenocrates, text, R. Heinze (Leipzig, 1892)

SECONDARY WORKS

Abramowski, L., Die 'Erinnerungen der Apostel' bei Justin, in Das Evangelium und die Evangelien, ed. P. Stuhlmacher, *WUNT* 28 (Tübingen, 1982)
Die Entstehung der dreigliedrigen Taufformel, *ZThK* 81 (1984)
Adam, A., Grundbegriffe des Mönchtums in sprachlicher Sicht, *ZKG* 65 (1953/4)
Aland, B., Gnosis und Kirchenväter, Ihre Auseinandersetzung um die Interpretation des Evangeliums, in *Gnosis, FS Hans Jonas*, ed. B. Aland (Göttingen, 1978)
Aland, K., Das Verhältnis von Kirche u. Staat in der Frühzeit, *ANRW*, 23, 1, (1979)
D'Alès, A., *La théologie de Tertullien* (Paris, 1905)
Le mot οἰκονομία dans la langue théologique de S. Irénée, *REG* 32, (1919)
Allen, R. E., *Plato's Parmenides*, trans. and analysis (Oxford, 1983)
Allo, E. B., *Saint Paul, Première épître aux Corinthiens*, 2nd edn (Paris, 1956)
Altendorf, E., *Der Kirchenbegriff Tertullians* (Berlin, 1932)
Amstutz, J., Ἁπλότης, (Bonn, 1968)
Andia, Y. de, Matt. 5.5, La beatitudine dei miti nell'interpretazione di San Ireneo, *RSLR*, 30 (1984)
L'hérésie et sa réfutation selon Irénée de Lyon, *Aug.*, 25, 3 (1985)
Homo vivens: incorruptibilité et divinisation selon Irénée de Lyon (Paris, 1986)
Andresen, C., Justin und der mittlere Platonismus, *ZNW*, 44 (1952/3)
Logos und Nomos, Die Polemik des Kelsos wider das Christentum (Berlin, 1955)
Zur Entstehung und Geschichte des trinitarischen Personbegriffes, *ZNW*, 52 (1961)
Apostolopoulou, G., *Die Dialektik bei Klemens von Alexandria* (Frankfurt, 1977)
Appold, M. L., *The oneness motif in the fourth gospel* (Tübingen, 1976)
Armstrong, A. H., Some advantages of polytheism, *Dionysius*, 5 (1981)

The Cambridge history of later Greek and early medieval philosophy (Cambridge, 1967)

Arnim, H. von, *De octavo Clementis Stromateorum libro* (Rostock, 1894)

Bacq, P., *De l'ancienne à la nouvelle alliance, Unité du livre iv de l'Adversus Haereses* (Paris, 1978)

Baier, W., S. Otto Horn, V. Pfnür, eds., *Weisheit Gottes – Weisheit der Welt, FS J. Ratzinger* (St Ottilien, 1987)

Balthasar, Hans Urs von, *Herrlichkeit, Eine theologische Aesthetik*, ii (Einsiedeln, 1962)

Barbel, J., *Christos Angelos* (Bonn, 1941)

Barnard, L. W., *Justin Martyr, his life and thought* (Cambridge, 1967)
Athenagoras (Paris, 1972)

Barnes, T. D., *Tertullian* (Oxford, 1971)

Barrett, C. K., *The Gospel according to John*, 2nd edn (London, 1978)
Essays on John (London, 1982)

Bauer, W., *Orthodoxy and heresy in earliest Christianity* (Philadelphia, 1971), eds. R. A. Kraft and G. Krodel, translated from the second German edition, ed. G. Strecker (Tübingen, 1964)

Baumgarten, J. M., The Book of Elkasai and Merkabah mysticism, *JSJ*, 17 (1986)

Beierwaltes, W., Deus est veritas, in *Pietas, FS B. Kötting*, eds. E. Dassmann and K. S. Frank, *JAC* (Münster, 1980)
Pagan Rome and the early Christians (Bloomington, 1986)

Bélanger, R., Le plaidoyer de Tertullien pour la liberté religieuse, *SR*, 14 (1985)

Benko, S. E., Pagan criticism of Christianity during the first two centuries AD, *ANRW*, 23/2 (1980)

Benoit, A., *Saint Irénée, introduction à l'étude de sa théologie* (Paris, 1960)
Irénée et l'hérésie, *Aug.*, 20 (1980)

Berardino, A. di, and B. Studer, *Storia del metodo teologico, i, età patr.*, (Casale Montferrato, 1992)

Bernard, J., *Die apologetische Methode bei Klemens von Alexandrien* (Leipzig, 1968)

Berthouzoz, R., *Liberté et grâce suivant la théologie d'Irénée de Lyon* (Fribourg, 1980)

Betz, H. D., *Lukian von Samosata und das Neue Testament* (Berlin, 1961)

Bill, A., *Zur Erklärung und Textkritik des i. Buches Tertullians 'Adversus Marcionem'* (Leipzig, 1911)

Blume, H. D. and F. Mann, eds. *Platonismus und Christentum, FS Hermann Dörrie* (Münster, 1983).

Boer, W. den, ed., *Romanitas et Christianitas, FS J. H. Waszinck* (Amsterdam, 1973)

Boff, L., *A gracia liberta dora no mundo* (Petropolis, 1976)

Böhlig, A., *Mysterion und Wahrheit* (Leiden, 1968)

Zum Hellenismus in der Schriften von Nag Hammadi (Wiesbaden, 1975)

Bornkamm, G., Das Doppelgebot der Liebe, *Geschichte und Glaube*, I (München, 1968)

Boulluec, A. le, *La notion d'hérésie dans la littérature grecque IIe–IIIe siècles*, 2 vols. (Paris, 1985)

Bousset, W., *Jüdisch–christlicher Schulbetrieb in Alexandria und Rom* (Göttingen, 1915)

Braun, R., *Deus Christianorum*, 2nd edn (Paris, 1977)

Tertullien et le Montanisme: Église institutionelle et église spirituelle, *RSLR*, 21 (1985)

Bréhier, E., *Les idées philosophiques et religieuses de Philon d'Alexandrie* (3rd edn (Paris, 1950)

Brontesi, A., *La soteria in Clemente d'Alessandria* (Rome, 1972)

Brox, N., *Offenbarung, Gnosis und gnostischer Mythos bei Irenaeus von Lyon* (Salzburg und München, 1966)

Burke, G. T., Celsus and Justin: Carl Andresen Revisited, *ZNW*, 76 (1985)

Campenhausen, H. von, Taufen auf den Namen Jesu? *VC*, 25 (1971)

The formation of the Christian Bible (London, 1972)

Cantalamessa, R., *La cristologia di Tertulliano* (Freiburg, 1961)

Chadwick, H., Justin Martyr's defence of Christianity, *BJRL*, 47, 2 (1965)

Early Christian thought and the classical tradition (Oxford, 1966)

Charlesworth, J. M., Christian and Jewish self-definition in the light of Christian additions to the Apocryphal writings, in *Jewish and Christian self-definition*, II, ed. E. P. Sanders (London, 1981)

Clark, E. A., *Clement's use of Aristotle* (New York, 1977)

Cohen, S. J. D., The significance of Yavneh: Pharisees, Rabbis and the end of Jewish sectarianism, *HUCA*, 55 (1984)

Collins, J. J., *Between Athens and Jerusalem: identity in the Hellenistic diaspora* (New York, 1983)

The apocalyptic imagination (New York, 1984)

Cornford, F. M., *Plato and Parmenides* (London, 1939)

Countryman, L. W., Tertullian and the regula fidei, in *The Second Century*, (1982)

Damme, D. van, Gott und die Märtyrer, *FZPhTh.*, 27 (1980)

Daniélou, J., Ακολουθία chez Grégoire de Nysse, *RevSR*, 27 (1953)

Philon d'Alexandrie (Paris, 1958)

The theology of Jewish Christianity (London, 1964)

Message évangélique et culture hellénistique, (Tournai, 1961); *Gospel message and Hellenistic culture* (London, 1973)

Dattrino, L., La dignità dell'uomo in Giustino Martirio e Ireneo di Lione, *Lat.*, 46 (1980)

Davies, W. D. and Louis Fickelstein, eds. *The Cambridge history of Judaism*, I (1984), II (1989)

Dillon, J., *The Middle Platonists* (London, 1977)

Dodds, E. R., The Parmenides of Plato and the origin of the Neoplatonic 'One', *CQ*, 22 (1928)

Dörrie, H., Hypostasis, Wort und Bedeutungsgeschichte, *NAWG* (1955)

Die Frage nach dem Transzendenten im Mittelplatonismus, *Les sources de Plotin, Entretiens sur l'antiquité classique*, Fondation Hardt, v (Geneva, 1960)

Die platonische Theologie des Kelsos in ihrer Auseinandersetzung mit der christlichen Theologie auf Grund von Origines c. Celsum, *NGPHkl* (1967)

Was ist spätantiker Platonismus?, *ThR*, 36, 4 (1971)

Droge, A. J., Justin Martyr and the restoration of philosophy, *ChH*, 56 (1987)

Ehrhardt, A., *The beginning* (Manchester, 1968)

Engelhardt, M. von, *Das Christentum Justins des Märtyrers, Eine Untersuchung über die Anfänge der katholischen Glaubenslehre* (Erlangen, 1878)

Escoula, L., Le verbe sauveur et illuminateur chez S. Irénée, *NRTh.*, 66 (1939)

Eynde, D. von den, *Les normes de l'enseignement chrétien, dans la littérature patristique des trois premiers siècles* (Gembloux et Paris, 1933)

Faye, E. de, *De l'influence du Timée de Platon sur la théologie de Justin Martyr* (Paris, 1896)

Etude sur les rapports du Christianisme et la philosophie grècque au IIe siècle (Paris, 1898)

Festugière, A. J., *L'idéal religieux des Grecs et l'évangile* (Paris, 1932)

Fontaine, J. and Kannengiesser, C., eds., *EPEKTASIS*, *Mélanges patristiques offerts au Cardinal Jean Daniélou* (Paris, 1972)

Fossum, J. E., *The name of God and the angel of the lord* (Tübingen, 1985)

Gen. 1:26 and 2:7 in Judaism, Samaritanism and Gnosticism, *JSJ*, 16 (1985)

Fredouille, J. C., *Tertullien, et la conversion de la culture antique* (Paris, 1972)

Frend, W. H. C., *Martyrdom and persecution in the early church* (Oxford, 1965)

The rise of Christianity (London, 1984)

Gadamer, H. G., *Dialogue and dialectic: eight hermeneutical studies on Plato* (New Haven and London, 1980)

Gaiser, K., *Platons ungeschriebene Lehre* 2nd edn (Stuttgart, 1968)

Goodenough, E. R., *The theology of Justin Martyr* (Jena, 1923)

By light, light: the mystic gospel of hellenistic Judaism (New Haven, 1935)

Goppelt, L., *Christentum und Judentum im ersten und zweiten Jahrhundert* (Gütersloh, 1954)

Grant, R. M., Irenaeus and Hellenistic culture, *HThR*, 42 (1949)
  The early Christian doctrine of God (Charlottesville, 1966)
  Gods and the one God (Philadelphia, 1986)

Greschke, G., *Gnade als konkrete Freiheit* (Mainz, 1972)

Gruenwald, I., *Apocalyptic and Merkavah mysticism* (Leiden, 1980)

Guthrie, W. K. C., *A history of Greek philosophy*, 6 vols. (Cambridge, 1962–81)

Gwatkin, H. M., *The Arian controversy* (London, 1958)

Hägglund, B., Die Bedeutung der 'regula fidei' als Grundlage theologischer Aussagen, *StTh.*, 12 (1958)

Hallman, J. M., The mutability of God: Tertullian to Lactantius, *TS*, 42 (1981)

Harl, M., *Origène et la fonction révélatrice du verbe incarné* (Paris, 1958)

Harnack, A. von, History of Dogma, 7 vols. (London, 1897–9)
  Militia Christi (Berlin, 1905)

Hasler, V. E., *Gesetz und Evangelium in der alten Kirche bis Origenes* (Zürich and Frankfurt, 1953)

Hatch, E., *The influence of Greek ideas and usages upon the Christian church* (London, 1914)

Heinze, J., Tertullians Apologeticum, *BSGW*, 62, 10 (Leipzig, 1911)

Hengel, M., *The son of God* (London, 1976)

Heussi, K., *Der Ursprung des Mönchtums* (Jena, 1936)

Hodgson, L., *The doctrine of the trinity* (London, 1944)

Hoek, A. van den, *Clement of Alexandria and his use of Philo in the Stromateis* (Leiden, 1988)

Holfelder, H. H., Εὐσέβεια καὶ φιλοσοφία, Literarische Einheit und politischer Kontext von Justins Apologie, *ZNW*, 68 (1977)

Holte, R., Logos Spermatikos, Christianity and ancient philosophy according to St Justin's Apologies, *StTh.*, 12 (1958)

Horbury, W., The benediction of the *minim* and early Jewish Christian controversy, *JThS*, 33, 1 (1982)

Hornus, J. M., Etude sur la pensée politique de Tertullien, *RHPhR*, 38 (1958)

Horst, P. W. van der, *The sentences of Pseudo-Phocylides* (Leiden, 1978)

Houssiau, A., *La christologie de saint Irénée* (Louvain, Gembloux, 1955)
  Le baptème selon Irénée de Lyon, *EThL*, 60 (1984)

Hurtado, L., *One God, one lord: early Christian devotion and ancient Jewish monotheism* (Philadelphia, 1988)

Hyldahl, N., Hegesipps Hypomnemata, *StTh.*, 14 (1960)

Philosophie und Christentum (Copenhagen, 1966)
Jackson, R., Studies in the epistemology of Greek atomists (Dissertation, Princeton, 1982)
Jaeger, W., *The theology of the early Greek philosophers* (Oxford, 1947)
Jossua, J. P., *Le salut: incarnation ou mystère pascale* (Paris, 1968)
Karpp, H., *Schrift und Geist bei Tertullian* (Gütersloh, 1955)
Käsemann, E., *Perspectives on Paul* (London, 1971)
  Commentary on Romans (Grand Rapids, 1980)
Kattenbusch, F., *Das apostolische Symbol, II, Verbreitung und Bedeutung des Taufsymbols* (Leipzig, 1900 and Hildesheim, 1967)
Kelly, J. N. D., *Early Christian Creeds* (London, 1952)
  Early Christian Doctrines (London, 1958)
Koffas, A., *Die Sophia-Lehre bei Klemens von Alexandreia* (Frankfurt, 1982)
Koschorke, K., *Die Polemik der Gnostiker gegen das kirchliche Christentum* (Leiden, 1978)
Krämer, N. J., *Der Ursprung der Geistmetaphysik* (Amsterdam, 1964)
  Plato and the foundations of metaphysics (New York, 1990)
Kretschmar, G., *Studien zur frühchristlichen Trinitätstheologie* (Tübingen, 1956)
Kuhn, P., *Gottes Selbsterniedrigung in der Theologie der Rabbinen* (München, 1968)
Kunze, J., *Die Gotteslehre des Irenaeus* (Leipzig, 1891)
Kutter, H., *Clemens Alexandrinus und das Neue Testament* (Giessen, 1897)
Ladaria, L. F., *El espiritu in Clemente Alejandrino* (Madrid, 1980)
Langerbeck, H., *Aufsätze zur Gnosis* (Göttingen, 1967)
Lassiat, H., *Promotion de l'homme en Jésus Christ* (Tours, 1974)
Lawson, J., *The biblical theology of St Irenaeus* (London, 1948)
Lebeau, P., Koinonia, la signification du salut selon S. Irénée, in *Epektasis, FS J. Daniélou*, eds. J. Fontaine and C. Kannengiesser (Paris, 1972)
Leipoldt, J., *Griechische Philosophie und frühchristliche Askese* (Berlin, 1961)
Lilla, S. R. C., *Clement of Alexandria: a study of Christian Platonism and Gnosticism* (Oxford, 1971)
Loewe, W. P., Irenaeus' soteriology: Christus Victor revisited, *AThR* 17 (1985)
Loofs, F., Theophilus von Antiochien Adversus Marcionem, und die anderen theologischen Quellen bei Irenaeus, *TU* 46, 2 (Leipzig, 1930)
  Leitfaden zum Studium der Dogmengeschichte 7th edn (Tübingen, 1968)
Lortz, J., Das Christentum als Monotheismus in den Apologeten des zweiten Jahrhunderts, in *Beiträge zur Geschichte des christlichen*

Altertums und der Byzantinischen Literatur, FS A. Ehrhard, ed. A. M. Koeniger (Bonn, 1922)

Tertullian als Apologet 2 vols. (Münster, 1927, 1928)

Lubac, H. de, *Histoire et esprit* (Paris, 1950)

Lüdemann, G. Zur Geschichte des altesten Christentums in Rom, *ZNW*, 70 (1979)

McCullagh, C. B., *Justifying historical descriptions* (Cambridge, 1984)

Maier, J., *Jüdische Auseinandersetzung mit dem Christentum in der Antike* (Darmstadt, 1982)

Malherbe, A. J., The Holy Spirit in Athenagoras, *JThS*, NS 20, 2 (1969)

Athenagoras on the location of God, *ThZ* 26 (1970)

Mambrino, J., Les deux mains de Dieu chez S. Irénée, *NRTh*, 79 (1957)

Markus, R. A., Pleroma and fulfilment: the significance of history in St Irenaeus' opposition to Gnosticism, *VC* 8 (1954)

Marmorstein, A., *The old rabbinic doctrine of God* (New York, 1968)

Essays in anthropomorphism (New York, 1968)

Matthews, W. R., *God in Christian thought and experience* (London, 1930)

May, G., *Schöpfung aus dem Nichts* (Berlin, 1978)

Mayer, A., *Das Gottesbild im Menschen nach Clemens von Alexandrien* (Rome, 1942)

Meeks, W. A. and R. L. Wilken, *Jews and Christians in Antioch* (Missoula, 1978)

Mees, M., Die frühe Christusgemeinde von Alexandrien und die Theologie des Klemens von Alexandrien, *Lat.*, 50 (1984)

Rechtgläubigkeit und Häresie nach Klemens von Alexandrien, *Aug.*, 25 (1985)

Méhat, A., *Etudes sur les Stromates de Clément d'Alexandrie* (Paris, 1966)

Meijering, E. P., *God, being, history: studies in patristic philosophy* (Amsterdam and Oxford, 1975)

Meis, A., El problema de Dios en Tertulliano, *TyV*, 21 (1980)

El problema del Mal en Origenes (Santiago, 1988)

Merki, H., ΟΜΟΙΩΣΙΣ ΘΕΩΙ. *Von der platonischen Angleichung an Gott zur Gottähnlichkeit bei Gregor von Nyssa* (Freiburg CH, 1952)

Moingt, J., *Théologie trinitaire de Tertullien*, 4 vols. (Paris, 1966–9)

Le problème du dieu unique chez Tertullien, *RevSR*, 44 (1970)

Moltmann, J., *The trinity and the kingdom of God* (London, 1981)

Momigliano, A., Some preliminary remarks on 'religious opposition' to the Roman empire, in *Opposition et résistances à l'empire d'Auguste à Trajan*, Fondation Hardt, Entretiens, XXXIII (Geneva, 1986)

Mondésert, C., *Clément d'Alexandrie. Introduction à l'étude de sa pensée religieuse à partir de l'Ecriture* (Paris 1944) (ed.)*Le monde grec ancien et la Bible, 1, Bible de tous les temps*, (Paris, 1984)

Montini, P., Elementi di filosofia stoica in S. Giustino, *Aquinas*, 28 (1985)

Morales, J., La investigacion sobre San Justino y sus escritos, *ScrTh.*, 16 (1984)

Fe y demostracion en el metodo teologico de San Justino, *ScrTh.*, 17 (1985)

Mortley, R., *Connaissance religieuse et herméneutique chez Clément d'Alexandrie* (Leiden, 1973)

From word to silence, 2 vols. (Bonn, 1986)

Moule, C. F. D., *The epistles of Paul the apostle to the Colossians and to Philemon* (Cambridge, 1957)

Fulfilment-words in the New Testament: use and abuse, in *Essays in New Testament interpretation* (Cambridge, 1982)

Munck, J., *Untersuchungen über Klemens von Alexandria* (Stuttgart, 1933)

Munier, C., Analyse du traité de Tertullien, de praescriptione haereticorum, *RevSR*, 59 (1985)

La structure littéraire de l'Apologie de Justin, *RevSR*, 60 (1986)

Nagel, P., *Die Motivierung der Askese in der alten Kirche und der Ursprung des Mönchtums* (Berlin, 1966)

Nielsen, J. T., *Adam and Christ in the theology of Irenaeus of Lyon* (Assen, 1968)

Niederwimmer, K., Die Freiheit des Gnostikers nach dem Philippus Evangelium, in *Verbum Veritatis, FS G. Stählin* (Wuppertal, 1970)

O'Malley, T. P., *Tertullian and the Bible* (Nijmegen, 1967)

Orbe, A., *Antropología de San Ireneo* (Madrid, 1969)

Osborn, E., *The philosophy of Clement of Alexandria* (Cambridge, 1957)

Justin Martyr (Tübingen, 1973)

Ethical patterns in early Christian thought (Cambridge, 1976)

The beginning of Christian philosophy (Cambridge, 1981)

Paul and Plato in second century ethics, *StPatr.*, XV, 1984

Word, spirit and Geistmetaphysik, The concept of spirit, Prudentia, Supplement, 1985.

Clément, Plotin et l'Un, in ΑΛΕΞΑΝΔΡΙΝΑ, *FS Claude Mondésert* (Paris, 1986)

Irenaeus and the beginning of Christian humour, in *The idea of salvation, Prudentia*, Supplement, 1989

Reason and the rule of faith in the second century AD, in *The making of orthodoxy, FS Henry Chadwick*, ed. R. Williams (Cambridge, 1989)

The Christian God and the Platonic One, *StPatr*, XX (Leuven, 1989) (with Colin Duckworth), Clement of Alexandria's Hypotyposeis: a French eighteenth century sighting. *JThS*, 36 (1985)

Otto, S., '*Natura*' *und* '*Dispositio*', *Untersuchung zum Naturbegriff und zur Denkform Tertullians* (München, 1960)

Padovese, L., La speranza 'del vero gnostico' secondo Clemente di Alessandria, *Laur.* 25 (1984)

Pannenberg, W., The appropriation of the philosophical concept of God as a dogmatic problem of early Christian theology, in *Basic questions of theology*, II (London, 1971)
Systematische Theologie, 2 vols. (Göttingen, 1980)

Passmore, J., The idea of a history of philosophy, *HThS*, 5 (1965)

Pelikan, J., *The Christian tradition*, I, *The emergence of the Catholic tradition* (*100–600*) (Chicago, 1971)

Peterson, E., ΕΙΣ ΘΕΟΣ (Göttingen, 1926)
Der Monotheismus als politisches Problem (Leipzig, 1935)

Pfeil, H., Die Frage nach der Veränderlichkeit und Geschichtlichkeit Gottes, *MThZ* 31, 1980

Pohlenz, M., *Vom Zorne Gottes* (Göttingen, 1909)
Klemens von Alexandreia und sein hellenisches Christentum, *NGPHkl* (1943)
Die Stoa: Geschichte einer geistigen Bewegung, 2 vols., Göttingen, 1980, 1984)

Prestige, G. L., *God in patristic thought* (London, 1952)

Prigent, P., *Justin et l'ancien testament* (Paris, 1964)

Prümm, K., Göttliche Planung und menschliche Entwicklung nach Irenäus' Adversus haereses, *Schol.* (1938)

Purves, G. T., *The testimony of Justin Martyr to early Christianity* (London, 1888)

Rambaux, C., *Tertullien face aux morales des trois premiers siècles* (Paris, 1979)

Raven, J. E., *Plato's thought in the making* (Cambridge, 1965)

Reinhardt, K., *Parmenides* (Bonn, 1960)

Renehan, R., The Greek philosophic background of Fourth Maccabees, *RMP*, 115 (1972)

Reynders, D. B., La polémique de Saint Irénée, principes et méthode, *RThAM*, 7 (1935)
Optimisme et théocentrisme chez Saint Irénée, *RthAM*, 8 (1936)

Rist, J. M., Plotinus on matter and evil, *Phron.*, 6 (1961)
Plotinus, the road to reality (Cambridge, 1967)
Human value (Leiden, 1982)

Rizzerio, L., La nozione di ἀκολουθία come 'logica della verità 'in Clemente di Alessandria, *RFNS*, 2, 79, 1987

Le problème des parties de l'âme et de l'animation chez Clément d'Alexandrie, *NRTh.* 111, 3 (1989)

Rodriguez, E., *La dunamis de Dios en San Justino* (Santiago, 1982)

Rordorf, W., La trinité dans les écrits de Justin Martyr, *Aug.*, 12 (1980)

Rorty, R., *Consequences of pragmatism* (Minneapolis, 1982)

Rorty, R., J. B. Schneewind and Quentin Skinner, eds. *Philosophy in history* (Cambridge, 1984)

Runia, D. T., *Philo of Alexandria and the Timaeus of Plato*, 2 vols. (Leiden, 1986)

Sanders, E. P., ed. *Jewish and Christian Self-Definition*, 3 vols. (London, 1980–2)

Schäfer, P., Die sogenannte Synode von Jabne, in *Studien zur Geschichte und Theologie des rabbinischen Judentums* (Leiden, 1978)
Der Bar-Kochba-Aufstand (Tübingen, 1981)
Hekhalot-Studien (Tübingen, 1988)

Scharl, E., *Recapitulatio Mundi* (Freiburg, 1941)

Schindler, A., ed. *Monotheismus als ein politisches Problem* (Gütersloh, 1978)

Schlossmann, S., Tertullian im Lichte der Jurisprudenz, *ZKG*, 27 (1906)

Schoedel, W. R., A neglected motive for second century trinitarianism, *JThS*, 31 (1980)

Schoedel, W. R. and R. L. Wilken, eds. *Early Christian literature and the classical intellectual tradition*, FS R. M. Grant (Paris, 1979)

Schoepflin, M., Servizio militare e culto imperiale: il 'de corona' di Tertulliano, *Apoll.*, 58 (1985)

Schofield, M. The antinomies of Plato's Parmenides, *CQ*, 27, 1 (1977)

Scholem, G. G., *Jewish Gnosticism, Merkabah mysticism and Talmudic tradition* (New York, 1960)

Schöllgen, G., Die Teilnahme der Christen am städtischen Leben in vorkonstantinischer Zeit, *RQ*, 77 (1982)

Schürer, E., G. Vermes, F. Millar, *The history of the Jewish people in the age of Jesus Christ* (175 BC–135 AD) (Edinburgh, 1973)

Schweizer, E., *Der Brief an die Kolosser* (Zürich, Einsiedeln, Köln, 1976)

Segal, A. F., *Two powers in heaven: early rabbinic reports about Christianity and Gnosticism* (Leiden, 1977)

Sherwin-White, A. N., *The letters of Pliny: a historical and social commentary* (Oxford, 1966)

Shortt, C. de L., *The influence of philosophy on the mind of Tertullian* (London, 1932)

Sider, R. D., *Ancient rhetoric and the art of Tertullian* (Oxford, 1971)

Siegfried, C., *Philo von Alexandrien als Ausleger des Alten Testaments* (Jena, 1875)

Siegwalt, G., Introduction à une théologie chrétienne de la récapitulation, *RThPh*, 113 (1981)

Simon, M., *Verus Israel* (Paris, 1964)

Simonetti, M., Il problema dell'unità di Dio da Guistino a Ireneo, *RSLR*, 22 (1986)

Il problema dell'unità di Dio a Roma da Clemente a Dionigi, *RSLR*, 22 (1986)

Skinner, Quentin., Meaning and understanding in the history of ideas, *HTh*., 8 (1969)

Spanneut, M., *Le stoïcisme des pères de l'église* (Paris, 1957)

Tertullien et les premiers moralistes africains (Gembloux, 1969)

Permanence du Stoïcisme (Gembloux, 1973)

Stead, G. C., Divine substance in Tertullian, *JThS* 14 (1963)

Divine Substance (Oxford, 1977)

Stier, J., *Die Gottes- und Logoslehre Tertullians* (Göttingen, 1899)

Story, C. I. K., *The nature of truth in the Gospel of Truth and in the writings of Justin Martyr* (Leiden, 1971)

Stout, Jeffrey, *The flight from authority* (Notre Dame, 1981)

Strecker, G., Christentum und Judentum in den ersten beiden Jahhunderten, in *Eschaton und Historie* (Göttingen, 1969)

Striker, G., Κριτηρίον τῆς ἀλήθειας, *NAWG*, (1974) 1.

Stuhlmacher, P., *Versöhnung, Gesetz und Gerechtigkeit* (Göttingen, 1981)

Stylianopoulos, T., *Justin Martyr and the Mosaic Law* (Montana, 1975)

Theiler, W., Einheit und unbegrenzte Zweiheit von Platon bis Plotin, in *Isonomia*, eds. J. Mau and E. G. Schmidt (Berlin, 1964)

Thornton, T. C. G., Christian understanding of the BIRKATH HA-MINIM in the Eastern Roman Empire, *JThS*, 38, 2 (1987)

Tibiletti, C., Vita contemplativa in Tertulliano, *Orph*., NS 2 (1981)

Un passo de Clemente Alexandrino su verginità e matrimonio, *Orph*., NS 5 (1984)

Trakatellis, D. C., *The pre-existence of Christ in the writings of Justin Martyr* (Ann Arbor, 1976)

Tremblay, R., *La manifestation et la vision de Dieu selon Saint Irénée de Lyon* (Münster, 1978)

Irénée de Lyon 'L'empreinte des doigts de Dieu' (Rome, 1979)

Tully, J., ed., *Meaning and context* (Cambridge, 1988)

Uglione, R., Il matrimonio in Tertulliano tra esaltazione e disprezzo, *EL*, 93 (1979)

Ungern-Sternberg, A. von, *Der traditionelle alttestamentliche Schrift beweis 'de Christo' und 'de evangelio'* (Halle, 1913)

Valentin, P., Héraclite et Clément d'Alexandrie, *RSR*, 46 (1958)

Vermander, J. M., La polémique de Tertullien contre les dieux du paganisme, *RevSR*, 53 (1979)

Viciano, A., *Cristo, salvador y liberador del hombre* (Pamplona, 1986)

Völker, W., *Fortschritt und Vollendung bei Philo von Alexandrien* (Leipzig, 1938)
  Der wahre Gnostiker nach Clemens Alexandrinus (Berlin, 1952)
Wallis, R., *Neoplatonism* (London, 1972)
Walzer, R., *Galen on Jews and Christians* (Oxford, 1949)
Waszinck, J. H., Der Platonismus und die altchristliche Gedankenwelt, *Recherches sur la tradition platonicienne*, Fondation Hardt, Entretiens, III (Geneva, 1955).
  Bemerkungen zum Einfluss des Platonismus im frühen Christentum, *VC*, 19 (1965)
Weissengruber, F., 'Samenkörner der Wahrheit' bei Clemens Alexandrinus, in *Ecclesia peregrinans*, FS *J. Lenzenberger*, ed. K. Amon (Wien, 1986)
Whittaker, John, *Studies in Platonism and patristic thought*, (London, 1984)
Wickert, U., Glauben und Denken bei Tertullian und Origenes, *ZThK*, 62 (1965)
Widmann, M., Der Begriff, οἰκονομία im Werk des Irenäus und seine Vorgeschichte (Dissertation, Tübingen, 1956)
  Irenaeus und seine theologische Väter, *ZThK*, 54 (1957)
Wiese, H., Heraklit bei Klemens von Alexandrien (Dissertation, Kiel, 1963)
Wiles, M. F., *The making of Christian doctrine* (Cambridge, 1967)
Wilken, R., *The Christians as the Romans saw them* (Yale, New Haven and London, 1984)
Williams, R., *Arius, heresy and tradition* (London, 1987)
Winden, J. C. M. van, Idolum and Idololatria in Tertullian, *VC* 36 (1952)
  An early Christian philosopher: Justin Martyr's dialogue with Trypho, chapters 1 to 9, PhP 1 (Leiden, 1971)
Witt, R. E., *Albinus and the history of Middle Platonism* (Cambridge, 1937)
Wittgenstein, L., *Philosophical investigations* (trans. G. E. M. Anscombe) (Oxford, 1963)
Wyrwa, D., *Die christliche Platonaneignung in den Stromateis des Clemens von Alexandrien* (Berlin, 1983)

Index of modern writers

Fossum, J. E.   24, 26, 179
Fredouille, J. C.   36, 276
Frend, W. H. C.   12, 13
Frye, Northrop   258

Gadamer, H.-G.   47, 262, 284
Gaiser, K.   46
Glatzer, N. N.   32
Goodenough, E. R.   24, 110, 139
Goppelt, L.   32
Grant, R. M.   3, 14, 175, 176, 232, 295, 296, 297
Gregg, R. C.   289–90
Groh, D. E.   289–90
Gruenwald, I.   25, 26, 179
Guthrie, W. K. C.   40, 46
Gwatkin, H. M.   290

Hackenschmidt, C.   299
Hägglund, B.   246, 247
Hallman, J. M.   132
Hanson, R. P. C.   71, 289
Harl, M.   71
Harnack, A. von,   225, 245, 269
Hasler, V. E.   200, 201, 205, 206
Hegel, G. W. F.   305
Heidegger, M.   271
Heinze, J.   128
Hengel, M.   140
Heussi, K.   232
Hodgson, L.   195
Holfelder, H. H.   270
Holte, R.   269
Horbury, W.   31
Hornus, J. M.   226
Houssiau, A.   166, 181
Hurtado, L.   24, 25
Hyldahl, N.   251

Jackson, Robin   244, 245
Jakoby, F.   140
Jebb, R.   22
Jonas, H.   19
Jossua, J. P.   153
Judge, E. A.   231

Kaibel, G.   71
Kant, I.   286
Karpp, H.   252
Käsemann, E.   84, 93, 289
Kattenbusch, F.   246
Kehm, G. H.   312

Kelly, J. N. D.   175, 177, 246, 289, 290
Kerst, R.   6
Kimelman, R.   31
Knox, W. L.   97
Koch, H.   136
Koffas, A.   220
Koschorke, K.   18, 226
Krämer, H.-J.   46, 48, 52, 60, 61, 62, 63, 311
Kretchmar, G.   179, 180, 181
Kuhn, P.   184
Küng, H.   140, 292
Kunze, J.   186
Kutter, H.   252

Ladaria, L. F.   131
Lampe, G. W. H.   147, 287
Langerbeck, H.   19
Lassiat, H.   153
Layton, B.   17, 286
Lebeau, P.   170
le Boulluec, A.   16, 281
Leipoldt, J.   232
Liddell, H. G.   147
Lightfoot, J. B.   83
Lilla, S. R. C.   52
Lloyd, A. C.   63, 67
Loewe, W. P.   153
Loofs, F.   6, 136, 146, 176, 178
Lortz, J.   127, 128
Lüdemann, G.   232

Mackie, J. L.   313
McIntyre, J.   288
McMullen, R.   8, 9
MacRae, G. W.   20
Maier, J.   30, 31
Malherbe, A. J.   114, 131
Mambrino, J.   183
Markus, R. A.   134
Marmorstein, A.   113, 114
Matthews, W. R.   194
May, G.   19
Mayer, A.   219
Meeks, W. A.   33
Mees, M.   16, 274
Meijering, E. P.   275
Meis Wörmer, A.   133
Merki, H.   213
Millar, F.   32
Minns, D. P.   136
Minter, D. W.   35

330

Index of subjects

333